Taverner, William.
Taking sides. Clashing
views in human sexuality
c2010.
33305220792794
gi   05/14/ 0

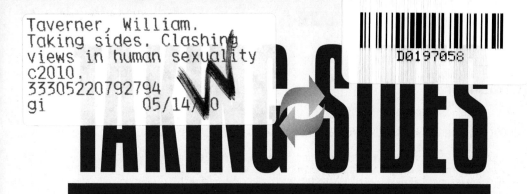

Clashing Views in

Human Sexuality

ELEVENTH EDITION

Selected, Edited, and with Introductions by

William J. Taverner

Ryan W. McKee
Montclair State University

The McGraw-Hill Companies

Connect
Learn
Succeed™

TAKING SIDES: CLASHING VIEWS IN HUMAN SEXUALITY ELEVENTH EDITION

Published by McGraw-Hill, a business unit of The McGraw-Hill Companies, Inc., 1221 Avenue of the Americas, New York, NY 10020. Copyright © 2010 by The McGraw-Hill Companies, Inc. All rights reserved. Previous edition(s) 2008, 2006, 2002. No part of this publication may be reproduced or distributed in any form or by any means, or stored in a database or retrieval system, without the prior written consent of The McGraw-Hill Companies, Inc., including, but not limited to, in any network or other electronic storage or transmission, or broadcast for distance learning.

Some ancillaries, including electronic and print components, may not be available to customers outside the United States.

Taking Sides® is a registered trademark of the McGraw-Hill Companies, Inc.
Taking Sides is published by the **Contemporary Learning Series** group within the McGraw-Hill Higher Education division.

1 2 3 4 5 6 7 8 9 0 DOC/DOC 0 9

MHID: 0-07-354563-5
ISBN: 978-0-07-354563-9
ISSN: 1098-5387

Managing Editor: *Larry Loeppke*
Senior Managing Editor: *Faye Schilling*
Senior Developmental Editor: *Jill Meloy*
Editorial Coordinator: *Mary Foust*
Production Service Assistant: *Rita Hingtgen*
Permissions Coordinator: *Shirley Lanners*
Editorial Assistant: *Cindy Hedley*
Senior Marketing Manager: *Julie Keck*
Marketing Communications Specialist: *Mary Klein*
Marketing Coordinator: *Alice Link*
Senior Project Manager: *Jane Mohr*
Design Specialist: *Tara McDermott*
Cover Graphics: *Rick D. Noel*

Compositor: Macmillan Publishing Solutions
Cover Image: © Photodisc/Getty Images/RF, © John Foxx Images/Imagestate, © Getty Images/ RF, The McGraw-Hill Companies, Inc./Andrew Resek, photographer, © Trilio Productions/Getty Images/RF (montage)

Library of Congress Cataloging-in-Publication Data

Main entry under title:
    Taking sides: clashing views in human sexuality/selected, edited, and with introductions by William J. Taverner.—11th ed.

    Includes bibliographical references and index.
    1. Sex. 2. Sexual ethics. I. Taverner, William J., *comp.*
                                              612.6

www.mhhe.com

Preface

In few areas of American society today are clashing views more evident than in the area of human sexual behavior. Almost daily, in the news media, in congressional hearings, and on the streets, we hear about Americans of all ages taking completely opposite positions on such issues as abortion, contraception, fertility, homosexuality, teenage sexuality, and the like. Given the highly personal, emotional, and sensitive nature of these issues, sorting out the meaning of these controversies and fashioning a coherent position on them can be a difficult proposition. The purpose of this book, therefore, is to encourage meaningful critical thinking about current issues related to human sexuality, and the debates are designed to assist you in the task of clarifying your own personal values in relation to some common, and often polar, perspectives on the issues presented.

This eleventh edition of *Taking Sides: Clashing Views in Human Sexuality* presents 40 lively and thoughtful statements by articulate advocates on opposite sides of a variety of sexuality-related questions. Each issue includes:

- A *question* (e.g., Issue 1 asks, Has sex become too casual?);
- An *Introduction* that presents background information helpful for understanding the context of the debate and information on the authors who will be contributing to the debate;
- *Essays* by two authors—one who responds yes, and one who responds no to the question; and
- A *Postscript* that poses additional questions to help you further examine the issues raised (or not raised) by the authors, including bibliographical resources.

It is important to remember that for the questions debated in this volume, the essays represent only two perspectives on the issue. Remember that the debates do not end there—most issues have many shades of gray, and you may find your own values congruent with neither author. Because this book is a tool to encourage critical thinking, you should not feel confined to the views expressed in the articles. You may see important points on both sides of an issue and may construct for yourself a new and creative approach, which may incorporate the best of both sides or provide an entirely new vantage point for understanding.

As you read this collection of issues, try to respect other people's philosophical worldviews and beliefs, and attempt to articulate your own. At the same time, be aware of the authors' potential biases and how they may affect the positions each author articulates. Be aware, too, of your own biases. We all have experiences that may shape the way we look at a controversial issue. Try to come to each issue with an open mind. You may find your values challenged— or strengthened—after reading both views. Although you may disagree with one or even both of the arguments offered for each issue, it is important that you read each statement carefully and critically.

Changes to This Edition

This edition of *Taking Sides: Clashing Views in Human Sexuality* includes substantial changes from the previous edition, including ten brand new issues or issues with updated articles.

Brand New Issues

- Issue 1: Has Sex Become Too Casual?
- Issue 3: Does Sexual Medicine Benefit Society?
- Issue 5: Is BDSM a Healthy Form of Sexual Expression?
- Issue 6: Is There Something Wrong with the Content of Comprehensive Sex Education Curricula?
- Issue 10: Should Libraries and Other Places That Provide Public Wi-Fi Restrict Sexual Content?
- Issue 12: Should Prostitution Be Legal?
- Issue 14: Should Pharmacists Have the Right to Refuse Contraceptive Prescriptions?
- Issue 15: Is Abortion Immoral?
- Issue 16: Should There Be Restrictions on the Number of Embryos Transferred during In-Vitro Fertilization?
- Issue 18: Is "Gender Identity Disorder" an Appropriate Psychiatric Diagnosis?
- Issue 19: Should Corporations Ensure Equal Rights for Their Lesbian, Gay, Bisexual, and Transgender Employees?

Issues with Updated Articles (note that some issues, not listed here, have questions that we have updated or rephrased)

- Issue 2: Can Sex Be Addictive?
- Issue 20: Should Same Sex-Marriage Be Legal?

In all, 22 of the 40 essays are brand spanking new. In addition, introductions and postscripts have been revised and updated where necessary.

A Word to the Instructor

An *Instructor's Manual*, with issue synopses, suggestions for classroom discussions, and test questions (multiple-choice and essay) is available from McGraw-Hill/CLS. This resource is a very useful accompaniment for this text. A general guidebook, *Using Taking Sides in the Classroom*, which discusses methods and techniques for integrating the pro/con approach into any classroom setting, is also available. An online version of *Using Taking Sides in the Classroom* and a correspondence service for *Taking Sides* adopters can be found at www.mhcls.com/usingts.

Taking Sides: Clashing Views in Human Sexuality is one of the many titles in the Taking Sides series. If you are interested in seeing the table of contents for any of the other titles, please visit the Taking Sides Web site at www.mhcls .com/takingsides or www.mhhe.com, or by contacting the authors at sexedjournal @hotmail.com or mckeer@mail.montclair.edu. Ideas for new issues are always welcome!

For more information, please contact McGraw-Hill Contemporary Learning Series or visit www.mhcls.com, or www.mhhe.com, or by contacting the author at taverner@ptd.net.

Acknowledgments
Thanks from William J. Taverner

First and foremost, I wish to thank my family. Putting together a collection of pro and con essays is no easy task, and the many hours I worked on this book were also hours that my family waited patiently for me to be done for the day. I thank my wife, Denise, and my children, Robert and Christopher, who always welcomed me with open arms whenever I was finished working. I thank my parents, Joan and Bill, and my brother and sister, Joey and Karen. My family's differing opinions about social issues is always a source for spirited discussion, and I love them all for their support and for their help in making me think critically about all these issues. I am amused to think how occasionally a member of the press will call for a quote about a sexual issue and accidentally reach the "other" William Taverner, and be surprised by the quote my father gives.

For the hard work that goes into this book, I am indebted to the expert publishing skills of all my colleagues at McGraw-Hill. Thank you, Larry Loeppke, for your encouragement. Thanks to Shirley Lanners for handling all the permissions requests. Thanks to Jill Meloy for your patience and for giving sound advice on the new issues, carefully reviewing every article and giving excellent feedback on what to keep and what to cut.

Thanks to colleagues and friends who suggested new issues or pointed us in the direction of great articles, gave good advice, or just continue to inspire me: Maggi Boyer, Steve Brown, Matthew Carara, Rob Courtney, Melissa Keyes DiGioia, Mark Eberle, David Hall, Joyce Korbylo, Konnie McCaffree, Mike McGee, Jason Merin, Sue Montfort, Art Robinson, Jessica Shields, Elizabeth Schroeder, and Susie Wilson. Thanks to my friend and colleague, Judith Steinhart, who several years ago introduced me to Ryan McKee. Judith insisted that I just *had* to meet Ryan, and I am glad I did. Ryan is a gifted researcher and writer whose thoughtful analysis shines in the commentaries that precede and follow many of the selections. Ryan assisted me with several prior editions of *Taking Sides,* and with him as coeditor, this is a very improved edition.

Thanks to Allyson Sandak, gifted writer and editor who serves as editor-in-chief of *Contemporary Sexuality* and who wrote the Instructor's Manual for this edition. Allyson assisted with editing and researching many of the new issues and writing first drafts for some of the introductions and postscripts.

Thanks also to my old friends who passed away earlier in the decade: Tim Cummings and Pete Kasenchak. Tim and Pete were two of the smartest people I knew and could debate the night away.

Finally, I wish to thank two colleagues who have been both mentors and friends for many years: Peggy Brick and Robert T. Francoeur. Peggy and I have collaborated on numerous sexuality education manuals, and I value her advice dearly. She is a patient and generous mentor who constantly inspires me to think critically about all matters, not just those related to sexuality education. Bob edited or coedited the first seven editions of *Taking Sides: Clashing Views on Controversial Issues in Human Sexuality.* I have had the privilege of working with Bob on three previous editions of this book and was introduced to both *Taking Sides* and Bob when I took his international studies course in Copenhagen, Denmark, 17 years ago. I am grateful for his kind guidance over the years and honored to carry on his legacy. Everyone should be so lucky as to have such knowledgeable and caring mentors.

Thanks from Ryan McKee

To begin, I would like to thank my wife, Jennifer, for her patience and encouragement throughout the *Taking Sides* editing process (and throughout our relationship). A project like this can lead to more than a few working dinners and late nights in front of the computer. It will be my pleasure to make up for this lost time with such a kind and loving partner. I also owe our dog, Luigi, a few walks and our cats, Wally and Tito, a few naps on the couch.

Thank you to William J. Taverner for including me in this fascinating and challenging process. When he asked me to contribute to the Instructor's Manual of the 9th edition of *Taking Sides,* I never imagined it would one day lead to this opportunity. His trust and support in welcoming me as a Co-Editor for the 11th edition was an honor. His contributions to the field of human sexuality education are invaluable, and I am fortunate to have him as a mentor, colleague, and friend. Thanks as well to Robert T. Francoeur, a former editor of *Taking Sides* and a brilliant sexologist, for giving me the opportunity to sit in on classes and follow in your footsteps at Fairleigh Dickinson.

Thanks to the folks at McGraw-Hill, especially Larry Loeppke, Shirley Lanners, and Jill Meloy, for making the process of editing my first book less intimidating of a process. And thanks to Allyson Sandak for her help with this edition—I look forward to working with her again!

Extra special thanks to my friends and colleagues in the doctoral Human Sexuality Education program at Widener University. My fellow students at Widener are incredibly gifted and dedicated to making the world a better place through their contributions in research, education, and the helping professions. In particular, I would like to thank Alice Holland for ideas and suggestions about new issues; Michal Naisteter for the links to sex worker advocacy organizations; Colin Sutton and Chris Park for sharing their BDSM reference lists; and Jayleen Galarza, Daniel Cronin, Chris Nenstiel, Jamie Aiken, Ashley Mader, and Briana Laskey for their book and song recommendations. I am privileged to be part of such an incredible program with outstanding professors. The future of sexology is bright thanks to their efforts.

I am especially grateful to Daphne Rankin and Judith Steinhart, two extraordinary women and sexuality educators who treated me like family when I moved to the big city of Richmond and the bigger city of Brooklyn. The opportunities I have enjoyed in this field would not have happened without the support and encouragement they both so kindly and selflessly gave. In addition, I would like to thank Steve Conley, Executive Director of the American Association of Sexuality Educators, Counselors, and Therapists, for his support and friendship over the years.

I also wish to thank my parents, Paul and Erma McKee, married nearly 55 years, for their love, support, and stability in what can at times be an unstable world. Lastly, to my sisters, brothers, nieces, and nephews, I owe an unpayable debt of gratitude for their inspiration, regardless of which sides they take.

To Robert T. Francoeur

Contents In Brief

Contents

David L. Rowland, Professor of Psychology and Dean of the Graduate School at Valparaiso University, Valparaiso, examines the benefits and risks of sexual medicine, and the future of the treatment of sexual problems. Leonore Tiefer, author and Clinical Associate Professor of Psychiatry at New York University School of Medicine, counters that the rise of "sexual medicine" brings with it risks that should not be ignored.

Issue 4.   Is Oral Sex Really Sex?   53

Sexuality educator Rhonda Chittenden says that it is important for young people to expand their narrow definitions of sex and understand that oral sex *is* sex. Chittenden offers additional educational messages about oral sex. Sexuality trainer Nora Gelperin argues that adult definitions of oral sex are out of touch with the meaning the behavior holds for young people. Rather than impose adult definitions of intimacy, educators should be seeking to help young people clarify and understand their own values.

Issue 5.   Is BDSM a Healthy Form of Sexual Expression?   68

Sex educator Wayne Pawlowski provides an explanation of BDSM and describes it as a normal, healthy expression of sexuality. J. Paul Fedoroff describes BDSM as a disorder and a pathology and links BDSM to criminal activity.

UNIT 2   SEX EDUCATION   93

Issue 6.   Is There Something Wrong with the Content of Comprehensive Sex Education Curricula?   94

The Administration for Children and Families, U.S. Department of Health and Human Services, presents their findings in a critical analysis of comprehensive sexuality education curricula. Elokin CaPece, Health Educator with Planned Parenthood Greater Memphis Region, disputes the research methods used and the findings of the report, highlighting what she sees as bias in the overall findings.

William J. Taverner, sexuality educator and editor of *Taking Sides,* argues that sexuality education should teach about abstinence, and introduces a new model to replace problematic abstinence education models of the past. Sexuality educator Maureen Kelly argues that the framing of abstinence by conservatives has essentially made the term politically volatile, and that the one-size-fits-all definition has rendered the term useless to educators.

David M. Hall, a graduate professor of human sexuality at Widener University, outlines and comments favorably on the "Sexual Health Report Card," a ranking of 100 universities in the United States by Trojan Condoms. Dr. Hall describes the various sexual health indicators for college campuses, as measured by the report, and argues for better sexuality education programs. Jens Alan Dana, a student and school newspaper editor at Brigham Young University, which was ranked lowest in the Trojan survey, argues that the rankings were unscientific, and based on a subjective set of criteria that were self-serving to Trojan's interests in marketing condoms.

UNIT 3   SEX AND SOCIETY   159

Cynthia Dailard, a senior public policy associate for the Alan Guttmacher Institute, outlines the potential for a new vaccination to prevent the spread of the human papillomavirus (HPV), a sexually transmitted infection that causes genital warts and most cases of cervical cancer. Dailard explains and summarizes the views of experts who believe that widespread vaccinations of preadolescent girls will dramatically reduce the incidence of HPV in the United States and abroad, especially in developing nations. *New York Times* columnist Roni Rabin acknowledges the potential for the HPV vaccination, but contends that cervical cancer can be staved off more economically by encouraging girls and women to have routine Pap smears.

The American Family Association, an organization that advocates for "traditional family values," argues that library filtering software is essential to protect children from harm. Donald Dyson, Ph.D., and Brent Satterly, Ph.D., professors at Widener University, argue that filtering software limits free access to information and state that Wi-Fi should be unrestricted in all settings, including libraries.

The Federal Communications Commission (FCC), a U.S. government agency charged with regulating the content of the broadcast airways, including television and radio, outlines what it defines as "indecent" broadcast material and describes its enforcement policy. Author Judith Levine traces the history of censorship in the United States, and argues that much of what the FCC has determined is "indecent" sexual speech is not, in fact, harmful to children.

Susan A. Milstein, Ed.D., CHES, associate professor in the Health Department at Montgomery College and advisory board member for Men's Health Network, argues that while the legalization of prostitution will not stop all of the social problems associated with the institution, the benefits of legalization make it the best option. Donna M. Hughes, Ph.D., professor at the University of Rhode Island and leading international researcher on trafficking of women and children, counters that the criminalization of prostitution not only reduces demand, but also slows the spread of international sex trafficking.

Dorian Solot and Marshall Miller, founders of the Alternatives to Marriage Project (www.unmarried.org), describe some of the challenges faced by people who choose to live together without marrying, and offer practical advice for couples who face discrimination. David Popenoe and Barbara Dafoe Whitehead, directors of the National Marriage Project (marriage. rutgers.edu), contend that living together before marriage is not a good way to prepare for marriage or avoid divorce. They maintain that cohabitation weakens the institution of marriage and poses serious risks for women and children.

UNIT 4   REPRODUCTIVE CHOICES   249

Eileen Kelly, a professor of Management at Ithaca College, argues that conscience clauses are necessary to protect the religious liberty and rights of pharmacists and others in the workplace. The National Women's Law Center, a national organization that works to promote issues that impact the lives of women and girls, highlight laws and public opinion while stressing that free and unrestricted access to contraception is in the best interest of women's health.

Douglas Groothuis, author and professor of philosophy at Denver Seminary, draws on the philosophical tradition to present his moral argument against abortion. Jennifer Webster, projects coordinator for the Network for Reproductive Options, asserts that the choice of abortion is a multifactoral decision that always expresses a moral consideration.

Mercedes Allen, educator, trainer, and founder of AlbertaTrans.org,
recognizes the bias in the DSM's classification of Gender Identity Disorder
as a mental disorder, but argues that changes run the risk of leaving the
trans community at risk of losing medical care and treatment. Kelley
Winters, Ph.D, writer and founder of GID Reform Advocates, argues the
inclusion of Gender Identity Disorder in the DSM adds to the stigma faced
by transpersons and that reclassification is necessary in order to
adequately address the population's health care needs.

Issue 19.   Should Corporations Ensure Equal Rights for Their Lesbian, Gay, Bisexual, and Transgender Employees?   321

David Hall outlines, from a chapter in his book *Allies at Work: Creating a
Lesbian, Gay, Bisexual and Transgender Friendly Works Environment,*
the need for corporations to work as allies in establishing equal rights for
LGBT employees. Glen E. Lavy suggests, on behalf of the Corporate
Resource Council, that by offering equal rights to LGBT employees,
corporations are doing much more than that—they are actually signing on
to support broader social changes sought by LGBT individuals.

Issue 20.   Should Same-Sex Marriage Be Legal?   358

The Human Rights Campaign (HRC), America's largest gay and lesbian
organization, explains why same-sex couples should be afforded the
same legal right to marry as heterosexual couples. John Cornyn, United
States senator from Texas, says a constitutional amendment is needed to
define marriage as permissible only between a man and a woman.
Senator Cornyn contends that the traditional institution of marriage needs
to be protected from activist courts that would seek to redefine it.

Correlation Guide

The *Taking Sides* series presents current issues in a debate-style format designed to stimulate student interest and develop critical thinking skills. Each issue is thoughtfully framed with an issue summary, an issue introduction, and a postscript. The pro and con essays—selected for their liveliness and substance—represent the arguments of leading scholars and commentators in their fields.

Taking Sides: Clashing Views in Human Sexuality, 11/e is an easy-to-use reader that presents issues on important topics such as *sex education, embryo implantation,* and *casual sex.* For more information on *Taking Sides* and other *McGraw-Hill Contemporary Learning Series* titles, visit www.mhhe.com/cls.

This convenient guide matches the issues in **Taking Sides: Human Sexuality, 11/e** with the corresponding chapters in one of our best-selling McGraw-Hill Human Sexuality textbooks by Yarber et al.

Taking Sides: Human Sexuality, 11/e by William Taverner and Ryan McKee	Human Sexuality: Diversity in Contemporary America, 7/e, by Yarber et al.
Issue 1: Has Sex Become Too Casual?	**Chapter 8:** Love and Communication in Intimate Relationships **Chapter 9:** Sexual Expression **Chapter 16:** HIV and AIDS
Issue 2: Can Sex Be Addictive?	**Chapter 3:** Female Sexual Anatomy, Physiology, and Response **Chapter 4:** Male Sexual Anatomy, Physiology, and Response **Chapter 9:** Sexual Expression **Chapter 10:** Variations in Sexual Behavior **Chapter 17:** Sexual Coercion: Harassment, Aggression, and Abuse
Issue 3: Does Sexual Medicine Benefit Society?	**Chapter 11:** Contraception, Birth Control, and Abortion **Chapter 13:** The Sexual Body in Health and Illness **Chapter 14:** Sexual Function Difficulties, Dissatisfaction, Enhancement, and Therapy **Chapter 16:** HIV and AIDS
Issue 4: Is Oral Sex Really Sex?	**Chapter 10:** Variations in Sexual Behavior
Issue 5: Is BDSM a Healthy Form of Sexual Expression?	**Chapter 10:** Variations in Sexual Behavior **Chapter 13:** The Sexual Body in Health and Illness
Issue 6: Is There Something Wrong with the Content of Comprehensive Sex Education Curricula?	**Chapter 11:** Contraception, Birth Control, and Abortion **Chapter 12:** Conception, Pregnancy, and Childbirth

(Continued)

Taking Sides: Human Sexuality, 11/e by William Taverner and Ryan McKee	Human Sexuality: Diversity in Contemporary America, 7/e, by Yarber et al.
Issue 7: Should Sex Ed Teach about Abstinence?	**Chapter 6:** Sexuality in Childhood and Adolescence **Chapter 11:** Contraception, Birth Control, and Abortion
Issue 8: Does the Availability of "Sexual Health Services" Make Some College Campuses Healthier than Others?	**Chapter 7:** Sexuality in Adulthood **Chapter 15:** Sexually Transmitted Infections
Issue 9: Should Children Have an HPV Vaccination Before They Enroll in School?	**Chapter 6:** Sexuality in Childhood and Adolescence **Chapter 15:** Sexually Transmitted Infections
Issue 10: Should Libraries and Other Places That Provide Public Wi-Fi Restrict Sexual Content?	**Chapter 17:** Sexual Coercion: Harassment, Aggression, and Abuse **Chapter 18:** Sexually Explicit Materials, Prostitution, and Sex Laws
Issue 11: Should the FCC Fine TV Stations That Broadcast "Indecency"?	**Chapter 18:** Sexually Explicit Materials, Prostitution, and Sex Laws
Issue 12: Should Prostitution Be Legal?	**Chapter 7:** Sexuality in Adulthood **Chapter 18:** Sexually Explicit Materials, Prostitution, and Sex Laws
Issue 13: Should Society Support Cohabitation before Marriage?	**Chapter 7:** Sexuality in Adulthood **Chapter 8:** Love and Communication in Intimate Relationships
Issue 14: Should Pharmacists Have the Right to Refuse Contraceptive Prescriptions?	**Chapter 11:** Contraception, Birth Control, and Abortion **Chapter 12:** Conception, Pregnancy, and Childbirth
Issue 15: Is Abortion Immoral?	**Chapter 11:** Contraception, Birth Control, and Abortion
Issue 16: Should There Be Restrictions on the Number of Embryos Transferred during In-Vitro Fertilization?	**Chapter 12:** Conception, Pregnancy, and Childbirth
Issue 17: Should Parents Be Allowed to Select the Sex of Their Baby?	**Chapter 5:** Gender and Gender Roles **Chapter 12:** Conception, Pregnancy, and Childbirth
Issue 18: Is "Gender Identity Disorder" an Appropriate Psychiatric Diagnosis?	**Chapter 5:** Gender and Gender Roles **Chapter 14:** Sexual Function Difficulties, Dissatisfaction, Enhancement, and Therapy
Issue 19: Should Corporations Ensure Equal Rights for Their Lesbian, Gay, Bisexual, and Transgender Employees?	**Chapter 17:** Sexual Coercion: Harassment, Aggression, and Abuse
Issue 20: Should Same-Sex Marriage Be Legal?	**Chapter 18:** Sexually Explicit Materials, Prostitution, and Sex Laws

Introduction

Sexual Attitudes in Perspective

To many, America can seem like one seriously divided country, with a blue northern and coastal perimeter, and a bright red center! On television and in print media, this is the overly simplified caricature of American politics and social attitudes. Are you from a *red state,* perhaps Georgia or maybe Texas? Then surely you are a Republican who supported John McCain in the 2008 presidential election. You also oppose abortion and same-sex marriage, and you probably love hunting and NASCAR. Are you from a *blue state,* perhaps California or maybe Massachusetts? Then surely you are a Democrat who voted for Barack Obama in 2008. You support a woman's right to choose, are a staunch civil libertarian, and may have plans to attend a friend's same-sex wedding. Oh, and you are also a vegan who bikes to work in order to reduce greenhouse gas emissions!

If you are scratching your head, thinking that neither profile describes you, you are not alone. Texas and Utah may be "red states," but how do we reconcile the fact that more than 5 million Americans in these two states voted for Obama, who was called the "most liberal" senator by opponents in the primaries and general election? Or that another 5 million people voted for the conservative McCain in the "blue state" of California? Or that many more millions voted in ways that were inconsistent with their assigned state color, leading to many "swing states" narrowly choosing Obama? Moreover, what do we know about the nearly 38 percent of eligible voters who did not vote at all in 2008? It's an important question as these nonvoters make up over 80 million Americans! The reality is that our opinions, attitudes, and values on social and sexual issues are as diverse as we are. They are formed by numerous factors that we will explore in this Introduction.

As you examine the 20 controversial issues in human sexuality in this volume, you will find yourself unavoidably encountering the values you have absorbed from our society, your ethnic background, your religious heritage and traditions, and your personal experiences. Because these values will influence your decisions, often without being consciously recognized, it is important to actively think about the role these undercurrent themes play in the positions you take on these issues.

How Social and Ethnic Factors Influence Our Values

American society is not homogeneous, nor is it even red or blue! People who grow up in rural, suburban, and large urban environments sometimes have subtle differences in their values and attitudes when it comes to gender roles, marriage, and sexuality, or trends that may reflect the views of the majority of people in communities. Growing up in different areas of the United States can influence one's views of sex, marriage, and family. This is even truer for men and women who were born, and raised, in another country and culture.

Many studies have shown how values can be affected by one's family income level and socioeconomic status. Studies have also indicated that one's occupation, educational level, and income are closely related to one's values, attitudes, sex role conceptions, child-rearing practices, and sexual identity. Our values and attitudes about sex are also influenced by whether we are brought up in a rural, suburban, or large urban environment. Our ethnic background can be an important influence on our values and attitudes. In contrast to the vehement debates among white, middle-class Americans about pornography, for instance, Robert Staples, a professor of sociology at the University of California, San Francisco, says that among African Americans, pornography is a trivial issue. "Blacks," Staples explains, "have traditionally had a more naturalistic attitude toward human sexuality, seeing it as the normal expression of sexual attraction between men and women. . . . Rather than seeing the depiction of heterosexual intercourse or nudity as an inherent debasement of women, as a fringe group of [white] feminists claims, many in the black community would see women as having equal rights to the enjoyment of sexual stimuli. . . . Since the double [moral] standard has never attracted many American blacks, the claim that women are exploited by exhibiting their nude bodies or engaging in heterosexual intercourse lacks credibility" (quoted in Philip Nobile and Eric Nadler, *United States of America vs. Sex* [Minotaur Press, 1986]). Of course, Staples's analysis may be too generalizing for *all* African American people, as certainly there are many African American citizens who hold strong attitudes against pornography. However, Staples's observations may offer some insights as to how race or ethnicity might factor in the formation of sexual attitudes and values. Although some middle-class whites may be very concerned about pornography promoting sexual promiscuity, Staples argues that many African Americans are far more concerned about issues related to poverty and employment opportunities.

Similarly, attitudes toward homosexuality vary among white, African American, and Latino cultures. In the macho tradition of Latin America, male homosexual behavior may be considered a sign that one cannot find a woman and have sexual relationships like a "real" man. In some African American communities, a similar judgment prevails, and gay and lesbian relationships are often unrecognized. In his book *On the Down Low: A Journey Into the Lives of "Straight" Black Men Who Sleep with Men* (Broadway, 2004), J.L. King explains this cultural ethic and how "straight" men live secret lives with their same-sex sexual encounters "on the down low," and not impacting their sexual orientation. Understanding this ethnic value becomes very important in appreciating the ways in which African Americans and Latinos respond to the crisis of AIDS and the presence of males with AIDS in their families. The family might deny that a son or husband has AIDS until the very end because others might interpret this admission as a confession that the person is homosexual. Or, a man on the "down low" might receive inadequate treatment from a doctor or health clinic clinician who does not ask the right questions. A clinician who asks him whether he is gay, will probably be told "no." A clinician who asks a number of questions, including whether he sometimes has sex with men, might be able to get a better picture of his sexuality and needs.

Another example of differing ethnic values is the issue of single motherhood. In ethnic groups with a strong tradition of extended matrilineal families, the concept of an "illegitimate" child born "out of wedlock" may not even exist. Unmarried mothers in these cultures do not carry the same stigma often associated with single mothers in other, less matrilineal cultures. When "outsiders" who do not share the particular ethnic values of a culture enter into such a subculture, they often cannot understand why contraception and sexuality education programs do not produce any substantial change in attitudes. They overlook the basic social scripting that has already taken place. Gender roles also vary from culture to culture. Muslim men and women who grow up in the Middle East and then emigrate to the United States have to adapt to the much greater freedom women have in the States. Similarly, American men and women who have served in the armed forces in Afghanistan, Iraq, Saudi Arabia, and other parts of the Middle East found they had to adapt to very different Muslim cultures that put many restrictions on the movement and dress of women in the military.

A boy who grows up among the East Bay Melanesians in the Southwestern Pacific is taught to avoid any social contact with girls from the age of 3 or 4, even though he may run around naked and masturbate in public. Adolescent Melanesian boys and girls are not allowed to have sex with each other, but boys are expected to have sex both with an older male and with boys of their own age. Their first heterosexual experiences come with marriage. In the Cook Islands, Mangaian boys are expected to have sex with many girls after an older woman teaches them about the art of sexual play. Mangaians also accept and expect both premarital and extramarital sex. These are all examples of differing cultural attitudes toward sexual norms. As peculiar as these norms may seem to many Americans is as peculiar as American sexual norms may seem to non-Americans.

But one does not have to look to exotic anthropological studies to find evidence of the importance of ethnic values. Even within the United States, one can find subtle but important differences in sexual attitudes and values among its diverse population of its native people, and of those who immigrated from all over the world.

Religious Factors in Attitudes toward Sex

In the Middle Ages, Christian theologians divided sexual behaviors into two categories: behaviors that were "natural" and those that were "unnatural." Because they believed that the natural function and goal of all sexual behavior and relations was reproduction, masturbation was unnatural because it frustrated the natural goal of conception and continuance of the species. Rape certainly was considered illicit because it was not within the marital bond, but because it was procreative, rape was also considered a "natural" use of sex. The same system of distinction was applied to other sexual relations and behaviors.

Premarital sex, adultery, and incest were "natural" uses of sexuality, while oral sex, anal sex, and contraception were "unnatural." Homosexual relations were both illicit and unnatural. These religious values were based on the view that God created man and woman at the beginning of time and laid down certain rules and guidelines for sexual behavior and relations. This view is still very influential in our culture, even for those who are not active in any religious tradition.

In recent years, several analysts have highlighted two philosophical or religious perspectives that appear throughout Judeo-Christian tradition and Western civilization. These perspectives have been synthesized into a model proposed by Dr. Robert T. Francoeur, coeditor of the *International Encyclopedia of Sexuality*. Understanding these two perspectives, or "worldviews" is important in any attempt to debate controversial issues in human sexuality.

Two Major Sexual Value Systems

Fixed or Absolutist World View

- Sexuality is basically an animal passion and must be controlled.
- The main goal of sex is marriage and reproduction. Sex is only acceptable in heterosexual marriages.
- Masturbation, oral sex, anal sex, and other non-genital sex all impede God's purpose for sex. They are forbidden.
- Same-sex relationships are forbidden.
- Gender roles are strictly defined, and the male is superior in relationships.
- The emphasis of sex should be on genital acts.

Process or Relativist World View

- Sexuality is a natural and positive life force with both sensual and spiritual aspects.
- Pleasure, love, and celebration of life are goals in themselves. Sex does not have to be confined to marriage.
- The purpose of sex is to celebrate life; masturbation, oral sex, anal sex, and other non-genital sex can express the celebratory and communal nature of sex.
- Same-sex relationships are accepted.
- Gender roles are equal and flexible.
- The emphasis should be on people and their relationships, rather than on what they do sexually.

Adapted from a summary of the work of sexologist and biologist Robert T. Francoeur by Linda L. Hendrixson.

Judeo-Christian tradition allows us to examine two distinct worldviews, the *fixed worldview* and the *process worldview*. The fixed worldview says that morality is unchanging. Right and wrong are always right and wrong, regardless of the situation or circumstances. The fixed worldview relies on a literal interpretation of its religious or ethical teachings, without regard for context. The process worldview examines issues of morality in an ever-changing world. What is right or wrong may require a contextual examination, and rules and ethics must constantly be reexamined in light of new information and the world's evolving context.

Take for example the question of masturbation. Where does the Christian prohibition of masturbation come from? If you search the words of the Bible (the wonderful Web site, www.biblegateway.com allows for such searches), you will discover that the words "masturbate" and "masturbation" are never mentioned! Yet much of what has been taught in Christianity regarding masturbation comes from the story of Onan:

> Then Judah said to Onan, "Go in to your brother's wife and perform the duty of a brother-in-law to her, and raise up offspring for your brother." But Onan knew that the offspring would not be his. So whenever he went in to his brother's wife he would waste the semen on the ground, so as not to give offspring to his brother. And what he did was wicked in the sight of the Lord, and he put him to death also.
>
> Genesis 38:8–10, English Standard Version

Many theologians point to this passage as evidence for a masturbation prohibition. The passage describes how Judah asked his brother Onan to help him to bear a child, and how Onan had sexual intercourse with his sister-in-law, but "waste[d] his semen." This phrase has been interpreted literally by fundamentalist Christians to say that semen must never be wasted, therefore, no masturbation. Indeed, Catholic theologians in the middle ages even examined whether sperm cells had souls! This interpretation led to prohibitions on masturbation and other sexual behaviors that do not produce pregnancy. The fixed worldview is that God did not want any semen wasted—what Onan did was "wicked", and so masturbation will always be wicked.

Process worldview Christians may read the same passage differently. They might ask "What was the thing Onan did that was 'wicked in the sight of the Lord'?" Was God condemning the wasting of semen? Or was God angry at Onan's selfishness—or disobedience—with his intentional failure to produce a child for his brother, as was his traditional obligation at the time? A process worldview Christian might also point out that even if the passage is to be interpreted as a masturbation prohibition because of the spilling of one's seed, the passage says nothing about female masturbation, which involves no release of any seed. Is female masturbation therefore permissible?

This example serves to illustrate only two possible values related to the sometimes controversial issue of masturbation. It may be tempting to stop there and look at only two perspectives, but consider that there are many other reasons people may support or oppose masturbation. The ancient Chinese Tao of love and sex advises that semen should be ejaculated very rarely for reasons related to mental and physical (not moral) health. Masturbation aside, the Tao advises that males should only ejaculate one time per every 100 acts of intercourse, so that female—not male—pleasure is maximized! Another position on masturbation may be its functionality, as viewed by sex therapists, for treating sexual dysfunction. Another perspective is to evaluate the morality of masturbation as to whether it causes physical harm. Because masturbation—a very common behavior from birth to death—causes no physical harm, it might be regarded as a healthy sexual alternative to other behaviors that may be dishonest or exploitative. There are many perspectives on this one topic, and there are similarly many perspectives beyond the two articles presented for every issue in this book.

Consider a non-Western, non-Christian example from recent history: the Islamic cultures of the Middle East and the politics of Islamic fundamentalists. On the fixed worldview side are fundamentalist Muslims who believe that the Muslim world needs to return to the unchanging, literal words of Mohammed and the Koran (the sacred book of the teachings of Allah, or God). Again, there is no gray area in a fixed worldview—what Allah revealed through Mohammed is forever the truth, and the words of the Koran must be taken as literally as the day they were first recorded. There is no room for mitigating factors or new or unique circumstances that may arise. The literal interpretation of the Koran calls for purging all Western and modern influences that have assimilated into Islamic society. Consequently, about 25 years ago, Islamic fundamentalists overthrew the shah of Iran, and assassinated the president of Egypt, both of whom had encouraged modernization of their countries. More recently, the September 11, 2001, terrorist attacks against the United States' World Trade Center and the Pentagon represented the rejection of Western influences at its ultimate, deadliest extreme.

On the other side are Muslims who view the world through a process worldview—an ever-changing scene in which they must struggle to reinterpret and apply the basic principles of the Koran to new situations. They consider as progress the new rights that women have earned in recent years, such as the right to education, the right to vote, the right to election of political office, the right to divorce their husbands, the right to contraception, and many other rights.

The fixed and process worldviews are evident throughout the history of American culture. Like Islamic fundamentalists, Christian fundamentalists believe that Americans need to return to traditional values. This worldview often shares a conviction that the sexual revolution, changing attitudes toward masturbation and homosexuality, a tolerance of premarital and extramarital sex, sexuality education in the schools, and the legality of abortion are contributing to a cultural decline and must be rejected. A classic expression of this value system surfaced in the aftermath of the September 11, 2001, terrorist attacks, when Christian conservative commentators Pat Robertson and the Reverend Jerry Falwell agreed that the destruction of the towers of the World Trade Center and the Pentagon were caused by the immoral activism of the American Civil Liberties Union and advocates for abortion and gay rights.

At the same time, other Americans argue for legalized abortion, civil rights for homosexuals, decriminalization of prostitution, androgynous sex roles in child-rearing practices, and the abolition of all laws restricting the right to privacy for sexually active, consenting adults. For a time, the process worldview gained dominance in Western cultures, but renewed influences of such fixed world groups as the Moral Majority and Religious Right have manifested in the recent elections of President Bush and other fundamentalist politicians.

The two worldviews described here characteristically permeate and color the way we look at and see everything in our lives. One or the other view will influence the way we approach a particular political, economic, or moral issue, and the way we reach decisions about sexual issues and relationships. However, one must keep in mind that no one is ever fully and always on one or the other end of the spectrum. The spectrum of beliefs, attitudes, and values proposed here is an intellectual abstraction. Real life is not that simple. You may find yourself holding fixed worldviews on some issues and process worldviews on others. Your views may represent neither worldview. Just as there are no pure blue and red states, there are no absolutes when it comes to sexual values. There is a continuum of values, with the fixed worldview on one end, and the process worldview on the other. Your sexual values for each issue presented in this text will likely depend on the issue, your personal experiences with the subject matter, and the values and beliefs that you have accumulated by important sources within your own life.

Personal connection with an issue may be a strong indicator of one's sexual values. If you are among the millions of Americans who has had a sexually transmitted infection, that firsthand experience will likely affect what you believe about condom availability programs or sexuality education. A family member that you love and respect, who taught you that pornography is wrong, will make it difficult for you to accept the proposition that it is okay. As we are all sexual beings, so many of the issues presented here provide an opportunity for a personal connection to an issue, beyond a simple academic exercise.

As you plunge into the 20 controversial issues selected for this volume, try to be aware of your own predispositions toward certain topics and to be sensitive to the kinds of ethnic, religious, social, economic, and other factors that may be influencing the position a particular author takes on an issue. Understanding the roots that support a person's overt position on an issue will help you to decide whether you agree with that position. Take time to read a little bit about the authors' biographies too, as their affiliations may reveal something about their potential biases. Understanding these same factors in your own thinking will help you to articulate more clearly and convincingly your own values and decisions.

Internet References . . .

SexHelp.com

SexHelp.com is a Web site that showcases resources championed by Patrick J. Carnes, authority on sexual addiction. The Web site provides links for further reading, self-assessments, discussion forums, and more.

http://www.sexhelp.com/

Sexual Intelligence

Sexual Intelligence provides information and commentary on contemporary sexual issues, written by sex therapist Dr. Marty Klein. The Web site also features a free monthly newsletter.

http://www.sexualintelligence.org

Goofyfoot Press

Visitors to this Web site will find links to chapters from the popular sex information resource, *The Guide to Getting It On,* and weekly commentary by author Paul Joannides.

http://www.goofyfootpress.com

National Coalition for Sexual Freedom

A resource that provides information about psychotherapeutic, medical, and legal services from "kink-aware" professionals.

www.ncsfreedom.org

FSD Alert

FSD Alert is an educational campaign that challenges myths promoted by the pharmaceutical industry and calls for research on the causes of women's sexual problems. Visitors will find developing information on Intrinsa at this Web site.

http://www.fsd-alert.org

International Society for Sexual Medicine

Established In 1982 to promote erectile dysfunction research, the ISSM today encourages research and education across a broad spectrum of human sexual functioning. The ISSM publishes the *Journal of Sexual Medicine.*

www.issm.info

Understanding Sexual Expression

*R*obert T. Francoeur, *author of* The Complete Dictionary of Sexology, *calls sexuality a "bio-psycho-socio and cultural phenomenon." Humans are sexual beings from birth through death, and our sexuality is shaped by our physical makeup (biological); our thoughts, feelings, and perceptions of our sexuality (psychological); and the way we interact with our environment (sociological and cultural). In many ways, sexuality may be as subjective as the individual who expresses it.*

Defining "sex" is no more universal. One of our favorite classroom activities is to ask students to take out their cell phones, call a few friends and family members, and ask them what "sex" means. The varied responses illustrate the many different viewpoints people have about the nature of sex.

This section examines the very nature of sex by presenting debates on issues related to sexual definitions, how we understand sexual behavior, and how sexual problems are addressed.

- Has Sex Become Too Casual?
- Can Sex Be Addictive?
- Does Sexual Medicine Benefit Society?
- Is Oral Sex Really Sex?
- Is BDSM a Healthy Form of Sexual Expression?

ISSUE 1

Has Sex Become Too Casual?

YES: Rebecca Hagelin, from "Parents Should Raise the Bar for Their Kids," http://townhall.com/columnists/RebeccaHagelin/2009/03/10/parents_should_raise_the_bar_for_their_kids (March 10, 2009)

NO: Lara Riscol, from "Purity, Promiscuity or Pleasure?" An original essay written for this volume (2009)

ISSUE SUMMARY

YES: Rebecca Hagelin, author and public speaker on family and culture, argues that sex education promotes casual sex and that schools and parents should do more to protect children.

NO: Lara Riscol, an author who explores the connections between society and sexuality, counters that blaming sex education is an oversimplification while arguing that sexuality has always been openly expressed throughout human history.

It seems that every generation envisions the younger, emerging generation as more permissive than their own. This pattern of observation can be seen at least throughout the past century. In the late 1800s, the mass production of the *bicycle* worried many adults who thought that they would allow young people to ride far away and engage in sexual trysts, free of the watchful eyes of their parents. The growing automobile industry similarly gave young people new opportunities to be alone and led to concerns among many adults that younger generations were becoming sexually permissive. In the "Roaring '20s," "flappers"—women who drank, danced, voted, and wore their hair short—were regarded by their elders as being especially permissive. In the 1930s through the 1950s, the growing number of movie theaters, dance halls, and coed universities worried adults that sex was becoming more and more casual.

Adults looked to the televised hip gyrations of Elvis Presley as a signal of emerging sexual permissiveness, and in the 1960s and 1970s many adults did not know what to make of young people and the Sexual Revolution, particularly with its "Free Love" messages. Some critics still point to the Sexual Revolution as being the originator of a "casual sex" mentality. Sociologist Ira Reiss refutes this notion by observing that it wasn't sexual *behaviors* that changed so much during this period; rather, the *attitudes* people expressed about sex began to change.

Still, modern commentators continue to describe sex as more casual than ever. Some have remarked on the high volume of sexual content on television, in the movies, on the Internet, almost everywhere, which often has no marital or relationship context. Others look to the ubiquitous "Girls Gone Wild" enterprise that features young women, often intoxicated, taking their tops off for the camera.

Is sex more casual today? In the following selections, author and commentator Rebecca Hagelin blames sex education for promoting casual sex and says that parents and schools should expect more of their children, instilling "concepts of self-worth," "basic morality," and abstinence education. Author Lara Riscol criticizes the Far Right for oversimplifying the issue and responds by comparing the social and sexual norms today to those at other times in history, noting that in many instances the norms today are better than norms of the past.

YES

Rebecca Hagelin

Parents Should Raise the Bar for Their Kids

Spring break is in full swing for many college students across the country. And believe me, when I say "full swing," I mean full-rockin', rollin' party-hearty swinging!

But given that nearly all of these students' lifestyles are still funded by their parents, and that nearly all are still under the legal drinking age, it makes me wonder: What are their parents thinking?

As a mom of two college men I actually find it fairly easy to boldly proclaim: "If you are livin' on my dime, then you are livin' by my rules."

My rules for them as adults are actually filled with freedom, coupled with the principle of "self government." They were raised with this consistent theme, and they understand that my husband and I practice the "abuse and lose" approach. (I.e., they have both freedom and our full support as long as they follow basic rules that provide for their safety, moral development, and future.)

Of course, I can hear the naysayers now: "But they're adults. You can't tell adult children what to do." To this I simply answer, "BALONEY!"

I am a much older adult, and I understand that an employer can impose certain codes and expectations for my behavior on me. That's the deal in life—you work for someone, you have to play by their rules. (Of course, I know they can't trample your basic rights, deny civil liberties, etc. So don't go there. You know what I'm talking about.)

The young college men in my life—of whom I am so very proud and blessed to be called their "mom"—also know that my husband and I are fully committed to them as individuals and will provide plenty of opportunities for good, safe fun.

Let's get back to Spring Break as an example. Instead of shrugging our shoulders and letting them go off to some distant beach where mayhem, alcohol, and "Girls Gone Wild" abound, I booked a house at our favorite beach, which is located on a barrier island on Florida's Gulf Coast. With no bridge (you have to get here by boat) and no bars, this break is a lot safer and a lot more meaningful than what many are experiencing.

One of my dear friends has a house nearby and her daughter, also on Spring Break, has brought about nine of her "best friends" too. So, there's plenty of social activity, fun, and friendship without the nonsense. The kids go

From *Townhall.com*, March 10, 2009. Copyright © 2009 by Rebecca Hagelin. Reprinted by permission of the author.

back and forth between our houses, so my friend and I both get to spend time with them and listen to their entertaining—and interesting—chatter.

Last night the gang was at my friend's house and the main topic of conversation proved an eye-opening, mind-numbing experience for her.

Most of the girls on this trip are freshmen, and somehow the conversation led to a shared humiliating experience now common at most college campuses: the mandatory co-ed, sex-ed course they all attended during their first few weeks on campus. They described the graphic nature of the class, and how embarrassed and outraged they were when they were shown how to put a condom on a banana.

But then it got worse—they were all encouraged to do the condom/banana exercise, too. The girls spoke of how a couple of their fellow students seemed to take great pride at their skill in demonstrating what seemed an all-too-familiar maneuver. However, my young friends said they were mortified and left the course feeling "trashy" and belittled by administration officials who expect them to all behave like wild animals in heat. "They seemed to be encouraging us to be sexually active," one member of the volleyball team said. "I was insulted and offended by the entire experience."

This particular young co-ed had gone to a private Christian high school, so she had managed to escape the low expectations that many educators bring to today's youth. She and her mom weren't aware that in today's public schools, millions of boys and girls are now, indeed, treated as if they are going to be sex-crazed creatures and, therefore, are actually encouraged to engage in risky behavior.

Face it: When an adult in authority stands in front of the classroom and directs graphic discussions of sex in every form, forces boys and girls to sit by each other throughout the humiliating lectures, and then further violates the child's natural tendencies to be private or modest, then you end up with kids who follow what they've been taught. On the other hand, when kids are treated with dignity, taught the value of abstinence, and how to avoid placing themselves in compromising situations in the first place, the research shows that more of them do, indeed, respond by adopting a lifestyle of self-control and more responsible behavior than those drowning in "sex ed". Also critical to the delayed on-set of sexual activity is parental involvement. I can not overstate the influence that loving, connected parents have on their teens and young adult children. You'll find loads of data and research on both points at www.abstinenceclearinghouse.com and www.familyfacts.org

Which, once again, brings me back to the plethora of wild Spring Break "pah-tays" going on around the country as you read this. I wonder: If more public junior high and high schools joined hands with more parents in teaching abstinence education, the concepts of self-worth, and basic morality, wouldn't our nation's kids have a higher view of themselves and rise to meet the expectations?

And if colleges and parents expected better of our kids, wouldn't more of them choose the higher ground? If more parents took the effort to provide safer—but still "way fun"—supervised beach trips and other options for college kids, would more of them opt for something other than the drunken orgies that many Spring Break trips have become? In short, are older adults getting exactly the type of behavior from young adults that we expect?

Granted, my personal "focus group" is small. But the data, my experience, and the e-mails I receive from thousands of people tell me this: Young adults are still malleable, still looking for direction, and still crave to rise above the status quo. But they need help and encouragement. They need to be told that they can be self-controlled people of strong character, and they need to be provided with opportunities to thrive, have fun, and become men and women they can be proud of.

Young adults rise or fall to the expectation levels set for them. Will you help raise the bar?

Purity, Promiscuity or Pleasure?

"**Y**ou would watch the girls give each other oral sex, do themselves with dildos, place cigars in their vaginas and rectums, suck on each others' breasts, and lick freshly poured beer off of one another's vulvas while their legs were tucked behind their necks." Often one fellow would get to have sex with one of the three performers directly before leering and cheering men.

No, this is not another spring break outrage making the latest round on cable news, but business as usual back in the good ol' days when live sex shows were easier to find than now. And I don't mean the '50s glory days of traditional values when *Ozzie and Harriet* reigned and the U.S. teen pregnancy rate hit an historic high, but in the prostitution heyday of the 1800s when feminists and medical experts warned against women riding bicycles lest the seat stir "libidinousness and immorality."

In the latest hot and seminal *Guide to Getting It On,* author Paul Joannides' longest chapter, "Sex in the 1800s," reminds us that the more things change, the more they stay the same. He compares the sexual contradictions of then "hardcore live sex shows and concerns about bicycle seats for adult women" to now "abstinence-only sex education and porn-filled Websites on the Internet." As today's technology flings sex front and center, in your face, round the clock, no escape, get me off of this d——n merry-go-round spinning ever faster into an erotic yawn of Girls Gone Wild, prostitots, MILFs, Bang Bus, booty call, and endless multimedia overexposures—America, "Land of the Free," remains stuck in a sexual schizophrenia of smut and sanctimony.

My first mental flash when reading about the famous centuries-ago sex show was VH1's latest season premiere of *Rock of Love Bus with Bret Michaels,* where Pamela Anderson wannabes vie for the lead singer of '80s hair band Poison. When one drunken contestant takes a vagina shot of booze from another, even a nonbeliever can fear the Apocalypse is near. Minus historical context and nuanced reasoning, I feel the appeal of Chicken Little conservatives crying the decline of Western civilization due to the sexual revolution and liberal moral relativism.

It's cheap and easy to dump hypersexualized floaties from our unfettered free market society on those who reject retro reactions to today's growing sexual, reproductive, gender, relationship, and family complexities. But could our nation's unmatched trouble with sex—runaway rates of teen and unplanned pregnancy, single parenthood, abortion, HIV and STDs, sexual "addiction," alienation and desire discrepancies, divorce—really be a black-and-white

An original essay by Lara Riscol. Copyright © 2009 by Lara Riscol. Reprinted by permission.

case of purity or promiscuity? How to reach the glorious human heights of pleasure—sacred to silly—when laden by potent conflicting forces intent on commercializing and politicizing sex?

Our dominantly Christian nation's schizophrenic approach to sex has deep roots. Likely former Governor Elliot Spitzer wouldn't have been so disgraced for feeding his costly call girl fetish in 1870, when New York City's second-largest economy was commercial sex. Yet America's prostitution-powered era wouldn't have tolerated a women's studies graduate auctioning off her virginity to finance her master's in family and marriage therapy, à la Natalie Dylan. Women weren't allowed the same transgressions as men. Of course women weren't allowed the same opportunities. Traditionalists argued that the intellectual rigors of higher education would shrink female reproductive organs and deny a real woman's one true calling: motherhood.

The God-fearing Victorian era of presumed moral restraint was nearly as sex segregated as Afghanistan today. Hooking up isn't so easy when you don't school, work, or socialize together. Young men routinely staved off masturbation at brothels where prepubescent virgins were in high demand; women were deemed unnatural if they displayed sexual desire, though ads for birth control abounded. Gender and sexuality has evolved along with technologies like automobiles, birth control, the Internet, economic shifts, and social equality. America, grounded in equality and plurality, rises from the right to life, liberty, and the pursuit of happiness. Our national stability and family honor doesn't rest on hypocritical sexual traditions like enforcing female virtue.

But that doesn't stop opportunistic purity posturing by family values conservatives, such as wedge-issue Republicans, the religious right, and Fox News, which airs so much B-roll of pulsating female flesh, while morally bloviating it inspired the NSFW FoxNewsPorn.com. The head of the "Biblically based" policy group Concerned Women for America says that proponents of sexual health education are financially motivated to encourage kids' having sexually transmitted diseases and abortions. A Morality in Media press release, "Connecting the Dots: The Link Between Gay Marriage and Mass Murders," links secular values, the sexual revolution, and the decline in morality to the gay rights movement, all sexual ills, including rape and the sexual abuse of children, and naturally the recent spate of mass murders.

Fox News megastar Bill O'Reilly, who a few years ago paid millions to make a sexual harassment suit go away, makes millions as lead culture-war bugle for traditional values against deviant secular progressives out to destroy America. In a recent column, "Kids Gone Wild," he decries the supposed sidelining of "Judeo-Christian principles of right and wrong" in policymaking. He shamelessly makes a slippery slope case against nuanced responses to sexual controversies by conflating child rape, unfettered abortion, gay marriage, and sexting—the latest shame name for teenagers and younger sharing provocative photos of themselves via cellphone, mostly girls sending and guys receiving.

But with child porn charges against juveniles now in at least five states, our sense of right and wrong can't be vindicated when we scar a kid as sex offender for a naughty consensual exchange. Some of the girls dragged into our criminal justice system posed in bikinis or thick, white bras. Flailing before budding sexuality and uncontainable technology, alleged adults lose all moral sense and lump the heinous crime of child pornography with a developing person's playful physical expression. Forget addressing the real potential harm to a child's well-being, such as high-tech bullying when a jerk "friend" recklessly or vindictively distributes private communication.

Yes, times are rapidly changing, and there's no going back to that elusive simpler time when men were predators and women gatekeepers, and anyone in between stayed in the closet. Despite hyperventilating sex-frenzied traditionalists, societal breakdowns go way beyond gay marriage, the hookup generation, Bill Clinton, or even Hugh Hefner. Although the "anything-goes, if it feels good do it" '60s is a tattered punching bag, liberalism not only ushered in free-love rebels, but also groundbreaking equality for women, queers, and ethnic minorities. Life can feel out of control as technology accelerates, rules of the game change, and our salacious 24/7 infotainment highway takes us to the edge of tolerance, but we face much graver threats today than friends with benefits, condoms on a banana, or two grooms in a tux.

With sexual debate stuck in such demonizing reductionism of traditional vs. secular, conservative vs. liberal, purity vs. perversion, abstinence vs. condoms, good vs. evil, no wonder we can't budge beyond nostalgia-fed moral panics to sane responses to modern challenges. A politically potent, multibillion-dollar industry of chastity crusaders seeks to save our national Gomorrah by corralling sex back into the procreative marital bedroom. But with virtually all of us doing some version of the dirty deed before, outside, between, or after marriage, America must expand the sexual conversation beyond purity balls or rainbow parties.

The two authors of the book, *Hooked: How Casual Sex Is Harming Our Kids*, recently lectured at a broadcast forum by the Christian-right Family Research Council, the powerful lobbying arm of media empire Focus on the Family. Beyond the usual physical dire consequences, Joe McIlhaney and Freda Bush stated the irreparable emotional damage of one having multiple sex partners. Dr. Bush drove home their scientific claims by describing how adhesive tape loses its sticky power after pulling it apart more than once. Like used adhesive tape, the more you have sex with someone other than your spouse, the more you lose your ability to bond. Oh, and sex means anything that incites physical arousal; no word on masturbation. Bottom line is there are only two types of sex: married (good) and unmarried (bad).

Their conclusion supports the absolutist agenda of the synergistic family values, traditional marriage and abstinence-only movements that push the conservative ideal of sex confined to a heteronormative lifetime of marital fidelity, to the exclusion of all other sexual expressions. But hawking sexual purity as a salve for personal ills and tonic for a stronger America amounts to selling snake oil.

For many, a magic pill to make bad and scary things go away sounds nice. But if prescribing to dogmatic absolutes worked, then the most religious and conservative red states wouldn't have the highest rates of teen pregnancy, divorce, and porn consumption. And the fallen Colorado megachurch Pastor Ted Haggard, former head of the National Association of Evangelicals, frequent

President George W. Bush confidant, and fierce opponent of same sex marriage, wouldn't have betrayed his family by spending three years with a male prostitute and crystal meth.

Ignoring the human frailties of adults and the capitalistic pornification of our public square, conservatives offer only one denial standard for all kids aged 8 to 28 if unmarried. Maybe in the Obama era, we're ready to grow up and stop making the most vulnerable ground zero in our lose–lose, sex-obsessed culture war. For the past eight years, we've been demonizing sexual science, distorting sex education, limiting access to information and health care services, and denying civil rights all for the sake of the children. Consequences be damned, we resist lessons of holistic sexual openness from our far sexually healthier Western allies. Instead we champion the A & B only of the "Abstinence, Be Faithful, Use Condoms" HIV campaign launched by war torn, polygamist Uganda, which now rewards virginal new brides with TV sets instead of goats.

Steeped in raunch culture that shames or sensationalizes young sex, we grasp onto Disney offerings of purity no matter how often or far our sexy virgins fall (Britney, Jessica Simpson, Mandy Moore), and as long as new ones keep us afloat (Miley Cyrus, Jonas Brothers). But sustaining the virgin–whore dichotomy after all these centuries perverts smart decision making for all. You can't answer a high-tech free society's hypersexualized reality with fictionalized extremism? As I wrote in a 2001 column, "The Britney and Bob Challenge," about America's sexual schizophrenia and refusal to move beyond sexuality's marital ideal or commodified reality: neither excess nor repression develops into sexual intimacy or connection, let alone responsibility.

In *17 Again*, Disney's *High School Musical* heartthrob Zac Efron dresses down sexy cheerleaders, saying boys don't respect them, and rebukes a condom-distributing teacher with "abstinence is best," he knows. Well his character knows because he's really his dad who lost his basketball scholarship because he knocked up his high school sweetheart and chose teen marriage and fatherhood. So even though abstinence-only didn't work any more for him than for Bristol Palin, the lesson remains "no sex unless married," not responsible sexual choices like protection or non-coital play.

In real life, Zac Efron dates his HSM co-star Vanessa Hudgens, who suffered momentary embarrassment when earlier sexy photos surfaced online. But after celebrating her 20th birthday, she and Zac comfortably posed when shopping at a Los Angeles sex-toy shop.

The *Today Show* recently pitted the feminist author of *The Purity Myth: How America's Obsession with Virginity is Hurting Young Women* against international abstinence advocate Lakita Garth, who promotes her success to staying a virgin until marriage at 36. Jessica Valenti points out that a women's worth is more than her hymen, and most fall between girls gone wild or chaste virgin. Like Zac and Vanessa versus their Disney image, most of us figure out how to achieve a full life *while* expressing our sexuality, married or not.

I saw Lakita Garth keynote an Abstinence Clearinghouse conference themed, "Abstinence: It's a Black and White Issue," as in "allowing no gray area between sexual integrity and irresponsibility." The flashy multimedia conference took me back to high school pep rallies and my cheerleader senti-mentality. Watching a bejeweled and stylin' Garth flash photos of herself with President Bush as she bragged about her virginity-won "bling," I momentarily felt sexually inadequate for my life's choices before marrying at almost 32. After all, I don't have any photos with a U.S. president. But by Star Parker, a self-described former welfare queen and abortion regular, reducing all of America's problems to the denial of God's sexual truth, I kept from getting further swept away by the idealism and heartfelt talent of the "Abstinence Idol" competition.

Though Kelly Clarkson, a self-proclaimed Christian virgin, won *American Idol's* first season, this year's likely winner, Adam Lambert, doesn't deny rumors of his being gay or bisexual. When Internet photos circulated of him kissing other men and dressed in drag, he responded, "I have nothing to hide. I am who I am." Other successful *American Idol* contestants include Clay Aiken, who finally came out as gay when he announced becoming a father with his male "friend," and Fantasia, a young single mom.

Oh, I like being an American and am glad my six-year-old son, husband, and I have so many more sexual and gender options today than in the 1800s or 1950s. The virginal ideal of the 1950s was beautiful, bubbly movie icon Sandra Dee, whose reality was an incest survivor, divorced at 22, and a lonely life of anorexia, alcoholism, and depression.

Because my son is so precious, I'll protect him by preparing him to make healthy sexual decisions throughout his life. I'm not going to feed him more of the same parental "do as I say, not as I do or did" crap, but will teach him moral reasoning over absolutes. I'll teach him to be is own moral agent, to value himself, to choose pleasure no matter how much purity or promiscuity extremes are forced upon him. I'll teach him that this is the United States of America and his sex does not belong to the church or state.

To reach humanity's highest ideals, permission trumps repression. With rights come responsibilities. My son may mess up, as I have, and will have to deal with consequences with respect and dignity. And I'll work for a world that uses all of its modern resources to ameliorate harm. As Mahatma Gandhi said, "Freedom is not worth having if it does not include the freedom to make mistakes."

POSTSCRIPT

Has Sex Become Too Casual?

Some commentators who view sex as having become too casual today point to explicitly sexual lyrics in popular music for sexualizing modern culture. Consider three sets of sexually explicit lyrics by different composers.

1. A composer encourages his listeners to shake their bodies "like a Polaroid picture," and the accompanying music video on YouTube makes it clear that the performer is referring to the shaking of one's buttocks and/or breasts.
2. A second composer processes her sexual encounter with another female while considering the consequences on her relationship with her boyfriend.
3. A third composer describes a woman tricking her boyfriend into performing analingus (mouth-to-anus sexual contact) on her.

Which of these three lyrical pieces would you consider to be the *most* promoting of casual sex? If you chose the first, you charged the contemporary group Outkast with promoting casual sex in their smash hit, "Hey Ya." Sample lyrics follow:

> *Shake it, shake, shake it, shake it (OHH OH)*
> *Shake it, shake it, shake, shake it, shake it, shake it (OHH OH)*
> *Shake it, shake it like a Polaroid Picture, shake it, shake it*
> *Shh you got to, shake it, shh shake it, shake it, got to shake it*
> *(Shake it Suga') shake it like a Polaroid Picture*

If you chose #2, you decided that Katy Perry was the most promoting of casual sex in her popular song from 2008, "I Kissed a Girl." Read on for an excerpt.

> *"I kissed a girl and I liked it, the taste of her cherry chapstick.*
> *I kissed a girl just to try it, I hope my boyfriend don't mind it.*
> *It felt so wrong, it felt so right. Don't mean I'm in love tonight.*
> *I kissed a girl and I liked it (I liked it)."*

If you chose the third—the piece describing analingus—then you thought that the lyrics of Geoffrey Chaucer, written more than 600 years ago, were the most promoting of casual sex. An excerpt from "The Miller's Tale" in *The Canterbury Tales* follows, in which Absalom's girlfriend gives him quite a surprise.

> *And through the window she put out her hole.*
> *And Absalom no better felt nor worse,*

But with his mouth he kissed her naked arse
Right greedily, before he knew of this.

Although many other examples of casual, sexually explicit passages can be found in some of the world's great literature—from ancient Greece's Aristophanes, to William Shakespeare, to the modern day—it still seems to many who would agree with Hagelin that today's society is more casual than ever about sex. What is it about modern-day society that fosters these impressions? Is Hagelin right that sex has become way too casual and parents and schools need to take greater responsibility in raising the bar of expectation for children? Is Riscol right that sexual values have been depraved at other times in history? How does Riscol's understanding of moral depravity differ from Hagelin's? With whom do you agree? After considering Hagelin and Riscol's viewpoints, how would you describe the sexual norms at your college in comparison with what you know about other generations or other times in history?

Suggested Readings

D. Herzog, *Sex in Crisis: The New Sexual Revolution and the Future of American Politics* (New York: Basic Books, 2007).

M. Klein, *America's War on Sex* (Santa Barbara, CA: Praeger, 2006).

J. McIllhaney and F.M. Bush, F. M., *Hooked: New Science on How Casual Sex is Affecting Our Children* (Chicago: Moody Publishers, 2008).

J.A. Sherman and N. Tocantins, N., *The Happy Hook-Up. A Single Girl's Guide to Casual Sex* (Berkeley, CA: Ten Speed Press, 2004).

B. Taverner, "Behind the Music: Music Literacy and Healthy Relationships," in S. Montfort and P. Brick, *Unequal Partners: Teaching about Power and Consent in Adult–Teen and Other Relationships* (Morristown, NJ: Planned Parenthood of Greater Northern New Jersey, 2007).

Special thanks to Dr. Robert T. Francoeur, co-editor of the *International Encyclopedia of Sexuality,* for his extensive notes on sexual customs in American history.

Source: www.litrix.com/canterby/cante004.htm

ISSUE 2

Can Sex Be Addictive?

YES: Patrick J. Carnes, from "Frequently Asked Questions," http://www.sexhelp.com/addiction_faq.cfm (November 11, 2009)

NO: Lawrence A. Siegel and Richard M. Siegel, from "Sex Addiction: Recovering from a Shady Concept," An original essay written for this volume (2006)

ISSUE SUMMARY

YES: Patrick J. Carnes, considered by many to be an expert on sexual addiction, answers some common questions about this phenomenon, as featured on the Web site http://www.sexhelp.com. Carnes discusses the nature of sexual addiction, including ways in which it might be manifested, and offers suggestions for treatment.

NO: Sex therapist Lawrence A. Siegel and sex therapist/educator Richard M. Siegel counter that sexual addiction is grounded in "moralistic ideology masquerading as science." They argue that while some sexual behaviors may be dysfunctional, the term "sexual addiction" pathologizes many common forms of sexual expression that are not problematic.

What is sex? Does it include masturbation? Does it include oral or anal intercourse, in addition to vaginal intercourse? Are nongenital touching behaviors, like kissing or massage, sexual in nature? And how about the viewing of erotic material or the reading of an erotic passage? Answers will depend on whom you ask.

Similarly, people have very different opinions about how much sex is *too much* sex. Consider this exchange from the 1977 Woody Allen movie, *Annie Hall*. Two characters, Alvy and Annie, have just been asked by their therapists if they have sex "often."

> *Alvie* Hardly ever. Maybe three times a week.

> *Annie* Constantly. I'd say three times a week.

Whether or not one can (or is) having too much sex might be a matter of perspective, as it seems to be for Alvie (wanting more) and Annie (wanting less).

14

On the other hand, some aspects of the sexological community will clearly tell you that there is a point at which sex can become too much. The website for Sex Addicts Anonymous (www.sexaa.org) states that addicts are "powerless over our sexual thoughts and behaviors and that our preoccupation with sex was causing progressively severe adverse consequences for us, our families, and our friends. Despite many failed promises to ourselves and attempts to change, we discovered that we were unable to stop acting out sexually by ourselves." The site points the visitor to links for additional resources and meeting information.

Much of the modern understanding of sexual addiction comes from the work of Patrick J. Carnes, who authored *Don't Call It Love: Recovery from Sexual Addiction*. Carnes co-founded the Society for the Advancement of Sexual Health in 1987, an organization dedicated to "helping those who suffer from out-of-control sexual behavior." Today, Carnes is considered a leading authority on sexual addiction in a field that includes prevention services, treatment services (including a 12-step recovery model), professional conferences, an academic journal (*Sexual Addiction and Compulsivity*), and more.

Other sexologists call the whole idea of sexual addiction nonsense and say that the very term "sexual addiction" invites comparison to other addictions in which the object of addiction (heroin, nicotine, alcohol, gambling, etc.) is inherently harmful. They explain that sex, as a normal biological drive, should not be placed in the same category. Efforts to create an addiction out of sex do nothing more than feed a hungry new addiction treatment industry that is erotophobic at its core.

In the following passages, Patrick J. Carnes explains the nature of sexual addiction, signs of possible sexual addiction, codependency, and different types of treatment. Sex therapists Lawrence Siegel and Richard Siegel reject the notion of "sexual addiction" as unscientific and moralistic.

Frequently Asked Questions

Like an alcoholic unable to stop drinking, sexual addicts are unable to stop their self-destructive sexual behavior. Family breakups, financial disaster, loss of jobs, and risk to life are the painful themes of their stories.

Sex addicts come from all walks of life—they may be ministers, physicians, homemakers, factory workers, salespersons, secretaries, clerks, accountants, therapists, dentists, politicians, or executives, to name just a few examples. Most were abused as children—sexually, physically, and/or emotionally. The majority grew up in families in which addiction already flourished, including alcoholism, compulsive eating, and compulsive gambling. Most grapple with other addictions as well, but they find sex addiction the most difficult to stop.

Much hope nevertheless exists for these addicts and their families. Sex addicts have shown an ability to transform a life of self-destruction into a life of self-care, a life in chaos and despair into one of confidence and peace.

Patrick J. Carnes, Ph.D.
Author of *Out of the Shadows*, 1992

- What is sexual addiction?
- What is sexual anorexia?
- Sexual dependency vs. other addictions
- How many people are affected by sexual addiction?
- What are multiple addictions?
- Are more sex addicts male or female?
- Why don't sexual addicts "just stop" their destructive behavior?
- What about AIDS and the sexual addict?
- How is Sexual Addiction diagnosed?
- What are the behavior patterns which may indicate sexual behavior?
- What is the role of Cybersex?
- What help is there for Sexual Addiction or Sexual Anorexia?
- What treatment is available for sex addiction?
- Are sexual addicts ever cured?
- Is there any help available for the partners of sex addicts?

What Is Sexual Addiction?

Sexual addiction is defined as any sexually-related, compulsive behavior which interferes with normal living and causes severe stress on family, friends, loved ones, and one's work environment.

From www.sexhelp.com, 2009. Copyright © 2009 by Patrick J. Carnes. Reprinted by permission.

Sexual addiction has been called sexual dependency and sexual compulsivity. By any name, it is a compulsive behavior that completely dominates the addict's life. Sexual addicts make sex a priority more important than family, friends, and work. Sex becomes the organizing principle of addict's lives. They are willing to sacrifice what they cherish most in order to preserve and continue their unhealthy behavior.

No single behavior pattern defines sexual addiction. These behaviors, when they have taken control of addicts' lives and become unmanageable, include: compulsive masturbation, compulsive heterosexual and homosexual relationships, pornography, prostitution, exhibitionism, voyeurism, indecent phone calls, child molesting, incest, rape and violence. Even the healthiest forms of human sexual expression can turn into self-defeating behaviors.

What Is Sexual Anorexia?

Sexual anorexia is an obsessive state in which the physical, mental, and emotional task of avoiding sex dominates one's life. Like self-starvation with food or compulsive dieting or hoarding with money, deprivation with sex can make one feel powerful and defended against all hurts. As with any other altered state of consciousness, such as those brought on by chemical use, compulsive gambling or eating, or any other addiction process, the preoccupation with the avoidance of sex can seem to obliterate one's life problems. The obsession can then become a way to cope with all stress and all life difficulties. Yet, as with other addictions and compulsions, the costs are great. In this case, sex becomes a furtive enemy to be continually kept at bay, even at the price of annihilating a part of oneself.

Specialists in sexual medicine have long noted the close parallels between food disorders and sexual disorders. Many professionals have observed how food anorexia and sexual anorexia share common characteristics. In both cases, the sufferers starve themselves in the midst of plenty. Both types of anorexia feature the essential loss of self, the same distortions of thought, and the agonizing struggle for control over the self and others. Both share the same extreme self-hatred and sense of profound alienation. But while the food anorexic is obsessed with the self-denial of physical nourishment, the sexual anorexic focuses his or her anxiety on sex. As a result, the sexual anorexic will typically experience the following:

- A dread of sexual pleasure
- A morbid and persistent fear of sexual contact
- Obsession and hyper vigilance around sexual matters
- Avoidance of anything connected with sex
- Preoccupation with others being sexual
- Distortions of body appearance
- Extreme loathing of body functions
- Obsessional self-doubt about sexual adequacy
- Rigid, judgmental attitudes about sex
- Excessive fear and preoccupation with sexual diseases
- Obsessive concern or worry about the sexual activity of others

- Shame and self-loathing over sexual experiences
- Depression about sexual adequacy and functioning
- Self-destructive behavior to limit, stop, or avoid sex

Sexual anorexics can be men as well as women. Their personal histories often include sexual exploitation or some form of severely traumatic sexual rejection—or both. Experiences of childhood sexual abuse are common with sexual anorexics, often accompanied by other forms of childhood abuse and neglect. As a result of these traumas, they may tend to carry dark secrets and maintain seemingly insane loyalties that have never been disclosed. In fact, sexual anorexics are for the most part not conscious of the hidden dynamics driving them.

Dr. Carnes, book *Sexual Anorexia* focuses on the suffering of the sexual anorexic. Sexual anorexia is as destructive as the illnesses that often accompany it, and behind which it often hides, such as alcoholism, drug addiction, sexual addiction, and compulsive eating. It resides in emotion so raw that most sufferers would wish to keep it buried forever were it not so painful to live this way. Sexual anorexia feeds on betrayal, violence, and rejection. It gathers strength from a culture that makes sexual satisfaction both an unreachable goal and a nonnegotiable demand. Our media focus almost exclusively on sensational sexual problems such as rape, child abuse, sexual harassment, or extramarital affairs. When people have problems being sexual, we are likely to interpret the difficulty as a need for a new technique or a matter of misinformation. For those who suffer from sexual anorexia, technique and information are not remotely enough. Help comes only through an intentional, planned effort to break the bonds of obsession that keep anorexics stuck.

This book is intended as a guide to support that effort. The early chapters help the reader understand sexual anorexia: how it starts, and how it gathers such strength. The last twelve chapters present a clinically tested and proven plan for achieving a healthy sexuality. This program has worked for many, many people. It is safe. It is practical. It works if the sufferer follows the guidelines and has the appropriate outside support. It will not be easy because the obsession was created in the first place by intimate violations and shattered trust. Yet step by step, healing can be effected so that the sufferer can learn to trust the self as well as others.

Recognition of Sexual Addiction by the Professional Health Care Community

Sexual addiction was first brought to the forefront in Dr. Patrick Carnes' 1983 book, *Out of the Shadows: Understanding Sexual Addiction* (Hazelden). Since then, thousands of people have come forward seeking help, and more and more professionals are being trained to identify and treat sexual addiction.

The Society for the Advancement of Sex Health was created in 1987 to serve as an independent clearing house for information on sexual addiction and treatment options. One of SASH's missions is to decrease the stigma surrounding sexual addiction problems and treatment. They may be contacted at:

The Society for the Advancement of Sex Health
P.O. Box 725544
Atlanta, Georgia 31139
1-770-541-9912
e-mail-sash@sash.net

Medical and clinical research appears each quarter in *Sexual Addiction and Compulsivity; The Journal of Treatment and Prevention* published by Taylor and Francis. For further information contact:

Taylor and Francis
1101 Vermont Ave., N.W., Suite 200
Washington, DC
1-800-272 -7737

For a recent listing of relevant articles about sex addiction see the *Sexual Resource* section.

Sexual Dependency vs. Other Addictions

Sexual addiction can be understood by comparing it to other types of addictions. Individuals addicted to alcohol or other drugs, for example, develop a relationship with their "chemical(s) of choice"—a relationship that takes precedence over any and all other aspects of their lives. Addicts find they need drugs merely to feel normal.

In sexual addiction, a parallel situation exists. Sex—like food or drugs in other addictions—provides the "high" and addicts become dependent on this sexual high to feel normal. They substitute unhealthy relationships for healthy ones. They opt for temporary pleasure rather than the deeper qualities of "normal" intimate relationships.

Sexual addiction follows the same progressive nature of other addictions. Sexual addicts struggle to control their behaviors, and experience despair over their constant failure to do so. Their loss of self-esteem grows, fueling the need to escape even further into their addictive behaviors. A sense of powerlessness pervades the lives of addicts.

How Many People Are Affected by Sexual Addiction?

Estimates range from 3 to 6 percent of the population.

What Are Multiple Addictions?

National surveys revealed that most sexual addicts come from severely dysfunctional families. Usually at least one other member of these families has another addiction (87%).

Dual addictions include sexual addiction and:

- Chemical Dependency (42%)
- Eating Disorder (38%)
- Compulsive Working (28%)
- Compulsive Spending (26%)
- Compulsive Gambling (5%)

Sexual Addiction and Abuse

Research has shown that a very high correlation exists between childhood abuse and sexual addiction in adulthood.

Sexual addicts, both men and women, who have reported experiencing:

- Emotional Abuse (97%)
- Sexual Abuse (83%)
- Physical Abuse (71%)

There is a growing body of evidence that early child abuse, especially sexual, is a primary factor in the onset of sex addiction. It appears that biological shifts occur in the brain, which heightens the brain's arousal mechanisms as well as limiting the ability to inhibit behavior.

Are More Sex Addicts Male or Female?

It remains unclear whether one gender has a higher incidence of sexual addiction that the other. Research by Dr. Carnes shows that approximately 20–25% of all patients who seek help for sexual dependency are women. (This same male-female ratio is found among those recovering from alcohol addiction, drug addiction, and pathological gambling.)

As once was the case with alcohol addiction, many people cannot accept the reality that women can become sexual addicts. One of the greatest problems facing female sexual addicts is convincing others that they have a legitimate problem.

The great irony is that sex addiction in women appears to be increasing. In recent, very large studies of on-line behavior, 40% of those struggling with sexually compulsive behavior are women.

Why Don't Sexual Addicts "Just Stop" Their Destructive Behavior?

Sexual addicts feel tremendous quilt and shame about their out-of-control behavior, and they live in constant fear of discovery. Yet addicts will often act out sexually in an attempt to block out the very pain of their addiction. This is part of what drives the addictive cycle. Like other forms of addiction, sex addicts are out of control and unable to stop their behaviors despite their self-destructive nature and potentially devastating consequences.

Key to understanding loss of control in addicts is the concept of the "hijacked brain." Addicts essentially have rewired their brains so that they do behaviors (drinking, drug use, eating, gambling, and sex) even when they are intending to do something quite different. The triggers to these maladaptive responses are usually stress, emotional pain, or specific childhood scenarios of sexual abuse or sexual trauma. Breakthrough science in examining brain function is helping us to understand the biology of this disease.

What about AIDS and the Sexual Addict?

As a function of their denial system, sexual addicts often ignore the severe emotional, interpersonal, and physical consequences of their behavior. Addicts are so entrenched in maintaining their behaviors that environmental cues which would signal caution and danger to most non-addicted people are lost to them. Such has been the case with the HIV virus and other dangerous, sexually transmitted diseases (STDs).

Sexual addicts are focused on getting a sexual "fix." They may occasionally consider the possible consequences of their activities, but in the throes of the addictive cycle, rational thinking is seldom, if ever, present. Often dismissing the potential danger of their behavior, addicts will embrace an anxiety-laden situation to enhance their sexual high. Avoiding reality and disregarding personal safety and health are typical symptoms of sexual addiction, and they put sexual addicts at grave risk for contracting one of the many disabling STDs, including HIV.

Fear of being infected with the HIV virus and developing AIDS is not enough to stop an addict intent on being anonymously sexual, picking up prostitutes, or having multiple affairs with unsafe sex partners. Even the potential of infecting a loved one with an STD is often not enough to stop addicts from acting out. In fact, sexual addicts may find ways to act out even more intensely after such sexual practices in order to help drown out the shame and guilt of an overloaded and repressed emotional life.

Despite the frequency and range of their acting-out experiences, sexual addicts are often poorly informed about sexuality in general. An important part of their recovery process is learning about healthy sexual practices: behaviors which are connecting and affirming rather than shaming and guilt inducing. In addition, sexual addicts often need to be taught about safe sexual practices, basic self-care, and health concerns.

How Is Sexual Addiction Diagnosed?

Often sexual addicts don't know what is wrong with them. They may suffer from clinical depression or have suicidal tendencies. They may even think they are losing their minds.

There are, however, recognizable behavior patterns which indicate the presence of sexual addiction. Diagnosis should be done by a mental health professional trained in carrying out such diagnoses.

To help professionals determine whether a sexual addiction is present, Dr. Carnes has developed the Sexual Addiction Screening Test (SAST), an assessment tool specially designed for this purpose. . . .

What Are the Behavior Patterns That May Indicate Sexual Behavior?

While an actual diagnosis for sexual addiction should be carried out by a mental health professional, the following behavior patterns can indicate the presence of sexual addiction. Individuals who see any of these patterns in their own life, or in the life of someone they care about, should seek professional help.

1. Acting out: a pattern of out-of-control sexual behavior
   Examples may include:
   - Compulsive masturbation
   - Indulging in pornography
   - Having chronic affairs
   - Exhibitionism
   - Dangerous sexual practices
   - Prostitution
   - Anonymous sex
   - Compulsive sexual episodes
   - Voyeurism
2. Experiencing severe consequences due to sexual behavior, and an inability to stop despite these adverse consequences
   Some of the losses reported by sexual addicts include:
   - Loss of partner or spouse (40%)
   - Severe marital or relationship problems (70%)
   - Loss of career opportunities (27%)
   - Unwanted pregnancies (40%)
   - Abortions (36%)
   - Suicide obsession (72%)
   - Suicide attempts (17%)
   - Exposure to AIDS and venereal disease (68%)
   - Legal risks from nuisance offenses to rape (58%)
3. Persistent pursuit of self-destructive behavior
   Even understanding that the consequences of their actions will be painful or have dire consequences does not stop addicts from acting out. They often seem to have a willfulness about their actions, and an attitude that says, "I'll deal with the consequences when they come."
4. Ongoing desire or effort to limit sexual behavior
   Addicts often try to control their behavior by creating external barriers to it. For example, some move to a new neighborhood

or city, hoping that a new environment removed from old affairs will help. Some think marriage will keep them from acting out. An exposer may buy a car in which it's difficult to act out while driving.

Others seeking control over their behavior try to immerse themselves in religion, only to find out that while religious compulsion may soothe their shame, it does not end their acting out.

Many go through periods of sexual anorexia during which they allow themselves no sexual expression at all. Such efforts, however, only fuel the addiction.

5. Sexual obsession and fantasy as a primary coping strategy
   Though acting out sexually can temporarily relieve addicts' anxieties, they still find themselves spending inordinate amounts of time in obsession and fantasy. By fantasizing, the addict can maintain an almost constant level of arousal. Together with obsessing, the two behaviors can create a kind of analgesic "fix." Just as our bodies generate endorphins, natural anti-depressants, during vigorous exercise, our bodies naturally release peptides when sexually aroused. The molecular construction of these peptides parallels that of opiates like heroin or morphine, but are many times more powerful.

6. Regularly increasing the amount of sexual experience because the current level of activity is no longer sufficiently satisfying
   Sexual addiction is often progressive. While addicts may be able to control themselves for a time, inevitably their addictive behaviors will return and quickly escalate to previous levels and beyond. Some addicts begin adding additional acting out behaviors. Usually addicts will have three or more behaviors which play a key role in their addiction—masturbation, affairs, and anonymous sex, for instance.

   In addition, 89% of addicts reported regularly "bingeing" to the point of emotional exhaustion. The emotional pain of withdrawal for sexual addicts can parallel the physical pain experienced by those withdrawing from opiate addiction.

7. Severe mood changes related to sexual activity
   Addicts experience intense mood shifts, often due to the despair and shame of having unwanted sex. Sexual addicts are caught in a crushing cycle of shame-driven and shame-creating behavior. While shame drives the sexual addicts' actions, it also becomes the unwanted consequence of a few moments of euphoric escape into sex.

8. Inordinate amounts of time spent obtaining sex, being sexual, and recovering from sexual experiences
   Two sets of activities organize sexual addicts' days. One involves obsessing about sex, time devoted to initiating sex, and actually being sexual. The second involves time spent dealing with the consequences of their acting out: lying, covering up, shortages of money, problems with their spouse, trouble at work, neglected children, and so on.

9. Neglect of important social, occupational, or recreational activities because of sexual behavior

As more and more of addicts' energy becomes focused on relationships which have sexual potential, other relationships and activities—family, friends, work, talents and values—suffer and atrophy from neglect. Long-term relationships are stormy and often unsuccessful. Because of sexual over-extension and intimacy avoidance, short-term relationships become the norm.

Sometimes, however, the desire to preserve an important long-term relationship with spouse or children, for instance, can act as the catalyst for addicts to admit their problem and seek help.

What Is the Role of Cybersex?

Today over 70% of sex addicts report having problematic on-line sexual behavior. Two-thirds of those engaged have such despair over their internet activities that have had suicidal thoughts. Sexual acting out online has been shown to manifest in similar off-line behavior. People who already were sex addicts find the internet accelerates their problem. Those who start in the on-line behavior quickly start to act out in new ways off-line. One of the pioneering researchers of this problem, the late Dr. Al Cooper, described on-line sexual behavior as the "crack-cocaine" of sexual compulsivity.

What Help Is There for Sexual Addiction or Sexual Anorexia?

1. Take our online test, the *SAST*
2. Contact a Certified Sex Addition Therapist (CSAT) for help. You can find a therapist in your area by calling 800-708-1796. . . .
3. Twelve step programs
4. Visit GentlePath.com to browse the online catalog for books and tapes, which will help you understand sex addiction and sexual anorexia.

Getting Help: The First Step

The first step in seeking help is to admit to the problem. Though marital, professional, and societal consequences may follow, admission of the problems must come, no matter the cost. Fear of these consequences unfortunately keeps many sexual addicts from seeking help.

Many sources of help are available to provide information, support, and assistance for sexual addicts trying to regain control of their lives. These include inpatient and outpatient treatment, professional associations, self-help groups, and aftercare support groups.

Sex Addicts Anonymous (SAA)
P.O. Box 70949
Houston, TX 77270
1-800-477-8191
e-mail: webmaster@saa-recovery.org

SASH
P.O. Box 725544
Atlanta, GA 31139
1-770-541-9912
e-mail: info@SASH.net

Sex Compulsives Anonymous (SCA)
P.O. Box 1585
Old Chelsea Station
New York, NY 10011
(001)210-828-7900
email: info@slaafws.org

Sex and Love Addicts Anonymous (SLAA)
1550 NE Loop 410, Ste. 118
San Antonio, TX 78209
212-439-1123
email: info@slaafws.org

National Council for Couple and Family Recovery
P.O. Box 410586
St. Louis, MO 63141
314-997-9808
email: nccfr@hotmail.com

What Treatment Is Available for Sex Addiction?

Treatment programs for sexual addiction include patient, outpatient, and aftercare support, and self-help groups. Treatment programs also offer family counseling programs, support groups, and educational workshops for addicts and their families to help them understand the facets of belief and family like that are part of the addiction.

Unlike recovering alcoholics who must abstain from drinking for life, sexual addicts are led back into a normal, healthy sex life much in the way those suffering from eating disorders must relearn healthy eating patterns.

The staff at Gentle Path is trained to help individuals develop healthy, effective coping skills through interacting with others experiencing similar problems. Gentle Path is designed to set addicts on the road to recovery, to provide relapse prevention techniques, and to help them stay in recovery with the help of aftercare and Twelve Step recovery support groups.

Are Sexual Addicts Ever Cured?

Like other types of addicts, some sexual addicts may never be "cured." Sexual addicts achieve a state of recovery, but maintaining that recovery can be a lifelong, day-by-day process. The Twelve Step treatment approach teaches addicts to take their recovery "one day at a time"—concentrating on the present, not the future.

Is There Any Help Available for the Partners of Sex Addicts?

Partners of sexual addicts, like partners of alcoholics, can also benefit from counseling and support groups. Normally these partners are codependents, and they, too, suffer from the extreme adverse effects of the addiction. Inpatient and outpatient programs, counseling, and support groups are all available to help them regain control of their lives and support the recovery of their partner.

Codependents can find support by contracting:

S-Anon Family Groups
P.O. Box 5117
Sherman Oaks, CA 91413
818-990-6910

Codependents of Sex Addicts (CoSA)
P.O. Box 14537
Minneapolis, MN 55414
612-537-6904

Lawrence A. Siegel and
Richard M. Siegel

 **NO**

Sex Addiction: Recovering from a Shady Concept

It seems, more than ever, that many Americans are more comfortable keeping sex in the dark or, as sex addiction advocates might actually prefer, *in* the shadows. We seem to have gotten no further than the Puritan claims of sex being evil and pleasure being threatening. "The Devil made me do it" seems to be something of a battle cry, especially when someone gets caught cheating on their spouse, having inappropriate dalliances with congressional pages, or visiting prostitutes. Even those not in relationships are easily targeted. We constantly hear about the "dangers" of Internet porn and how every Internet chat room is just teeming with predators just waiting to devour our children. Daily masturbation is considered by these folks as being unhealthy and a marked pathology. As a society, we seem able to be comfortable with sex only as long as we make it uncomfortable. As one of the leading sexologists, Marty Klein, once wrote:

> "If mass murderer Ted Bundy had announced that watching Cosby Show reruns had motivated his awful crimes, he would have been dismissed as a deranged sociopath. Instead, Bundy proclaimed that his 'pornography addiction' made him do it, and many Right-wing feminists and conservatives treated this as the conclusion of a thoughtful social scientist. Why?"[1]

The whole idea of "sex addiction" is borne out of a moralistic ideology masquerading as science. It is a concept that seems to serve no other purpose than to relegate sexual expression to the level of shameful acts, except within the extremely narrow and myopic scope of a monogamous, heterosexual marriage. Sexual diversity? Interests in unusual forms or frequency of sexual expression? Choosing not to be monogamous? Advocates of "sex addiction" would likely see these as the uncontrollable acts of a sexually pathological individual; one who needs curing.

To be clear, we do not deny the fact that, for some people, sexual behavior can become problematic, even dysfunctional or unmanageable. Our objection is with the use of the term "sexual addiction" to describe a virtually unlimited array of—in fact, practically ANY—aspect of sexual expression that falls outside of the typically Christian view of marriage. We believe that the term

An original essay written for this volume. Copyright © 2007 by Lawrence A. Siegel and Richard M. Siegel. Reprinted by permission.

contributes to a generally sex-negative, pleasure-phobic tone in American society, and it also tends to "pathologize" most forms of sexual expression that fall outside of a narrow view of what "normal" sex is supposed to look like. This is a point made clear by sex addiction advocates" own rhetoric. Three of the guiding principles of Sexaholics Anonymous include the notion that (1) sex is most healthy in the context of a monogamous, heterosexual relationship; (2) sexual expression has "obvious" limits; and (3) it is unhealthy to engage in any sexual activity for the sole purpose of feeling better, either emotionally or to escape one's problems. These principles do not represent either science or most people's experience. They, in fact, represent a restrictive and repressive view of sex and sexuality and reflect an arrogance that sex addiction proponents are the keepers of the scepter of morality and normalcy. Moreover, the concept of "sex addiction" comes out of a shame-based, arbitrarily judgmental addiction model and does not speak to the wide range of sexual diversity; both in and outside the context of a committed relationship.

A primary objection to the use of the term "sex addiction," an objection shared with regard to other supposed behavioral "addictions," is that the term *addiction* has long ago been discredited. Back in 1964, the World Health Organization (WHO) declared the term "addiction" to be clinically invalid and recommended in favor of dependence, which can exist in varying degrees of severity, as opposed to an all-or-nothing disease entity (as it is still commonly perceived).[2] This is when we began to see the terms *chemical dependency* and substance abuse, terms considered to be much more appropriate and clinically useful. This, however, did not sit well with the addiction industry. Another objection to the concept of "sex addiction" is that it is a misnomer whose very foundation as a clinically significant diagnosis is built on flawed and faulty premises. For example, a common assertion put forth by proponents of sex addiction states that the chemical actions in the brain during sexual activity are the same as the chemical activity involved in alcohol and drug use. They, therefore, claim that both sexual activity and substance abuse share reward and reinforcement mechanisms that produce the "craving" and "addictive" behaviors. This assertion is flawed on several levels, not the least of which is that it is based on drawing conclusions from brain scan imaging that are devoid of any real interpretive foundation; a "leap of faith," so to speak. Furthermore, it is somewhat of a stretch to equate the neurophysiological mechanisms which underlie chemical dependency, tolerance, and withdrawal with the underlying mechanisms of what is most often obsessive-compulsive or anxiety-reducing behaviors like gambling, shopping, and sex. Another example often cited by sex addiction proponents is the assertion that, like alcohol and drugs, the "sex addict" is completely incapable of controlling his or her self-destructive behavior. Of course, this begs the question of how, then, can one change behavior they are incapable of controlling? More importantly, however, is the unique excuse this "disease" model provides for abdicating personal responsibility. "It's not my fault, I have a disease." Finally, a major assertion put out by sex addiction advocates is that anyone who is hypersexual in any way (e.g., frequent masturbation, anonymous "hook ups," infidelity, and cybersex) must have been abused as children or adolescents. Again, the flaws here are obvious and serve to continue to relegate any type of frequent sexual engagement to the pathological and unseemly.

Every clinician knows that "addiction" is not a word that appears anywhere in the Diagnostic and Statistical Manual, or "DSM," the diagnostic guidebook used by psychiatrists and psychologists to make any psychopathological diagnosis. Nor does it appear in any of the International Classification of Diseases (ICD-10), codes used for classifying medical diagnoses. "Abuse" and "dependence" do appear in the DSM, relevant only to substance use patterns, but "addiction" does not. Similarly, there is an ICD-10 code for "substance dependence," but not addiction. Why? Perhaps because the word means different things to different people, especially when used in so many different contexts. Even without acknowledging the many trivial uses of the addiction concept, such as bumper stickers that proclaim, *"addicted to sports, not drugs,"* cookies that claim to be *"deliciously addicting,"* Garfield coffee mugs that warn *"don't talk to me until after my first cup,"* or T-shirts that say *"chocoholic,"* there aren't even consistent *clinical* definitions for the concept of addiction. A 1993 study, published in the American Journal of Drug and Alcohol Abuse, compared the diagnostic criteria for substance abuse and dependence between the DSM and ICD-10. The results showed very little agreement between the two.[3]

Pharmacologists, researchers who study the effects of drugs, define addiction primarily based on the presence of tolerance and withdrawal. Both of these phenomena are based on pharmacological and toxicological concepts of "cellular adaptation," wherein the body, at the very cellular level, becomes accustomed to the constant presence of a substance, and readjusts for "normal" function; in other words, whatever the "normal" response was before regular use of the substance began returns. This adaptation first accounts for tolerance, wherein an increasing dose of the substance to which the system has adapted is needed to maintain the same level of "normal." Then it results in withdrawal, wherein any discontinuation of the substance disrupts the "new" equilibrium the system has achieved and symptoms of "withdrawal sickness" ensue. This is probably most often attributed to addiction to opiates, such as heroin, because of its comparison to "having a monkey on one's back," with a constantly growing appetite, and its notorious "cold turkey" withdrawal. But perhaps it is most commonly observed with the chronic use of drugs with less sinister reputations, such as caffeine, nicotine or alcohol.

Traditional psychotherapists may typically define addiction as a faulty coping mechanism, or more accurately, the *result* of using a faulty coping mechanism to deal with some underlying issue. Another way to consider this is to see addiction as the symptom, rather than the disease, which is why the traditional therapist, of any theoretical orientation, is likely to want to find the causative issue or issues, and either teach the patient more effective coping mechanisms or resolve the unresolved issue(s) altogether.

Another definition of addiction has emerged, and seems to have taken center-stage, since the development of a pseudo-medical specialty known as "addictionology" within the last twenty or so years. Made up primarily of physicians, but including a variety of "addiction professionals," this field has helped to forge a treatment industry based on the disease model of addiction that is at the core of 12-Step "fellowships," such as Alcoholics Anonymous and Narcotics Anonymous. Ironically, despite the resistance to medical or psychiatric treatment historically expressed in AA or NA, their philosophy has become the mainstay of the addictionological paradigm.

If the concept of chemical addictions, which have a neurophysiological basis that can be measured and observed, yields no clinical consensus, how, then, can we legitimize the much vaguer notion that individuals can be "addicted" to behavior, people, emotions, or even one's own brain chemistry? Other than to undermine responsibility and self-determination, we really can't. It does a tremendous disservice to our clients and patients to brand them with a label so full of judgment, arbitrary opinion, and fatuous science. It robs individuals of the ability to find their own levels of comfort and, ultimately, be the determining force in directing their own lives. There is a significant and qualitative difference between the person who acts because he or she can't (not a choice, but a position of default) and the person who is empowered to choose not to. As clinicians, we should be loathe to send our clients and patients down such a fearful, shameful road.

In 1989, Patrick Carnes, founder of the sex addiction movement, wrote a book entitled "Contrary to Love." The book is rife with rhetoric and personal ideology that reveals Carnes's lack of training, knowledge, and understanding of sexuality and sexual expression; not surprising for someone whose background is solely in the disease model of alcoholism. This, while seemingly a harsh judgment, is clearly reflected in his Sex Addiction Screening Test (SAST). Even a cursory glance at the items on the SAST show a deep-seeded bias against most forms of sexual expression. Unlike other legitimate screening and assessment tools, there is no scientific foundation that would show this tool to be credible (i.e., tests of reliability and validity). Instead, Carnes developed this "test" by simply culling his own ideas from his book. Annie Sprinkle, America's first adult-film-star-turned-PhD-sexologist, has written a very good web article on the myth of sex addiction. In it, she also describes some of the shortcomings of the SAST. While not describing the complete test here, a listing of some of the assessment questions are listed below, along with commentary.[4]

1. *Have you subscribed to sexually explicit magazines like* Playboy *or* Penthouse? This question is based on the assumption that it is unhealthy to view images of naked bodies. Does that mean that the millions of people who subscribe to or buy adult magazines are sex addicts? Are adolescent boys who look at the *Sports Illustrated* Swim Suit edition budding sex addicts? By extension, if looking at *Playboy* or *Penthouse* is unhealthy and pathological, then those millions of people who look at hardcore magazines or Internet porn should be hospitalized!
2. *Do you often find yourself preoccupied with sexual thoughts?* This is totally nebulous. What does "preoccupied" mean? How often does one have to think about sex in order to constitute preoccupation? Research has shown that men, on average, think about sex every eight seconds; does that mean that men are inherently sex addicts?
3. *Do you feel that your sexual behavior is not normal?* What is normal? What do they use as a comparison? As sexologists, we can state

unequivocally that the majority of people's sexual concerns relate, in one way or another, to the question "Am I normal?" This is incredibly vague, nebulous, and laughably unscientific.

4. *Are any of your sexual activities against the law?* This question is also steeped in a bias that there is only a narrowly acceptable realm of sexual expression. It assumes that any sexual behavior that is against the law is bad. Is being or engaging a prostitute a sign of pathology? What about the fact that oral sex, anal sex, and woman on top are illegal in several states?

5. *Have you ever felt degraded by your sexual behavior?* Again, there is a serious lack of quantification here. Does regretting a sexual encounter constitute feeling degraded? Does performing oral sex for your partner, even though you think it's degrading, constitute a pathology or compromise? What if one's partner does something during sex play that is unexpected and perceived as degrading (like ejaculating on someone's face or body)? What if someone enjoys feeling degraded? This question pathologizes at least half of the S/M and B/D communities. Moreover, anyone who has had a long and active sexual life may likely, at one point, to have felt degraded. It is important to note that this question does not ask if one consistently puts oneself in a position of being degraded but, rather, have you ever felt degraded. We suspect that most people can lay claim to that.

6. *Has sex been a way for you to escape your problems?* Is there a better way to escape one's problems temporarily? This is a common bias used against both sex and alcohol use: using sex or alcohol to provide relief from anxieties or problems is inherently problematic. It also begs the question: why are things like sex and alcohol not appropriate to change how one is feeling but Zoloft, Paxil, Xanax, and Klonopin are? The truth of the matter is that sex is often an excellent and healthy way to occasionally experience relief from life's stressors and problems.

7. *When you have sex, do you feel depressed afterwards?* Sex is often a great way to get in touch with one's feelings. Oftentimes, people do feel depressed after a sexual experience, for any number of reasons. Furthermore, this doesn't mean that sex was the depressing part! Perhaps people feel depressed because they had dashed expectations of the person they were involved with. Unfulfilled expectations, lack of communication, and inattentiveness to one's needs and desires often result in post-coital feelings of sadness and disappointment. In addition, asking someone if they "feel depressed" is arbitrary, subjective, and clinically invalid.

8. *Do you feel controlled by your sexual desire?* Again, we are being asked to make an arbitrary, subjective, and clinically invalid assessment. There is an undercurrent here that seems to imply that a strong sexual desire is somehow not normal. Human beings are biologically programmed to strongly desire sex. Our clients and patients might be better served if we addressed not their desires, but how and when they *act* upon them.

Again, it needs noting that the concept of "sex addiction" is one with very little clinical relevance or usefulness, despite it's popularity. Healthy sexual expression encompasses a wide array of forms, functions, and frequency, as well as myriad emotional dynamics and personal experiences. Healthy behavior, in general, and sexual behavior, in particular, exists on a continuum rather than a quantifiable point. Using the addiction model to describe sexual behavior simply adds to the shame and stigma that is already too often attached to various forms of sexual expression. Can sexual behaviors become problematic? Most certainly. However, we must be careful to not overpathologize even problematic sexual behaviors because, most often, they are symptomatic expressions rather than primary problems.

For many years, sexologists have described compulsive sexual behavior, where sexual obsessions and compulsions are recurrent, distressing, and interfere with daily functioning. The actual number of people suffering from this type of sexual problem is relatively small. Compulsive sexual behaviors are generally divided into two broad categories: *paraphilic and non-paraphilic.*[5] Paraphilias are defined as recurrent, intensely arousing fantasies, sexual urges, or behaviors involving non-human objects, pain and humiliation, or children.[6] Paraphilic behaviors are usually non-conventional forms of sexual expression that, in the extreme, can be harmful to relationships and individuals. Some examples of paraphilias listed in the DSM are pedophilia (sexual attraction to children), exhibitionism (exposing one's genitals in public), voyeurism (sexual excitement from watching an unsuspecting person), sexual sadism (sexual excitement from dominating or inflicting pain), sexual masochism (sexual excitement from being dominated or receiving pain), transvestic fetishism (sexual excitement from wearing clothes of the other sex), and frotteurism (sexual excitement from rubbing up against or fondling an unsuspecting person). All of these behaviors exist on a continuum of healthy fantasy play to dangerous, abusive, and illegal acts. A sexologist is able to view these behaviors in varying degrees, knowing the difference between teacher-student fantasy role play and cruising a playground for victims; between provocative exhibitionist displays (including public displays of affection) and illegal, abusive public exposure. For those with a "sex addiction" perspective, simply having paraphilic thoughts or desires of any kind is reason to brand the individual a "sex addict."

The other category of compulsive sexual behavior is non-paraphilic, and generally involves more conventional sexual behaviors which, when taken to the extreme, cause marked distress and interference with daily functioning. This category includes a fixation on an unattainable partner, compulsive masturbation, compulsive love relationships, and compulsive sexuality in a relationship. The most vocal criticism of the idea of compulsive sexual behavior as a clinical disorder appears to center on the overpathologizing of these behaviors. Unless specifically trained in sexuality, most clinicians are either uncomfortable or unfamiliar with the wide range of "normal" sexual behavior and fail to distinguish between individuals who experience conflict between their values and sexual behavior, and those with obsessive sexual behavior.[7] When diagnosing compulsive sexual behavior overall, there is little consensus even among sexologists. However, it still provides a more useful clinical framework for the professional trained in sexuality and sexual health.

To recognize that sexual behavior can be problematic is not the same as labeling the behaviors as "sexually compulsive" or "sexual addiction." The reality is that sexual problems are quite common and are usually due to non-pathological factors. Quite simply, people make mistakes (some more than others). People also act impulsively. People don't always make good sexual choices. When people do make mistakes, act impulsively, and make bad decisions, it often negatively impacts their relationships; sometimes even their lives. Moreover, people do often use sex as a coping mechanism or, to borrow from addiction language, medicating behavior that can become problematic. However, this is qualitatively different from the concept that problematic sexual behavior means the individual is a "sexual addict" with uncontrollable urges and potentially dangerous intent. Most problematic sexual behavior can be effectively redirected (and cured) through psycho-sexual education, counseling, and experience. According to proponents of "sex addiction," problematic sexual behavior cannot be cured. Rather, the "sex addict" is destined for a life of maintaining a constant vigil to prevent the behavior from reoccurring, often to the point of obsession, and will be engaged in a lifelong process of recovery. Unfortunately, this view often causes people to live in fear of the "demon" lurking around every corner: themselves.

References

1. Klein M. The myth of sex addiction. Sexual Intelligence: An Electronic Newsletter (Issue #1). March, 2000. . . .

2. Center for Substance Abuse Treatment (CSAT) and Substance Abuse and Mental Health Services Administration (SAMHSA). Substance use disorders: A guide to the use of language. 2004.

3. Rappaport M, Tipp J, Schuckit M. A comparison of ICD-10 and DSM-III criteria for substance abuse and dependence. American Journal of Drug and Alcohol Abuse. June, 1993.

4. Sprinkle, A. Sex addiction. Online article. . . .

5. Coleman E. What sexual scientists know about compulsive sexual behavior. Electronic series of the Society for the Scientific Study of Sexuality (SSSS). Vol 2(1). 1996. . . .

6. American Psychiatric Association. Diagnostic and Statistical Manual of Mental Disorders. 4th edition, TR. Washington: American Psychiatric Publishing. June, 2000.

7. Coleman E. What sexual scientists know about compulsive sexual behavior. Electronic series of the Society for the Scientific Study of Sexuality (SSSS). Vol 2(1). 1996. . . .

POSTSCRIPT

Can Sex Be Addictive?

The framing of sex as a compulsive and addictive behavior is nothing new. The idea that masturbation and frequent intercourse could send a person into a downward spiral of unhealthiness was presented in advice columns, "health" journals, and other periodicals during the Victorian Era and the early 1900s. Consider the following excerpt about masturbation from John Harvey Kellogg's *Plain Facts for Old and Young*, written in 1891:

> As a sin against nature, it has no parallel except in sodomy. It is known by the terms self-pollution, self-abuse, masturbation, onanism, voluntary pollution, and solitary or secret vice. The habit is by no means confined to boys; girls also indulge in it, though it is to be hoped, to a less fearful extent than boys, at least in this country. Of all the vices to which human beings are addicted, no other so rapidly undermines the constitution, and so certainly makes a complete wreck of an individual as this, especially when the habit is begun at an early age. It wastes the most precious part of the blood, uses up the vital forces, and finally leaves the poor victim a most utterly ruined and loathsome object.
>
> Suspicious signs are: bashfulness, unnatural boldness, round shoulders and a stooping position, lack of development of the breasts in females, eating chalk, acne, and the use of tobacco.

Nineteenth-century preacher Sylvester Graham also described a litany of ailments that would affect the masturbator or anyone who had "frequent" intercourse before age 30. If the names Kellogg and Graham ring a bell, it may be because they created cornflakes and graham crackers—food products that were thought to suppress the sexual urges of some of the earliest "sex addicts" (which could have been just about anyone)!

More recently, attempts at measuring sexual addiction have taken on a more scientific tone, although critics of this term pose that it is simply the same old Victorian idea, repackaged for a new century. At the heart of this controversy, however, is the true meaning of a word many have trouble defining: addiction.

Think of the many things that might be considered addictive—alcohol, caffeine, tobacco, other drugs—and assess whether or not they are part of your life, or the lives of your family or friends. What makes something addictive? Is it how often a person indulges in it? Is it the degree to which it seems recreational or compulsive? Is it how much control a person has in deciding whether or not to engage in it? Or, is addiction more about what might be considered a social vice?

How about non-chemical behaviors that some might consider compulsive? Are people who surf the Internet for hours "addicted"? How about a political "junkie" who constantly scours newspapers and blogs for new information? The person who never misses an episode of their favorite TV crime-fighting drama, or who has every episode of *The Family Guy* on DVD? What about the guy who spends every Sunday (and Monday night) glued to the TV watching football, or the woman who builds her life around her favorite soaps? The person who constantly checks and updates his Twitter or Facebook account? Can a person be addicted to his or her artistic or musical pursuits? Are these harmless habits ways to relax and blow off steam? Which behaviors escape the realm of "addiction" because they are more socially functional?

Does something become addictive only when it is undesired or otherwise interferes with one's life? Does this apply to spending more time with one's hobbies than a significant other, family, or job might like? Does skipping class to play video games or engage in online gambling put one at the cusp of addiction? Considering sexual behaviors, is it possible to be addicted to masturbation or other sexual behaviors, as Carnes asserts? Is looking at online porn for hours different than playing an online game for hours? Is skipping class to have intercourse with a partner a sign of addiction? Is there a line between healthy sexual expression and compulsion or addiction? And if so, where is that line drawn?

Did you agree with Carnes' examples of behaviors that may indicate sexual addiction? Do you agree or disagree with Siegel and Siegel's critiques of Carnes' assessment criteria? Is sex addiction a serious problem, as Carnes asserts? Or is the assigning of an "addiction" status to otherwise healthy and consensual activities simply adding to the modern trend of the medicalization of sexuality, while recalling an era when sexuality was demonized?

Suggested Readings

P. Carnes, *Don't Call It Love: Recovery from Sexual Addiction* (Bantam Books, 1992).

P. Carnes, *Out of the Shadows: Understanding Sexual Addiction* (Compcare Publications, 1992).

B.J. Dew & M.P. Chaney, "Sexual Addiction and the Internet: Implications for Gay Men," *Journal of Addictions & Offender Counseling* (vol. 24, 2004).

B. Dodge et al., "Sexual Compulsivity among Heterosexual College Students," *The Journal of Sex Research* (vol. 41, 2004).

R. Eisenman, "Sex Addicts: Do they Exist?" *Journal of Evolutionary Psychology* (2001).

M. Griffiths, "Sex on the Internet: Observations and Implications for Internet Sex Addiction," *The Journal of Sex Research* (vol. 38, 2001).

M. Klein, *America's War on Sex* (Praeger, 2006).

M.F. Schwartz, "Sexual Addiction: An Integrated Approach," *Archives of Sexual Behavior* (vol. 33, 2004).

ISSUE 3

Does Sexual Medicine Benefit Society?

YES: David L. Rowland, from "Will Medical Solutions to Sexual Problems Make Sexological Care and Science Obsolete?" *Journal of Sex and Marital Therapy* (vol. 33, 2007)

NO: Leonore Tiefer, from "Beneath the Veneer: The Troubled Past and Future of Sexual Medicine," *Journal of Sex and Marital Therapy* (vol. 33, 2007)

ISSUE SUMMARY

YES: David L. Rowland, Professor of Psychology and Dean of the Graduate School at Valparaiso University, Valparaiso, examines the benefits and risks of sexual medicine, and the future of the treatment of sexual problems.

NO: Leonore Tiefer, author and Clinical Associate Professor of Psychiatry at New York University School of Medicine, counters that the rise of "sexual medicine" brings with it risks that should not be ignored.

If you watch much television, chances are you have seen ads for Viagra, a drug that treats erectile dysfunction in men. In fact, 2008 marked the 10-year anniversary of the "little blue pill." Since its release, several additional erectile dysfunction drugs, including Levitra and Cialis, have made the process of getting erections much easier for millions of men around the world. The products have been so successful that pharmaceutical companies have, for years, been attempting to replicate their success with medications for a variety of sexual dysfunctions in women (including hypoactive sexual disorder, otherwise known as low libido). Authors of a study from 1999 found that 43 percent of women between the ages of 18 and 59 had some type of sexual dysfunction (Laumann et al., 1999). This number raised many eyebrows. Pharmaceutical companies raced to invest billions of dollars into research for elusive remedies. It was thought that the profits from women's treatments would rival, if not surpass, those of male treatments.

Clinical trials of a women's version of Viagra, as well as several other potential medications, ended with mixed results. Intrinsa, a testosterone patch designed to increase women's libido, showed promise but was denied Food and Drug Administration (FDA) approval (the patch was approved in several European countries, however). The desire for the product was there; the desired results, on the other hand, were not.

Why has the search for a women's prescription treatment proven so challenging? If men can have some of their sexual issues taken care of with a prescription medication, critics argue, why have women's sexual problems proven so difficult to treat? Some women's health advocates take issue over the disparity between FDA-approved drugs available for men and women. Some saw sexism and a fear of women's sexuality at play in the FDA's decisions. Others theorized there were subtle differences between the ways men and women experienced arousal. A pill may have a difficult time differentiating between such body–mind nuances.

Another camp holds that pharmaceutical treatments for such complex issues (for both men and women) may be off base to begin with. Many therapists and sexologists warn against what they see as the "medicalization" of sexual problems. An overreliance on prescription drugs is seen as a one-size-fits-all approach that ignores larger issues. Some point to the far more common psychogenic causes of sexual dysfunction that cannot be treated by medication. They contend that nonmedical treatments (improving partner communication, for example) would be far more effective. They charge that pharmaceutical companies are making a hefty profit through the "medicalization" of sexuality. Others argue that the estimated number of sexual dysfunction cases is inflated and that the vast majority of real cases of both female and male sexual dysfunction are caused by psychological or interpersonal factors that are better treated with nonmedical intervention.

In the following selections, Dr. David L. Rowland offers the argument that the medicalization of sexuality is likely to continue. While this could have negative consequences, Rowland sees the benefits of continued mental health care and counseling, combined with well-researched medical options as a major advancement in the treatment of sexual problems. Dr. Leonore Tiefer argues that pharmaceutical companies aim not to solidify a holistic approach to sexual health, but rather to increase profits for drug companies.

Reference

E. Laumann, A. Paik, and R. Rosen, (1999). "Sexual Dysfunctions in the United States," *Journal of the American Medical Association* (vol. 281, 1999).

YES

David L. Rowland

Will Medical Solutions to Sexual Problems Make Sexological Care and Science Obsolete?

Developments in the field of sexology indicate a trend toward the medicalization of sexual issues which is likely to continue over the next decades. With the introduction of new pharmacological treatments, the resulting shift from the biopsychosocial model to the disease model will become increasingly accepted and solidified over the next decade. Some of this shift may be beneficial in that the healthcare needs of the patient/client may at times be better served through this route. However, concern arises when such shifts are likely to limit the meaningful choices presented to the patient and to dampen support for basic psycho-behavioral and neurophysiological sexological investigation. Such developments challenge sexologists and sex therapists to define their treatment outcomes more clearly and, relying on stronger evidence-based studies, define the critical role of the therapist in achieving these outcomes.

Recent Trends

Recently much ado has been made about the "medicalization" of sexual problems and with it, the increasing use of (and in some cases, return to) the disease model as the standard for treatment (Tiefer, 2002; Winton, 2000). Indeed, over the past 5–10 years, a dramatic shift has occurred in the treatment of sexual problems; most notable is the treatment of sexual dysfunction where the use of pharmaceuticals such as PDE-5 inhibitors (Viagra™ [Pfizer, New York, New York, USA], Levitra™ [GlaxoSmithKline, Brentford, Middlesex, UK], Cialis™ [Lilly ICOS, Indianapolis, Indiana, USA]) has dominated clinical and research protocols. Other sexual problems such as gender identity disorders and the sexual paraphilias, if not already undergoing change, are likely to do so over the next 10–20 years.

Why raise this issue, and why raise it now? Over the past decade, the study of sexuality and sexual problems has experienced a resurgence of interest. Not since Masters and Johnson (1970) and Kaplan (1974) has there been so much talk about—and progress in the understanding of—sexual problems and sexual health. New journals have been founded, new professional societies have been established, new research funds have been invested, new research

From *Journal of Sex & Marital Therapy*, vol. 33, October 2007, pp. 385–396. Copyright © 2007 by Routledge/Taylor & Francis Group. Reprinted by permission via Rightslink.

programs have been implemented, and new treatments have been touted. But in this new era of the study and treatment of sexuality, the discipline has, for the most part, re-emerged as a medical one, specifically known as "sexual medicine." In fact, sexual medicine has become the commonplace and defining term for most of the recent developments in the field, taking precedence over more traditional and broadly defined terms such as "sexological science" and "sex therapy," designations that have become stagnant or even invisible to the public over the past decades.

The resurging interest in sexual health—now under the guise of sexual medicine—has been driven, to a large extent, by recent pharmacological developments. These developments have significant implications for patients, healthcare providers, and for the field of sexology as a whole.

Defining the Terms

The shift in paradigms in the treatment of sexual problems *from sexological* care to sexual medicine has been swift and near total, at least for erectile dysfunction (ED). Important to the understanding of the issues discussed in this article is the distinction between "sexual medicine" and "sexological science and care."

Sexual medicine (i.e., "medical solutions") relies heavily on the disease model, one that assumes an underlying pathophysiology that requires fixing or adjustment. This model focuses on physical (surgical) or biomedical treatments, and the underlying research methodology supporting these treatments typically involves a strong emphasis on clinical trial research. From the patient's perspective, entry to the healthcare system is through the physician's door, either the primary care physician (PCP) or the specialist (e.g., urologist, gynecologist, psychiatrist).

In contrast, sexological science and care have come to represent a broadly defined interdisciplinary approach to the research, diagnosis, and treatment of sexual problems—commonly known as the biopsychosocial model. While this terminology has sometimes been overused, in essence it refers to an approach that emphasizes an integration of cultural, relationship, psychological, and biological factors in both treatment and research investigations. An underlying assumption of this approach has been that patients may enter the healthcare system through any number of different doors, but that the healthcare provider will take a systemic approach to the problem, investigating a variety of possible domains that impinge upon the disorder and recommending a range of treatment options that guide the patient toward both improved sexual functioning and sexual satisfaction.

Past Developments, Future Trends

Consider the likely developments that underlie the transformation from sexology to sexual medicine. Over the past years, there has been an increasing trend among pharmaceutical companies to invest in drugs that address quality of life issues (vs. life and death issues)—Viagra™ is a clear example of this, but others exist as well: in the U.S. these drugs are being marketed under trade-names such as Nasonex™ (Schering-Plough, Kenilworth, New Jersey, USA) for nasal and sinus problems, Lunesta™ (Sepracor, Marlborough, Massachusetts, USA) for insomnia, Nexium™ (AstraZeneca, Wilmington, Delaware, USA) for acid reflux, Requip™ (GlaxoSmithKline, Brentford, Middlesex, UK) for restless leg syndrome, and so on. Although the motivations of the pharmaceutical companies are many and varied, economic opportunity is clearly one of them. An aging population, the consequent increasing prevalence of ED, and the strong interest in and moderate success with intracavernosal injection therapy set the stage for the transformation. This transformation for ED became a fait accompli with the arrival of the first PDE-5i, Viagra™, followed shortly there-after by Cialis™ and Levitra™. These oral medications ensured easy, economic, and efficacious treatment options for men with either (or both) pathophysi-ologically or psychologically based erectile dysfunction.

The interest in and use of these pharmacologic options is evident from the dollar sales amounts for these drugs beginning with their introduction in 1998 to 2005. A steady rate of increase occurred for Viagra™ from 1998 to 2003, fol-lowed by a further jump in 2004 when Levitra™ and Cialis™ were introduced (2004–2005 include estimated sales for all three drugs). Between 1998 and 2004, 123 million prescriptions had been written for an estimated 23 million men, with most recent assessments suggesting that 90% of men seeking treatment for ED are now being treated with PDE-5 inhibitors (Althof, 2006).

Thus, a sexual problem that once involved the shared interests and exper-tise of sex therapists and physicians/urologists has now become the near-exclu-sive domain of the medical profession. Forthcoming developments in the field indicate that the pattern for ED will not be unique; this trend is likely to expand to other sexual problems, as the initial impetus stimulated from the PDE-5i's gains further momentum from drugs such as dapoxetine and Intrinsa™ (Proctor & Gamble, Cincinnati, Ohio, USA)—agents that show promise in the treatment of ejaculatory, arousal, and desire disorders in either or both men and women. Specifically, dapoxetine, having undergone extensive clinical trials in the U.S. and Europe, has been shown to delay ejaculation by 1–3 minutes in men with premature ejaculation and to increase their sense of control over ejaculation (Pryor et al., 2006). Intrinsa™, a transdermal androgenic preparation for the treatment of low arousal and desire in women, has recently received approval from the European regulatory agency (see Davis et al., 2006). The search for other agents that impact sexual functioning has reached a new pace: the melanocortin agonist bremelanotide is under investigation as a treatment for problems related to men's and women's sexual desire and arousal; agents that affect serotonergic, dopaminergic, nitergic, vipergic, and GABAergic systems, all known to play roles in sexual response (Giuliano & Clement, 2005), are likely to be developed further over the next few decades as well.

As more pharmacological treatments become available, men and women will increasingly turn to them for solutions to their sexual problems. The resulting shift in the point of entry for sexual health, with PCP and medical specialists becoming both the front and main doors to the system, will become increasingly accepted and solidified over the next decade. Some of this shift is appropriate and beneficial in that the healthcare needs of the patient/client may at times be better served through this route. However, concern arises when such shifts are likely to limit the meaningful choices presented to the patient, to be driven by economic considerations, and to dampen support for basic psycho-behavioral and neurophysiological sexological investigation.

Benefits and Liabilities

The emergence of sexual medicine—exemplified in the pharmacological treatment of sexual problems—is a two-sided issue having both benefits and liabilities. Furthermore, the benefits and liabilities are different for patients, vs. the field of sexology and the advancement of knowledge, vs. the nonmedical healthcare professional.

For the Patient

The patient benefits from pharmacological options in an obvious way: increased access (through the PCP) to efficacious treatment options that are generally less intrusive and more affordable (particularly with third-party reimbursement) (Table 1). But more subtle benefits have also accrued. As a result of the introduction and promotion of Viagra™ and its counterparts, patients with ED have been given a clear point of entry into the healthcare system and can do so feeling less stigmatized—the problem has been relegated to the domain of physical health and removed from the more stigmatizing realm of mental or psychological health.

Yet, the disadvantages of these developments are also becoming increasingly apparent. The new "one door" entry point to the healthcare system is likely to limit the patients' options, or at least reinforce treatment biases that occur due to the entry points initially selected (PCP vs. sex therapist, for example). Specifically, the patient and partner are less likely to understand the value and, in some instances, need to address psychological and relationship elements of their problem. Furthermore, a portion of those seeking help may not find the pharmacological treatment satisfactory—either they do not respond to

Table 1

Positive and Negative Impact on the Patient

Positive	Negative
• Clear entry point into healthcare system likely to bias/limit the options	• Entry point
	• Not a cure, just a treatment
• Destigmatization of the condition through depersonalization	• Dependency on the medication for sexual response
• Increased treatment options	• Address physiological but not psychological or relational components
• Demonstrated efficacy	
• Easy and accessible solutions	• Nonresponders and adherence issues
• Third-party reimbursement	

the drug, or after trying the drug they realize that fixing the genital response does little to fix the larger problem of regaining a satisfying sexual life with their partner. The surprisingly low levels of adherence to medications such as Viagra™ attest to such issues (see Althof, 2006). Finally, although the issue has not been investigated thoroughly, the question arises as to whether those using such medications to enhance their sexual responsiveness will eventually become dependent on them for their propensity to respond, thereby diminishing the role of the partner, one's own emotional response and feelings of excitement, the specific situation, and so on, all of which play important roles in sexual arousal and response (Rowland, 2006).

For the Field of Sexological Science

It is probably safe to say that research in the field of sexual response and dysfunction had been languishing in the U.S.—and perhaps to a lesser extent in Europe—in the late 1980s through the mid-90s (Hawton, 1992, Schover & Leiblum, 1994). In the U.S., only a handful of struggling researchers had been investigating factors affecting sexual response and dysfunction—indeed some of the major research centers had been disbanded or substantially diminished in size through attrition, and many of the surviving research programs were hindered by lack of funding. Unquestionably, the possibility of pharmacological solutions brought renewed vitality and interest to sex research; with it came new resources from the pharmaceutical industry and more rigorous research designs necessary for regulatory agency approval (Table 2). This research has not only helped identify biological contributions to sexual response (e.g., nitric oxide, serotonin), but it has also stimulated discussion and, to some extent, consensus about defining, diagnosing, and assessing specific sexual problems and their treatment (e.g., International Index of Erectile Function (IIEF), Rosen et al., 1997).

Nevertheless, because most of this new research has been supported by the pharmaceutical industry, the research agenda is driven by the need to generate data for regulatory agency approval, with new found economic resources shifted primarily toward carrying out expensive clinical trials. Little funding appears to have been allocated for basic research on the etiology or causes of the sexual problem–whether primarily biological or psychological—or even exploring the efficacy of nonpharmacological treatments such as sex and/or cognitive-behavioral therapies. As a cogent illustration of this pattern, shows how the pharmaceutical industry has affected the amount of research and discussion about one male sexual dysfunction—premature ejaculation (PE). The average number of publications has increased sharply over the past 6 years—concomitant with a flurry of research testing the ejaculatory-retarding effects of the serotonin selective reuptake inhibitors (SSRI) anti-depressants and the newly developed compound dapoxetine. The percentage of articles on PE dealing with biological and pharmacological factors has increased greatly. In contrast, the number of published articles dealing with psychological and behavioral covariates of PE has remained about the same, with the overall percentage accounted for by these articles now representing only a small part of the total.

Table 2

Positive and Negative Impact on the Field of Sexology

Positive	Negative
• Rigorous research paradigms	• Successful treatments can inhibit basic research
• Identify specific (NO, 5-HT) biochemical systems	• Economic resources shifted toward clinical trials
• Stimulated research on assessment and psychological impacts	• Research agenda driven by regulatory agencies
• Solution with demonstrated efficacy	• Rekindles mindless psychological-biological dichotomy
• Renewed vitality for the field (e.g., sexual medicine departments), along with new resources	• Does not encourage integrated treatment paradigms

Other liabilities for the field of sexology are inherent in the trend toward sexual medicine. Clinical trial research seldom allows for investigation of multi-dimensional or integrated treatment paradigms and, when drugs are eventually proven effective and approved by regulatory agencies, successful treatment options can have the effect of dampening further research into teasing out cause–effect relationships. Finally, the successful therapeutic use of chemical agents in treating sexual problems by altering neural functioning has rekindled the misguided dichotomy of biological vs. psychological causes of sexual dysfunction (Rowland & Motofei, 2007).

For the Nonmedical Healthcare Professional

With the development of new pharmacological solutions and a shift in the direction of research toward clinical trials, the nonmedical healthcare practitioner is facing a rising tide. Sexologists, for example, are left with a set of therapeutic tools of unproven efficacy and reliability, and the therapeutic process they advocate is less accessible and affordable for most people with sexual problems (Table 3). Under such conditions, the sexologist is likely to have even less access to resources from the community, government, and third-party reimbursers. Consequently, the influence of sexology on the study and treatment of sexual problems will continue to wane, and ultimately this general trend portends the eventual demise of the nonmedical sex specialist. Indeed, given the confluence of all of the above factors, the future for the sexological health practitioner appears quite bleak.

Reframing the Issue

The question to ponder, then, is this: given the aforementioned projection in treatment approaches, the current tendency for the research agenda to be driven by pharmaceutical interests, and the economic incentives for both the

Table 3

Positive and Negative Impact on the Nonmedical Healthcare Professional

Positive	Negative
???	• Therapeutic tools of "unproven" efficacy and reliability
	• Therapeutic approaches that are less accessible and affordable
	• Fewer resources from community, government, and third-party reimbursers
	• Decreasing impact on the field of sexuality and treatmen
	• Demise of the nonmedical sexual specialist

pharmaceutical and medical interests, will basic sexological research continue to languish as it is overshadowed by "clinical trial" research, and will sexological care (as opposed to "medical care for sexual problems") become a thing of the past?

Rather than lamenting these recent developments, the better strategy is to reframe the issue: what opportunities lie in this challenge to sexologists and the field of sexological science? Indeed, based on the experience with drugs like Viagra™, it is becoming increasingly clear that replacement of the sexological model with the medical model has generated its own set of problems. For example, the medical community and pharmaceutical industry increasingly realize that "sexual and relationship satisfaction" are multi-dimensional constructs, that sexual/genital *performance* accounts for only a portion of the variation in these endpoints, and that attainment of true sexual health and satisfaction will require an integrated approach that includes psychological-relationship factors in the conceptualization, investigation, and development of new treatment paradigms. Who better can bring such perspective and skills to the study of sexuality than sexologists?

Sexological Healthcare

With any therapeutic process that involves a significant psychological-relationship component, medical personnel are often handicapped by their lack of training and time to handle the interpersonal dimensions of sexual relationships and satisfaction. Furthermore, therapists have long understood the need to address *content* (the "prescribed" treatment, whether medical or counseling), *process* (the way in which it is delivered within the context of the patient–provider relationship), and *systemic* factors (e.g., patient characteristics, patient values, and context variables such as partner variables, patient–partner relationship, and so on) in developing optimal treatment outcomes.

In this regard, sexologists are well positioned to advocate and implement integrated treatment protocols that maximize patient and partner satisfaction. They can, for example:

1. Assist in identifying, beforehand, patients (i.e., patient characteristics) most likely to benefit solely from pharmacological treatment;
2. Clarify how content vs. process can affect the outcome of treatment protocols, particularly insofar as treatment adherence and overall relationship satisfaction are concerned (perhaps initially using models based on other disorders);
3. Develop minimalist (e.g., 1–3 sessions) yet effective co-treatment plans;
4. Help deliver treatments that integrate psychological-behavioral approaches with medical approaches to ensure seamless delivery of optimal care;
5. Work side-by-side with medical practitioners to ensure third-party reimbursement, or alternatively, lobby for prescription rights, thereby allowing integration of services and the opening of new doors to treatment.

Naturally, to achieve such collaboration with the medical community, sexologists will need to be flexible, innovative, and, to some extent, political in their approach. Equally important, they will need to demonstrate empirically the unique value and effectiveness of their tools, a process that can be realized only by an intentional, intense, and agreed-upon research agenda.

Sexological Science and Research

As illustrated previously in this article, the great majority of current research on premature ejaculation is pharmacological and/or biological. Similar trends would likely emerge for some of the other sexual dysfunctions, were they systematically explored. For example, much of the seminal research on behavioral treatments for PE was done in the 1970s and 80s; little has been done since that time to confirm or expand on the treatment protocols offered by Masters and Johnson or Kaplan (Hawton, 1992). Furthermore, clinical trial research, while important to determining treatment (drug) efficacy and securing approval of the regulatory agencies, often provides little or no understanding about basic etiologies and causes of dysfunctions, or of effective alternative (and sometimes competing) treatment strategies.

Sexologists must therefore work to reinvigorate a balanced research agenda that:

1. Creates an international data base to support recommendations regarding the role and impact of counseling and sex therapy on endpoints relevant to specific dysfunctions and overall sexual satisfaction;
2. Establishes the impact of an integrated cognitive-behavioral and sex therapy program on the treatment of sexual problems; current data are outdated, based on poorly defined outcome measures and the result of poorly controlled studies;
3. Specifies how both therapeutic content and process affect treatment outcomes;

4. Differentiates therapies that work from those that do not;
5. Ranks therapeutic techniques and processes—those specific to the sexual problem and those more general (education, communication)—according to their level of impact, validation, and cost;
6. Identifies the points at which the therapist's role makes most sense in the treatment of sexual dysfunctions;
7. Along with basic medicine/science advocates, supports basic scientific research into psychological, behavioral, and relationship aspects of sexual dysfunctions;
8. Counters the belief that the double-blind, placebo-controlled design is superior to other modes of experimental research in yielding credible data and conclusions, particularly when the problems are multifactorial and when ethical concerns argue against the use of such research designs.

One way to facilitate the research agenda above is by establishing a consensus panel, supported by the medical community (general practitioners and specialists), professional societies, and the pharmaceutical industry, which combines a research agenda with research advocacy and expert interpretation of findings. As a subtext to this effort, sexologists and sex therapists should work through their professional societies to secure positions on pharmaceutical advisory boards—groups that can have significant influence on the variables included for assessment and analysis in clinical trials.

Conclusions

Not since Masters and Johnson has the time been so ripe for the development of a research agenda for sexological science. Developments in the field of sexual medicine provide both challenge to and opportunity for sex therapists—to define for both the professional audience and the public at large through evidenced-based research, their relevance and/or importance to the therapeutic process in the treatment of sexual problems. Specifically, not since the early 1980s have the opportunities been better for the following:

1. a revived research agenda investigating the role of psychological-behavioral factors in the etiology and treatment of sexual problems, and in adherence to treatment protocols;
2. reclaiming the value of a clinical research model that, rather than being driven by the medical model and regulatory approval, assesses the multi-dimensional nature of sexual problems;
3. a revised yet significant role for the sexologist in the development and implementation of integrated treatment protocols;
4. educating the public at large regarding the value of nonbiological variables in treatment protocols that lead to better sexual satisfaction and relationships; and
5. securing funding to take advantage of these opportunities.

The call for the action agenda above undoubtedly requires vision, leadership, and raw effort. However, this window of opportunity might well close permanently by the end of the next decade.

Leonore Tiefer  **NO**

Beneath the Veneer: The Troubled Past and Future of Sexual Medicine

My presidential address to the International Academy of Sex Research in 1993, 5 years *before* Viagra was released to the world, was entitled "Three Crises Facing Sexology" (Tiefer, 1994). One of the crises, a subject on which I had been publishing since 1986, 12 years before Viagra, was the medicalization of sexology (Tiefer, 1986). Ah, the joys of being ahead of one's time! Using sociological notions of medicalization and disease-mongering (Conrad, 2007; Payer, 1992), I have analyzed, over the past 20 years, how urologists, funded by an ambitious pharmaceutical industry assisted by favorable government policies such as direct-to-consumer advertising and poor oversight of conflicts of interest, created a new but thin subspecialty, "sexual medicine" (Tiefer, 2004, 2006a).

In the present essay under comment, Rowland (2007) errs in regarding this new "sexual medicine" as if it were an established clinical subspecialty, rather than merely the brand-name for a product being aggressively promoted by a multi-billion dollar industry. His analysis of the weaknesses of "sexual medicine" would be alarming if not for this fundamental error. It's as if he went to extraordinary lengths to analyze the advantages and disadvantages of alchemy. Over the past decade the pharmaceutical industry has spent billions to persuade professionals and the public that its leaden sex research is actually gold, in fact "gold standard." Much of the research in Rowland's figures is the result of this industry pseudoscience. Fortunately, the huge marketing machine of sponsored research, sponsored professional continuing education, sponsored lunches, sponsored organizations, sponsored dinner talks, sponsored workshops, sponsored awards, sponsored speakers' bureaus, sponsored conferences, sponsored journals, and other forms of gifts and entanglements by which the pharmaceutical industry pushes its brands is at last beginning to unravel (Abramson, 2004; Angell, 2004; Avorn, 2004; Critser, 2005; Kassirer, 2005; Moynihan, 2003a, 2003b; Moynihan & Cassels, 2005).

The rising tide of regulatory reform promises effectively to limit industry-expert entanglements and end direct-to-consumer drug advertising, off-label prescribing, and the epidemic of conflicts-of-interest among scientists and physicians. I expect that, then, the new subspecialty of sexual medicine will rapidly deflate in size and prominence. I hope the American Psychiatric Association will awaken to the biases at the heart of the human sexual response

From *Journal of Sex & Marital Therapy*, vol. 33, October 2007, pp. 473–477. Copyright © 2007 by Routledge/Taylor & Francis Group. Reprinted by permission via Rightslink.

cycle model and eliminate its list of specific sexual dysfunction disorders. As sex drugs continue to multiply, and there I agree with Rowland that the future will be full of more and more drugs (legal, illegal, prescription, nutraceutical, herbal, and over-the-counter, delivered through skin, nose, mouth, and all other orifices), sexologists will find their true calling in multi-method sexuality research, community-based sex coaching and education, academic and professional sex education, and treatment of people whose sex lives have been damaged by traumatic events, media hype, drug side effects, and false promises of all sorts.

In 1994, without the perspectives on advertising, conflicts of interest, sponsorship, etc. offered by the recent investigative work cited above, I called for rapprochement between sex research promoting a psychobiosocial model and that promoting a reductionistic view of sexuality (what Rowland calls "the medical model"). I called for multi-modal research to carve out "a complex middle ground" against "the medical juggernaut" (Tiefer, 1994, p. 373). Such rapprochement didn't happen, and eventually I understood that I had fallen into a fundamental error that I believe Rowland currently makes. What I hadn't grasped was that the medical juggernaut was not about developing good science or problem management from a biomedical perspective, but that the medical juggernaut was fundamentally about biological reductionism and pharmaceutical promotion. Too often, social and psychological research was used as window dressing to add a veneer of psycho-bio-social sophistication, but it remained unintegrated into research design or teaching materials in any meaningful way. While every organ, disease, and function system in the body was linked to sexual problems with a page or paragraph of its own, mental and social factors would repeatedly be summed up in one "psychological factors" paragraph as "anxiety" or "communication problems." No matter how much lip service was given to the importance of psychological factors, drug prescription was the first and often the only recommendation. This was the clear evidence that we were in the land of veneer, not multi-disciplinary integration. Recently, in the new sexual medicine organizations and journals, lip service is again being paid to collaboration and rapprochement, but the same oversimplifications reveal the same motives.

It is true that sexual problems are legion in our violent, inequitable, anxious, and speeded-up world, but fortunately we already have a sufficient armamentarium to help people relax, gain insight, develop skills, overcome trauma, and strengthen their capacities for cooperation, sensuality, pleasure, and intimacy. New diagnostic language is not needed, adequate research models are already available, and in my opinion, energy might be better spent at this point in preventing sexual problems than in developing new treatments. The quest for the "new" is probably more related to marketing than therapeutics, and truly useful work for sexologists might be to lend our professional clout to the politics of comprehensive sex education, reliable contraception and abortion services, parent education, and anti-stigma human rights training.

Although Rowland omits any mention of this, there are enormous new developments in sexuality scholarship over the past two decades in the new cultural studies of sexuality emerging from the social study of gender, as exemplified by journals like The Journal of the History of Sexuality (started in 1990) and books on men and masculinity. An obsessive focus on clinical trials research has allowed clinical sexologists to avoid familiarization with theoretical and empirical contributions arising from science and technology studies, globalization studies, gay and lesbian studies, the sociology of sexual identities and institutions, qualitative research on sexual meanings in diverse sexual cultures, and the impact of sexualized media (e.g., Seidman, Fischer, & Meeks, 2006). The disastrous substitution of clinical trials for genuine research and theoretical development in sexology since the mid-1990s may give rise to significant intellectual lacunae for many years to come. I hope it does not prove to have been a fatal choice.

This opportunity to comment on Rowland's essay rings one other historical bell for me, and I think it is important to take a little space to recognize stages in the process of medicalization.1 A watershed event in the progress of the medicalization of sexuality and the dismantling of the psycho-bio-social approach was the National Institutes of Health (NIH) Consensus Development Conference on "Impotence" held in 1992 (Impotence, 1992). Although this was the first (and to the date only) NIH Consensus Conference on a sexual topic, it signaled a urology agenda to build a new specialty of "sexual medicine."

The scientific evidence prepared for the conference was compiled in a 1986–1992 bibliography of 956 items (Beratan, 1992). Of the 19 database search strategies described, only three included anything clearly sexological (e.g., "psychosexual disorders" or "libido"). All the others had to do with "penis," "impotence," "erection," various diseases (e.g., diabetes), or medical treatments. The 21 "experts" speaking at the conference, each allotted 20 minutes, included five sexologists, one epidemiologist, and 15 urologists or basic scientists whose research focus was the biology of the penis. Three urologists (one, Goldstein, now founding editor of the Journal of Sexual Medicine) gave eight of the 27 presentations. The panel of "nonexperts" who heard the presentations and prepared the final report consisted of 14 members, including 6 urologists and 1 sexologist.

Inevitably, the final NIH report was suffused with a medical model orientation that reified "impotence" and exhaustively investigated details of physiology. It threw psychological factors into long nontechnical lists of "risk factors" such as "lack of sexual knowledge, poor sexual techniques, inadequate interpersonal relationships" (Impotence, 1992, p. 11). The report mentioned the patient's sexual partner only in passing and discussed nothing about differences among partners. It dealt with erectile troubles as an individual man's problem, and recommended that diagnostic evaluations be multi-disciplinary, "when available" (p. 13). The triumph of biological reductionism was the message of the 1992 report.

I suggested to Arnold Melman, then co-editor of the International Journal of Impotence Research, that the NIH Consensus Conference final report be published in his journal along with comments from sexologists and urologists. I hoped that the 31 sexologists whose names I provided would weigh in with trenchant commentaries about the dangers of the rush towards medicalization, but only 14 chose to respond, and they were generally polite in pointing out omissions and biases. The 18 invited urologists, by contrast, understandably, were generally euphoric. More to the point, sexologists took no concerted action to limit or rechannel the medicalization juggernaut. Fast forward 15 years and we have the current situation Rowland describes.

The creation of "sexual medicine" was the result of an unhindered confluence of events and social trends which Rowland should acknowledge (Tiefer, 2004, 2006b). Urologists needed a new subspecialty as new biotechnologies eliminated most kidney stone and benign prostate surgeries. Government policies promoting new academic–industry partnerships encouraged applied science on university and medical campuses, and escalated industry sponsorship of research and professional education. Government regulations relaxed drug approval and advertising policies as the result of industry lobbying and AIDS activism, and the industry shifted towards lifestyle drug development to reach the baby boomer market. Health and science media discovered the popularity of explicit sexual subjects. Conservative policies limited comprehensive sex education and cut back social science sexological funding.

I do not believe that sex therapy "stagnated" so much as it existed in an apolitical bubble, unaware of and uninterested in the many social trends poised to limit its development. It celebrated "objective" science and therapeutics, oblivious to the fact, extensively examined in the new sexuality studies, that sex is permanently political. It would be nice to hope that increased awareness of the current dilemmas identified by Rowland, and attention to the many factors that have brought it about, will lead to new directions. The New View Campaign is an educational network of sexologists and allies promoting just such new directions.

POSTSCRIPT

Does Sexual Medicine Benefit Society?

Is the medicalization of sexuality problematic? Perhaps a more interesting question is "For whom is the medicalization of sexuality problematic?" In his essay, Rowland breaks down the positives and negatives of medicalization for each of the stakeholders—the patient, sexologists (researchers), and nonmedical healthcare providers (therapists, counselors). Are there benefits for everyone? According to Rowland, who benefits the most? The least? Do you agree with his assessment of the state of sexology and sex therapy?

Tiefer takes a strong stance not only against Rowland's conclusions but also against his acknowledgment of sexual medicine as a valid field. Does the fact that much of the research on sexual dysfunction is sponsored by pharmaceutical companies, as Tiefer states, make the field of sexual medicine "merely the brand name for a product being aggressively promoted by a billion-dollar industry"? Are dysfunctions being created in order to make billions? Or is the neophyte field of sexual medicine simply trying to understand what dysfunctions are and are not best treated through prescription drugs.

One of the most interesting, yet least discussed aspects of the controversy over the medicalization of sexuality is the future of sex therapy. If people are able to have their sexual issues treated chemically by their general practitioners, OB-GYNs, and urologists, what role will the therapist fill? Rowland suggests steps that can help sexologists and therapists find their place in collaboration with the new direction of sexual medicine. Do you agree with his suggestions? If collaboration does not happen, do you agree that the future for the field of therapy-oriented sexological health care is "bleak"?

Can a prescription that increases a man's capacity for erection lead to increased satisfaction if the relationship he is in is deteriorating? Can increased capacity for physiological sexual arousal in a woman lead to more sex if her partner works too much and ignores her when they are together? These are important questions that sex and relationship therapists are asking about the influx of new treatments for sexual dysfunction. If relationship issues were addressed first, would there be a need for medical treatments?

How comfortable would you be taking medications for sexual problems? Would you rather deal with these issues through counseling first? Or would you be more comfortable raising the issue in your doctor's office than on a therapist's couch? If Rowland is correct, the future of sexology may depend on your answers.

In their new book, *Older, Wiser, Sexually Smarter,* sexuality educator Peggy Brick and her colleagues argue that many of the physical changes that people experience related to their sexuality as they grow older are not inherently problematic and do not necessarily require medication or treatment. Rather, they necessitate a new understanding of one's sexuality and, perhaps, new sexual behaviors that may not be quite the same as when the person was age 18. What do you think of this viewpoint? Can sexuality be experienced differently as one grows older?

Suggested Readings

P. Brick, J. Lunquist, A. Sandak, and B. Taverner, *Older, Wiser, Sexually Smarter: 30 Sex Ed Lessons for Adults Only* (Morristown, NJ: Planned Parenthood of Greater Northern New Jersey, 2009).

S. Katz, "Return of Desire: Fighting Myths about Female Sexuality," *AlterNet* (July 23, 2008).

L. Lyon, "Women Lacking Libido Aren't Sick," *U.S. News & World Reports* (March 27, 2008).

L. Tiefer, *Sex is Not a Natural Act & Other Essays* (Westview Press, 2008).

ISSUE 4

Is Oral Sex Really Sex?

YES: Rhonda Chittenden, from "Oral Sex *Is* Sex: Ten Messages about Oral Sex to Communicate to Adolescents," *Sexing the Political* (May 2004)

NO: Nora Gelperin, from "Oral Sex and Young Adolescents: Insights from the 'Oral Sex Lady,'" *Educator's Update* (September 2004)

ISSUE SUMMARY

YES: Sexuality educator Rhonda Chittenden says that it is important for young people to expand their narrow definitions of sex and understand that oral sex *is* sex. Chittenden offers additional educational messages about oral sex.

NO: Sexuality trainer Nora Gelperin argues that adult definitions of oral sex are out of touch with the meaning the behavior holds for young people. Rather than impose adult definitions of intimacy, educators should be seeking to help young people clarify and understand their own values.

$\mathbf{I}$n 1998, President Bill Clinton famously stated, "I did not have sexual relations with that woman, Miss Lewinsky." As it later became evident that the president, in fact, did have *oral* sex with intern Monica Lewinsky, a national debate raged over the meaning of sex. What, people asked, does "sexual relations" mean? What about "sex?" Do these terms refer to vaginal intercourse only, or are other sexual behaviors, like oral sex, included?

Some welcomed this unprecedented opportunity to have an open, national discussion about sex in an otherwise erotophobic, sexually repressed culture. Sexuality education professionals lent their expertise, offering suggestions to help parents answer their children's questions about the new term, "oral sex," they might hear on the evening news or at family gatherings. Others feared such openness would inevitably lead to increased sexual activity among teens. Perhaps the media viewed this as a foregone conclusion when they began airing hyped reports indicating a rise in teen oral sex, based on anecdotal, rather than research-based, evidence.

Feature reports, often intended to alarm viewers, have introduced even more new terms into our sexual lexicon. "Friends with benefits" describes a partner pairing based on friendship and casual oral sex. "Rainbow parties" involve events where girls wear different colors of lipstick and boys try to get as many colored rings on their penises as they can. But how much of this is really happening, and how much of this just makes for good television?

Even if *some* of what the reports say is true, many adults—parents, teachers, public health officials, and others—are concerned. Some are worried about the potential rise in sexually transmitted infections that can be passed orally as well as vaginally or anally. Others lament the inequity of oral sex as young people may experience it—with females *giving* oral sex far more than they are *receiving* it. Still others may have religious or other moral reasons that drive their concerns.

The apprehension among many adults is rooted in the very meaning of sex and oral sex. Since many adults hold oral sex to be an intensely intimate act—one that is even more intimate than vaginal intercourse—it is difficult for them to observe what they interpret as casual attitudes toward this behavior.

In the following selections, sexuality education professionals Rhonda Chittenden and Nora Gelperin examine the meaning of sex and oral sex in the context of giving young people helpful educational messages. Chittenden articulates several reasons why it is important for young people to know that oral sex is sex, and offers several other important messages for adults to convey to young people. Gelperin argues that it is not for adults to decide the meaning of such terms for young people. Rather, educators can help young people critically examine the meaning of such words and activities for themselves. She further argues against having overly dramatized media accounts dictate public health approaches.

YES

Rhonda Chittenden

Oral Sex *Is* Sex: Ten Messages about Oral Sex to Communicate to Adolescents

As a teen in the early-80s, I was very naïve about oral sex. I thought oral sex meant talking about sex with one's partner in a very sexy way. A friend and I, trying to practice the mechanics, would move our mouths in silent mock-talk as we suggestively switched our hips from left to right and flirted with our best bedroom eyes. We wondered aloud how anyone could engage in oral sex without breaking into hysterical laughter. In our naïveté, oral sex was not only hilarious, it was just plain stupid.

Twenty years later, I doubt most teens are as naïve as my friend and I were. Although the prevalence of oral sex among adolescents has yet to be comprehensively addressed by researchers,[1] any adult who interacts with teens will quickly learn that, far from being stupid or hilarious, oral sex is a common place activity in some adolescent crowds.

Some teens claim, as teens have always claimed about sex, that "everyone is doing it." They tell of parties—which they may or may not have attended—where oral sex is openly available. They describe using oral sex as a way to relieve the pressure to be sexual with a partner yet avoid the risk of pregnancy. Some believe oral sex is an altogether risk-free behavior that eliminates the worry of sexually transmitted infections. There is a casualness in many teens' attitudes towards oral sex revealed in the term "friends with benefits" to describe a non-dating relationship that includes oral sex. In fact, many teens argue that oral sex really isn't sex at all, logic that, try as we might, defies many adults. Most pointedly, teens' anecdotal experiences of oral sex reveal the continuing imbalance of power prevalent in heterosexual relationships where the boys receive most of the pleasure and the girls, predictably, give most of the pleasure.

Not willing to wait until research confirms what many of us already know, concerned adults want to address the issue of adolescent oral sex *now*. We know that young people long for straightforward and honest conversations about the realities and complexities of human sexuality, including the practice of oral sex. But where do we start with such an intimidating topic? The following ten messages may help caring and concerned adults to initiate authentic conversations about oral sex with young people.

From *Sexing the Political*, May 2004. Copyright © 2004 by Rhonda Chittenden. Reprinted by permission of the author.

1. Oral sex *is* sex.   Regardless of how casual the behavior is for some young people, giving and receiving oral sex are both sexual behaviors. This is made obvious simply by defining the act of oral sex: Oral sex is the stimulation of a person's genitals by another person's mouth to create sexual pleasure and, usually, orgasm for at least one of the partners. It's that straightforward.

Even so, many young people—and even some adults—believe that oral sex is not "real sex." Real sex, they say, is penis-vagina intercourse only. Any other sexual behavior is something "other" and certainly not *real* sex. This narrow definition of sex, rooted in heterosexist attitudes, is problematic for several reasons.

First, such a narrow definition is ahistorical. Art and literature reveal human beings, across human history and culture, consensually engaging their bodies in loving, pleasurable acts of sex beyond penis-vagina intercourse.[2] In Western culture, our notions of sex are still shackled by religious teachings that say the only acceptable sex—in society and the eyes of God—is procreative sex. Of course, the wide accessibility of contraceptives, among other influences, has dramatically shifted our understanding of this.[3] Even still, many people are unaware that across centuries and continents, human beings have enjoyed many kinds of sex and understood those acts to be sex whether or not they involved a penis and a vagina.

Next, by defining sex in such narrow terms, we perpetuate a dangerous ignorance that places people at risk for sexually transmitted infections (STIs), including HIV. Many people, including teens, who define sex in such narrow terms incorrectly reason that they are safe from HIV if they avoid penis-vagina intercourse. Because saliva tends to inhibit HIV, it's true that one's chances of contracting HIV through oral sex with an infected partner are considerably small, compared to the risk of unprotected vaginal or anal sex. Of course, this varies with the presence of other body fluids as well as the oral health of the giver. However, if one chooses to avoid "real sex" and instead has anal sex, the risk for HIV transmission increases.[4] In reality, regardless of what orifice the penis penetrates, all of these sex acts are real sex. In this regard, the narrow definition of sex is troubling because it ignores critical sexual health information that all people deserve, especially those who are sexually active or intend to be in the future.

Finally, this narrow definition of sex invalidates the sexual practices of many people who, for whatever reasons, do not engage in penis-vagina intercourse. Obviously, these people include those who partner with lovers of the same sex. They also include people who, regardless of the sex of their partners, are physically challenged due to illness, accident, or birth anomaly. To suggest to these individuals that oral sex—or any other primary mode of shared sexual expression—is not real sex invalidates the range of accessible and sensual ways they can and do share their bodies with their partners.

Clearly, we must educate young people that there are many ways to enjoy sex, including the sensual placement of one's mouth on another person's genitals. Oral sex may be practiced in casual, emotionally indifferent ways, but this does not disqualify it as a legitimate sex act. Oral sex *is* sex—and, in most states, the law agrees.

2. Without consent, oral sex may be considered sexual assault. Adults who work with teens know that oral sex often takes place at parties where alcohol and other drugs are consumed. It's imperative, then, that when adults talk to teens about oral sex, we confront the legal realities of such situations. Of course, drinking and drug use are illegal for adolescents. In addition, according to Iowa law, if alcohol or drugs are used by either partner of any age, consent for oral sex (or any sex) cannot be given. Without consent, oral sex may be considered sexual assault.[5] Other states have similar laws.

While giving some adolescents reason to reflect on their substance use, this information may also help them to contextualize their past experiences of oral sex. It may affirm the often uneasy and unspoken feelings of some teens who feel they were pressured into oral sex, either as the giver or receiver. It may also illuminate other risks that often occur when sex and substance use are combined, especially the failure to use protection against pregnancy, and in the case of oral sex, sexually transmitted infections.

3. Practice safer oral sex to reduce the risk of sexually transmitted infections. Because many young people don't consider oral sex to be real sex, they don't realize that sexually transmitted infections that are typically transmitted through genital-genital contact can also be transmitted through oral-genital contact. Although some are more easily transmitted through oral sex than others, these infections include chlamydia, gonorrhea, herpes, and, in some cases, even pubic lice. The lips, tongue, mouth cavity, and throat, are all vulnerable to various sexually transmitted bacteria and viruses.[6] With pubic lice, facial hair, including mustaches, beards and eyebrows, can be vulnerable.[7]

Aside from abstaining from oral sex, young people can protect themselves and their partners from the inconvenience, embarrassment, treatment costs, and health consequences of sexually transmitted infections by practicing safer oral sex. The correct and consistent use of latex condoms for fellatio (oral sex performed on a penis) and latex dental dams for cunnilingus (oral sex performed on a vulva) should be taught and encouraged. Manufacturers of condoms, dental dams, and pleasure-enhancing lubricants offer these safer sex supplies in a variety of flavors—including mint, mango, and banana—to increase the likelihood that people will practice safer oral sex.[8] Certainly, adolescents who engage in oral sex should be taught about the correct, pleasure-enhancing uses of these products, informed of the location of stores and clinics that carry them, and strongly encouraged to have their own supply at hand.

4. Oral sex is a deeply intimate and sensual way to give sexual pleasure to a partner. Although casual references to oral sex abound in popular music, movies and culture, many young people have never heard an honest, age-appropriate description of the profoundly intimate and sensual nature of oral sex. Especially for the giver of oral sex, the experience of pleasuring a partner's genitals may be far from casual. Unlike most other sex acts, oral sex acutely engages all five senses of the giver.

As is suggested by the availability of flavored safer sex supplies, for the giver of oral sex, the sense of taste is clearly engaged. If safer sex supplies are not used, the giver experiences the tastes of human body fluids—perhaps semen, vaginal fluids, and/or perspiration. In addition, the tongue and lips feel the varied textures of the partner's genitals, and, depending on the degree of body contact, other touch receptors located elsewhere on the body may be triggered. With the face so close to their partner's genitals, the giver's nose can easily smell intimate odors while the eyes, if opened, get a very cozy view of the partner's body. Lastly, during oral sex the ears not only pick up sounds of voice, moaning, and any music playing in the background, they also hear the delicate sounds of caressing another's body with one's mouth. Obviously, if one is mentally engaged in the experience, it can be quite intense! Honest conversations with adolescents about the intimate and sensual nature of oral sex acknowledge this incredibly unique way human beings share pleasure with one another and elevate it from the casual references of popular culture.

5. Boys do not have to accept oral sex (or any sex) just because it is offered. As I talked with a group of teenagers at a local alternative high school, it became painfully clear to me that some teen girls offer oral sex to almost any guy they find attractive. As a consequence of such easy availability, these teen boys, although they did not find a girl attractive nor did they desire oral sex from her, felt pressured to accept it simply because it was offered. After all, what real man would turn down sex? Popular music videos, rife with shallow depictions of both men and women, show swaggering males getting play right and left from eager, nearly naked women. These same performances of exaggerated male sexual bravado are mirrored on the streets, in the hallways, and in the homes of many boys who may, for various reasons, lack other more balanced models of male sexuality.

When I told the boys that they were not obligated to accept oral sex from someone to whom they were not attracted, it was clearly a message they had never heard. I saw open expressions of surprise and relief on more than a few young faces. This experience taught me that adults must give young men explicit permission to turn down oral sex—and any sex—they do not want. We must teach them that their manhood is not hinged on the number of sex partners they amass.

6. Making informed decisions that respect others and one's self is a true mark of manhood. In May 2002, when Oprah Winfrey and Dr. Phil tried to tackle this subject on her afternoon talk show, they not only put the onus of curbing the trend of casual adolescent oral sex on the girls, they threw up their hands and said, "What do the guys have to lose in this situation? Nothing!"

Nothing? I would suggest otherwise. To leave teen boys off the hook in regard to oral sex fails them miserably as they prepare for responsible adult relationships. In doing so, we set up boys to miss out on developing skills that truly define manhood: healthy sexual decision making, setting and respecting personal boundaries, and being accountable for one's actions. We also leave them at risk for contracting sexually transmitted infections. In addition, although our culture rarely communicates this, men who accept oral sex whenever it is offered risk losing the respect of people who do not admire or appreciate men who have indiscriminate sex with large numbers of partners. Clearly, adults—and especially adult men—must be willing to teach boys, through words and actions, that authentic manhood is a complex identity that cannot be so simply attained as through casual sex, oral or otherwise.[9]

7. Giving oral sex is not an effective route to lasting respect, popularity or love.   For some teen girls, giving oral sex is weighted with hopes of further attention, increased likeability, and perhaps even a loving relationship.[10] For them, giving oral sex becomes a deceptively easy, if not short-term, way to feel worthy and loved. Adults who care about girls must empower them to see beyond the present social situation and find other routes to a sense of belonging and love.

One essential route to a sense of belonging and love is the consistent experience of non-sexual, non-exploitive touch. Some adolescent girls seek sex as a way to find the sense of love and belonging conveyed by touch. If a girl's touch needs go unfilled by parents or other caregivers, sex is often the most available means for fulfilling them.[11] Adults who work with girls must acknowledge the deeply human need for touch experienced by some adolescent girls. Although outside the scope of this discussion, girl-serving professionals can provide creative ways for girls to experience safe, non-sexual touch as part of their participation in programs without violating program restrictions on physical touch between staff and clients.

On the other hand, it is possible—and developmentally normal—for teen girls to experience sexual desire. Although our cultural script of adolescent sexuality contradicts this, it may be that some girls, especially older teens, authentically desire the kind of sensual and sexual intimacy oral sex affords. If this is the case, it is essential that adults do not shame girls away from these emergent desires. Instead, they should explore the ways oral sex may increase one's physical and emotional vulnerabilities and strategize ways that girls can stay healthy and safe while acknowledging their own sexual desires.

8. Girls can refuse to give oral sex.   Unlike Oprah and Dr. Phil, I do not believe the onus for curbing casual adolescent oral sex rests solely or even primarily on teen girls. Teen boys can and should assert firmer boundaries around participating in oral sex. The cultural attitudes that make girls and women the gatekeepers of heterosexual male sexual behavior, deciding when and if sex will happen, are unduly biased and burdensome. By perpetuating these attitudes, Oprah and Dr. Phil missed a grand opportunity to teach the value of mutuality in sexual decision-making and relationships, a message many young people—and adults—desperately need to hear.

That said, it is disturbing to hear stories of adolescent girls offering casual oral sex to teen boys. Again, the models of a balanced female sexuality in the media and in the lives of many girls are often few and far between. This, coupled with the troubling rates of sexual abuse perpetrated against girls in childhood and adolescence, makes the establishment of healthy sexual boundaries a problem for many girls.

Therefore, adults must go beyond simply telling girls to avoid giving oral sex for reasons of reputation and health, as was stressed by Dr. Phil. We must empower girls, through encouragement, role plays, and repeated rehearsals, to establish and maintain healthy boundaries for loving touch in their friendships and dating relationships, an experience that may be new to some. Moreover, we must be frank about the sexual double-standards set up against girls and women that make them responsible for male sexual behavior. And, we must create safe spaces where girls can encourage and support each other in refusing to give boys oral sex, thus shifting the perceived norm that "everyone is doing it."

9. Young women may explore their own capacities for sexual pleasure rather than spending their energies pleasuring others. Some girls will argue that oral sex is just another exchange of friendship, something they do with their male friends as "friends with benefits." I would argue, however, that, in most cases, the benefits are rather one-sided. Rarely do the teen boys give oral sex to the teen girls in exchange. Neither research nor anecdotal evidence indicates a trend of boys offering casual oral sex to girls. It seems that the attention the girls get *en route* to oral sex make it a worthwhile exchange for them, even as they are shortchanged on other "benefits."

If, indeed, girls are fulfilling their valid need for attention and acceptance through giving oral sex, and if they don't consider what they are doing to be "real sex," it stands to reason that many girls engaged in oral sex may not be experiencing genuine sexual desire or pleasure at all. It wouldn't be surprising if they're not. After all, few girls receive a truly comprehensive sexuality education, one that acknowledges the tremendous life-enhancing capacities for desire and pleasure contained in the female body. Our sex education messages are often so consumed by trying to prevent girls from getting pregnant and abused that we fail to notice how we keep them as the objects of other people's sexual behaviors. In doing so, we keep girls mystified about their own bodies and thus fail to empower them as the sexual subjects of their own lives.[12]

Adults can affirm girls' emerging capacities for desire and pleasure by, first, teaching them the names and functions of all of their sexual anatomy, including the pleasure-giving clitoris and G-spot. When discussing the benefits of abstinence, adults can suggest to girls that their growing sexual curiosity and desires may be fulfilled by learning, alone in the privacy of one's room, about one's own body—what touch is pleasing, what is not, how sexual energy builds, and how it is released through their own female bodies. If girls could regard themselves as the sexual subjects of their own lives rather than spending vast energies on being desirable objects of others, perhaps they would make healthier, firmer, more deliberate decisions about the sexual experiences and behaviors they want as adolescents.[13] Not only might girls make better decisions around oral sex, they may feel more empowered to negotiate the use of contraception and safer sex supplies, a skill that would serve them well through their adult years.[14]

10. Seek the support and guidance of adults who have your best interests at heart. Young people do not have to figure it all out on their own. Human sexuality is complicated, and most of us, adults and adolescents, do better by sometimes seeking out the support, guidance, and caring of others who want to see us enjoy our sexualities in healthy, life-enhancing ways. Adults can let young people know we are willing to listen to their concerns around issues of oral sex. We can offer teens support and guidance in their struggles to decide what's right for their lives. We can become skilled and comfortable in addressing risk-reduction and the enhancement of sexual pleasure together, as companion topics. And, finally, adults can use the topic of oral sex as a catalyst to dispel myths, discuss gender roles, and communicate values that affirm the importance of mutuality, personal boundaries, and safety in the context of healthy relationships.

References

1. L. Remez, "Oral Sex Among Adolescents: Is it Sex or Is It Abstinence?" *Family Planning Perspectives,* Nov/Dec 2000, p. 298.

2. R. Tannahill, *Sex in History* (New York: Stein and Day, 1980), pp. 58–346.

3. M. Carrera, *Sex: The Facts, The Acts, and Your Feelings* (New York: Crown, 1981), pp. 49–51.

4. Centers for Disease Control and Prevention, "Preventing the Sexual Transmission of HIV, the Virus that Causes AIDS, What You Should Know about Oral Sex," Dec. 2000. . . .

5. Iowa Code, Section 709.1, Sexual abuse defined (1999). . . .

6. S. Edwards and C. Carne, "Oral Sex and the Transmission of Viral STIs," *Sexually Transmitted Infections,* April 1998, pp. 95–100.

7. Centers for Disease Control and Prevention, "Fact Sheet: Pubic Lice or 'Crabs'," June 2000. . . .

8. Several online retailers sell safer sex supplies, including flavored condoms and lubricants. . . .

9. P. Kivel, *Boys Will Be Men: Raising Our Sons for Courage, Caring and Community.* (Gabriola Island B.C., Canada: New Society, 1999), pp. 177–184.

10. S. Thompson, *Going All the Way: Teenage Girls' Tales of Sex, Romance, and Pregnancy* (New York: Hill & Wang, 1995), pp. 17–46.

11. P. Davis, *The Power of Touch* (Carlsbad, CA: Hay House, 1999), p. 71.

12. M. Fine, "Sexuality, Schooling, and Adolescent Females: The Missing Discourse of Desire," *Disruptive Voices: The Possibilities of Feminist Research,* Ann Arbor: University of Michigan, 1992), pp. 31–59.

13. M. Douglass & L. Douglass, *Are We Having Fun Yet? The Intelligent Woman's Guide to Sex* (New York: Hyperion, 1997), pp. 170–171.

14. TARSHI (Talking About Reproductive and Sexual Health Issues), *Common Ground Sexuality: Principles for Working on Sexuality* (New Dehli, India: TARSHI, 2001), p. 13.

 **NO**

Oral Sex and Young Adolescents: Insights from the "Oral Sex Lady"

A Brief History

I've been the Director of Training at the Network for Family Life Education for three years, but recently I've become known as the "Oral Sex Lady." (My parents are so proud.) It all began when I started receiving more frequent calls from parents, teachers and the media concerning alleged incidents of 11–14-year-olds engaging in oral sex in school buses, empty classrooms or custodial closets, behind the gym bleachers and during "oral sex parties." People were beginning to panic that youth were "sexually out of control." Most people believe young teens should not engage in oral sex, but that's not our current reality. So in response, I developed a workshop about oral sex and young teens, which I have since delivered to hundreds of professionals throughout the country. This process has helped me refine my thinking about this so-called oral sex "problem." Now, when I arrive at a meeting or workshop I smile when I'm greeted with, "Hey, aren't you the Oral Sex Lady?!"

What's the "Problem"?

The 1999 documentary "The Lost Children of Rockdale County" first chronicled a syphilis outbreak in suburban Conyers, Georgia, due to a rash of sex parties. Since then, more anecdotal and media stories about middle school students having oral sex began to surface. Initially, a training participant would tell me about an isolated incident of a young girl caught performing oral sex on a boy in the back of the school bus. During a workshop in Minnesota, I was educated about "Rainbow Parties" in which girls wear different-colored lipstick and the goal for guys is to get as many different-colored rings on their penises by night's end. In Florida, there were stories of "chicken head" parties where girls supposedly gave oral sex to boys at the same time, thus bobbing their heads up and down like chickens. During a workshop in New Jersey, I learned that oral sex was becoming the ultimate bar mitzvah gift in one community, given under the table during the reception, hidden by long tablecloths. (At one synagogue, the caterer was ultimately asked to shorten the tablecloths as a method of prevention!) The media began to pick up on these stories and

From *Educator's Update*, 2004. Copyright © 2004 by Nora Gelperin. Reprinted by permission of the author.

run cover stories in local and national newspapers and magazines. One could conclude from the media buzz that the majority of early adolescents are frequently having oral sex at sex parties around the country. But what was *really* going on and what can the research tell us?

What is missing from the buzz is any recent scientific data to support or refute the claims of early adolescents having oral sex at higher rates than in previous years. Due to parental rights, research restrictions, and lack of funding, there is no rigorous scientific data conducted on the behavior of early adolescents to establish the frequency or incidence of oral sex. So we are left with anecdotal evidence, research conducted on older adolescents, media reports and cultural hype about this "new" phenomenon. We don't know how frequent this behavior is, at what ages it might begin, how many partners a young teen might have, whether any safer sex techniques are utilized, or the reasoning behind a teen's decision to engage in oral sex. What is universal among the anecdotes is that girls are giving oral sex to boys without it generally being reciprocated and it's mostly the adults that find this problematic. But what can we learn from all this?

Major Questions to Consider

Is Oral Sex Really "Sex"?

One of the most common themes I hear during my workshop is that adults want to convince teens that oral sex is really "sex." The adult logic is that if we can just convince teens that oral sex is "really" sex, they will take it more seriously and stop engaging in it so recklessly. This perspective seeks to universally define oral sex from an adult perspective that is out of sync with how many teens may define it. Many teens view oral sex as a way to maintain their "virginity" and reduce their risk for pregnancy and infections. According to a recent Kaiser Family Foundation report, 33 percent of 15–17-year-old girls report having oral sex to avoid having intercourse. In the same report, 47 percent of 15–17-year-old girls and boys believe that oral sex is a form of safer sex. Most people believe that young adolescents should not engage in oral, anal, or vaginal sex. As a backup, we should make sure teens understand that if they are going to engage in sexual behaviors, oral sex is less risky for many infections than vaginal or anal sex if latex barriers like flavored condoms and sheer glyde dams[1] are used, and it cannot start a pregnancy.

If You've Only Had Oral Sex, Are You Still a Virgin?

From my experience facilitating workshops on oral sex, professionals really struggle with this question and many of the 32,000 teens per day who come to our *SEX, ETC*. Web site . . . do too. The concept of virginity, while troublesome to many adults, is still central to the identity of many teens, particularly girls. Many adults and teens define virginity as not having had vaginal intercourse, citing the presence or absence of the hymen. Some adults then wrestle with the idea of what constitutes actual intercourse—penetration of a penis into a vagina, orgasm by one or both partners, oral sex, anal sex, penetration of any body opening? For heterosexual couples, virginity is something girls are often pressured to "keep" and boys are pressured to "lose." The issue also becomes much more volatile when a teen may not have given consent to have intercourse the first time—does this mean that he/she is no longer a virgin? Gay and lesbian teens are also left out when virginity is tied to penis-vagina intercourse, possibly meaning that a gay or lesbian teen might always be a "virgin" if it's defined that way. Educators can help teens think more critically about their definitions of sex, intercourse, and virginity and the meanings of these words in their lives.

How Intimate Is Oral Sex?

Many adults in my workshops express their belief that oral sex is just as intimate as other types of penetrative sexual behaviors. Some adults believe oral sex is even *more* intimate than vaginal or anal intercourse because one partner is considered very vulnerable, it involves all of the senses (smell, taste, touch, sight, and sound) and requires a lot of trust. Many teens, although certainly not all teens, believe oral sex is *less* intimate than vaginal intercourse. Through my experience as an on-line expert for our *SEX, ETC.* Web site, I hear from hundreds of teens every month who submit their most personal sexual health questions. Some of these teens believe oral sex is very intimate and acknowledge the same issues that adults raise while others find it less intimate than vaginal intercourse. From a teen's perspective, it is less intimate because:

- oral sex doesn't require that both partners be nude;
- oral sex can be done in a short amount of time (particularly if performed on adolescent boys);
- oral sex can maintain virginity;
- oral sex doesn't involve eye contact with a partner;
- oral sex doesn't require a method of contraception;
- oral sex doesn't require a trip to the gynecologist; and
- most teens believe oral sex doesn't carry as much of a risk for sexually transmitted infections as vaginal or anal intercourse.

Some girls even feel empowered during oral sex as the only sexual behavior in which they have complete control of their partner's pleasure. Others feel pressured to engage in oral sex and exploited by the experience. So while many adults view oral sex as extremely intimate, some teens do not.

This dichotomy presents challenges for an educator in a group that may assign a different value to oral sex than the educator. Oral sex also requires a conversation about sexual pleasure and sexual response, topics that many educators are not able to address with young teens. The salient issue is how teens define behaviors, not how adults define behaviors, since we are operating in their world when we deliver sexuality education. I believe our definitions and values should be secondary to those of teens because ultimately teens need to be able to operate in a teen culture, not our adult world.

What Can an Educator Do?

As sexual health educators, our role is to provide medically accurate information and encourage all adolescents to think critically about decisions relating to their sexuality. We should ask middle school–age adolescents to sift through their own beliefs and hear from their peers, many of whom might not agree about oral sex, virginity, intimacy or the definition of sex. Finding ways to illuminate the variety of teens' opinions about oral sex will more accurately reflect the range of opinions instead of continuing to propagate the stereotype that "all teens are having oral sex." Additionally, instead of focusing exclusively on the ramifications of oral sex and infections, we should address the potential social consequences of having oral sex. Since early adolescents are not developmentally able to engage in long-term planning, focusing on the long-term consequences of untreated sexually transmitted infections (STIs) is not developmentally appropriate. Educators should be cognizant of what is developmentally appropriate for early adolescents and strive to include information about sexual coercion, correct latex condom and sheer glyde dam use, and infection prevention.

So Are They or Aren't They?

Without research, this question will remain unanswered and we must not rely on overly dramatized media accounts to dictate public health approaches. Instead we should focus on giving young adolescents developmentally appropriate information, consider their reasoning for wanting to engage in oral sex, explore their definitions of sex, virginity, and intimacy, and develop programs that incorporate all of these facets. We need to advocate for more research and reasoned media responses to what is likely a minority of early adolescents having oral sex before it becomes overly dramatized by our shock-culture media. Finally, we must not forget that the desire for early adolescents to feel sexual pleasure is normal and natural and should be celebrated, not censored. From my experience as the "Oral Sex Lady," teens are much more savvy than we adults think.

Note

1. Sheer glyde dams are squares of latex that are held in place on the vulva of a female during oral sex to help prevent sexually transmitted infections. They are the only brand of dental dam that is FDA approved for the prevention of infections.

POSTSCRIPT

Is Oral Sex Really Sex?

"Sex is more than sexual intercourse. This means teaching young people that there are many ways to be sexual with a partner besides intercourse, and most of these behaviors are safer and healthier than intercourse. The word 'sex' often has a vague meaning. When talking about intercourse, the word 'intercourse' [should be] used."

This statement is taken from a list of principles for sexuality education developed by The Center for Family Life Education, included in the U.S. chapter of the *International Encyclopedia of Sexuality*. Do you agree or disagree with this principle? How does it compare with your own definition of "sex"? Do you agree with Chittenden that young people need to recognize oral sex as "really sex"? Or are you inclined to side with Gelperin as she asserts that adult values and definitions should be secondary, and that young people need to form their own definition of oral sex?

Chittenden presents specific messages she believes young people need to hear about oral sex. What do you think about these messages? Are they messages you would want to give to a son or daughter, or to a younger sibling? What other advice would you want to give to a loved one who was thinking about having oral sex?

Whereas Chittenden identifies specific messages that need to be articulated to young people, Gelperin seems more inclined to advocate a values clarification process and educational strategies based on the developmental needs of a given audience. What merits do these different approaches have? Would you advocate a combination of these approaches? Or would your own educational approach be very different?

Gelperin expresses great concern about the hype surrounding media reports of oral sex. What do you think about such reports? How do they compare with the social climate in your schools or community as you were growing up?

Since both Chittenden and Gelperin are sexuality education professionals, you may have noticed several overlapping themes, such as the concern both expressed about condom use and protection from sexuality transmitted infections. What other similarities did you observe?

Is it more important to have a uniform definition of "sex," that includes (or does not include) oral sex, or for people to create their own personal definitions that have meaning for themselves and/or their partners? Some reproductive health professionals have ascertained that if you cannot define "sex," then you cannot define its supposed opposite, "abstinence." In other words, young people need to understand what sex is before they can determine what it is they are being encouraged to abstain from. How has a culturally vague notion of "sex" and "abstinence" contributed to the widespread failure of abstinence-only education programs?

Suggested Readings

W.C. Chambers (2007). "Oral Sex: Varied Behaviors and Perceptions in a College Population," *Journal of Sex Research, 44(1):28–42.*

G. D'Souza, et al. (2009). "Oral Sexual Behaviors Associated with Prevalent Oral Human Papillomavirus Infection," *Journal of Infectious Diseases, 199:1263–1269.*

L.D. Lindberg, et al. (2008). "Noncoital Sexual Activities among Adolescents," *Journal of Adolescent Health, 43(3):231–238.*

L. Remez, "Oral Sex Among Adolescents: Is It Sex or Is It Abstinence?" *Family Planning Perspectives* (November/December 2000).

R. Stein, "Oral Sex Isn't Keeping Kids Virgins," *Washington Post* (May 20, 2008).

P. Schehl, "Middle Schoolers Facing Tough Issues," *Mount Vernon News* (January 20, 2009).

J. Timpane, "No Big Deal: The Biggest Deal of All—Young Adults and the Oral Sex Code," *Philadelphia Inquirer* (October 28, 2002).

D. Trice, "Teens Have Sex But Don't Have the Facts," *Chicago Tribune* (March 17, 2008).

ISSUE 5

Is BDSM a Healthy Form of Sexual Expression?

YES: Wayne Pawlowski, from "BDSM: The Ultimate Expression of Healthy Sexuality," an original essay written for this volume (2009)

NO: J. Paul Fedoroff, from "Sadism, Sadomasochism, Sex, and Violence," *The Canadian Journal of Psychiatry* (vol. 53, no. 10, 2008)

ISSUE SUMMARY

YES: Sex educator Wayne Pawlowski provides an explanation of BDSM and describes it as a normal, healthy expression of sexuality.

NO: J. Paul Fedoroff describes BDSM as a disorder and a pathology and links BDSM to criminal activity.

Bondage/Discipline, Dominance/submission, and Sadism/Masochism (BDSM) all involve the eroticization of the exchange of power. For some, there is no bigger turn on than taking control in a sexual encounter. For others, giving away all power may be the ultimate thrill. These choices may manifest in many different ways. Bondage play involves the restriction of movement by rope, chains, or other instruments. Submission may take the form of being spanked or confined to a cage. A sadist may enjoy striking a submissive partner with an object like a whip or cane. To some, these behaviors may sound like an exhilarating Friday night. For others, the behaviors may seem extreme or even dangerous. There is even much debate among health care professionals and sexuality educators. The subjective nature of classifying behaviors and fantasies, along with the social stigma attached to BDSM, can make it difficult to find accurate and representative statistics on the subject. A 1993 study found that 14 percent of men and 11 percent of women had engaged in some sadomasochistic sexual activities in their lives (Janus & Janus, 1993). A recent Australian study found that 1.8 percent of sexually active people (2.2% of men, 1.3% of women) reported involvement in BDSM in the past year (Richters et al., 2008). Much of what we know about those who practice BDSM comes from studies of those who attend BDSM clubs or functions, or who are members of BDSM organizations (Weinberg, 2006) rather than from studies of the general population.

According to the DSM-IV, the reference book used by psychiatrists to diagnose mental disorders, both sadism and masochism are considered paraphilias (sex-related disorders), as long as the thoughts or behaviors cause "clinically significant distress or impairment in social, occupational, or other important areas of functioning." Sadism is defined as the use of "sexual fantasies, urges or behaviors involving infliction of pain, suffering or humiliation to enhance or achieve sexual excitement"; and masochism is defined as the use of "sexual fantasies, urges, or behaviors involving being beaten, humiliated, bound, or tortured to enhance or achieve sexual excitement" (APA, 1994).

Despite the caveat that an interest in BDSM must cause "distress" in order to be considered a problem, many find any interest in sadistic or masochistic sexuality to be unhealthy. Making for surprising bedfellows, conservatives and radical feminists have often found themselves on the same side of the argument against BDSM. The conservative group Concerned Women for America have pressured hotel chains to prevent BDSM organizations from holding conventions in their hotels (CWFA, 2003). Large BDSM groups like Black Rose in Washington, DC, often rent out entire hotels for weekend conventions that host hundreds of BDSM practitioners. Across the ideological spectrum, many radical feminists also criticize BDSM, holding that any form of sexual dominance reinforces sexual hierarchy, thereby contributing to the well-established patriarchal dominance.

But does sex play involving dominance and submission always signal violence and oppression? Are these types of behaviors and fantasies always dangerous? Or are they simply part of the larger tapestry of incredibly diverse sexual expressions, capturing the imaginations of some, but not others?

Suggested Readings

American Psychiatric Association. (1994). Diagnostic and statistical manual of mental disorders, (4th ed.). Washington, DC: American Psychiatric Association.

Concerned Women for America (CWFA). (2003). "Cancel Sexual Torture Convention, CWA Urges Adam's Mark Chicago–Northbrook Hotel." Press release accessed from http://www.cwfa.org/articledisplay .asp?id=3270&department=FIELD&categoryid=misc

M. Freedenberg. (2008). "Kink Dreams: Peter Acworth's Fetish Porn Empire Takes over the San Francisco Armory to Create a New Kind of Dotcom." Accessed at http://www.sfbg.com/entry.php?entry_id=7161&catid= 4&volume_id=398&issue_id=425&volume_num=43&issue_num=27

R. Goldman, "Love Hurts: Sadomasochism's Dangers: Man Spends Three Days in a Coma after Kinky Sex—But Unsafe Play Can Result in Death" (2008). Accessed at http://abcnews.go.com/Health/story?id=4285958&page=1

S. Janus & C. Janus, The Janus Report on Sexual Behavior (New York: Wiley, 1993).

J. Richters et al., "Demographic and Psychosocial Features of Participants in Bondage and Discipline, 'Sadomasochism' or Dominance and Submission (BDSM): Data from a National Survey," Journal of Sexual Medicine. (vol. 5, no. 7, 2008).

D. Schoetz, "Wife Held in Kinky Hubby's Bondage Death: Police Say Woman Left Her Husband for 20 Hours Bound, Gagged Before He Suffocated" (2008). Accessed through http://abcnews.go.com/US/story?id=4703433

YES

Wayne V. Pawlowski

BDSM: The Ultimate Expression of Healthy Sexuality

What is BDSM? We will get to definitions in a moment, but let's start off by saying that it (BDSM) is perhaps one of the most misunderstood forms of sexual expression today. It is not only misunderstood, it is feared; prosecuted as abuse/assault; depicted as something engaged in by mentally disturbed, sexual predators who torture, rape, kill, and dismember their victims; and the behaviors associated with it are classified as mental disorders in the psychiatric diagnostic criteria of the *Diagnostic and Statistical Manual of Mental Disorders* (commonly known as the DSM) and the *International Classification of Diseases* (ICD). Given all of this, individuals who engage in BDSM behaviors rarely talk about their interests with people outside of the "BDSM Community." The end result is that BDSM and BDSM behaviors remain "in the closet" and misunderstood.

It is known that BDSM behaviors occur among all genders, sexual orientations, races, ages, sexual identity groups, social groups and economic groups. And, they have occurred throughout recorded history and across cultures. Beyond these general statements, however, there is very little solid and reliable research as to the number of individuals who engage in and/or who fantasize about BDSM behaviors. And, in part because of its secrecy, there is almost no research data describing the population of individuals who are regular or periodic BDSM "players" and/or who are members of the "BDSM Community." As a result, the misunderstanding and myths about BDSM continue to pervade the culture and the psychiatric view of BDSM behaviors.

Much has been written and discussed about:

- The weaknesses of the psychiatric diagnostic criteria for BDSM behaviors,
- The lack of research and data to back up the diagnostic criteria,
- The inaccurate and inconsistent application of diagnoses of BDSM behaviors,
- The gender bias in the diagnostic descriptions (overwhelmingly male),
- The discrepancies between the descriptions of BDSM behaviors in the *Diagnostic and Statistical Manual* and the *International Classification of Diseases,* and,

An original essay written for this volume. Copyright © 2009 by Wayne Pawlowski. Reprinted by permission.

- The lack of a clear and consistently applied distinction between individuals who engage in BDSM behaviors *consensually and safely* verses those who force, rape, torture, and/or otherwise engage in non-consensual, violent behaviors.

The bottom line is that the *Diagnostic and Statistical Manual* is not a useful place to go to try to understand BDSM, or the people who engage in BDSM behaviors. In addition, as with other previously "pathologized" behaviors that the *Diagnostic and Statistical Manual* eventually "de-pathologized" (masturbation and same-sex sexual behavior, to name two), BDSM behaviors as they are engaged in by those who identify with the "BDSM Community" bear little to no resemblance to the behaviors described in the psychiatric diagnostic criteria. The subtleties and distinctions among BDSM behaviors as practiced and understood by those who engage in those behaviors (hereafter, for brevity sake, referred to as "practitioners") are lost on the majority of the psychiatric community (those who write the psychiatric diagnostic criteria), the legal community (police, courts, lawyers), and the culture as a whole.

So, in order to understand how BDSM and engaging in BDSM behaviors can be the ultimate, healthy expression of self and of sexuality we must first step away from the psychiatric diagnostic criteria and from the legal and cultural misperceptions and interpretations. Next we must clarify what BDSM is and isn't, then we must examine BDSM behaviors in the context of "normal," "conventional" behaviors, and lastly, we must try to let go of our preconceived biases and see the incredibly healthy aspects of how BDSM play is conducted and experienced.

What BDSM Is and Isn't

BDSM is an acronym for a wide range of behaviors, both sexual and non-sexual. It is actually a complex interplay of three separate and distinct "worlds" of behavior, none of which are inherently overtly sexual but most of which can and often do play out in powerfully erotic ways. BDSM includes the world of *BD*, the world of *Ds* and the world of *SM*. While these three worlds can and frequently do overlap (hence the acronym "BDSM"), they can and frequently do travel totally and completely separately from each other.

Recognizing that the language used to describe BDSM is in flux and that different regions of the US and the world will use different terms to describe the same behaviors, let us attempt to clarify the three "worlds" mentioned above.

BD is the world of "bondage and dominance," "bondage and domination," or, "bondage and discipline" (remember, language varies from place to place and person to person so all three descriptions are simply different words used to define *BD*.). *BD* always involves some sort of restraint—bondage—and is frequently, but not always, paired with some sort of domination and/or punishment/discipline.

Ds is the world of "Dominance and submission" or "Domination and submission." (Remember the note above about variations in language.) And, yes, the upper case "D" and lower case "s" are intentional. *Ds* involves some sort of "superiority" and "inferiority"; the domination of one individual over another and/or the submission of one individual to another.

SM is the world of "sadism and masochism" or "sadomasochism." *SM* involves some sort of playing with and/or giving (sadism) and receiving (masochism) of pain and/or other sensations.

So, BDSM encompasses a wide range of behaviors and activities. Common elements that are "played with" in most BDSM behaviors are power (exchanging it, taking it, and/or giving it up), the mind (psychology), and sensation (using or depriving use of the senses and working with the chemicals released by the body when pain and/or intense sensations are experienced).

BDSM play often occurs as much psychologically as it does physically so "using" the mind, the brain, and the imagination is a powerful and well-exercised skill among BDSM practitioners. It is the psychological aspect of BDSM that gives BDSM play its meaning and context. Sometimes, BDSM play is *primarily* psychology rather than physical. When it is, things like domination and submission may not look at all like what people expect. In fact, predominantly psychological BDSM "behaviors" may not be at all "visible" or evident to an observer even when they are occurring in a very public arena. More will be said about the psychological aspects of BDSM later in this article.

As with every other aspect of their lives, practitioners of BDSM make ongoing decisions about what role BDSM behaviors will play in their general lives and in their sexual lives. Their BDSM behaviors may be "real" or role play, one-time-only, 24/7, on-going, short-term, long-term, periodic, primarily erotically sexual, primarily non-sexual, a part of one relationship only, or a part of every relationship. There is no single way that BDSM behaviors are integrated into practitioners' lives, sexual lives, and/or love making in the same way that there is no single way that other more "conventional" behaviors are integrated into the lives, sexual lives, and/or love making of people in general.

Normal/Conventional or Abnormal/ Unconventional

For most non-practitioners, BDSM is viewed as "unconventional" and/or "exotic" behavior at best or abnormal and dangerous at worst. In fact, BDSM play is nothing more or less than an extension of the "normal," "conventional" behaviors that most "traditional" couples engage in with great frequency. Most behaviors in life are engaged in along a continuum from mild/gentle to moderate to extreme/intense. (See Figure 1.) BDSM is simply the more extreme/intense end of the continuum of normal, conventional behavioral expression.

Figure 1

Continuum of Expression of Conventional Behaviors

◄ - ►

Mild   Moderate   Extreme

BD Behaviors

During love making it is not uncommon for one partner to "hold" the other partner "in place" at a particular moment (e.g., holding a partner's head in place during oral sex), or to tie a partner's hands with underwear or a scarf. Many couples view these behaviors as nothing more than playful and exciting ways to enhance their intimacy. Most would not view them as BDSM. They are, however, all forms of "restraint" and "restraint" in BDSM parlance is "bondage." These playful and exciting behaviors are simply the mild or gentle end of a continuum of behaviors that may, at the extreme end, involve having someone completely immobilized, caged, or chained to a wall. (See Figure 2.) The only difference between holding a person's head in place and having someone completely immobilized is the level of intensity and drama of the behaviors, the psychological meaning of the behaviors, the way the behaviors "look," and how the behaviors are experienced by the participants. The behaviors themselves are the same; one partner is restraining another. And, again, restraint is another word for bondage and bondage is a part of the world of *BD*.

Figure 2

Continuum of BD Behaviors

Partner's hands tied   Partner handcuffed Partner immobilized/
with scarf. to bed. caged.

◄---►

Mild   Moderate   Extreme

Ds Behaviors

A partner may playfully and lightheartedly say, "You get no sex from me unless you bring me a glass of wine and light some candles first!" This is a conventional, light-hearted occurrence among many "traditional" couples; sex is playfully "withheld" and later "granted" upon the completion of a task. As we saw with *BD*, this playful behavior is nothing less than the gentle end of *Ds*. It is servitude, "requiring" one partner to "serve" the other with sex as the "reward." The more intense end of this behavior might be a full-time live in "slave" who is "allowed" to have sex with the Dominant partner as a result of satisfactorily completing his/her chores. (See Figure 3.) Again, both of

Figure 3

Continuum of Ds Behaviors

No sex without a glass of wine.   Full-time live-in slave.

◄---►

Mild   Moderate   Extreme these behaviors are essentially the same as they both involve servitude. What is different about them is the intensity and drama of the behaviors, their psychological meaning, how they "look," and how they are experienced by the participants.

SM Behaviors

A light slap on the buttocks or gently pinching a partner as orgasm nears is common "conventional" behavior among "traditional" couples. But, as with the *BD* and *Ds* examples, this light slap and gentle pinch are nothing less than the mild or gentle end of the *SM* continuum . . . playing with sensations. The moderate place on this continuum might be lightly spanking a partner. The extreme end of the continuum might be severely whipping or flogging a partner. (See Figure 4.) Again, all of these behaviors are the same in that they involve administering some sort of sensation to a partner in order to heighten erotic feeling. What is different about them is the intensity of the behaviors, their psychological meaning, how they "look," and how they are experienced by the participants.

Figure 4

Continuum of SM Behaviors

Light slap on buttocks	Light spanking	Severe whipping
◄ - ►		
Mild	Moderate	Extreme

Some readers might be horrified to think of or to interpret their "normal," "conventional," "vanilla," "ordinary" behaviors as BDSM behaviors . . . but in fact, they are just that. Perhaps they are the mild or gentle end of BDSM; but they are BDSM nonetheless. Or, to put it the other way, BDSM behaviors are nothing more than the extreme end of "normal," "ordinary," "conventional" behaviors.

The importance of the "psychological meaning" of behavior was mentioned earlier and it cannot be emphasized enough how important psychological meaning is to BDSM practitioners. The experience of any behavior and how the behavior "feels," comes directly from the meaning that has been given to the behavior by the people involved in it. It also comes from the context in which the behavior occurs. If a behavior is labeled and/or identified as a BDSM behavior for a particular couple, it will be EXPERIENCED as a BDSM behavior by that couple. If the exact same behavior is not given that label or identified in that way, it will be experienced completely differently; likely it will be experienced as ordinary, conventional behavior.

It was mentioned earlier that predominantly psychological BDSM behavior may not be visible even if it is occurring in a very public arena. An example of this is someone sitting alone on a park bench. That individual may well be doing nothing more or less than sitting alone on a park bench. However, if that individual is a submissive that has been ordered to sit there until his/her Dom returns, that submissive will be engaging in an intense and powerful BDSM experience. The behavior alone looks very conventional—sitting on a park bench—but the psychological meaning of that sitting is profoundly influenced by the meaning assigned to it by the individuals involved.

Healthy Sexuality and Healthy Relationships

Because the meaning of behavior comes from knowing and understanding its context, for BDSM behaviors to "work" they must be discussed, analyzed, clearly understood, and agreed upon. This means individuals must share with their partners their wants, needs, desires, fantasies, limits, fears, etc. It means they must *communicate* and *negotiate* in great detail and clarity about what they want, what they like, what they are willing to do, what they are not willing to do, what the relationship means to them right now, and what it might mean tomorrow; and, after-the-fact, they must communicate again about what the experience was like for them.

All of this requires the development of self-awareness, communication skills, listening skills, high self-esteem, awareness of boundaries (one's own and others'), awareness of personal likes and dislikes, negotiation skills, etc.

What could be healthier than for individuals to be encouraged to develop and practice all of these things? And then, what could be better for couples than to engage in this level of communication, negotiation, and feedback as they enter into and develop relationships?

As part of their belief in and need for communication, openness, and full consent, BDSM practitioners have developed a number of guiding principles which are taught and followed by the "community" and by those who seriously engage in BDSM activities. These principles include *SSC* (Safe, Sane, Consensual) and/or *RACK* (Risk Aware Consensual Kink), *Hurt Not Harm, Negotiation, Relationship of Equals, Safe Words, After Care, Self-Affirming Not Self-Destructive,* and *Never Under the Influence.*

This paper does not allow for a full explanation of each of these principles, but the list itself conveys the BDSM Community's interest in and desire to talk openly and honestly about safety, limits, can-do's, can't-dos, how to monitor and take care of each other while in the midst of play, how to take care of each other when play is done, etc. All of this illustrates the fact that BDSM practitioners are not the disturbed, compulsive, driven, dangerous individuals who engage in pathological behaviors as described in the *Diagnostic and Statistical Manual* and as seen on TV. Instead, in reality, they are serious, cautious, thoughtful, caring individuals who negotiate with equal partners to engage in behaviors that are mutually satisfying, mutually desired, and enacted as safely as possible. They believe that two people can only enter into a BDSM relationship if they both fully understand each other, they both fully understand what they are going to do together, and, they both fully and completely consent to what will happen before, during, and after the behavior. These beliefs, qualities, interactions, and behaviors epitomize healthy sexuality and sexually healthy relationships.

J. Paul Fedoroff  **NO**

Sadism, Sadomasochism, Sex, and Violence

The true prevalence of sexual sadism (and its variants) is unknown. However, all clinicians will knowingly or unknowingly encounter patients with this disorder. Regretfully, few programs offer adequate education in normal sexuality and even less provide training in the assessment and treatment of pathologic sexual interests. This review synthesizes current theories about possible etiologies of criminal sexual sadism and the resulting implications for diagnosis and treatment of this sexual disorder. Included is a review of theories of criminally sadistic sexual motivations, response patterns, and physiology, including possible neurophysiologic factors and more complex interactions. This review focuses primarily on published English-language scientific studies of sexual sadism. It should be noted that my use of the term sadism refers to nonconsensual sexual aggression.

Highlights

- While some scientific evidence supports an interaction between sexual behaviours and aggression, the purported association between sex and violence in media reports is misleading. This is due to a focus on sensational cases, lack of consistency in diagnostic criteria, inconclusive study designs, overgeneralization, and reliance on opinion.
- Sexual arousal from consensual interactions that include domination should be distinguished from nonconsensual sex acts. Nonconsensual sex may be opportunistic, disinhibited, or sexually motivated. Often motivations are mixed.
- Future research needs to integrate studies to account for how neurophysiologic and neurohormonal events translate into psychologic experiences that in turn are modified by social variables within specific populations across the lifespan.
- The frequency of reported sex crimes is decreasing. The efficacy of treatment for paraphilias of all types is improving. Further research into the relation between sex and violence will aid in decreasing sex crimes but more importantly will aid in understanding how to facilitate safe, healthy, and happy sexuality for everyone.

Sadism and masochism occupy a special place among the perversions, for the contrast of activity and passivity lying at their bases belong to the common traits of the sexual life. —Sigmund Freud[1], p. 23

From *Canadian Journal of Psychiatry,* by J. Paul Fedoroff 53(10), October 2008, pp. 637–646.
Copyright © 2008 by Canadian Psychiatric Association. Reprinted by permission.

How one thing depends upon another is the greatest mystery about life in my opinion, and no doubt if we could see the network of cause and effect spun and spinning around us, it would be a very interesting and wonderful spectacle.[2], *p. 1*

The topics of sex and violence are of almost universal interest. A Google search using the word sex produces 687 million hits. A search linking sex with synonyms for violence results in 274 million searchable links. A more specific review of the scientific literature was conducted using SUM search, which combines a metasearch strategy with contingency searching of major databases including PubMed and PsycLIT. In our review, the following key words were linked with the word sexual: violence, sadism, homicide, coercion, and predator. This search, limited to human subject research published in the English language within the last 10 years, resulted in 4211 journal article citations. These citations were combined with 148 journal articles identified by the key word sadomasochism, followed up by referral to articles and books cited in the materials listed above.

To capture articles not yet cited within standard research databases, the results were combined with a recent review of the published literature on sexual violence.[3] Full details of the search strategies and results for this article are available on request.

Introduction

These incidence and prevalence of sex crimes in North America is declining,[4] and no one knows why.[5] In Canada, the rate of sexual assault in 2004 was 74 incidents per 100,000, representing a 33% drop from 1985. Since then, published rates report a further decrease to 72 per 100,000.[6]

Despite this welcome trend, the association between sexually motivated behaviours and violence is unknown. Sexual offences of all types result in devastating consequences, not only for victims but also for perpetrators (a third of whom are themselves victims of sexual abuse).[7] No clinician who cares for adult patients has the luxury of avoiding contact (knowingly or otherwise) with perpetrators and potential perpetrators whose activities may be modified to the extent that sex crimes can be prevented.

Appropriate interventions require adequate education. In a survey of 141 medical schools in North America, 54% provided 10 hours teaching on the general topic of sexual medicine[8]; however, most medical schools provided prospective physicians with less than 2 hours of sex education.[9] These numbers are important because physicians are often the first people confronted with situations in which clinical judgments are crucial. The vignette in Table 1 is an example of the questions posed during typical sexual attitude restructuring exercises advocated by experts in medical education.

The purpose of this review is to examine the relation between sex and violence, to explain some of the contradictory views of researchers, to provide a rational basis for answers to the questions posed in Table 1, and to advocate for evidence-based evaluation and treatment of men and women with potentially problematic sexual interests and behaviours. This review is intended primarily

ABBREVIATIONS USED IN THIS ARTICLE

BDSM	Bondage–Discipline, Dominance–Submission, Sadism–Masochism
DSM	Diagnostic and Statistical Manual of Mental Disorders
ICD	International Classification of Diseases
LH	luteinizing hormone
MRI	magnetic resonance imaging
PET	positron emission tomography
RCBF	regional cerebral blood flow

Table 1

Case History

You are a psychiatry resident on call in a busy downtown emergency room. A young patient is brought to the ER by ambulance with a fractured femur. Radiologic examination indicates this is a third fracture. You are asked whether a psychiatric consultation is indicated.

What is your answer if:

- The injuries were sustained during high school football games?
- The injuries were sustained during consensual, sadomasochistic sex play?
- The injuries were sustained during nonconsensual sexual activity?
- The patient is a child; is female; is intellectually disabled; does or does not think there is a problem?

Finally, what would your answer be in each case if the patient were the sexual partner of another individual with the same medical injury?

for psychiatrists in general practice. Reviews of topics of more interest to sub-specialists are available, such as sexually aggressive women,[10] sexually aggressive juveniles,[11, 12] intellectually delayed sex offenders,[13] and neurological comorbidity in sexual violence.[14]

Diagnostic Criteria

DSM-IV-TR criteria for sexual sadism (302.84) are reproduced in Table 2.[15, p. 574] Examining the A criteria, several questions arise:

- Why 6 months?
- What does recurrent mean?
- What does intense mean?
- Is it meaningful to discuss sexual urges independent of sexual fantasies?

Table 2

DSM-IV-TR Criteria for Sexual Sadism (302.84)

Over a period of 6 months, recurrent, intense sexually arousing fantasies, sexual urges, or behaviors involving acts (real, not simulated) in which the psychological or physical suffering (including humiliation) of the victim is sexually exciting to the person.

The person has acted on these sexual urges with a non-consenting person, or the sexual urges or fantasies cause marked distress or interpersonal difficulty.[15, p. 574]

- Why distinguish between real and simulated acts?
- Appearing to be a fairly inclusive criteria, why is humiliation specifically identified in addition to psychological and physical suffering?

Few experts follow the DSM-IV-TR criteria.[16] For example, in a series of survey studies involving respected and experienced forensic psychiatrists, investigators found that "the diagnosis of sexual sadism was not being applied in the Canadian prison system in a way that matched any of the criteria identified in the literature."[17, p. 2]

These findings also applied to internationally renowned psychiatrists, in which a kappa coefficient for reliability across diagnosis was only 0.14.[18]

Table 3 lists the ICD-10 criteria for sadomasochism.[19] There are several obvious differences between these criteria and those of the DSM-IV-TR. First, the conditions of sexual sadism and sexual masochism are combined. Second, there is an indication that elements of sadomasochism may be present in so-called normal sexual life. Third, there is an explicit differentiation between sexually motivated sadomasochistic acts and those motivated by cruelty or anger in a sexual context.

The differences between the DSM and ICD diagnostic criteria underline a major cause of confusion in the literature as it is often hard to know what is meant by the term sadist. Also, most studies use samples of convenience consisting of men convicted of violent sexual crimes. Examination of samples of this type begs the question of the relation between sexual sadism and sexual violence.

Table 3

ICD-10 Criteria for Sadomasochism (F 65.5)

A preference for sexual activity that involves bondage or the infliction of pain or humiliation. If the individual prefers to be the recipient of such stimulation this is called masochism; if the provider, sadism. Often an individual obtains sexual excitement from both sadistic and masochistic activities.

Mild degrees of sadomasochistic stimulation are commonly used to enhance otherwise normal sexual activity. This category should be used only if sadomasochistic activity is the most important source of stimulation or necessary for sexual gratification.

Sexual sadism is sometimes difficult to distinguish from cruelty in sexual situations or anger unrelated to eroticism. Where violence is necessary for erotic arousal, the diagnosis can be clearly established. Includes: masochism, sadism.[19, p. 172]

Etiologic Theories

Sexual Motivation

In a recent paper,[20] 12 series of serial sexual murderers were reviewed.[20-31] The men in these surveys were judged to have shown evidence of "positive feelings of sexual pleasure, even exhilaration- rather than anger or other unpleasant states . . ." that represented the "driving psychological force in the crimes."[20, p. 902]

On the basis of a review of studies on the sexual physiology in nonsadistic men, these authors assert that anger is incompatible with sexual arousal because sympathetic catecholamines associated with anger (for example, norepinephrine) are also associated with penile detumescence.[32, 33]

Unfortunately, all but one of the 12 reports involved reviewing historic cases, with several involving descriptions by authors with no clinical experience. It is possible that the descriptions of sexual pleasure as the prime motivating force may more accurately reflect the views of the reports' authors than those of the study's participants.

In addition, many sex crimes involve activities that do not require an erection.[34,35] The act of planning and carrying out a sex crime may itself be associated with subjective sexual arousal.[36] Presumably these phases of the crime are independent of penile tumescence and not incompatible with other emotions such as anger directed at the victim. Several studies have indicated that anger itself can be a major factor contributing to the commission of sex crimes.[37-39]

Sexual Fantasies, Experiences, and Behaviours

If serial violent sex offenders are primarily motivated by sexual arousal, how unique to offenders is sexual arousal in response to sadistic stimuli or scenarios? Meyers et al.'s review of 3 studies[20, p. 904] in which a percentage of presumably noncriminal male college students were aroused by fantasies of "infliction of pain on others"[40] and found pictures of women with "distressed faces"[41] more sexually arousing, and in which the degree of arousal increased together with the degree of distress depicted in pictures of "semi-nude women in bondage."[42]

These and other studies have been summarized.[43] Among the general male population, 39% have had fantasies of "tying up" and 30% of "raping a woman."[44, p. 571] Among male college students, 51%[44, p. 130] indicated they would rape a woman if they thought they could get away with it, and perhaps most controversially, 25%[44, p. 134] of the male and female college students in the sample thought women would enjoy being raped if no one knew about it.[45]

Most rapes involve the use of alcohol. In one representative study, according to 61% of the victims, the offender was under the influence of alcohol.[46] It is unknown whether the percentages of students apparently approving of rape in the previous study would have been higher had the surveys been done after the respondents had consumed alcohol.

One of the most influential studies of sexual murderers involved a sample of only 36 men, interviewed in custody by FBI special agents.[47] Authors of the FBI study hypothesized that offenders begin with deviant fantasies that graduate to minor crimes that in turn become increasingly serious. This "degeneration hypothesis" was originally advanced by Marquis Donatien-Alphonse Francois de Sade, after whom the term sadism was eponymously named.[48] This influential uncontrolled FBI study has supported the theory that men who commit extreme sex crimes can be identified and classified on the basis of unique characteristics, including deviant sexual fantasies.[40, 49, 51–53]

Problems with the sensitivity and specificity of sexual fantasies characteristic of sadistic sex offenders have been reviewed.[54] One study of 94 men with no history of sexual offences found 33% reported rape fantasies and 14.9% reported humiliation fantasies.[44] Although men far outnumber women convicted of sadistic sex crimes, surveys have found no difference in frequency of sadistic fantasies in men and women.[55–57] In fact, nonscientific reports indicate that women's fantasies may be becoming more sadistic even though the number of sadistic women convicted of sex crimes has remained constant or even dropped.[58] Variables identified as characteristic of criminal sadists by Burgess[49] were compared with frequencies of these variables in a sample of 18 undergraduate men and 32 undergraduate women. None of the university students were known to have committed crimes of any type. Among 11 childhood experiences identified as characteristic of criminal sadists, only a history of convulsions was more frequent in Burgess' criminal sadist group. Three childhood experiences were more common in the university group: daydreaming, accident proneness, and headaches. The university group also reported more adolescent experiences than the sexual sadists, including: poor body image, sleep problems, and headaches. Sexual sadists were more likely to report eneuresis and convulsions during adolescence. In adulthood, the university group continued to show more worrisome behavioural indicators than did Burgess' criminal sexual sadists: daydreaming, poor body image, sleep problems, and headaches.

A similar lack of specificity was found for the childhood behavioural indicators previously identified to be associated with criminal sadists. The only exceptions were self-identified compulsive masturbation and fire-setting, which were significantly more prevalent in the sadist group.

It should be noted that more differences emerged between the 2 groups during adolescence and adulthood. Unfortunately, data concerning the time of onset of criminal behaviour in the offender sample were not available. Still, the failure to find consistent clear differences between the criminal sadists and the university student group, even though the university student group consisted of both men and women, suggests that experiences and behaviours, at least as identified in the FBI sample, are unreliable.

Sexual Response Patterns

If criminal sadists cannot be reliably distinguished from noncriminal men on the basis of sexual fantasies, childhood experiences, or behaviours, can they be distinguished on the basis of laboratory testing of penile tumescence in response to stimuli designed to simulate or approximate sadistic scenarios? This possibility was also investigated.[59–65] Marshall[66] pointed out that results of these early studies have yielded inconsistent results when arousal in response to rape was compared between groups consisting of rapists and normal men. In response to rape stimuli, rapists were found to show penile tumescence responses that were either more than,[64, 67–69] equal to,[59, 60, 70–74] or less than[61] those of the control group. It may be that differences in results may be due to differences in the number of sadists in each group.[75, 76]

A second explanation for variance in ability to distinguish between rapist and nonrapists on the basis of penile tumescence testing may be due to the types of stimuli used in the test procedure.[77, 78] Two potentially important variations include the degree of brutality of the audiotape stimuli[79] or the degree of humiliation.[80] In all likelihood, an interaction exists between the degree of sadism in the man tested and the type of stimuli presented. In a group of rapists with few sadists, manipulation of sadistic elements in the stimuli presented during penile tumescence testing would not be expected to assist in discrimination from nonrapist, nonsadistic controls. This is in fact what was found.[81]

In a study involving[41] sexual offenders diagnosed with sexual sadism and 18 sexual offenders without sadism, Boer[65] found that on a "composite index" of phallometric responses, "only 17.1% of sadists appeared deviant and yet 44% of the so-called nonsadists displayed deviant responses."[p. 2] This raises the question of whether sadistic interest necessarily increases risk of sexual offences.

Penile tumescence (phallometric) testing is at best a crude measure of sexual interest because it measures only one aspect of sexual arousal (penile erection) and because it does not measure propensity to act on sexual interests.[82]

Physiology

More proximal measures of physiologic associations associated with sexual violence have been investigated. Testosterone is a hormone that has received great interest based on the observations that most sex offenders are male and that men have more testosterone than women. In a sample of 4462 male war veterans, serum testosterone was associated with antisocial behaviours.[83]

However, the only reported association with sexual behaviours was between high testosterone levels and "more than 10 sex partners in one year"[p. 210] and the association between high testosterone and antisocial behaviours was moderated by increases in socioeconomic status. An association between high salivary-free testosterone levels and aggression was also shown in a sample of 89 prison inmates.[84]

However, sexual aggression was not measured in this study. This deficiency was partially addressed in a third study, which included cross-validation with earlier samples of prisoners.[85] Although inmates with higher testosterone levels were described as more confrontational, only 5% of the 692 prisoners had committed a nonstatutory rape, and a total of 4% of men in this sample had been convicted for some type of child molestation. The percentage of sex offenders of both types was higher in the group of prisoners with the highest testosterone levels but the majority of men with high testosterone (86%) were not sex offenders.

These findings are consistent with an earlier study[86] specifically intended to investigate testosterone and violence involving 50 sex offenders in which no relation was found between plasma testosterone and violent sexual behaviour. In a review of the literature on testosterone and sexual behaviour in men, it was concluded that fluctuations in testosterone have little effect on sexual behaviour as long as the fluctuations are within the normal range and as long as a minimum amount of the hormone is present.[87]

In spite of the equivocal findings in the previously reviewed studies, considerable evidence supports the interrelation between high testosterone levels and social dominance and with low levels of social reciprocity. For example, testosterone levels in 2100 Air Force veterans decreased when they married but rose again when they divorced.[88] A more recent investigation examined serum testosterone levels in 501 adult male sex offenders.[89] Men with higher testosterone were reported to have historically committed the most invasive sex crimes and were reported to be more likely to recidivate.

However, the significance of testosterone in predicting sexual offence recidivism while controlling for age was absent in men who had completed treatment. Results of this study are hard to interpret for numerous reasons: while few in number, men with below average testosterone were excluded from the sample; high testosterone was defined as any level above the upper range (presumably even if within the standard error of the lab test); and recidivism rates were not reported for either group.

While the evidence supports some association between testosterone and aggression, a causal relation between testosterone and sexual violence has not been shown. (For a more extensive review of the association of testosterone and aggression, including a review of animal research, see Demetrikopoulos and Siegel.[90])

Until recently, most researchers have assumed that only free testosterone is biologically active.[91] However, boundtestosterone and gonadotropin-releasing hormones may also have important effects.[91] For example, in a new study examining the relation between aggression and both free and total testosterone levels in 848 convicted sexual offenders, a positive correlation was found for total testosterone, but a negative correlation was found between free testosterone levels and recidivism.[92] In addition, a significant correlation was found between LH and recorded violence of the index offence. These results are similar to those of another study that failed to find a significant correlation between testosterone and aggression or impulsivity in a sample of rapists but which did find a significant correlation with impulsivity.[93] LH, the hormone secreted by gonadotrope cells in the anterior pituitary, is significant to this discussion because it stimulates Leydig cells in the testes to produce testosterone. It may be that some offenders suffer from a breakdown in the normal hypothalamic—pituitary—testes biofeedback loop. This may explain LH elevation in the absence of recorded abnormalities in testosterone levels.

LH, other hormones, and bioamines were all implicated in normal sexual function in men and women.[94] Surprisingly, given the frequent descriptions of sadists as being heartless, cold-blooded, and loners (compare Brittain[95]), and given the presumed association of oxytocin with bonding (compare Carter[96]), there have been no investigations of this hormone in men and women with sadism and (or) psychopathy (another syndrome with similar descriptors).

Neurological Explanations and Investigations

Several surveys of sexual sadists have noted a high frequency of signs indicative of neurological abnormalities. The Gratzer survey[97] found 55% of the sadists in that sample had abnormal neurological findings, primarily suggestive of temporal lobe abnormalities. This is particularly significant because sexual arousal in males presented with visual stimuli has been shown to be associated with bilateral activation of the inferior temporal cortex, the right insular and inferior frontal cortex, and the left anterior cingulate cortex.[98] Considerable evidence supports the role of temporal—limbic neural pathways in sexual arousal[99] as well as in aggression (see Siegel[100] for a review).

Neuroimaging studies of violent offenders has been summarized in a chapter on brain imaging.[101] Among 8 studies, only one dealt explicitly with criminally sadistic offenders.[102] This study included 22 sadistic offenders, 21 nonsadistic sex offenders, and 36 nonviolent, nonsex offenders. Sadistic offenders were more likely than nonsadistic offenders or the control group to have right-sided temporal horn abnormalities (41%, compared with 11% and 13%, respectively).

However, significantly more nonsadistic offenders (61%) had neuropsychological impairments on the Luria-Nebraska test battery, compared with the sadists (17%) or the control group (17%). While the other studies reviewed in this series did not explicitly examine sadists, it is notable that temporal lobe abnormalities were also described in other sex offender groups.[103–105] Raine[101] also summarized 6 PET scan, regional cerebral blood flow, and MRI studies.

However, of these, only one studied a diagnosed sexual sadist. A flurodeoxglucose PET scan of a sexual sadist was compared with scans of 2 male university students with no known paraphilic interests.[106] All 3 men were presented with an erotic (nonsadistic) audiotape. Although all 3 men showed evidence of sexual arousal as evidenced by simultaneous circumferential penile plethysmography, the 2 men without sadism showed more right hemisphere lateralization than the man with sadism. Unfortunately, the investigators did not present the study participants with stimuli that were differentially sexual stimulating (for example, sexually sadistic materials).

As in other studies reviewed above, temporal lobe dysfunction was noted in one PET scan study involving violent patients[107] and in another, involving computed tomography, MRI scans of patients with organic brain syndrome who were violent.[108] In addition, neuroimaging studies showed selective frontal lobe dysfunction in murderers,[101] violent study participants,[107] and sex offenders including rapists.[105]

Complex Interactions

A frequently cited study compared offender and offence characteristics of 29 men known to have committed sadistic criminal offences with a control group consisting of 28 men with nonsadistic criminal sex offences.[97] These in turn were compared with a previously published uncontrolled sample of 30 men diagnosed sexual sadism.[50] Many characteristics listed in the Dietz et al. paper[50, p. 50] were found to occur with equal frequency in nonsadistic offenders.

The 4 characteristics found more frequently among sadists in both studies but not in the control group on nonsadistic offenders were: physical abuse in childhood; cross-dressing; history of peeping (voyeurism); and obscene phone calls or indecent exposure. With the exception of cross-dressing, which is a comparatively rarely reported activity among nonsadistic sex offenders, the other 3 characteristics are fairly high-frequency sex offences that are perhaps notable only for the fact that they often do not in themselves result in referral to specialized forensic assessment units.

Cross-dressing occurs with high frequency in 2 groups of men: those with gender identity disorder and those with transvestic fetishism.

Gender identity confusion in men with sadism has been noted in other descriptive studies (for example, see Langevin[38] and Langevin et al.[109]). Extreme cases of gender identity confusion were reported in men who have been described as sadists and whose crimes included dismembering female body parts, cannibalizing, and even attempting to wear body parts of their victims. Perhaps the most well known was Edward Theodore Gein, after whom the fictional sadistic killer in The Silence of the Lambs was modelled.[110]

The high frequency of transvestic fetishism (DSM-TR 302.3) is interesting for a different reason. Transvestic fetishism is a paraphilic sexual disorder characterized by sexual arousal from wearing clothes of the opposite sex.[111] Transvestic fetishism often cooccurs with sadomasochism. Evidence of both disorders is often found in men who fatally self-asphyxiate themselves.[112]

This finding is notable for 2 reasons. The first is the fact that criminal sexual sadists are often described as resorting to strangulation as a frequent or preferred method of incapacitating or killing their victims. In the Dietz study,[50, p. 50] cause of death in 130 victims was 32.3% by ligature strangulation, 26.1% by manual strangulation, 1.5% by hanging, and 0.8% by suffocation (although it should be noted that 57 of the murders by hanging or manual strangulation in this series were committed by 2 of the men in the study).

Is there a reason why criminal sadists appear to be so interested in asphyxia or strangulation? Obvious answers may be that these murder methods are compatible with sexual arousal from control of another person.

A second intriguing explanation results if the problem of sexual sadism is reformulated from one of problems owing to deviant sexual interest to one of problems arising from failure to become sufficiently aroused by conventional scenarios. In men with normal sexual function, at the time of orgasm, serum norepinephrine increases up to 12 times the baseline level.[113–115] Similar changes in biogenic amines were also shown in women at the time of orgasm.[116]

If an individual was unable to reach orgasm owing to insufficient autonomic sympathetic activity during sexual activity, it is conceivable that an individual might try to heighten release of norepinephrine. One of the most effective ways to do so is by breath holding or self-asphyxia. This strategy of purposefully engaging in dangerous or frightening activities to accentuate subjective simulation was noted in various paraphilic disorders including sexual sadism[117] and specifically transvestic fetishism.[118]

This theory gains some support from a study in which patients with Huntington disease were found to develop paraphilic behaviours only after the onset of inhibited orgasm.[119] For at least some sexual sadists, cruel or humiliating acts may produce sufficient autonomic arousal during sexual activity to facilitate or enhance orgasm thereby reinforcing the problematic behaviour.

Treatment

Reviews concerning the treatment of violent sex offenders, especially sexual sadists, tend to be pessimistic. However, this may be due more to the fact that convicted sadists are less likely than other offenders to be released from custody. The section of the Criminal Code of Canada dealing with applications for designation as a dangerous offender lists one of the criteria as the predicate crime was "of such a brutal nature as to compel the conclusion that the offender's behaviour in the future is unlikely to be inhibited by normal standards of behavioral restraint."[120]

Clinicians have been shown to be more likely to make a diagnosis of sadism if the patient had committed an offence that was brutal (compare Marshalland Kennedy,[16] Marshall and Hucker,[17] and Marshall et al.[18]). Therefore an offender with a diagnosis of sadism presumably is more likely to fulfill criteria for designation as a dangerous offender. This designation allows the sentencing judge to impose an indeterminate sentence, the most severe in Canadian law.

Offenders designated as dangerous offenders receive lower priority in treatment programs (as they are not likely to be released imminently). Therefore they are less likely to be able to show they have responded to treatment. Regretfully, the fact that treatment response has not been demonstrated is frequently misinterpreted as meaning that treatment is not available or effective.

In fact, available evidence suggests that at least some sexual sadists do respond to treatment. Case studies of successful treatment of sexually violent men with or without sadism have been published (for example, see Kafka[121]). One case report is of interest because it involved a man who entered treatment for a nonsexual and certainly nonsadistic problem.[122] After treatment with buspirone (prescribed for anxiety) he spontaneously reported that sadistic fantasies involving torture of his sister had disappeared. The fantasies had been clearly sadistic, focusing on humiliation and cruelty. He reported that he would fantasize about breaking his sister's bones while masturbating and that he would imagine the sound of her femur snapping at the time of orgasm.

Because he had kept a detailed and dated diary that included his fantasies, it was possible to independently verify that his sadistic fantasies had decreased in both frequency and severity in association with treatment. While case reports are usually of limited scientific value, this one is unique in that the medication was prescribed in a triple-blind fashion (that is, the prescribing physician did not know about the sexual disorder, the patient did not know the medication might help his sadistic fantasies, and neither knew the patient's diary would be used to assess his response to treatment).

Effective treatment of any condition is dependent on accurate diagnosis. A major issue in any assessment of treatment options is that sexual sadism (according to DSM-IV) and sadomasochism (according to ICD-10) explicitly require that the disorder must be of sufficient severity or kind to cause problems owing to nonconsensual harm of some type.

However, many individuals self-identify themselves as sadists or masochists while strongly advocating only consensual sexual activities. Examples of this issue come from self-identified members of the so-called BDSM community. BDSM is a portmanteau acronym for Bondage–Discipline, Dominance–Submission, as well as Sadism–Masochism. Clearly these headings define various sexual interests. As a side note, the Marquis de Sade, had he sought psychiatric attention, would have most likely been diagnosed as a sexual fetishist or paraphilias not otherwise specified rather than as a true sadist, as his primary preoccupation involved processes of elimination and because his writing appears to have been strongly motivated by his views on politics and religion rather than on sex.

In contrast to sadists as defined by the DSM-IV or ICD-10, most individuals who belong to BDSM communities repeatedly cite a rule concerning sexual relations: "safe, sane and consensual."[123, p. 3] While patients who meet psychiatric criteria for sexual sadism or sadomasochism may be sane (in the sense of not ordinarily meeting criteria for insanity defences), by definition, without treatment they are neither safe nor consensual. These and other issues concerning the noncriminal BDSM community have recently been summarized.[124]

Returning to Table 1, the diagnosis of sadism, based solely on observed behaviour is problematic, particularly if the behaviour is assessed without attention to the context in which the behaviours occurred and without regard to an assessment of the mental state of the patient. For example, individuals with intellectual disability (who often have impaired verbal ability to negotiate consent) are vulnerable to being misdiagnosed as sadistic (as the crucial characteristic of sadism is nonconsensual sexual activity). This concern has led to a reanalysis and proposed revision of DSM diagnostic criteria in this population.[125]

Recalling that the essential feature of sadism is nonconsensuality, prior to initiating treatment, other possible causes of nonconsensual behaviour should be investigated, including dis-inhibition (such as, owing to stroke or dementia), intoxication, personality disorders, and major psychiatric disorders. Nonpsychiatric conditions such as criminality should also be eliminated or at least accounted for.

Assuming the person being assessed meets diagnostic criteria for sadism after elimination of competing or complimentary explanations for observed or reported activities, treatment is similar to that of other sexually motivated problematic behaviours.

Several guidelines for treatment approaches have been published (compare Marshall et al.[126] and Serin[127] for reviews). The efficacy of these treatment options was also recently summarized.[128] A useful algorithm to assist in decisions about intrusiveness of intervention is also available.[129]

Table 4

Recommendations for Future Research

Study groups should be homogenous.

Study groups should be constituted in a way that allows generalization to clinical populations.

Sexual sadism should be distinguished from violence.

Studies should test falsifiable hypotheses.

Alternate or complimentary hypotheses should be entertained.

Summary

Recommendations for future research are summarized in Table 4.

This review indicates that sexual sadism, as currently defined, is a heterogeneous phenomenon. To date, research has often failed to clearly define the population under study and therefore conclusions are limited. This makes generalization from research findings to specific patients problematic. Of particular concern is the possibility that correlations and outcomes from studies consisting of samples of convenience may be interpreted as verified causal relations between unconventional sexual interests and nonconsensual sexual violence. Understanding the ways in which sexually sadistic interests are established and maintained will certainly aid not only in the development of increasingly effective treatments but also in the establishment of strategies to aid in the prevention of harmful sexual behaviours and the promotion of healthy and fulfilling lives for everyone.

Funding and Support

Dr Fedoroff's work on this manuscript was partially supported by the University of Ottawa Medical Research Fund, and the Canadian Institute of Health Research.

The Canadian Psychiatric Association proudly supports the In Review series by providing an honorarium to the authors.

Acknowledgments

Dr Fedoroff gratefully acknowledges the assistance of Ms Jennifer Arstikaitis and Ms Beverley Fedoroff, who both assisted with the literature search, and Dr J Bradford for his helpful editorial comments.

POSTSCRIPT

Is BDSM a Healthy Form of Sexual Expression?

In February 2008, a regular visitor at a New York City bondage club was found unconscious after being left alone while bound and partially suspended in air (Goldman, 2008). He spent three days in a coma before awaking in a nearby hospital. The following April, a Tennessee man died of suffocation after his wife left him alone, bound and gagged, for over 20 hours (Schoetz, 2008). It is unknown, however, how many people safely explored these or other BDSM-related fantasies during these months. To know this, we would first have to decide what behaviors or thoughts should be included under this umbrella. In fact, many who enjoy such acts may not identify as part of the scene or culture. Where, exactly, does one draw the line between being sexually aggressive and being "into" domination? Is the couple who occasionally play with pink fuzzy handcuffs necessarily "into" bondage? Does enjoying a smack on the behind make one a masochist, or must one be ritualistically paddled and scolded to carry that title?

Powlowski attempts to place BDSM behaviors along a continuum in order to cast them as merely less conventional expressions of common sexual activities. Do you agree with his analysis? Why or why not? He continues by attempting to counter the "pathology" label given by the DSM and "as seen on TV" depictions of BDSM. Do you feel any BDSM activities are pathological? Some? None? All? How did you decide?

Fedoroff focuses on the links between sadism and violent crime. Early in his article, Fedoroff stressed that his definition of sadism "refers to non-consensual sexual aggression." Why is this important? He presents several studies that support his arguments, including studies of college students. Did any of the research presented surprise you? Why or why not?

During recent tours pop stars Britney Spears and Rhianna have incorporated steamy, bondage-inspired costumes and dance routines into their stage shows. When allegations of domestic violence arose between Rhianna and her partner, many online commentators pointed to her BDSM outfits as "evidence" of "risky" lifestyle choices. Critics also condemned Spears for allowing her own children to attend her shows. Are bondage-inspired costumes an outward expression of a troubled personality or relationship? Does an interest in BDSM reflect poorly on a person's ability to raise a child? Are the celebrities simply looking to push the envelope? Or is this type of entertainment merely a reflection of an increased public interest in BDSM? *Time* magazine, one of the nations' most popular weekly news magazines, ran an in-depth feature on BDSM in 2004. Kink.com, an online BDSM porn site, made over $16 million in

2007.[8] Should we as a society be concerned about the apparent mainstreaming of BDSM, or "kink" culture? Or should we celebrate the growing visibility and acceptance of diverse sexual expressions?

The line between pleasure and pain has been the subject of erotic writings for centuries. Centuries-old artwork from around the world depicts sadistic and masochistic sexual acts. Is this proof that BDSM is a natural expression of our sexuality? Or simply proof that sexual exploitation is not a modern phenomenon? People of all genders have written about and enjoyed the erotic overtones of power exchange. While some feminists have brought attention to power imbalance in dominant/submissive relationships, do these same critiques apply to same-sex couples? To submissive males with female partners? Does the eroticization of power (or the lack thereof) signify sexual enlightenment or disordered thinking?

Suggested Readings

L. Alison, P. Santtila, N.K. Sandnabba, and N. Nordling, "Sadomasochistically Oriented Behavior: Diversity in Practice and Meaning," *Archives of Sexual Behavior* (vol. 30, no. 1, 2001), 1–12. Accessed March 1, 2009, from SpringerLink database.

A. Moore, "Rethinking Gendered Perversion and Degeneration in Visions of Sadism and Masochism, 1886–1930," *Journal of the History of Sexuality* (vol. 18, no. 1, 2009). doi: 10.1353/sex.0.0034.

P.J. Kleinplatz and C. Moser (eds.), *Sadomasochism: Powerful Pleasures* (New York, NY: Harrington Park Press, 2006).

B.J. Sagarin, B. Cutler, N. Cutler, K.A. Lawler-Sagarin, and L. Matuszewich, "Hormonal Changes and Couple Bonding in Consensual Sadomasochistic Activity," *Archives of Sexual Behavior* (vol. 38, 2008). doi: 10.1007/s10508-9374-5.

Internet References . . .

The Abstinence Clearinghouse

The Abstinence Clearinghouse is a national, nonprofit organization that promotes the practice of sexual abstinence through the distribution of educational materials and by providing speakers on the topic.

www.abstinence.net

Answer

Answer is a nationally known sexuality education resource that promotes comprehensive sexuality education by training educators and connecting young people through *Sex, Etc.* magazine and Web site (www.sexetc.org).

http://answer.rutgers.edu

Go Ask Alice!

Go Ask Alice is the health question-and-answer Internet service produced by Columbia University's Health Promotion program. The service works to provide readers with reliable, accessible information about various aspects of health, including sexuality, sexual health, and relationships.

www.goaskalice.columbia.edu

The American Journal of Sexuality Education

The *American Journal of Sexuality Education* is a peer-reviewed journal that provides sexuality educators and trainers at all skill levels with current research about sexuality education, sample lesson plans, scholarly commentary, educational program reports, and media reviews.

http://www.tandf.co.uk/journals/WAJS

Sexuality Information and Education Council of the United States

Sexuality Information and Education Council of the United States (SIECUS) advocates for the right of all people to accurate information, comprehensive education about sexuality, and sexual health services, and has served as a national voice for sexuality education for more than 40 years.

www.siecus.org

Sex Education

M<i>any debates involving sexuality are centered around the sexual information that young people are exposed to in the academic environment. The government allocates billions of dollars for sexuality education and there is much debate about when, where, and how these funds should be distributed. This section examines three contemporary issues involving students and schools.</i>

- Is There Something Wrong with the Content of Comprehensive Sex Education Curricula?
- Should Sex Ed Teach about Abstinence?
- Does the Availability of "Sexual Health Services" Make Some College Campuses Healthier Than Others?

ISSUE 6

Is There Something Wrong with the Content of Comprehensive Sex Education Curricula?

YES: The Administration for Children and Families (ACF), Department of Health and Human Services (HHS), from "Review of Comprehensive Sex Education Curricula" (Washington, DC: U.S. Government Printing Office, 2007)

NO: Elokin CaPece, from "Commentary on the *Review of Comprehensive Sex Education Curricula* (2007)," *American Journal of Sexuality Education* (vol. 3, no. 3, 2007)

ISSUE SUMMARY

YES: The Administration for Children and Families, U.S. Department of Health and Human Services, presents their findings in a critical analysis of comprehensive sexuality education curricula.

NO: Elokin CaPece, Health Educator with Planned Parenthood Greater Memphis Region, disputes the research methods used and the findings of the report, highlighting what she sees as bias in the overall findings.

Over the past decade, the United States has invested almost $2 billion in abstinence-only-until-marriage (AOUM) programs. These are programs that forbid providing accurate information about contraceptives to prevent unplanned pregnancy, and condoms to prevent sexually transmitted infections. Concurrently, the federal government has also elected *not* to fund comprehensive sex education that would provide safer sex and contraceptive information, as well as other age-appropriate information recommended by public health policy experts.

Initially, criticism of AOUM was largely ideological. "Why subject children to explicit information about sex when they should be waiting for marriage?" AOUM advocates would argue. "Why fund programs that withhold critical, potentially life-saving information from teens?" sexuality education advocates would respond. There were also concerns about using public funds—and public schools—to establish a singular moral (and, in some cases, religious) standard sexual behavior. *Only* in monogamous, heterosexual marriages, taught AOUM programs.

As the ideological battle was waged, the money continued to pour in for AOUM programs. The annual spending more than doubled during the administration of George W. Bush, rising from $97.5 million per year at the time of his election to $242 million in his last year in office. Eyebrows were raised at this enormous amount of spending, and American taxpayers—who overwhelmingly support sexuality education—were chagrined as the national economy tanked.

In the midst of the perennial debate over funding, several important, independent criticisms of AOUM programs came to light. In 2004, a federally commissioned review of 13 AOUM curricula found that 80 percent of the curricula material provided "false, misleading, or distorted information about sexual health" (United States House of Representatives Committee on Govt. Reform, 2004). In some cases, the distortions were so severe as to have been pulled out of thin air, and without reference, such as the assertion of one curriculum that "girls who have sex before marriage are six times as likely to commit suicide than virgins" (Taverner, 2008).

Research also found the programs to be ineffective. In 2007, the independent research group Mathematica Policy, Inc. found that teens who participated in AOUM programs "were no more likely than control group youth to have abstained from sex" (Mathematica Policy Research, Inc., 2007). Doug Kirby, one of the nation's most respected researchers on adolescent sexual health, also found no impact of AOUM programs on teen sexual behavior (Kirby, 2007). Two researchers found that AOUM programs were not only ineffective, but also potentially harmful. In a study of virginity pledge programs involving more than 20,000 young Americans, the researchers found that 88 percent of those who made a pledge failed to keep that pledge, and were one-third less likely to use a condom in intercourse (Brückner & Bearman, 2005).

There was a backlash among conservatives who championed AOUM programs all along. As evidence documenting the failure of AOUM programs grew (and a number of states—17 to date—actually began *rejecting* the federal funds), Senator Tom Coburn (R-Oklahoma) and former Senator Rick Santorum (R-Pennsylvania) commissioned a new federal study to scrutinize the content of comprehensive sexuality education programs. Under their direction, the United States Administration for Children and Families and the Department for Health and Human Services sought to similarly discredit sexuality education, by focusing primarily on the types of words that appear in the text of sexuality education curricula. The *Yes* essay that follows is an excerpt from the report.

In response, sexual health educator Elokin CaPece criticizes the report as "irresponsible research" and critiques its research methods and findings. She criticizes the report for its clear and inappropriate bias against the subject examined and for establishing unreasonable criteria for describing the "failure" of sexuality education programs.

YES

The Administration for Children and Families (ACF), Department of Health and Human Services (HHS)

Review of Comprehensive Sex Education Curricula

Introduction

"Comprehensive Sex Education" curricula for adolescents have been endorsed by various governmental agencies, educational organizations, and teenage advocacy groups as the most effective educational method for reducing teenage pregnancy and helping prevent the spread of sexually transmitted diseases (STDs) among America's youth. The National Institutes of Health (NIH) defines Comprehensive Sex Education (CSE) as "teaching both abstinence and the use of protective methods for sexually active youth"; NIH states that CSE curricula have been "shown to delay sexual activity among teens." Non-governmental groups that support CSE have also made statements linking CSE curricula to abstinence as well as reduction of pregnancy and sexually transmitted infections (STIs).

The Administration for Children and Families, within the Department of Health and Human Services undertook an examination of some of the most common CSE curricula currently in use. The purpose of this examination was to inform federal policymakers of the content, medical accuracy, and effectiveness of CSE curricula currently in use.

Background

In 2005, Senators Santorum and Coburn requested that the Administration for Children and Families (ACF) review and evaluate comprehensive sex education programs supported with federal dollars. The Senators wrote to the Assistant Secretary for Children and Families,

> In particular, we would appreciate a review that explores the effectiveness of these programs in reducing teen pregnancy rates and the transmission of sexually transmitted diseases. In addition, please assess the effectiveness of these programs in advancing the greater goal of encouraging teens to make the healthy decision to delay sexual activity. Please also include an evaluation of the scientific accuracy of the content of these programs. Finally, we would appreciate an assessment of how the actual content of these programs compares to their stated goals.

From a report published by Administration for Children & Families (ACF)/U.S. Dept. of Health and Human Services. May 2007, pp. 3–12. http://www.acf.hhs.gov/programs/fysb/content/docs/comprehensive.pdf

In response, ACF contracted with the Sagamore Institute for Policy Research to review some of the most common CSE curricula currently in use. ACF also requested and received comments on these reviews from the Medical Institute for Sexual Health (MISH).

Research Questions and Methodology

In response to the request from Senators Santorum and Coburn, the curriculum reviews evaluated four questions:

1. Does the content of the comprehensive sex education curricula mirror the stated purposes?
2. What is the content of comprehensive sex education curricula?
3. Do comprehensive sex education curricula contain medically inaccurate statements?
4. Do evaluations of these curricula show them to be effective at (a) delaying sexual debut and (b) reducing sex without condoms?

The initial charge of this project was to evaluate the content and effectiveness of the "most frequently used" CSE curricula. After a thorough search, which included contacting publishers, researchers, distributors, and advocacy groups, it was determined that a list ranked by "frequency of use" or "number of copies purchased" was not in existence nor could one be produced.

Instead, curricula were chosen for this study based on the frequency and strength of endorsement received from leading and recognized sexuality information organizations and resources. A curriculum was considered to be "endorsed" if a source recommended it or promoted it as a "program that works." The curricula mentioned most frequently were chosen for this study if they were school-based (i.e., not solely for community organizations), widely available, and described by at least one source as "comprehensive" or "abstinence-plus." Additional weight was given to curricula described as evidence-based or as a "program that works."

It should be noted that some of the curricula reviewed do not state in their materials that they have an abstinence focus—i.e., that they are "comprehensive sex education," "abstinence plus," or in some other way focused on abstinence. However, if a curriculum were endorsed as "comprehensive" or "abstinence plus" by a leading sexuality information organization and resources, it was assumed that the curriculum would be purchased and used for the purpose of providing comprehensive sex education. Additionally of note, some of the curricula have recently published revisions with added abstinence components. In every case, the most recent version of the curricula available was studied.

Nine curricula met the criteria for this study and were subsequently reviewed:

1. *Reducing the Risk: Building Skills to Prevent Pregnancy, STD & HIV (4th Edition)*, by R. Barth, 2004.
2. *Be Proud! Be Responsible!*, L. Jemmott, J. Jemmott, K. McCaffree, published by Select Media, Inc. 2003.

3. *Safer Choices: Preventing HIV, Other STD and Pregnancy (Level 1),* by J. Fetro, R. Barth, K. Coyle, published by ETR Associates, 1998; and *Safer Choices: Preventing HIV, Other STD and Pregnancy (Level 2),* by K. Coyle and J. Fetro, published by ETR Associates, 1998.
4. *AIDS Prevention for Adolescents in School,* by S. Kasen and I. Tropp, distributed by the Program Archive on Sexuality, Health, and Adolescence (PASHA), 2003.
5. *BART=Becoming a Responsible Teen (Revised Edition),* by J. Lawrence, published by ETR (Education, Training, Research) Associates, 2005.
6. *Teen Talk: An Adolescent Pregnancy Prevention Program,* by M. Eisen, A. McAlister, G. Zellman, distributed by PASHA, 2003.
7. *Reach for Health, Curriculum, Grade 8,* by L. O'Donnell, et al., by Education Development Center, Inc., 2003.
8. *Making Proud Choices.* L. Jemmott, J. Jemmott, K. McCaffree, published by Select Media, Inc., 2001, 2002.
9. *Positive Images: Teaching Abstinence, Contraception, and Sexual Healthy,* by P. Brick and B. Taverner, published by Planned Parenthood of Greater Northern New Jersey, Inc., 2001.

The curriculum review consisted of four components. First, each curriculum underwent an extensive content analysis, i.e., a word-by-word count of instances in which certain words or themes (e.g., condoms, abstinence) are mentioned. Content analyses offer insight into the weight respective curricula give to key themes. Appendix A contains the complete content analysis for each curriculum reviewed.

Second, the stated purposes of the curricula were compared to the actual emphases of the curricula, as demonstrated by the content analysis.

Third, curriculum content was evaluated for medical accuracy, primarily the accuracy of statements about condoms (including statements on a common spermicide, nonoxynol-9, that was previously recommended to be added to condoms).

Lastly, evaluations of each curriculum—which offer insights into curriculum effectiveness at delaying sexual debut and increasing condom use—were located and summarized.

Appendix B contains a curriculum-by-curriculum review of the each curriculum's content, medical accuracy, and evaluations of each curriculum.

Findings

The curriculum reviews yielded the following findings:

- **Does the content of the curricula mirror their stated purposes?** While the content of the curricula reviewed adheres to their stated purposes for the most part, these curricula often do not spend as much time discussing abstinence as they do discussing contraception and ways to lessen risks of sexual activity. Of the curricula reviewed, the curriculum with the most balanced discussion of abstinence and safer-sex still discussed condoms and contraception nearly seven times more than abstinence. Three of the nine curricula reviewed did not have a stated purpose of promoting abstinence; however, two of these three curricula still discussed abstinence as an option (although, again, discussion of condoms and safer sex predominated). As a last note, it is important to recognize that, although some of the curricula do not include abstinence as a stated purpose, some sexuality information organizations and resources recommend these curricula as comprehensive sex education.

- **What is the content of comprehensive sex education curricula?** As mentioned in the previous paragraph, these curricula focus on contraception and ways to lessen risks of sexual activity, although abstinence is at times a non-trivial component. Curriculum approaches to discussing contraception and ways to lessen risks of sexual activity can be grouped in three broad areas: (1) how to obtain protective devices (e.g., condoms), (2) how to broach a discussion on introducing these devices in a relationship, and (3) how to correctly use the devices. Below are a few excerpts from the curricula in these three areas.

    - **How to obtain protective devices:** "How can you minimize your embarrassment when buying condoms? . . . Take a friend along; find stores where you don't have to ask for condoms (e.g., stocked on open counter or shelf); wear shades or a disguise so no one will recognize you; have a friend or sibling who isn't embarrassed buy them for you; make up a condom request card that you can hand to the store clerk (Show example)" (*AIDS Prevention for Adolescents in School*, p. 63).

    - **How to broach a discussion on introducing these devices in a relationship:** "Teacher states: "Pretend I am your sexual partner. I am going to read more excuses (for not using condoms) and I want you to convince me to use a condom" (*Making Proud Choices*, p. 157).

    - **How to correctly use the devices:** "Have volunteers come to the front of the room (preferably an equal number of males and females). Distribute one card to each. Give them a few minutes to arrange themselves in the proper order so their cards illustrate effective condom use from start to finish. Non-participants observe how the group completes this task and review the final order. When the order is correct, post the cards in the front of the room. CORRECT ORDER: (Sexual Arousal, Erection, Leave Room at the Tip, Roll Condom On, Intercourse, Orgasm/Ejaculation, Hold Onto Rim, Withdraw the Penis, Loss of Erection, Relaxation). Ask a volunteer to describe each step in condom use, using the index and middle finger or a model of a penis" (*Positive Images*, p. 102).

- **Do the curricula contain medically inaccurate statements?** Most comprehensive sex education curricula reviewed contain some level of medical inaccuracy. Of the nine curricula reviewed, three had no medically inaccurate statements. The most common type of medical inaccuracy involved promotion of nonoxynol-9, a common spermicide; three curricula had medical inaccuracies involving nonoxynol-9. While condoms with nonoxynol-9 (N-9) had previously been recommended for reducing the risk of HIV and other STD in the 1990s, research over the last decade has demonstrated that nonxynol-9 is at best ineffective against STDs and HIV, and at worse increases risk.

Other inaccuracies included: (a) one curriculum that used the term "dental dam" instead of the FDA-approved "rubber dam"; (b) one curriculum that quoted first year condom failure rates for pregnancy at 12%, when the correct statistic is 15%; and (c) one curriculum that stated that all condoms marketed in the United States "meet federal assurance standards" (which is not true).

In terms of inaccurate statistics related to condom effectiveness, eight of the nine curricula did not have any inaccuracies. The one curriculum which did have inaccuracies, *Making Proud Choices,* had three erroneous statements.

Although there were few inaccurate statements regarding condom effectiveness, the curricula do not state the risks of condom failure as extensively as is done in some abstinence-until-marriage curricula, nor do they discuss condom failure rates in context. Indeed, there were misleading statements in every curriculum reviewed. For example, one curriculum states, "When used correctly, latex condoms prevent pregnancy 97% of the time." While this statement is technically true, 15% percent of women using condoms for contraception experience an unintended pregnancy during the first year of "typical use," and 20% of adolescents under the age of 18 using condoms for contraception get pregnant within one year.

For perspective, it may be helpful to compare the error rate reported here with statistics cited in the December 2004 report entitled "The Content of Federally Funded Abstinence Education Programs," which is typically called the Waxman Report. This report found that, of thirteen abstinence-until-marriage curricula reviewed, eleven contained medically inaccurate statements; in all thirteen curricula (nearly 5,000 pages of information), there were 49 instances of questionable information. It could easily be argued that the comprehensive sex education curricula reviewed for this report have a similar rate of error compared with abstinence-until-marriage curricula.

- **Do evaluations of these curricula show them to be effective at (a) delaying sexual debut and (b) reducing sex without condoms?** According to the evaluations reviewed, these curricula show some small positive impacts on (b) reducing sex without condoms, and to a lesser extent (a) delaying sexual debut. Specifically, there were evaluations for eight of the nine curricula reviewed. Of those eight curricula, seven showed at least some positive impacts on condom use; two showed some positive impacts on delay of sexual initiation. One curriculum (*Teen Talk*) showed the only negative impact: for sexually inexperienced females, there was a negative impact on first intercourse and on consistent use of contraceptives. Often the impacts observed in evaluations are small, and most often the impacts do not extend three or six months after a curriculum has been used. It is important to note that evaluations of the curricula do have limitations. All curricula were evaluated by the curriculum authors themselves (although all evaluations were peer-reviewed and published in established journals). Also, the sample sizes are small in some of the evaluations, and research design issues decrease the ability to draw conclusions from some of the evaluations. Appendix B contains details on the evaluations of these curricula.

Conclusion

Research on the effectiveness of nine commonly used comprehensive sex education curricula demonstrates that, while such curricula show small positive impacts on increasing condom use among youth, only a couple of curricula show impacts on delaying sexual debut; moreover, effects most often disappear over time. The fact that both the stated purposes and the actual content of these curricula emphasize ways to lessen risks associated with sexual activity—and not necessarily avoiding sexual activity—may explain why research shows them to be more effective at increasing condom use than at delaying sexual debut. Lastly, although the medical accuracy of comprehensive sex education curricula is nearly 100%—similar to that of abstinence-until-marriage curricula—efforts could be made to more extensively detail condom failure rates in context.

Appendix A: Content Analysis

Provided below is a word-by-word count of the number of times specific words or themes appears in each of the reviewed curricula.

RTR = Reducing the Risk
Be Proud = Be Proud, Be Responsible
SC1 = Safer Choices 1
SC2 = Safer Choices 2
AIDS = AIDS Prevention for Adolescents in School
BART = Becoming A Responsible Teen
Teen Talk
Reach = Reach for Health
MPC = Making Proud Choices
PI = Positive Images

	RTR	Be Proud	SC 1	SC 2	AIDS	BART	Teen Talk	Reach	MPC	PI
100% safe/effective	4	22	7	1	4	0	5	12	1	7
abortion/termination/ interruption	1	0	0	1	0	0	8	0	0	18
abstinence/abstain	90	50	5	5	0	19	32	15	18	87
alcohol	3	14	2	3	5	12	2	0	18	21
alternatives to sexual intercourse	45	10	64	40	1	7	0	5	12	16
anal sex	11	33	10	2	4	16	0	1	57	8
avoid/avoiding (behaviors/consequences)	20	9	24	1	0	14	11	9	42	18
birth control	27	5	25	25	9	5	58	10	37	37
boyfriend (s)	24	13	1	3	11	8	2	11	23	7

(continued)

	RTR	Be Proud	SC 1	SC 2	AIDS	BART	Teen Talk	Reach	MPC	PI
casual sex	0	0	0	0	0	0	0	0	0	0
cervical cap	0	0	1	0	0	0	8	0	5	15
chlamydia	5	0	16	7	1	0	5	2	6	1
committed relationship	0	2	0	0	0	1	0	1	0	1
condom/contraceptive failure	1	3	5	5	0	0	0	0	2	7
condom/condoms	183	495	383	389	136	262	22	8	650	235
contraception/contraceptive	18	3	31	38	2	0	131	3	39	381
diaphragm	0	0	3	2	0	0	31	0	7	26
douche/douching	8	0	11	10	0	0	14	5	10	2
Drug/drugs	32	58	20	8	36	45	2	2	81	75
ejaculate (tion, s, ed, "cum")	6	14	10	11	0	5	9	18	24	12
emotional (consequences)	2	0	0	0	0	0	1	2	1	0
erection (erect)	1	12	9	9	3	0	8	7	15	19
fantasy (ies, ize)	0	3	0	0	0	0	2	9	5	0
French kissing	2	1	1	0	0	0	0	0	1	1
fun (of sex)	0	24	0	1	0	0	0	0	19	0
genital warts/warts	1	0	8	4	0	0	6	1	11	1
girlfriend	31	13	3	3	6	8	3	6	24	3
gonorrhea	5	1	16	7	2	0	12	3	20	2
health/healthy	27	39	58	60	16	72	77	54	35	180
healthier/healthiest	2	2	0	0	0	1	0	1	3	1
Herpes	4	1	15	6	0	0	20	5	18	1
HIV/AIDS	451	477	369	253	28	473	20	7	210	48
IUD	0	0	4	6	0	0	0	0	0	5
kiss, kissing, kissed, kisses	29	30	15	14	2	8	0	4	33	6
love, loved, loves	51	9	35	19	6	16	0	14	22	14
lovers	1	1	0	0	0	0	0	0	1	1
making love (love making)	0	0	1	1	0	0	0	0	1	1
marriage	3	0	4	1	0	0	0	1	0	9
marry, married	3	0	0	5	1	0	4	0	0	4
masturbation, masturbate	4	5	0	0	0	3	8	2	9	13
masturbation: mutual/partner	1	2	0	0	0	0	1	0	3	0
maximum protection	0	1	0	0	0	0	0	0	0	0
morning after pill (emergency contraception)	0	0	6	12	0	0	1	0	0	24
negative, negatively, (ism)	2	18	12	27	6	10	4	22	14	18

	RTR	Be Proud	SC 1	SC 2	AIDS	BART	Teen Talk	Reach	MPC	PI
negotiation (to use condoms)	1	37	4	1	14	35	1	0	52	1
no risk	0	0	0	0	0	2	0	0	3	1
not having sex	8	0	7	7	7	1	2	3	0	0
oral sex	10	36	9	2	3	13	0	2	73	4
orgasm	1	15	0	0	0	0	6	1	8	11
outercourse	0	2	0	0	0	0	0	0	0	13
parents/parenthood	104	0	97	118	5	34	11	13	13	65
pill (contraceptive)	45	13	37	35	7	4	27	3	31	59
pleasure, able, ing (re: sex)	0	31	2	1	1	0	3	3	8	8
practice (s, ed, ing) (techniques, skills, using condoms)	2	5	13	14	0	6	19	47	70	20
pregnant, pregnancy	348	30	167	242	3	8	155	113	184	241
prophylactics	1	0	1	1	0	0	2	0	0	0
protect (s, ed), protection	254	25	314	145	7	24	7	20	82	80
protective (products)	1	10	6	0	0	0	0	0	0	1
purchasing (buying) condoms	2	6	11	12	8	10	4	0	12	5
rape	0	1	0	0	0	0	0	0	2	3
rape: date	0	0	0	0	0	0	0	0	2	1
refuse, refusal (skills)/ delaying sex tactics	110	11	84	76	1	13	2	48	46	0
reproductive, reproduction	0	0	5	4	0	0	33	18	2	80
risk reduction	0	0	0	1	0	2	0	0	3	0
risk (high)	4	4	0	0	4	5	4	0	5	3
risk (low, lower)	1	0	0	0	0	1	1	0	1	2
risk, risks, risking	273	166	133	112	32	149	31	38	118	140
riskier	0	0	0	0	0	2	0	0	0	0
risky	8	25	9	5	21	42	2	2	18	2
rubber (s)	8	3	2	2	0	5	24	0	4	4
safe, safely	11	41	8	7	3	67	8	4	40	12
safer	0	74	297	345	2	55	0	0	61	38
safest	6	1	45	26	2	0	1	0	1	0
sex	290	334	442	287	64	168	91	168	440	83
sexual	71	152	106	81	101	94	78	116	146	232
intercourse (sexual)	46	47	81	46	77	23	22	28	58	237

(continued)

	RTR	Be Proud	SC 1	SC 2	AIDS	BART	Teen Talk	Reach	MPC	PI
sexual orientation (gay, lesbian, homosexual, same sex)	5	19	7	2	0	6	1	2	9	13
sexuality	18	0	17	19	1	3	32	115	1	98
sexually	47	46	18	23	11	33	38	49	60	85
sexy	2	1	0	1	1	0	0	4	2	0
spermicide (s, dal)	14	11	35	19	4	15	25	4	43	23
sponge	0	0	0	0	0	0	4	0	0	28
STD (s)	230	44	221	178	2	8	47	77	281	2
STI	0	0	0	0	0	0	0	0	0	64
syphilis	0	2	15	4	2	0	12	0	17	1
unprotected sex/intercourse	54	26	43	0	0	23	13	8	30	5
contraceptive film	3	0	6	5	0	0	0	0	6	4
venereal disease (VD)	0	0	0	0	0	0	3	0	0	0
withdrawal (withdraws, pull out)	10	3	12	0	0	6	9	4	13	17

Elokin CaPece  **NO**

Commentary on the *Review of Comprehensive Sex Education Curricula* (2007)

In the last several years research on the effectiveness of sex education programs that target preteens and teens has evolved into a very sophisticated and professional discourse. In 2002, a review of 73 studies of programs (including but not limited to comprehensive sex education programs) pulled out a set of characteristics that were found in programs that reduced sexual risk-taking, promoted condom use, and/or delayed sexual onset. These programs focused on behaviors that prevented unintended pregnancy or sexually transmitted infection (including HIV), utilized already-established practices for reducing risk-taking behaviors, gave a clear message that emphasized the prevention behaviors and frequently reinforced that message, provided basic and accurate information, included modeling, role-playing, and refusal skills practice, employed a high degree of student participation in a wide range of educational styles, were tailored to the age, culture, and sexual experience of their audience, lasted a sufficient length of time, and were taught by facilitators who had adequate training and believed in the program's effectiveness. This same review attempted to include abstinence-only program studies in its analysis but found that only three published studies met the criteria for his review and two of these had "important methodological limitations." The article did not make any claims about the effectiveness or ineffectiveness of such programs (due to the lack of reliable research and the wide variance in program formats), but concluded that the characteristics found common in effective comprehensive sex education programs should be considered best practices for abstinence-only programs of comparable design as well (Kirby, 2002, 51–54).

In 2004 a federally funded and commissioned review of 13 abstinence-only curricula (representing two-thirds of the programs funded by abstinence-only federal money at the time of the review), commonly known as the Waxman Report, found that 80% of the curricular material reviewed contained "false, misleading, or distorted information about reproductive health (United States House of Representatives Committee on Government Reform [U.S. Committee on Govt. Reform], 2004, i)." The most common inaccuracies were an exaggeration of contraceptive failure rates, inaccurate information

From *American Journal of Sexuality Education*, by Elokin CaPece, vol. 3, no. 3, September 2008, pp. 295–312. Copyright © 2008 by Routledge/Taylor & Francis Group. Reprinted by permission.

about the risks of abortion, the stating of religious belief as scientific fact, the treatment of gender role stereotypes as scientific fact, and general scientific errors (U.S. Committee on Govt. Reform, 2004, i–ii).

In 2007 Mathematica Policy, Inc. released a study of four federally funded abstinence-only programs. These programs were chosen because they represented the wide range of types of educational programming that fell under the banner of abstinence-only and because they served rural and urban communities in every region of the U.S. The report found that these programs had just as much of an impact on teens as no sex education programming at all had. Teens in the abstinence-only programs behaved in statistically similar ways to teens in the control group (who were receiving no sex education programming) (Mathematica Policy Research, 2007, 59–60).

These reviews represent the macro-level of sex education research. On the micro-level there are individual program evaluations, the quality of which has been transformed in the last ten years. In 1997 SIECUS published a manual written by researchers critiquing the research done on sex education programs as poorly designed, weakly implemented, and not well funded (Haffner & Goldfarb, 1997, 4). In 2002 Doug Kirby noted that while very few program evaluations had experimental or quasi-experimental designs and rarely were evaluations replicated in the late 1990s, by 2000 he had enough well-researched material to examine comprehensive sex education programs, reproductive health clinic services, service learning programs, and Children's Aid Society Carrera programs (Kirby, 2002). Today, the research standards put forth by SIECUS influence how many sex education programs are designed, implemented, and evaluated.

Background Information on the 2007 Comprehensive Sex Education Review

The 2007 *Review of Comprehensive Sex Education Curricula* was commissioned by Rick Santorum, former U.S. senator from Pennsylvania and Tom Coburn, U.S. senator from Oklahoma and conducted by The Administration for Children and Families (ACF) and The Department of Health and Human Services (HHS). Like the 2003 Waxman Report (commissioned by Representative Henry Waxman from California), the new report was commissioned with the intention of helping political leaders make informed decisions about sex education funding. Nine curricula were reviewed, and they were chosen by the "frequency and strength of endorsement" by sexuality and sexual health organizations (The Administration for Children and Families [ACF] & The Department of Health and Human Services [HHS], 2007, 4). These curricula were evaluated for four criteria: whether the content mirrored the curricula's stated purpose, the content itself, whether the content was medically accurate, and whether evaluations of these curricula demonstrated that they were effective at delaying sexual onset and reducing sex without condoms (ACF & HHS, 2007, 4). [See Table 1 at the end of this section for a list of the reviewed curricula.]

The remaining sections of this article will focus on the content of the review (and its appendices), specifically looking at instances of clear and interfering bias, the use of research methodologies that are not in line with presented findings, inappropriately critical benchmarks for failure, and inaccurate referencing of outside works.

Table 1

Curricula Reviewed in the 2007 Review

Title	Author	Year
Reducing the Risk: Building Skills to Prevent Pregnancy, STD, & HIV (4th Edition)	R. Barth	2004
Be Proud! Be Responsible!	L. S. Jemmott & J. B. Jemmott	2003
Safer Choices: Preventing HIV, Other STD and Pregnancy (Level 1 & Level 2)	J. Fetro, R. Barth, K. Coyle	1998
AIDS Prevention for Adolescents in School	S. Kasen & I. Troop	2003
BART = Becoming a Responsible Teen (Revised Edition)	J. Lawrence	2005
Teen Talk: An Adolescent Pregnancy Prevention Program	M. Eisen, A. McAlister, G. Zellman	2003
Reach for Health Curriculum, Grade 8	L. O'Donnell, et al.	2003
Making Proud Choices	L. Jemmott, J. Jemmott, K. McCaffree	2002
Positive Images: Teaching Abstinence, Contraception, and Sexual Health	P. Brick & B. Taverner	2001

Clear and Interfering Bias

The first criterion used to evaluate the selected comprehensive sex education curricula highlighted whether or not these curricula do what they say they will. The content of each of the curricula was compared to that curriculum's stated objectives. In several places the authors express dissatisfaction with their own measure primarily because that measure privileges ideologies they hold a bias against. Right off the bat the authors issue a warning that most of the curricula do not claim to be abstinence-based or to exclusively privilege abstinence over other safe sex practices (ACF & HHS, 2007, 4). This does not stop them from later critiquing the examined curricula for just that. They gloss over their stated measure (whether the curricula content mirror's its purpose) in favor of discussing an underlying measure:

> While the content of the curricula reviewed adheres to their stated purposes for the most part, these curricula do not spend as much time discussing abstinence as they do discussing contraception and ways to

lessen sexual activity . . . As a last note, it is important to realize that, although some of the curricula do not include abstinence as a stated purpose, some sexuality information organizations and resources recommend these curricula as comprehensive sex education (ACF & HHS, 2007, 6).

This is one place where the clear bias of the authors (toward curricula that privilege abstinence exclusively over other forms of contraception) interfered with their stated goals. If you set out to measure whether a curriculum stuck to its stated purposes, and it did, then that's a passing measurement.

A second place where clear and interfering bias presented itself was in the content section of the review. Incredibly, the content analysis for all nine curricula could be summed up in four paragraphs, all of which were related to condom use. In the section that is supposed to describe the content of the curricula, there is no discussion of abstinence, other forms of contraception, STIs, HIV, or healthy relationship programming. Instead, the authors explain that "these curricula focus on contraception and ways to lessen risks of sexual activity," then that is boiled down to three main foci: how to get condoms, how to integrate condom use into a relationship, and how to use condoms. The three subsequent paragraphs are excerpts from curricula in these three main areas. All in all, the section succeeded in likening the promotion of condom use with the marketing of cigarettes to children (ACF & HHS, 2007, 6–7).

A third place where bias creeps into the review is in the section on medical inaccuracy. In the section on condom failure rates a curriculum that uses a correct statistic on the failure rate of a condom with perfect use is considered "misleading":

> Indeed, there were misleading statements in every curriculum reviewed. For example, one curriculum states, "When used correctly, latex condoms prevent pregnancy 97% of the time." While this statement is technically true, 15% percent [sic] of women using condoms for contraception experience an unintended pregnancy during the first year of "typical use" and 20% of adolescents under the age of 18 using condoms for contraception get pregnant within one year. (ACF & HHS, 2007, 7–8)

The curriculum excerpt they chose for this part of the medical inaccuracy section is . . . accurate. According to *The Essentials of Contraceptive Technology,* 1997 [which they would have been using for their failure rates in *Safer Choices* (1998)] condoms do have a 3% failure rate with perfect use (Hatcher, 1997, 4–19). In addition, they quote *Contraceptive Technology* (2005)'s rate for "typical use" (which is clearly different from perfect use) and then throw in a statistic from a longitudinal study from 1986 (ACF & HHS, 2007, 7–8). While a longitudinal study is a great place to see a "typical use" rate in action, the authors are clearly comparing apples to oranges in a biased fishing expedition to find medical inaccuracies.

Use of Research Methodologies That Do Not Match Their Findings

The first two research questions use evidence from a keyword content analysis. The keywords used in the content analysis and how often they were found in each of the curricula are provided for the reader (ACF & HHS, 2007, 10–12). The content analysis is a valid methodology in sociology, provided it is done properly and that it only generates findings that are within its limits. According to Bernard Berelson, content analysis can be used to compare the content of communication to specific objectives, construct and apply communication standards, make assumptions about the intentions and/or beliefs of the communicators, and to reveal the focus of attention in a communication (Krippendorff, 2003, 44–47). That said, it is easy to see the difference between a methodologically sound content analysis and the content analysis in the 2007 Review.

The 2007 review was chiefly concerned with the treatment of abstinence in sex education curricula and, specifically, whether it got more time and was privileged over other sex risk-reduction strategies:

> While the content of the curricula reviewed adheres to their stated purposes for the most part, these curricula do not spend as much time discussing abstinence as they do discussing contraception and ways to lessen sexual activity (ACF & HHS, 2007, 6).

This assertion, that the studied curricula do not contain as much information about abstinence as they do about contraception is supported by the key word content analysis:

> The content analysis counted words used in each curriculum. Of the words counted, variations on the word "condom" occurred 235 times and variations on the word "contraception" occurred 381 times, while variations on the word "abstinence" occurred 87 times (ACF & HHS, 2007, 6, in footnote).

While content analysis can be used to highlight the focus of a communication, the construction of the analytical tool is critical for usable results. The 2007 review content analysis tool was designed in such a way that it could not help but indicate that condoms/contraceptives were more discussed than abstinence. A breakdown of the keywords used with attention placed on what would count as an "abstinence reference" versus a "condom/contraceptive reference" reveals:

- 21 keywords explicitly related to condoms/contraceptives
- 2 keywords explicitly related to abstinence
- 8 keywords were ambiguous but could have been tied to one or the other
- 3 keywords were conversation descriptors were condoms were designated as the subject (for example: "negotiation (to use condoms)"
- 0 keywords had abstinence designated as the subject (ACF & HHS, 2007, 10–12)

The keywords notably did their own injustice to abstinence by not look-ing for it in as many ways as they looked for condoms. There was the keyword "negotiation (to use condoms)" but not "negotiation (to abstain from sex)", and similarly "practice (s, ed, ing) (techniques, skills, using condoms)" but no "practice (s, ed, ing) (techniques and skills for abstaining)".

That said, even if the keyword search had been carefully designed to balance abstinence and condom terminology, it still would not have been an appropriate assessment tool for curricula. When looking at teaching tools, it is important to remember that often the themes and "take home" messages in a lesson are not completely spelled out. One example of this can be found in *Positive Images,* one of the reviewed curricula. In a lesson titled "Choices and Consequences", this scenario is described:

> Jerome's family has strong values, including the belief that intercourse should be saved for marriage. Jerome respects both his parents and his religion (Brick & Taverner, 2001, 51–56).

This scenario is part of an activity where students are urged to advise Jerome on the contraceptive option best for him where the best answer is clearly abstinence. Activities like this get no acknowledgement as abstinence-promoting lessons when content analysis is used. Often in educational tools the use of a word in a lesson plan is not nearly as effective as the use of a theme. The measurement tool did not take into account the language and treatment of abstinence in comprehensive sex education before trying to measure it. With this measuring tool, there was no way abstinence would have come out ahead.

Inappropriately Critical Benchmarks For Failure

It is obvious from the tone of the review that the authors were looking for their chosen curricula to fail. Frequently in an effort to achieve that goal the article contains inappropriately critical benchmarks for failure. The main place this occurs is in the section on medical inaccuracies. This section starts out with the sentence, "Most comprehensive sex education curricula reviewed contain some level of medical inaccuracy (ACF & HHS, 2007, 7)." From there they break down exactly which curricula contained what inaccuracies:

- One-third of the curricula contained no medical inaccuracies.
- One-third of the curricula had errors in their discussion of nonoxyl-9 (N-9).
- One of the curricula called a "rubber dam" a "dental dam". This cur-riculum was one of the three with an N-9 error.
- In the last one-third (the 3 that had "medical inaccuracies", but none related to N-9), one was a 1998 curriculum whose condom failure rate did not match the rate quoted in *Contraceptive Technology* 2006, and the other (which they footnoted as *Positive Choices* but which they corrected in their appendix as *Positive Images*) was quoted as saying

that all condoms marketed in the U.S. today meet federal quality standards.

- Eight out of the 9 curricula did not contain incorrect condom failure rates. The one that the reviewers cited as having an incorrect rate was a 1998 curriculum compared to a 2006 failure rate (ACF & HHS, 2007, 7–8).

Some of these "medical inaccuracies" are themselves inaccurate. "Dental dam" is an acceptable name for a "rubber dam" and is used by both health educators and contraceptive suppliers. One of the most popular "rubber dam" products in the U.S., the Trustex/LIXX Dental Dam, has "dental dam" on the box (Total Access Group, 2005–2006, 1, 9). Another "medical inaccuracy" that can be dismissed is the erroneous condom failure rate in *Safer Choices* (1998). A curriculum can only be expected to be accurate according to the information available at least a year before its release, so *Safer Choices* statistics should only be compared with the condom statistics available in 1997 or before. In *The Essentials of Contraceptive Technology* (1997), which is the correct reference for this curriculum, the statistic is 14%, so *Safer Choices* was off by one, but so was the Review (Hatcher, 1997, 4–19).

When these are dismissed, 4 out of 9 of the curricula have one medical inaccuracy each. Those involving nonoxynol-9 are serious, but as they involve developing research on the subject that was not confirmed by the CDC until 2002 (and even then this confirmation only led to a recommendation to no longer purchase N-9 products) this does not constitute what the authors cite as a "serious medical error" (Centers for Disease Control and Prevention [CDC], 2002, 3–4; ACF & HHS, 2007, 18). This also does not take into account the live teaching of these curricula by trained professionals. It is reasonable to assume that, when reproductive health care clinics were advised to use up their stores of N-9 condoms and then stop purchasing more, that reproductive health educators would either omit or modify the N-9 phrase in their curricula to the new guidelines (CDC, 2002, 3–4). This leaves *Positive Images,* which states that all condoms marketed in the U.S. are federally approved. Though there are products marketed as condoms that are not federally approved for pregnancy and disease prevention (e.g. condoms made of lambskin), the majority of condoms readily available to the general public, even those with novelty enhancements, do follow FDA guidelines for pregnancy and disease prevention. Again, this is another instance where it can be assumed a trained curriculum implementer would elaborate based on knowledge and experience. That said, it is uncertain whether condom product sales can even count as "medical inaccuracy."

When critically examined, 5 out of the 9 curricula had no reasonable medical inaccuracies, and 4 of the 9 had one to two sentences of technical inaccuracy, medical or otherwise, in their entire content. Compared to textbooks on other subjects geared towards middle and high school age American children, this is an amazing level of accuracy (for common inaccuracies in middle and high school textbooks see Beaty, 2007; Loewen, 1996).

Medical inaccuracies were addressed in the appendices as well, and there "inaccuracy" was expanded to include content excerpts that did not make it into the executive summary findings. The appendix entry for *Reducing the Risk* was an excellent example of this. It had three quotes from the curriculum on condom failure rates. Two of the three stated that when condoms were used "correctly and consistently" or "correctly . . . every time a couple has sex" they "provide good protection" or "work almost all of the time" (ACF & HHS, 2007, 14–15). The authors followed the quotes with the statement that, "'Good', 'almost all the time', and 'very effective' are subjective terms (ACF & HHS, 2007, 15)." Even with an explicit reference to perfect use and admittance that condoms were not 100% safe or effective, these descriptors were still picked out for failure. The third quote stated that condoms were "very effective" at preventing STI transmission, including "gonorrhea, Chlamydia and trichomoniasis", but they added that "further studies are being done in this area (ACF & HHS, 2007, 14)." Even after the caveat, the authors criticized this quote for not acknowledging a specific 2001 study that did not find enough evidence to claim that condoms reduced trichomoniasis risk (ACF & HHS, 2007, 15). All of this fell under a statement claiming that these quotes "did not provide explicit details of condom failure rates". When reading a review, one assumes that quotes pulled from the text are the best representation in that text of the subject under discussion. However, someone reading this who was unfamiliar with *Reducing the Risk* would have no idea that the curriculum has a whole appendix dedicated to the subject of "Condom Use Effectiveness" (Barth, 2004, 23–24). These extremely critical benchmarks appear in every curriculum entry in the appendix. In *Reach for Health* (2003), a quote giving an incidence rate for HPV was deemed inaccurate because it did not match a report that came out in 2004, a *year after it* (ACF & HHS, 2007, 32).

Inappropriately critical benchmarks for failure went beyond the medical inaccuracies sections. The first two research questions, 1) comparing curriculum content to its stated purpose and 2) examining the content on its own, both contained failure language because the curricula did not place enough of an emphasis on abstinence. From the language, "enough of an emphasis" for the authors was at least more content on abstinence than on contraceptive methods. As discussed in the section on methodology, it is inappropriate to consider the content of these curricula as inadequate solely from the results of the keyword content analysis.

The final research question, whether evaluations of the curricula demonstrated that they were effective at delaying sexual onset and increasing condom use, also suffered from inappropriately critical analysis. This section also only merited one paragraph, which started with a summary of the research findings:

> According to the evaluations reviewed, these curricula show some small positive impacts on (b) reducing sex without condoms and to a lesser extent (a) delaying sexual debut (ACF & HHS, 2007, 8).

According to their appendices, here is a breakdown of the reviewed research results for the 8 curricula that had research:

- 6 out of the 8 had positive impacts at their first review
- 4 out of 8 had one or more subsequent reviews

- 4 out of the 4 with subsequently reviews still had positive impacts (though 2 of the 4 had greatly diminished impacts at the time of second review)
- 2 of the 8 had positive impacts on delaying sexual initiation
- 6 of the 8 had positive impacts on condom use (ACF & HHS, 2007, 10–40)

Left out of this analysis was the range of other risky behaviors that many of these curricula were shown to reduce, including number of sexual partners, frequency of sex, and increased knowledge about contraceptives and HIV (ACF & HHS, 2007, 13–40). The authors summarized these impacts as "often . . . small, and most often the impacts do not extend three or sex months after a curriculum has been used," though they immediately footnoted that with examples of 2 curricula that had demonstrated positive impacts after three months (of which there were four) and neglected to note that only 4 of the curricula studied had subsequent studies (which means that it is impossible to say that the remaining 5 out of 9 did not have enduring impacts) (ACF & HHS, 2007, 8). They followed up with a comment on the limitations of the research, specifically that "all curricula were evaluated by the authors themselves (ACF & HHS, 2007, 8)." This makes it sound like all of the evaluations were done only by the authors, when the reality was much more complex:

- 4 out of 8 only had research that was solely conducted by one or more of the authors
- 3 out of 8 had research that was conducted by one or more of the authors plus one or more independent researchers
- 2 out of 8 had at least one published research study conducted solely by independent researchers
- 4 out of 8 had research where independent researchers were represented either in a study collaborating with one or more of the authors or in a study without an author on the research team (ACF & HHS, 2007, 10–40)

A detailed look at their appendices revealed that at least half of the curricula had some sort of outside input in the research, and one-fourth had at least one study conducted by a completely unaffiliated research team (with "affiliated" meaning they were not a part of the curriculum's design). To represent this with the phrase "conducted by the curriculum's author", which appears in some permutation in every appendix with a research section, is inappropriately critical, not to mention misleading and technically inaccurate. Furthermore, it is important to note that having a curriculum designer on its research team, or having a researcher on a curriculum design team, is not necessarily a bad thing. Sex education curricula benefit when researchers are on board in the design phase to make sure they reflect current best practices, and research on sex education benefits when curriculum designers work with researchers to ensure that all of the curriculum's target behavior goals are measured.

All-in-all, every section of the review contained some example of inappropriately critical benchmarks for failure. But while the reviewers apparently went through selected portions of each curriculum with a fine tooth comb, their reading of outside sources was not as detailed.

Inaccurate Referencing of Outside Works

Often in the 2007 Review outside sources were brought in to prove the inaccuracy of the studied curricula. The bringing in of outside sources also went hand-in-hand with inaccurate referencing. Take this excerpt from the section on medical inaccuracy:

> For example, once curriculum states, "When used correctly, latex condoms prevent pregnancy 97% of the time." While this statement is technically true, 15% of women using condoms for contraception experience an unintended pregnancy during the first year of "typical use" and about 20% of adolescents under the age of 18 using condoms for contraception get pregnant within one year (ACF & HHS, 2007, 7–8).

Contraceptive technology has always used two measures to capture how effective contraceptive methods are in real-life situations: "perfect" and "typical". "Perfect" refers to how effective a particular method is when that method is employed consistently and correctly. "Typical" refers to how effective that method is when it is employed inconsistently or when user-error is taken into account (Hatcher, 2004, 225–228). "When used correctly" or "When used correctly and consistently" are reasonably clear and accurate ways to explain "perfect use" statistics to preteens and teens according to the Centers for Disease Control (CDC, 2003, 2). Proving a "perfect use" statistic wrong with a "typical use" statistic, especially in a context when the potential condom users are being taught how to use condoms correctly and how to obtain them consistently (and thus prepared to be "perfect" users) is both an instance of inaccurate referencing and an inappropriately critical benchmark for failure.

A second instance of inaccurate referencing compared the "medical inaccuracies" of selected comprehensive sex education curricula found in the 2007 Review with those found in selected abstinence-only curricula in the 2004 Waxman Report:

> For perspective, it may be helpful to compare the error rate reported here with statistics cited in the December 2004 report entitled "The Content of Federally Funded Abstinence Education Programs," which is typically called the Waxman Report. This report found that, of the thirteen abstinence-until-marriage curricula reviewed, eleven contained medically inaccurate statements; in all thirteen curricula, (nearly 5,000 pages of information), there were 49 instances of questionable information. It could easily be argued that the comprehensive sex education curricula reviewed for this report have a similar rate of error compared with abstinence-until-marriage curricula (ACF & HHS, 2007, 8).

This reference to the 2004 Waxman Report is brought up again in the conclusion:

Lastly, although the medical accuracy of comprehensive sex education curricula is nearly 100%—similar to that of abstinence-until-marriage curricula—efforts could be made to more extensively detail condom failure rates in context (ACF & HHS, 2007, 9).

At the beginning of this article, the 2004 Waxman Report itself was quoted stating that 80% of the curricular material reviewed contained "false, misleading, or distorted information about reproductive health (U.S. House of Representatives Committee on Govt. Reform, 2004, i). These quotes ignore the fundamental differences in the quality and quantity of errors found in the Waxman Report versus the 2007 Review. These quality and quantity differences can be broken down into several categories:

- **Quantity:** The inaccuracies cited in the 2007 Review curricula were one to two sentences at most, while the inaccuracies cited in the Waxman Report were often whole blocks of text or reoccurring themes in the text (ACF & HHS, 2007, 7–8; U.S. House of Representatives Committee on Govt. Reform, 2004, 8–22).
- **Reference Use:** In the 2007 Review curricula, inaccuracies in the curricula were either instances where the reviewers were not satisfied with specific phrasing or where statistics and details did not match current research either because the research was published right at or after the curriculum, or because the body of research had still not come to a satisfactory consensus. In the Waxman Report, inaccuracies were consistently defended with research that was either extremely outdated or rejected by federal bodies at large (ACF & HHS, 2007, 7–8; U.S. House of Representatives Committee on Govt. Reform, 2004, 8–22).
- **Ability of Implementer to Circumvent:** The inaccuracies in the 2007 Review curricula were the types of errors that could be corrected by a trained professional implementer (for example: when studies consistently showed that N-9 was ineffective, a trained implementer could easily leave out N-9 info or give updated, correct information for N-9). While some of the inaccuracies of the Waxman Report were of that type, most were thematic, making them impossible for a trained implementer to completely eliminate (for example, repeated emphasis on exaggerated condom failure rates throughout curricular materials in statistics, phrasing, and activities) (ACF & HHS, 2007, 7–8; U.S. House of Representatives Committee on Govt. Reform, 2004, 8–22).

Any assumption of similarity between the reviewed abstinence-only curricula and the reviewed comprehensive sex education curricula is, at best, wishful thinking on behalf of those who wish to debunk comprehensive sex education. Of the six inaccuracies cited in the 2007 Review's executive summary, three were N-9 statements (one to two sentences) that reflected the research at the time of publication (where the curricula was a few years old or N-9 statements were still not conclusive across the body of research), one was the use of manufacturer and layman terminology instead of FDA terminology, one was a condom failure rate that was correct when compared with a referent published before the curriculum, and one was a condom accessibility statement that could easily be corrected by the implementer. In addition, there were several instances of phrasing and statistic use around condom failure rates that were technically correct and used CDC-approved language about condom effectiveness, but that the authors took issue with.

The errors found by the Waxman Report for abstinence-only curricula were fundamentally different. The treatment of condom use is an excellent example of this fundamental difference. Studied abstinence-only curricula consistently used a 1993 study (commonly referred to as the Weller Study) which was rejected by the Department of Health and Human Services in 1997. Of the studied curricula, only one was put out at a time where use of the Weller Study might have been acceptable (*Sex Can Wait,* published in 1997). Even so, the Weller Study was a poor reference for condom failure rates when compared with the primarily used and endorsed *Contraceptive Technology,* which was available before 1997. Several abstinence-only curricula had activities which explicitly taught students that condoms did not work and had holes big enough for STIs to pass through. Many included erroneous research that STI rates have not fallen as condom use rates rose. STI risks were exaggerated in many curricula alongside exaggerated condom failure rates (U.S. House of Representatives Committee on Govt. Reform, 2004, 8–11, 21). For pregnancy prevention, curricula confused "perfect" and "typical" use and had activities designed to convince preteens and teens that condoms do not work to prevent pregnancy. Some have gender role lessons that imply that contraceptive use is a man's decision and that if women make demands in relationships (contraceptive demands included) that they will lose their partners (U.S. House of Representatives Committee on Govt. Reform, 2004, 11–12, 17–18). These types of errors were designed to scare teens to abstinence, but as a consequence create a dangerous false consciousness about condoms and contraceptive use in relationships that is too pervasive for an implementer to single-handedly correct.

In light of a careful reading of the 2007 Review and the 2004 Waxman Report, any comparison between the results of the two is both inaccurate and misleading. Abstinence-only programs benefit from their counterparts' exceptional performance in terms of medical accuracy. Comprehensive sex education programs are pulled down by the assumption that they are "similar to that of 'abstinence-until-marriage curricula'" (ACF & HHS, 2007, 9).

Conclusion

The 2007 *Review of Comprehensive Sex Education Curricula* was a timely addition to the current sex education discourse. As such, the Review garnered press attention and its conclusions were put out to the public at large. But the real impact of this study was not the attention it received from the press, but the ability it gave to supporters of abstinence-only education to say that comprehensive sex education did not work. One example of this comes from Project Reality, a publishing company that puts out two abstinence-only curricula, *A.C. Green's Game Play* and *Navigator,* both products which received negative reviews in the Waxman Report. Project Reality covered the 2007 Review's release, and has a handy fact sheet to help people browsing its website under-stand the findings of the Review. Its summary of the "overall findings of inter-est" included:

> Of the curricula reviewed, the curriculum with the most balanced dis-cussion of abstinence and safer sex still discussed condoms and contra-ception nearly **seven times more than abstinence.** (their emphasis)
>
> Every curricula reviewed contained misleading statements about condom effectiveness—leading teens to believe condoms are more effective than they actually are.
>
> All curricula were evaluated by the program authors themselves.
>
> **Seven of the nine curricula reviewed instructed and encour-aged teens to shop for condoms themselves.** (their emphasis)
>
> **THERE WAS NO REFERENCE IN ANY OF THESE COMPREHEN-SIVE SEX ED CURRICULA TO THE EMOTIONAL RISKS ASSOCIATED WITH SEXUAL ACTIVITY.** (their emphasis) (Project Reality, 2007)

Irresponsible research on the federal level affects how people on the local level chose what sex education is appropriate for their youth. The 2007 *Review of Comprehensive Sex Education Curricula* is not responsible research for all the reasons stated. The sooner it can be removed from the discourse and replaced with research that is less biased, uses reasonable benchmarks for success and failure, and which appropriately references other works, the better.

POSTSCRIPT

Is There Something Wrong with the Content of Comprehensive Sex Education Curricula?

Organizations supporting abstinence-only-until-marriage (AOUM) programs lauded the government's report and seized on the opportunity to criticize sexuality education. One AOUM-promoting organization, Operation Keepsake, based in Twinsburg, Ohio, complained that the words "abstinence" or "abstain" were mentioned only 321 times in sexuality education curricula, compared to 928 mentions of "protection." The conservative group Concerned Women for America responded to the report by calling sex education "Rated X." Most conservative organizations expressed alarm that condoms and contraceptives were mentioned so much more frequently than abstinence. Several organizations, including the National Abstinence Education Association, responded to the report by taking aim at *Making Sense of Abstinence,* a manual that was not even among those curricula examined. In the spirit of full disclosure, *Making Sense of Abstinence* was co-authored by William J. Taverner, one of the editors of this *Taking Sides* book. (His explanation of his innovative approach to abstinence education is explored in another issue in this book.) A principal objection of *Making Sense of Abstinence* was its discussion of outercourse—kissing and touching behaviors that do not involve the genitals. Taverner is also the co-author of one of the "curricula" that was examined in the report *Positive Images: Teaching about Abstinence, Contraception, and Sexual Health,* which is a collection of lessons and not a curriculum at all.

Meanwhile, organizations supporting sexuality education rose to the defense of these programs. The Guttmacher Institute, which publishes the peer-reviewed journal *Perspectives on Sexual and Reproductive Health,* said, "The analysis was poorly conducted and would never pass peer review by an established journal. Its findings should not be viewed or described as a credible or unbiased assessment of the content of sexuality education curricula."

What's your opinion of the content of the sexuality education curricula examined? Did the federal government use appropriate research methods? Which words or concepts, if any, do you think should be excluded from a teenager's sexuality education?

What insights might be gained from examining the words that appear in a curriculum? Is such an examination a reasonable barometer for programs' contents? "HIV" or "AIDS" are words that appeared most frequently in the content analysis, yet the government's report did not comment on this, choosing instead to emphasize the number of times phrases such as "100 percent safe" were mentioned compared to "condoms" or "contraceptives."

Other frequently cited words that received little attention in the government's descriptive summary were "pregnant" and "pregnancy"; "sex," "sexual," and "sexual intercourse"; and "STDs". Why did the report elect not to comment on these frequently mentioned words?

What do you think of the report's description of "medical inaccuracies" contained within sexuality education curricula? Were these legitimate concerns? Was CaPece's critique of the government's critique fair or biased? Were her explanations of the "medical inaccuracies" valid? How might you critique her analysis?

Suggested Readings

"Study: More 'Condoms than 'Abstinence' in Sex Ed," *Washington Times* (June 13, 2007).

D. Kirby, *Emerging Answers 2007: Research Findings on Programs to Reduce Teen Pregnancy and Sexually Transmitted Diseases* (Washington, DC: National Campaign to Prevent Teen and Unplanned Pregnancy, Available at http://www.thenc.org./ea2007 (2007)

C. Lee, "HHS Counters with Its Own Sex Ed Critique," *The Washington Post* (June 21, 2007).

Mathematica Policy Research, Inc., *Impacts of Four Title V, Section 510 Abstinence Education Programs* (Princeton, NJ: Trenholm, 2007).

National Abstinence Education Association, *Straight from the Source: What So-Called "Comprehensive" Sex Education Teaches to America's Youth* (Washington, DC: National Abstinence Education Association, 2007).

E. Schroeder and J. Kuriansky, *Sexuality Education: Past, Present, & Future Issues* (Westport, CT: Greenwood Press, 2009).

B. Taverner and S. Montfort, *Making Sense of Abstinence: Lessons for Comprehensive Sex Education* (Morristown, NJ: Planned Parenthood of Greater Northern New Jersey, 2005).

ISSUE 7

Should Sex Ed Teach about Abstinence?

YES: William J. Taverner, from "Reclaiming Abstinence in Comprehensive Sex Education," *Contemporary Sexuality* (2007)

NO: Maureen Kelly, from "The Semantics of Sex Ed: Or, Shooting Ourselves in the Foot as We Slowly Walk Backwards," *Educator's Update* (2005)

ISSUE SUMMARY

YES: William J. Taverner, sexuality educator and editor of *Taking Sides*, argues that sexuality education should teach about abstinence, and introduces a new model to replace problematic abstinence education models of the past.

NO: Sexuality educator Maureen Kelly argues that the framing of abstinence by conservatives has essentially made the term politically volatile, and that the one-size-fits-all definition has rendered the term useless to educators.

Should sex education teach students about abstinence? It sounds like a fairly straightforward question. Many who favor an abstinence-only approach to sex education might say, "Yes! Abstinence is the only 100 percent effective method for preventing pregnancy and the transmission of sexually transmitted infections (STIs). It should be the only thing we teach our students!" Others, who favor a comprehensive approach, might say, "Well, abstinence is an important concept, and we should include it in the discussion, as well as addressing other contraceptive methods and ways to prevent STIs." Some may say, "Since so many young people are already having sexual intercourse,

---

Editor's note: One of the arguments in this issue, "Should Sex Ed Teach about Abstinence?" is given by William J. Taverner, who is also the an editor of this Taking Sides reader. For a fair and balanced examination of both the "YES" and "NO" perspectives, Ryan W. McKee is the sole writer of the Introduction and Postscript to this issue.

why bother teaching abstinence?" Still others may say, "Wait—what exactly do you mean by abstinence?"

Surprising as it may sound, the definition of abstinence isn't as clear-cut as one might think. And who holds the power to define the term at a particular point in time greatly adds to the confusion—and acceptance—of that definition. The strict, eight-point definition of abstinence education that *both* Taverner and Kelly reject says that federally funded abstinence-only-until marriage education must:

1. Have as its exclusive purpose the teaching of the social, physiological, and health gains to be realized from abstaining from sexual activity;
2. Teach that abstinence from sexual activity outside of marriage is the expected standard for all school-age children;
3. Teach that abstinence from sexual activity is the only certain way to avoid out-of-wedlock pregnancy, sexually transmitted diseases, and other associated health problems;
4. Teach that a mutually faithful monogamous relationship in the context of marriage is the expected standard of human sexual activity;
5. Teach that sexual activity outside of the context of marriage may have harmful psychological and physical effects;
6. Teach that bearing children out of wedlock is likely to have harmful consequences for the child, the child's parents, and society;
7. Teach young people how to reject sexual advances and how alcohol and drug use increases vulnerability to sexual advances; and
8. Teach the importance of attaining self-sufficiency before engaging in sexual activity.

Sex educators often feel constrained by definitions and regulations handed down by agencies or governments. In some cases, they work within the system, following guidelines and adhering to definitions they may or may not agree with, but feel compelled to uphold. Others find creative ways to challenge definitions and expectations while still working within the specified framework. Some may disagree so strongly with the definitions that they reject them outright and actively seek systematic change. These are not uncommon occurrences in the paths of social movements. Which tactic is more effective is generally a matter of debate among academics, activists, and historians.

In the following essays, William J. Taverner, the director of the Center for Family Life Education, outlines a new framework for teaching about abstinence as a vital component of sexuality education. Maureen Kelly, vice president for education and training for Planned Parenthood of the Southern Finger Lakes, maintains that the framing of abstinence by conservatives has essentially made the term politically volatile, and that the one-size-fits-all definition has rendered the term useless to educators.

YES

William J. Taverner

Reclaiming Abstinence in Comprehensive Sex Education

T wo e-mails I received came from separate ends of the ideological universe, as it relates to the abstinence-only-until-marriage versus comprehensive sex education culture wars, but both had a similarly hostile tone. The subject of this electronic wrath was the new theoretical and pedagogical concepts introduced in a sex education manual I coauthored with Sue Montfort, *Making Sense of Abstinence: Lessons for Comprehensive Sex Education* (Taverner & Montfort, 2005).

The first e-mail followed a very short editorial in the *Wall Street Journal* that commented on one of the themes of the manual—that it was necessary to discuss with youth the way they *define* abstinence, so as to better help them be successful with this decision. The e-mail began as follows:

> *Dear Mr. Taverner:*
> *Abstinence means NO SEX. Only a pointy head liberal could think there was some other definition, and it is pointy headed liberals that give liberalism a bad name. It takes the cake that you would . . . write some papers on trying to define abstinence. I have done that in four words above.*

More later on this writer's comments about defining abstinence—and on my seemingly pointy head, too! The more recent e-mail followed the announcement of the annual sex ed conference of The Center for Family Life Education (CFLE) that went to thousands of sex educators by e-mail. Themed on the manual, the announcement was titled "The Abstinence Experience: Teaching about Abstinence in the Context of Comprehensive Sex Education." The conference featured sex education leaders from prominent organizations— Answer (Formerly the Network for Family Life Education), the California Family Health Council, Montclair State University, the Sexuality Information and Education Council of the United States (SIECUS), and trainers from the CFLE. This e-mail read, simply:

> *Please REMOVE my email address from this mailing list. I am 100% against ABSTINENCE!*

This is not the first time someone has asked to be taken off the e-mail list. People ask to be unsubscribed when they are no longer working in the field of

From *Contemporary Sexuality,* April 2007, pp. 9–14. Copyright © 2007 by American Association of Sex Educators, Counselors & Therapists—AASECT. Reprinted by permission.

sex education, or when they only do so peripherally, or when their inboxes are generally too clogged. Usually the request to unsubscribe is polite. But beyond the rude tone of this request, the last sentence stopped me in my tracks:

I am 100% against ABSTINENCE!

The capitalized ABSTINENCE was the writer's doing, not mine. Did I read this right? Or did he mean he was against abstinence *education?* Maybe he meant *abstinence-only-until-marriage-education?* But I *did* read it correctly; in fact, I cut and pasted the writer's remarks to this article! He was against *ABSTINENCE.* How could that be? If a person chooses to abstain from sexual intercourse, or any other sexual behaviors, or drugs, alcohol, chocolate, or whatever, how could *anyone* be against that? And yet this is a common theme I have experienced since we wrote *Making Sense of Abstinence.* It seems some comprehensive sex educators and advocates are *turned off* by the word "abstinence." The atmosphere among some might best be described as anti-abstinence. The anecdotal evidence:

- Upon reviewing the final manuscript for our new abstinence manual, one well-respected reviewer asked not to be identified in the acknowledgments. She explained that while she thought the manual was great, she also thought it would be a bad career move to become too closely associated with the "world of abstinence."
- One prominent sex education leader urged us to reconsider the title of both our manual and our conference. He did not think we should be promoting abstinence, instead favoring the term "delaying intercourse." (Imagine a title such as *Making Sense of Delaying Intercourse*— what could more clearly illustrate the disconnect between adults and teens who *never* think of themselves as "delaying intercourse," but who *do* sometimes choose abstinence?)
- A CFLE educator having a casual conversation with a colleague asked if that colleague would be coming to our annual conference. The colleague said he had not yet received our flyer. The CFLE educator was surprised, since we had sent the flyers out over a month ago, and this individual had been on our mailing list for many years. Upon hearing the title of the conference, he replied, "That was *you*? I threw that out when I saw the word 'abstinence'! "

What was going on here? Sue Montfort and I spent a year and a half writing *Making Sense of Abstinence.* It was nominated for four sex ed awards, to date, winning two. It had been showcased by SIECUS at a Congressional Briefing in Washington, D.C. And yet while most colleagues were embracing this new model for abstinence education, some were clearly shunning the idea of *any* abstinence education.

My first real understanding of the distaste some sexologists have for the word "abstinence" came to light as I proudly stood by my "Making Sense of Abstinence" poster session at a conference of the American Association of Sexuality Educators, Counselors, and Therapists (AASECT). As colleagues walked by the four-panel poster that my intern, Laura Minnichelli, had created, many veered off their paths suddenly, as if the word "abstinence," would jump off the poster and bite them. Some looked briefly at the poster and gave a look of disgust, perhaps wondering how an "abstinence" poster infiltrated a sexology conference. Those who stopped to ask about it seemed puzzled initially. They saw the poster's worksheets on masturbation, outercourse, the lack of efficacy of virginity pledge programs, and they gradually came to recognize that this was a *different* type of abstinence program. As these thoughtful individuals left, they offered words of thanks and encouragement that there was *finally* a sex ed program out that there was reframing abstinence education.

There is no doubt that any self-respecting sex educator has good reason to be skeptical of a new abstinence manual. I can understand and even appreciate the sideways looks that sexologists give after ten years of federal funding for abstinence-only-until-marriage programs, and 25 years since the first "chastity education" federal funds were issued. Over $1 billion has produced curricula that are directive, simplistic and insulting to teens—programs that want to tell teens *what to think,* not how to *think for themselves.*

Abstinence-only-until-marriage programs virtually ignore the nearly 50% of teens who *are* having intercourse (Centers for Disease Control, 2006). They tell these teens to get with the program, but have no advice, otherwise, for teens that *don't* get with the program. At worst, they give misleading or inaccurate information about condom and contraceptive efficacy. These programs ignore lesbian and gay teens (and their families) who are told to abstain until marriage, but who don't have a legal right to marry, except those who are residents of Massachusetts. These programs produce virginity pledge programs, where 88% of teens who pledge virginity fail to keep that pledge, and are one-third less likely to use condoms at first intercourse (Brückner & Bearman, 2005).

There are many reasons to bemoan the current state of abstinence education, as it has been done so poorly. Just read Congressman Henry Waxman's report (U.S. House of Representatives, 2004). Perhaps consider the wisdom of Dr. Michael Carrera, who reminds us that expecting outcomes when we tell kids to "just say no," is no different than expecting a person's clinical depression to be treated by saying, "Have a nice day!" Or teacher/columnist Deborah Roffman, who compares abstinence-only education to the sex-hungry media: both, Roffman explains, tell teens exactly what to do. The media scream, "Always say yes," abstinence-only programs admonish, "Just say no," but *neither* encourage teens to *think* for themselves. That is, of course, the whole point of learning.

Certainly there are many reasons that justify the collective distaste for the current abstinence education paradigm among sex educators. The state of abstinence-only education is just awful, from the moralizing, shame, and fear-based tactics, to the sideshow industry that markets abstinence slogans on billboards, t-shirts, mugs, and even chewing gum. ("Abstinence gum—for *chewzing* an abstinent lifestyle.")

But all complaints about abstinence-only-until-marriage education aside, what is wrong with educating about the *choice* of abstinence? Doesn't the polling research say that American parents want their children to learn about abstinence? When comprehensive sex educators trumpet the latest polling data from groups like the Kaiser Family Foundation that says parents support comprehensive sex education, how do we miss the fact that the same polling data reveals parental desire for their kids to learn about abstinence? What are we doing about this, and how can we react to the word "abstinence" so negatively when we are supposedly teaching it as a *part* of comprehensive sex education?

A New Model

The pedagogical concepts introduced in *Making Sense of Abstinence* make it unlike any abstinence education manual produced to date. There are four key themes that are woven throughout the manual's sixteen lessons: (1) abstinence education needs to help young people *define* abstinence in ways that help them understand and apply their decisions in real life; (2) abstinence education needs to include decision-making, skills-building opportunities; (3) abstinence education is not just talking about which behaviors to *avoid*, but also the behaviors that are *permitted* in a person's decision; (4) abstinence education needs to help young people protect their sexual health and transition safely when they decide to no longer abstain.

Defining Abstinence

Remember the guy who called me a "pointy headed liberal"? Define abstinence? Well, DUH! Abstinence means "no sex," right? Next time you are with a group of professionals, or a group of students, ask them to take out their cell phones and call three people. Have their friends, colleagues, coworkers, children, parents, etc. define the terms "sex" and "abstinence." You will be amazed, as I always am, with the discordant results you get. Do the definitions address only vaginal intercourse? Oral or anal intercourse? Other touching behaviors? Masturbation? What reasons or motivations emerge? Religious? Parental? Pregnancy prevention? Prevention of sexually transmitted infections? Assessing one's readiness? Marriage? Protecting one's mental health? When one person defines "sex," as "a loving, intimate, physical connection between two people," does that mean that kissing is sex? And, thus, abstinence is no kissing? When one says, simply, that "abstinence means no sex," does this mean one must also avoid the aforementioned feelings of intimacy and love?

If this seems like a trivial exercise, consider the following definitions of abstinence printed or posted by a variety of health-promoting organizations:

> *"Abstinence is . . . not having sex with a partner. This will keep the sperm from joining the egg."* . . .

> *"Abstinence is . . . no intercourse. Not even any semen on the vulva. Pretty straight-forward."* (Kinsey Institute's Sexuality Information Service for Students)

> Hmmm. So abstinence means no *vaginal* intercourse. But wait . . .

> *"For protection against infection . . . abstinence means avoiding vaginal, anal, and oral-genital intercourse, or participating in any other activity in which body fluids are exchanged."* . . .

So, the motivation here is avoiding infections that may be transmitted via body fluid exchange. This could include oral, anal, or vaginal intercourse. It also seems to refer tacitly to another fluid through which HIV could be transmitted: breast milk. So, does one practice abstinence by not breastfeeding her child? From the *Dictionary of Sexology* (Francoeur, 1997):

> *"A definition of abstinence may include not engaging in masturbation."*

and

> *"The practices of tantric yoga recommend short periods of abstinence to concentrate one's sexual energy and prepare for more intense responses when sexual intercourse is resumed."*

Ah, so abstinence is periodic, for the purpose of making sex *better!* How about some input from abstinence-only programs:

> *"Abstinence is . . . voluntarily refraining from all sexual relationships before marriage in order to uplift your own self-worth and provide the freedom to build character, develop career potentials and practice true love."* (As cited by Kempner, 2001)

Abstinence for career potential? Never came up in my job interviews, but who knows today? Back to reality, Thoraya Obaid, executive director of the United Nations Populations Fund, reminds us that abstinence is not always a choice:

> *"Abstinence . . . is meaningless to women who are coerced into sex."*

As I collected all these definitions, I was surprised when glossaries on websites for lesbian, gay, bisexual, and transgender teens repeatedly came up empty on definitions for abstinence. I asked my friend and colleague, Lis Maurer, about this. Lis is the director of Ithaca College's Center for LGBT Education and Outreach Services, and she explained:

> *I remember a high school class where we were taught about abstinence. Afterward, several of us non-straight students got together and reacted. Some said, "OK—we're totally in the clear!" Others said, "No, we were ignored—they really don't know we exist!" and yet others were just completely confused, as if the lecture was in some other language.*

Finally, . . . sums up all this confusion quite nicely:

> *"Abstinence is . . . avoiding sex. Sex, of course, means different things to different people."*

Indeed. What might abstinence mean to a teen?

> *"I'm proud that my boyfriend and I have decided to be abstinent. We have oral sex, but definitely not real sex, you know?"*

The importance of helping teens define abstinence cannot be under-scored enough. A recent evaluation of one abstinence-only program found that teens developed more positive attitudes toward abstinence following the program. That seems like good news, but the study went on to explain that "abstinence" meant "abstaining from sexual intercourse," which meant, "the male's penis is in the female's vagina. Some slang names for sexual intercourse are 'having sex,' 'making love,' or 'going all the way.' " (Laflin et al., 2005). So while these teens were developing their positive feelings toward abstinence, they were learning nothing about how abstinence might *also* mean avoiding other sexual behaviors, including anal and oral intercourse that could transmit a sexually transmitted infection. The teen cited said earlier could easily have been a participant in this abstinence-only education program.

The evidence is clear that teens need opportunities to discuss what absti-nence means to them. They need worksheets, activities, and discussion oppor-tunities to reflect on their reasons for choosing abstinence, and specifically what behaviors they will avoid while abstaining. If they ultimately decide *not* to avoid oral sex, anal sex, etc., then they need further information about pro-tection from sexually transmitted infections.

Decision-Making, Skills-Building Lessons

Maybe you've seen a billboard sign that says, "VIRGIN: Teach Your Kid It's Not a Dirty Word!" Or maybe you're familiar with the slogan, "Quit your urgin', be a virgin!" One of the abstinence slogans that always gets a chuckle is "Good cowgirls keep their calves together." The list goes on and on, and many of them are cute, catchy, and memorable. But none of them speak to the complex decision-making skills that really need to be developed in young people to help them make decisions that are meaningful and responsible in their lives.

Young people need opportunities to develop concrete steps for "using" abstinence effectively. Abstinence is not just a state of being; it is a method to be *used.* This is an important distinction. The former implies passivity; i.e., no need to think about anything when abstinence is the foregone conclusion. The latter encourages young people to think about *how* they are going to be effective with their decisions, to develop the skills to be successful with their decisions, and to re-evaluate their decisions as need be.

Abstinence skills include learning to plan for sexual abstinence, and prac-ticing assertive communication, so that one can better stand up for one's deci-sions. It involves learning about sexual response, so that one can understand and manage their sexual feelings in ways that are consistent with their values and decisions. It involves negotiation and enforcing boundaries with one's partner. It involves so much more than "Just say no!" or other simplistic, "educational" approaches that are far more directive than they are educational.

A relatively new model, supported by the federal government seeks to improve upon abstinence-only programs by teaching an "ABC" model. ABC stands for "*A*bstinence," "*B*e faithful," and "Use Condoms," and unfortunately it is not much more comprehensive than its abstinence-only cousin. The United States exported its ABC's to Uganda for the purposes of HIV prevention. The hierarchical ABC approach stresses Abstinence first; while Be faithful reserved for those who can't seem to practice Abstinence; and Condoms are reserved strictly for the sex workers.

A closer look at this new sloganistic approach exposes a model that is devoid of critical thinking and skills building. For example, what if a person is using "B" but their partner isn't. That person is likely to learn about three new letters, "S," "T," and "D." Further, what if a person ditches "A," in favor of "B" without using C? Does anyone in these programs ever mention the possibility of an unplanned or unwanted "P"? Simplistic models like this continue to reveal the importance of helping young people think through their abstinence decisions and become effective abstinence users.

It's Not Just What You Avoid . . .

Why is it that we are not talking about masturbation when we are teaching about abstinence? Twelve years ago a U.S. surgeon general was fired for suggesting this might be a good idea. Masturbation is one of the safest sexual behaviors around, perhaps the safest. There is no risk of getting pregnant, no risk of getting a sexually transmitted infection, no risk of getting *anything*, except pleasure. As Woody Allen said, "Don't knock masturbation. It's having sex with someone you love!"

So why does masturbation have such a stigma in America. I have a clue that maybe it has something to do with the things that have been written about it. Sylvester Graham, a New York preacher, wrote in 1834 that a masturbator grows up:

> "with a body full of disease, and with a mind in ruins, the loathsome habit still tyrannizing over him, with the inexorable imperiousness of a fiend of darkness." (Graham, 1834)

And, in 1892, a prominent nutritionist, John Harvey Kellogg, wrote this:

> "As a sin against nature, [masturbation] has no parallel except in sodomy. The habit is by no means confined to boys; girls also indulge in it, though it is to be hoped, to a less fearful extent than boys, at least in this country. Of all the vices to which human beings are addicted, no other so rapidly undermines the constitution, and so certainly makes a complete wreck of an individual as this, especially when the habit is begun at an early age. It wastes the most precious part of the blood, uses up the vital forces, and finally leaves the poor victim a most utterly ruined and loathsome object.
>   Suspicious signs are: bashfulness, unnatural boldness, round shoulders and a stooping position, lack of development of the breasts in females, eating chalk, acne, and the use of tobacco." (Kellogg, 1892)

No wonder the anxiety! It didn't matter that neither statement was true. People still flocked to buy the recommended antidotes, Sylvester's Graham crackers and Kellogg's Corn Flakes, both of which were supposed to suppress the urge to masturbate (and neither of which contained sugar or cinnamon in those days!).

More than a century later, our American culture still retains myths and misinformation. Perhaps if we can make young people feel a little less anxious about a behavior in which so many already engage, we can help them recognize masturbation as an important, safe *alternative* to intercourse.

Abstinence education needs to discuss other safe sexual behaviors, including outercourse, that get young people thinking about non-genital activities that are safe, and will keep them free of sexually transmitted infections and pregnancy. These behaviors—masturbation and outercourse—have inexplicably been omitted from abstinence-only curricula. It is as if we really think that if we don't mention these topics, teens won't think of it either! Have we really become that disconnected with our nation's youth? We really need to examine *why* information about masturbation and outercourse is omitted in abstinence education. Is it to keep information about sexual pleasure from young people? What gives educators the right to withhold *any* information from young people, especially information that might help keep them safe, while feeling positively about themselves?

Susie Wilson, who ran the Network for Family Life Education (now Answer), gave a review of *Making Sense of Abstinence,* and she put it better than I could have:

> "[Students] will learn that there is a long continuum of behaviors between "saying no" and "doing it" that will keep them safe, not sorry. Educators will feel more secure about teaching tough topics such as oral sex, masturbation and outercourse, when they see they are allied with discussion about personal values, decision-making and communication."

This is exactly what we are trying to do with our our model for abstinence education.

Help Young People Protect Themselves If/When Their Decisions Change

A final, critical part of abstinence education is the need to help young people protect themselves if and when their abstinence decisions change. It is no longer enough for us to bury our heads in the sand and just hope that teens remain abstinent through high school, college, and into young adulthood (or up until age 29, as the new federal abstinence-only guidelines suggest). We need to equip them with the skills to make that transition safely.

One way is to help them identify signs of *"sexual readiness"*. Students might read stories about other teens who are making sexual decisions, and assess and discuss how ready (or not) these teens are against any number of sexual readiness checklists. Consider these two teen quotes:

> "At times I get all hot with my partner and I feel like I really want to have sex. At other times, I know that I shouldn't have sex until I am ready. The problem is that sometimes I feel like I am ready and other times I feel like I am not ready. What should I do?"

and

"I've been going out with this guy—he's 18. Everything was romantic at first, but now he's gotten real pushy. Last time we were alone, he gave me a beer. I didn't feel like drinking, but he kept pushing it on me, so I drank it just to shut him up. Now he's pushing the sex thing on me. It's like we don't talk about anything but sex. I know he's tired of waiting for me, but I think things are getting out of hand, and I'm not sure I'm ready."

Both teens deserve much more than a catchy slogan. They need tools and discussion to help them identify how one knows when one is ready, and how to identify coercion in a relationship, and how to leave coercive relationships. We need to help young people actively think of their decisions in their sexual lives. Sexual intercourse is not something that people are just supposed to stumble into, without thinking of their decisions and their potential consequences. By contrast, the current culture of abstinence-only education supports teens making virginity pledges, which simply do not work. 88% of teens who make such a pledge break it! (Brückner & Bearman, 2005). And those teens are less likely to use protection, because they've never learned about condoms or contraceptives, or they've been taught only about failure rates.

In training teachers, I often say that "Sex education *today* is not necessarily for *tonight*." This is very applicable when it comes to abstinence education. We need to think about sex education in the context of a lifetime of sexual decision making, and abstinence as a conscious decision that is one's right to assert at anytime in their life. At the same time, we need to help teens gain knowledge and develop skills to protect their sexual health if and when they decide to no longer abstain, whether it is tonight, or in college, or when they celebrate a commitment ceremony, or after they walk down the aisle.

Young people need more from sex education. They need education that includes the *choice* to abstain. They need accurate information, not evasive, undefined terms, or misleading, or false information. Young people need and deserve respect, not to be subjected to scare tactics. They need to develop skills to be successful with abstinence; not to hear catchy slogans. They need to be met where they are, and recognized for their ability to make responsible decisions about their sexual lives. They need abstinence education, but they deserve better than what they've been getting so far.

References

Brückner, H. & Bearman, P. (2005). "After the promise: the STD consequences of adolescent virginity pledges," *Journal of Adolescent Health*, No. 36: 271–278.

Centers for Disease Control and Prevention. (2006). *Youth risk behavior surveillance—United States, 2005*. Atlanta, GA: Centers for Disease Control.

Francoeur, R.T. (1997). *The Complete Dictionary of Sexology*, New York: Continuum.

Graham, S. (1834). *A Lecture to Young Men on Chastity.* Boston, MA: Pierce.

Kellogg, J.H. (1892). *Plain Facts for Old and Young.* Burlington, IA: I.F. Segner.

Kempner, M.E. (2001). *Toward a Sexually Healthy America: Abstinence-Only-Until-Marriage Programs that Try to Keep Our Youth 'Scared Chaste.'* New York: Sexuality Information & Education Council of the United States.

Laflin, M.T., Sommers, J.M., & Chibucos, T.R., "Initial Findings in a Longitudinal Study of the Effectiveness of the *Sex Can Wait* Sexual Abstinence Curriculum for Grades 5–8," *American Journal of Sexuality Education,* 1(1):103–118.

Taverner, B. & Montfort, S. (2005). *Making Sense of Abstinence: Lessons for Comprehensive Sex Education.* Morristown, NJ: The Center for Family Life Education, Planned Parenthood of Greater Northern New Jersey.

U.S. House of Representatives, Committee on Government Reform (2004). *The Content of Federally Funded Abstinence-Only Education Programs,* prepared for Rep. Henry A. Waxman. Washington, DC: The House, December 2004.

Maureen Kelly

 **NO**

The Semantics of Sex Ed: Or, Shooting Ourselves in the Foot as We Walk Slowly Backwards

Should Sex Ed Teach about Abstinence?

No. And when I say no, I need to add two important caveats. First, I need to add quotation marks around the word "abstinence" because my answer pertains to the word "abstinence" not the life-affirming concept of personal choice and sexual decision-making across a vast span of sexual possibilities (more coarsely and simplistically placed on a continuum from not-doing to doing "it," whatever "it" may be). Second, when I refer to "abstinence" I am specifically referring to the strict eight-point definition of what "abstinence education" must include which is laid out in the 1996 federal Welfare Reform Law's abstinence-only-until-marriage provision. One highlight on the list of target groups for abstinence-only-until-marriage programs is all unmarried people under the age of thirty. Federally funded abstinence education for unmarried thirty year olds? Just say no.

Why do I take such issue with a word? In the dozen-plus years that I have worked as a professional sex educator I have watched secrets and lies take a growing hold on sex ed policies and programs. The highjacking of the word "abstinence" and the claiming of the moral high ground by opponents to sex ed is a striking example.

It's almost a cliché how the whole sex ed vs. abstinence ed debate has unraveled. It's just one more intentionally crafted pro vs. anti political dichotomy that infiltrates citizen's daily lives and choices. And one of the more cunning aspects of the "abstinence" conversation in America is that the Friday-night-wrestling-smack-down nature of the debate does not acknowledge that, once again, a political debate completely misses the obvious and neglects to uncover the fact that the extreme permutations of the political concept of "abstinence" as applied to health information content and funding, is a failure. Seek out the data! Read the reports! What did Waxman say? Look to Western Europe for innovative and effective roadmaps! But please, don't succumb to fear and politics and allow "abstinence" to be the only right, moral, good choice to make or lesson to teach; take a risk. Stir the pot. We need

An original essay written for this title, 2006. Copyright © 2006 by Maureen A. Kelly. Reprinted by permission.

to elevate this debate but I believe to do that we have to abandon the word "abstinence." However, when the pot is stirred, fear takes hold and people seem to freak out a bit.

When chatting about plans for an upcoming educational presentation, one teacher actually said "I didn't want a controversy, so I invited the abstinence people in." There's just so much wrong with this! First, I am amazed that a certified teacher does not find the contrary controversial! Isn't it far more controversial to deny information to youth, mislead kids about health facts, and to hold all youth to a singular heterosexual standard? And the sneaky underlying assumption is also flawed. To assume that good sex educators do not talk about sexual decision-making (of which NOT doing "it" is always an option!) is just wrong. Talking about personal sexual choices and teaching tips and tools for making effective and responsible and safe sexual decisions—yes *and no* decisions—are cornerstones of good sex ed. Again, it's dirty politics that tarnish this conversation, that make us focus our energy and worry on words and perceptions and fear of controversy or repercussions, not on young people. They are the ones losing!

The problem here is language. Semantics. Let's look at *abstinence*. Now, as a concept, abstinence is without moral judgment, without coercion and does not withhold information. Abstinence is simply about *not doing something*. People abstain from a lot of things. Certain foods, voting, paying taxes, alcohol; the scope of *abstinence* as a concept is deep and broad and has a rich social, religious, and political history filled with social protest and acts of resistance. The "abstinence" vis-à-vis sex ed discussion certainly has all that too!

As you may notice, I've been pissed off about this word for a while now. My anger bubbles up from a place of disbelief about how some people can't see the truth. I am incensed when I see people who, once exposed to the truth, whatever that truth may be—the war, gay marriage, taxes, sex ed—don't act in accordance with that truth but rather, stick fiercely to their strongly held beliefs even when they are in direct conflict with the facts.

I am also deeply troubled by the reality that many of us—sex ed advocates and educators—have gotten sucked into the defensive, no-win abstinence debate. We have science, data, a majority of parents, common sense and all of Western Europe on our side in support of smart and sane sex ed but we are losing. We are losing because we are hemorrhaging from our defensive wounds.

And, thanks to George Lakoff (UC Berkeley linguistics professor and Rockridge Institute Fellow) I have shifted from a full pissed off boil to a smarter, more informed and productive simmer. Here's why: I've been mad at the wrong things. I have been mad at issues and people, not frameworks. Although I flirt with stepping above the fray and getting glimpses of why people act (and vote) the way they do, I haven't quite grasped the depth and breadth of the real battle being waged. What has facilitated this transformation are insights from Mr. Lakoff's 2004 book *Don't Think of an Elephant: Know Your Values and Frame the Debate—The Essential Guide for Progressives* combined with reactions and reflections about how the brilliance of framing—and reframing—can help us win the sex ed war.

First and foremost, we must begin by understanding the power of mental structures—the power of *frames*. Frames are the ties that bind; they are the unconscious connectors that define our actions, reactions, perceptions and worldview. Frames are about way more than just the words; ideas are the foundation for the frame and the words are the messengers that deliver the ideas. And simply enough, in order to change the world, we must understand and acknowledge the power of these frames—as words *and* ideas—and then go about the vital business of changing them; *reframing is social change.*

> Reframing is changing the way the public sees the world. It is changing what counts as common sense. Because language activates frames, new language is required for new frames. Thinking differently requires speaking differently.[1]

The progressive movement as a whole, and we, as sex ed advocates and educators, are caught in a defensive cycle marked by reaction to words and ideas and philosophies that do not represent our view, our thinking and what we know to be true and right. As we do this we are unwittingly giving credibility to a frame that we do not believe.

Our opponents brilliantly crafted a powerful frame around "abstinence" that conjures a happy, ideal fairyland where kids are safe and protected from the mean, scary and unpredictable world. Who the heck wouldn't want that? I *love* the idea of protecting the young people I care about from bad things; it's a natural urge. So, when I say "no, I am against abstinence" (as a political and social means of control and a troubling marriage of church and state) I am in essence rejecting their frame yet still defining myself through their frame. That's where it gets really confusing! By being opposed to their idea but using their words, I end up standing for nothing.

Because, when I say "I am against abstinence," I am in effect saying, "I want kids to be unsafe, unprotected and get exposed to mean, scary and unpredictable things" (because that's what happens when you make your argument based on your opposition's language rather than your own inspiration). And none of us want that! We are caught in a defensive loop trying to explain that, yes, we believe in abstinence (safe, happy protected kids) but we want abstinence-plus or abstinence-based education (if they do end up having sex, they should have access to information and supplies that protect them); this approach is totally wrong. We are, by default, accepting our opponents' framework while trying to add our own footnote. And we have forgotten that most people don't read footnotes.[2]

One particularly troubling outcome of our tacit acceptance of our opponent's framing of abstinence is that we can easily be dismissed as confused and inconsistent (if we are for abstinence, as their frame defines it, how in the world can we be for birth control education for youth as well?). We seem to forget that "abstinence" as used by our opponents is not at all akin to the actual definition of the word, but rather it evokes a feeling, a philosophy and an idea—a frame—that is diametrically opposed to our view. The simple act of using the word "abstinence"—*no mater how we might mean it*—activates their frame, not ours. We are shooting ourselves in the foot as we walk slowly backwards.

> This gives us a basic principle of framing, for when you are arguing against the other side; do not use their language. Their language picks out a frame—and it won't be the frame you want.[3]
>
> Framing is about getting language that fits your worldview. It is not just language. The ideas are primary—and the language carries those ideas, evokes those ideas.[4]

Another problem; our in-fighting divides us and keeps us vulnerable. Why are some of us taking abstinence money and others lobbying their States to give it all back to the Feds? Why do some of us want to feverishly reclaim the language of "abstinence" while others want to totally eradicate it from our parlance? We have to ask these questions, talk about them and commit to finding and applying a common approach. We must get beyond the "my way is the right way" division of our field. We are stuck and until we step above this soul sucking and divisive in-fighting to discover and capitalize on the unity of our movement, our fight will remain amongst ourselves and do little to change the world. As all this swirls around us, we are rendering our own work less and less effective, articulate and strong because *we are fighting among ourselves in service of their vision, not ours.* We must stop our own in-fighting, stop fighting their war for them, stop using the word "abstinence" and take a bold and brave step right off the battlefield and say, why the heck are we fighting here any way? It's a bad war, not based on truth and it's not good for our country or our kids, period.

So, what should we do about this? We need to intentionally and thoughtfully become the object-center of our debate; we need to reframe our arguments for and definitions of sex ed in reference to *our* values, vision and morality; not in reference to our opponents'. We must remember that when we attack our opponents' stance by disagreeing with it but building on it rather than offering a viable alternative, we fail to move our agenda forward. *Our agenda?* Yes! Our Agenda. We do have one and we need to talk about it more.

And to do that, we have to take one more step inside Lakoff's world. We need to understand the dynamic of the strict father vs. nuturant parent paradigm. It is this paradigm that exposes the stark differences of vision and value between our opponents and us. It is precisely why, when I listen to the rhetoric of our opponents, I cringe. Why? I don't subscribe to the Strict Father frame. I'm more of a nurturant chick. At my core, I don't buy into the Father Knows Best, teach kids what to think not how to think, pick-yourself-up-by-your-bootstraps, stop your crying or I'll give you something to cry about, one nation under god, don't have sex until you're married paradigm. Conversely, I'm more of a fan of empathy and nurturance, open, two-way communication, honesty, choice, trust, integrity, opportunity and freedom.

To be effective in re-framing our version of what sex ed should be, we must understand that we cannot simply borrow from the strict father foundation of the abstinence-only-until-marriage frame, but rather, we must create and propose new and radical ideas that evoke a distinct and powerful frame that encompasses the spirit of nurturance. By nature, that cannot be a frame based on an abstinence-plus message; in fact, to be most effective, it will be an antithetical concept compared to the spirit of current abstinence messages touted by the strict father moralists.

Our version of sex ed is about asking, choosing, discussing, considering, exploring, learning, and offering open, honest access to information and exposure to diverse options. Now, that's a real alternative to the abstinence-only-until-marriage model! Maybe ours is called the teach-me-trust-me-and-mentor-me model? Or maybe the Freedom, Opportunity and Awareness Act of 2007? To be successful in reframing our work, we must understand that the battle for sex ed is a sub-battle that shares values and vision with the progressive movement as a whole. And, as we get better at gathering around our common goals—and investing less in the self-defeating, chase your own tail, me-first conundrum that is identity politics—we will triumph. Our ideas resonate with people; we simply need to find the words that resonate as much as our ideas.

But fear sells. So, we need to tell the truth and bust the myth that "abstinence will save the world" because it's just not true. The fear is real and visceral for those who worry that if we talk to kids about sex they will transmogrify into sex-crazed, insatiable fiends without remorse, protection or forethought (sounds more like a member of congress than a teen who got honest and complete sex ed). The great irony is, that despite their hearts being in the right place *(we all want our kids to be OK, safe and smart!),* they have it all wrong. The fact is, the more we talk about sex in age-appropriate, frank, honest, accurate ways, the *safer our kids are.* Yes, despite the fears and worries of well-meaning people, *when we don't give our kids sex ed, we end up with much bigger problems than when we do.* Just look at our teen pregnancy, STD, and abortion rates for that evidence!

And then, take a look at western Europe as an example of what could be. Young people in Germany, the Netherlands and France are given a lot of education and access to information about s-e-x. But here's the kicker—these European kids that are getting all this sex ed early and often, they are having less sex, with fewer partners, at a later age than their US peers, with less negative outcomes, fewer abortions, fewer teen births, and fewer STDs.[5] No kidding. It seems that the more we take the shame and taboo-filled mystique from sex and help it assume a normal, natural, spoken about and human part of our lives, the better off we all are.

So what do I propose as alternatives to abstinence-only-until-marriage programming for our kids? Simple: teach the facts, tell the truth, and include everyone. We need to work side by side to remove the shame and secrecy that shrouds our conversation and education about sex. It's the shame and secrecy that truly put our kids at risk, not sex ed.

I would like to eradicate the use of the word "abstinence" while explicitly and frequently teaching about the concept of choice vis-à-vis sex. Teach about when or whether to have sex. Teach about sexual choices and safety and responsibility. Teach about saying yes and teach about saying no. Just TEACH!

The complexities of sex, relationships, and communication require depth and breadth in teaching style; not a one-size-fits-all-just-say-no approach.

We have to talk about it and prepare for it, because sex is a part of life.

Notes

1. Page xi, *Don't Think of an Elephant! Know Your Values and Frame the Debate: The Essential Guide for Progressives,* George Lakoff, Chelsea Green Publishing, 2004.

2. Just checking. . .

3. Page 3, op cit.

4. Page 4, ibid.

5. Advocates for Youth, . . . "European Approaches to Adolescent Sexual Behavior & Responsibility," 1999.

POSTSCRIPT

Should Sex Ed Teach about Abstinence?

The debate over abstinence-only-until-marriage education was highlighted recently after it was revealed that Bristol Palin, the teenage daughter of vice preseidential candidate Sarah Palin, was pregnant. After initially making comments critical of abstinence-only education (of which her mother, the Rebublican Governor of Alaska, is a strong supporter), Palin began making appearances promoting abstinence-only education for young people. Meghan McCain, the daughter of Republican presidential candidate and Senator John McCain, caused waves among conservatives when she spoke out against abstinence-only education in a series of television appearances and blog posts.

Academics, educators, and activists may often agree on a desired outcome, but may strongly disagree on the best approach to meet that end. In her essay, Maureen Kelly argues that sex educators' use of the "frame" of abstinence only helps to serve a conservative agenda that promotes abstinence as the *only* acceptable means of contraception and STI prevention. She challenges the way in which abstinence was defined by the federal government and rejects the use of the term. Taverner embraces the term while working to challenge its definition from within the existing structure. Is Taverner shooting himself, and the movement for comprehensive sex education, in the foot, as Kelly suggests, by using the terminology of a system he seeks to question? Should Kelly and other sex educators reclaim the language of abstinence as part of comprehensive sex education, as Taverner suggests?

Should sex educators challenge preconceived notions of topics like abstinence while working within federal guidelines for abstinence-only education? What would be the benefits of such an approach? What would be the consequences? How can an educator challenge students to think about the definition(s) of abstinence and apply the possible meanings to their own decisions? In his essay, Taverner mentions a colleague proposing "delayed intercourse" as an alternative term to abstinence. Do you think Kelly would accept this term?

A new bill is being considered by Congress that would allow federal funding for more comprehensive approaches to sexuality education that *both* Taverner and Kelly might champion. This bill would require programs to:

1. Be age appropriate and medically accurate;
2. Not teach or promote religion;
3. Teach that abstinence is the only sure way to avoid pregnancy or sexually transmitted diseases;
4. Stress the value of abstinence while not ignoring those young people who have had or are having sexual intercourse;

5. Provide information about the health benefits and side effects of all contraceptives and barrier methods as a means to prevent pregnancy;
6. Provide information about the health benefits and side effects of all contraceptives and barrier methods as a means to reduce the risk of contracting sexually transmitted diseases, including HIV/AIDS;
7. Encourage family communication about sexuality between parent and child;
8. Teach young people the skills to make responsible decisions about sexuality, including how to avoid unwanted verbal, physical, and sexual advances and how not to make unwanted verbal, physical, and sexual advances; and
9. Teach young people how alcohol and drug use can affect responsible decision making.

How does this approach differ from the current federal guidelines listed in the introduction to this issue? In what ways are they similar? Which approach would you want for your children? Which of these items do you agree with? Disagree with? What do you think of the government saying that sexual behaviors should happen only within the context of marriage? Or claiming that people will suffer harmful psychological effects if they have sexual behaviors outside of marriage? Furthermore, how does a gay or lesbian person handle the message "abstinence until marriage" in a country that, except for a handful of states, makes same-sex marriages illegal?

Think back to your own sexuality education in high school. Did it include learning about condoms, contraception, and other aspects of human sexuality? Was abstinence taught? And if so, was it within the framework of the federal guidelines described by Kelly, or was it more comprehensive, as Taverner describes? If you had to give your high school sex education a grade, what would it be?

Suggested Readings

Advocates for Youth and Sexuality Education Council of the United States, *Toward a Healthy America: Roadblocks Imposed by the Federal Government's Abstinence-Only-Until-Marriage Education Program* (2001).

J. Blake, *Words Can Work: When Talking to Kids about Sexual Health* (Blake Works, 2004).

H. Brückner and P. Bearman, "After the Promise: The STD Consequences of Adolescent Virginity Pledges," *Journal of Adolescent Health* (no. 36, 2005).

M.E. Kempner, *Toward a Sexually Healthy America: Abstinence-Only-Until-Marriage Programs that Try to Keep Our Youth 'Scared Chaste'* (New York: Sexuality Information & Education Council of the United States, 2001).

D. Satcher. *The Surgeon General's Call to Action to Promote Sexual Health and Responsible Sexual Behavior* (Washington, DC: United States Department of Health and Human Services, 2001).

B. Taverner and S. Montfort, *Making Sense of Abstinence: Lessons for Comprehensive Sex Education* (Morristown, NJ: The Center for Family Life Education, Planned Parenthood of Greater Northern New Jersey, 2005).

U.S. House of Representatives, Committee on Government Reform. *The Content of Federally Funded Abstinence-Only Education Programs*, prepared for Rep. Henry A. Waxman (Washington, DC: The House, December 2004).

ISSUE 8

Does the Availability of "Sexual Health Services" Make Some College Campuses Healthier Than Others?

YES: David M. Hall, from "The Positive Impact of Sexual Health Services on College Campuses," an original essay written for this volume (2007)

NO: Jens Alan Dana, from "A Different Sort of Measure," an original essay written for this volume (2006)

ISSUE SUMMARY

YES: David M. Hall, a graduate professor of human sexuality at Widener University, outlines and comments favorably on the "Sexual Health Report Card," a ranking of 100 universities in the United States by Trojan Condoms. Dr. Hall describes the various sexual health indicators for college campuses, as measured by the report, and argues for better sexuality education programs.

NO: Jens Alan Dana, a student and school newspaper editor at Brigham Young University, which was ranked lowest in the Trojan survey, argues that the rankings were unscientific, and based on a subjective set of criteria that were self-serving to Trojan's interests in marketing condoms.

Have you ever considered what makes a college campus "sexually healthy"? College students are used to being graded all the time in the courses they take. A report card filled with "A's" naturally signifies excellence; one with "F's" is failing, with many possibilities in between. In 2006, the makers of Trojan brand condoms gave a report card to 100 college campuses, grading them in terms of their sexual health, as measured by seven categories:

1. **Web site**—Does the school offer a helpful and informative sexual information Web site? Consider, for example the "Go Ask Alice!" Web site operated by New York's Columbia University, which was not evaluated in this study.

2. **Condoms**—Does the school offer condoms (at the health center, or elsewhere), with directions to help its students avoid sexually transmitted infections and unwanted pregnancy?
3. **Contraception**—Are other methods of contraception available on campus, including emergency contraception? Is information about the benefits and drawbacks of different types of contraception provided?
4. **HIV & STD Testing**—Are HIV and other tests for sexually transmitted infections available on campus? Are they free? Are results timely?
5. **Sexual Assault Counseling**—Are sexual assault counseling services available on campus? Is there a hotline or Web site for students who have been sexually assaulted?
6. **Advice Column**—Does the student newspaper feature a forum that addresses sexual issues?
7. **Counseling Services/Other Outreach**—Does the college offer other services, such as peer counseling, campus events, or other outreach?

Based on these criteria, at least one college was graded in each of the 50 states. Yale finished #1, the only college with straight A's. But Ivy League status was not a clear indicator of sexual health as Trojan measured it: Dartmouth finished #63 and Harvard and Brown finished #43 and #44. The results were also not regional: The top five were from all parts of the country, from the East Coast to the West Coast, and middle America too!

There were some commonalities in the lower ranking schools. Ranked #99 was the Catholic institution Notre Dame, and at #100 was Brigham Young University, run by the Church of Latter Day Saints. Christian leaders cried "Foul!" saying that the Trojan standards were not fair indicators of "sexual health" to campuses that championed Christian values of sexual abstinence before marriage. Christian minister Albert Mohler declared that schools who scored well on the Trojan report card actually abdicated their "in loco parentis" responsibility to guide the morality of their students.

In the following essays, David M. Hall, a professor who teaches a graduate course on the history and ethics of human sexuality, outlines and comments on the importance of the findings of the Trojan Sexual Health Report Card, and advocates for sexuality education. Jens Alan Dana, an editor for *The Daily Universe,* the student newspaper of Brigham Young University, responds that the rankings were unscientific, and based on a subjective set of criteria that were self-serving to Trojan's interests in marketing condoms.

YES

David M. Hall

The Positive Impact of Sexual Health Services on College Campuses

Sexual Health of Teenagers and Young Adults

The average age of first sexual intercourse is 17.4 for girls and 16.9 for boys. Among high school students, 17 percent of males and 12 percent of females have already had four or more sexual partners. Those ages 18–24 are more likely to choose the birth control pill over a condom as their primary method of contraception (Kaiser Family Foundation, 2006). By the age of 21, almost 20 percent of Americans require treatment for a sexually transmitted infection (STI) (Van Vranken, 2004). The majority of teens and college students are sexually active. While this is true in every region of America, the quality of sexuality information and resources varies significantly from one school to another.

It is clear that too many teens and college students are making sexual decisions that can have an adverse impact on their future. Considering this fact, colleges and universities have a responsibility to help their students make sexual decisions consistent with their goals. Trojan condoms generated significant attention for venturing into this debate with a study of their own, ranking the sexual health on 100 college campuses. The results of this research were published in newspapers and blogs across America. Due to Trojan's support for safer sex information and resources, those opposed to providing students with scientifically accurate sexuality information were quick to criticize this study.

The Trojan National Survey of Sexual Health on College Campuses

Trojan condoms, the popular condom manufacturer, ranked 100 universities for their effectiveness in fostering healthy sexuality on college campuses. These rankings were of schools across America that are both large in population and familiar to the general public. Trojan stated that these results represented 23 percent of U.S. undergraduate students at four-year colleges (Bruno, 2006).

An original essay written for this volume. Copyright © 2007 by David M. Hall. Reprinted by permission.

Trojan gave each of the 100 schools a grade point average (GPA) and rank based on the following seven categories:

1. **A college or university website that offers sexuality information and advice.** Specific criteria included whether the website is easy to find, easy to navigate, informative (e.g., hours, location, services, costs, departments, testing, assault reporting, and counseling), offers online advice, provides STD/STI information and treatment, and provides email communication with staff.
2. **The availability of condoms and safer sex information and advice.** Specific criteria included whether condoms are available from the college health center, the cost of condoms, and providing instructions and cautions for condom use.
3. **The availability of contraception and safer sex information and advice.** Specific criteria included discussions of benefits and drawbacks of contraception, the availability of emergency contraception, and health notices and updates.
4. **On-campus testing for HIV and other STDs.** Specific criteria included the type of testing, timeliness of the results, the cost of testing, and whether this is provided on or off-site.
5. **Counseling and services for survivors of sexual assault.** Specific criteria included a separate sexual assault website, sexual assault services, counseling, and a 24-hour hotline.
6. **A school newspaper or web-based column featuring advice regarding sexuality issues or relationships.** Specific criteria included a feature in the student newspaper or an online forum, addressing issues from the student body, and providing links to national columns such as "Go Ask Alice."
7. **Education through campus community outreach such as counseling services, peer counseling, campus events, and other programs.** Specific criteria included peer counseling programs, specialized counseling programs, campus education programs, special events, and guest speakers.

Based on an examination of these criteria, Trojan revealed the top ten schools of the 100 surveyed for having policies that promote positive sexual health on campus: (1) Yale University, 4.0 GPA; (2) University of Iowa, 3.6 GPA; (3) University of Michigan-Ann Arbor, 3.6 GPA; (4) Stanford University, 3.6 GPA; (5) Oregon State University, 3.4 GPA; (6) Princeton University, 3.4 GPA; (7) University of New Hampshire, 3.4 GPA; (8) Duke University, 3.4 GPA; (9) Ohio State University, 3.3 GPA; and (10) University of Illinois at Urbana-Champaign, 3.1 GPA.

The schools that scored at the bottom of the Trojan study are (90) Minnesota State University–Mankato, 0.9 GPA; (91) University of Nevada–Reno, 0.9 GPA; (92) University of Wyoming, 0.9 GPA; (93) University of Louisville, 0.7 GPA; (94) Texas Tech, 0.7 GPA; (95) Clemson University, 0.6 GPA; (96) University of Memphis, 0.3 GPA; (97) Oklahoma State University, 0.1 GPA; (98) University of Utah, 0.1 GPA; (99) University of Notre Dame, 0.0 GPA; and (100) Brigham Young University (0.0 GPA).

According to a Trojan's press release announcing the study results, Vice President of Marketing Jim Daniels provided the following rationale for programs that provide for the sexual health of college students: "We live in a country with the highest rates of new STIs and unintended pregnancies of any Western nation, and we applaud those schools that provide fact-based, accurate and comprehensive information about sexual health to all students. While we understand there are a variety of reasons some schools do not provide these resources to students, we feel that comprehensive education and access to information is the best way to ensure people make smart decisions about protection should they choose to be sexually active" (Bruno, 2006).

Daniels continued by explaining the implications of this research and recommended action: "We know that 18- to 24-year-olds use condoms only for one in four sex acts, and we believe that it is important for those who choose to be sexually active and are at risk for STIs to understand the risks, and use a condom for every sex act. With this survey, we hope to shine a light on the need for greater discussion about these issues, which can help lead to lower rates of infection and unintended pregnancies" (Bruno, 2006).

The survey reveals valuable data for constructing a sexually healthy undergraduate campus. The Trojan study found that of the schools they examined, 93 percent offered some type of student testing of HIV and STI but only 24 percent offered this testing for free. Only 32 percent of schools had any sort of sex column available online or through the college newspaper. Only 24 percent of the colleges and universities surveyed provided free condoms for students (Bruno, 2006). The survey demonstrated that too few schools are acknowledging and supporting the sexual health needs of their students.

Discussion

Of course critics of this research stress the flaws of this study, and some of their criticisms are valid. First, it is in Trojan's economic best interest to encourage the use of condoms. A corporation certainly would not release a scientific study unless it strengthened the argument for the consumption of their product. Second, there are other criteria that could be useful for a thorough examination of the sexual health of a campus. For example, an examination of required course content related to sexuality information would have been preferable to gathering information about student programs with optional and haphazard attendance.

While this research has its flaws—and though critics are adamant about stressing the study's flaws—it is critical to note that all studies have flaws. Of course weaknesses in the research should be acknowledged by anyone examining the results. Furthermore, it is difficult to rank in a hierarchy the sexual health of 100 colleges.

However, the flaws of this study are secondary concerns from the standpoint of examining sexual health on college campuses. The criteria examined in the Trojan study merits consideration about the sexual health of a school community. The seven criteria from this study, though imperfect, if implemented properly can foster sexual literacy and improved sexual decision making consistent with one's future goals.

The criterion of this research is in stark contrast to the hundreds of millions of taxpayer dollars being spent on abstinence-only education. Studies have demonstrated that teens who pledge abstinence fail to see that translate into lower rates of contracting STIs (Bruckner and Bearman, 2005). Furthermore, Marty Klein (2006) illustrated that abstinence-only education disadvantages teens and young adults because it is preparing millions of youths for what they will not experience: abstinence until marriage.

It is the well intentioned but misguided supporters of abstinence-only education who are leading critics of Trojan's research. A closer examination of the seven criteria of the Trojan study is merited considering the reactionary criticism of this study.

First, evaluating a school's website is a valuable and necessary inclusion when rating the sexual health of a school. College students obtain a wide variety of information online. Scientifically accurate sexuality information available via a website is significantly less threatening for many students when compared with asking questions in person. Unfortunately, the average web surfer may be unaware of which websites offer credible and scientifically accurate information. A school-based website addresses this problem. Any college or university that offers this information to their students can disseminate quality sexuality information at the student's convenience.

Second, access to condoms and scientifically accurate information about condoms is critical. As noted earlier, young people prefer using the birth control pill over condoms (Kaiser Family Foundation, 2006). While the birth control pill provides significant protection from pregnancy, it fails to protect students from contracting HIV and other STIs. Disseminating condoms and scientifically accurate information allows sexually active students the opportunity to minimize their chances of contracting HIV and other STIs. Furthermore, free condoms ensure that students obtain the safer sex protection that they need regardless of their socioeconomic status.

Third, information about other forms of contraception allows sexually active heterosexual students to dramatically reduce their chances of an unintended pregnancy. A reduction in unintended pregnancies leads to a subsequent reduction in abortions. Contraception allows students to maximize their birth control options in the event that they choose to be sexually active. Free access to contraception ensures that students obtain the necessary pregnancy reduction methods regardless of their socioeconomic status.

Fourth, HIV and STI testing are critical to avoid students further spreading these viruses and infections. Those who are sexually active and at-risk should get tested so that they can take the necessary steps to protect others with which they might otherwise be sexually active. If these tests are free and guarantee confidentiality or anonymity, students will be further encouraged to obtain regular tests.

Fifth, students who are survivors of sexual assault have a variety of needs that a college or university has the responsibility to provide. They have emotional needs that are critical to address through counseling due to the pain and humiliation of their experience. They may need emergency contraception in the event that the victim is a woman who has been vaginally raped by a man. They may want to get tested for a STI. If they have reason to believe that the rapist is HIV positive, they may want to take post exposure prophylaxis for one month to reduce by 79 percent their chance of contracting HIV (New Mexico AIDS Education and Training Center, 2006).

Sixth, it is disheartening to learn that only one-third of schools had any type of sex advice column. Peer education about abstinence, contraception, HIV, sexual transmitted infections, sexual assault, dating violence, lesbian and gay issues, transgender issues, and other human sexuality topics can be extraordinarily influential. Peers have a unique level of credibility in educating about these sensitive issues. The anonymity of a website and newspaper column allows students to explore these issues without having to ask potentially embarrassing questions.

Seventh, counseling and education programs are critical in helping students make informed sexual decisions. While website and newspaper information are valuable tools for raising awareness, effective sexuality education must also work to change behavior. In effective sexuality education, cognitive, affective, and behavioral learning domains are addressed (Hedgepeth and Helmich, 1996). Campus programs can be particularly effective in addressing the behavioral learning domain. Seminars, workshops, and other campus events can help students develop the skills to make decisions in the best interest of their sexual health.

The Trojan study might have been further enhanced by examining what qualities are found in effective sexuality education programs. Simply meeting Trojan's criteria does not mean that the education is effectively impacting sexual decision making and behavior. According to the National Campaign to Prevent Teen Pregnancy (2003), effective sexuality education programs . . .

1. **Have a specific, narrow focus on behavioral goals.** For example, spend significant time on goals such as delaying sexual intercourse or using condoms.
2. **Are based on theoretical approaches that have been effective in influencing other risky health-related behavior.** This can be evidenced by including the reasoned action theory, cognitive behavior theory, and planned behavior theory. These theories are used to identify the risks and the reasons for behavioral change.
3. **Provide clear messages about sex and protection against STDs or pregnancy.** For example, consistently convincing students that not having sex or using condoms is the best thing to do.
4. **Provide basic, not detailed, information.** An example of this can be emphasizing the basic facts that young people need to avoid unprotected sex rather than details about all forms of contraception.
5. **Address peer pressure.** An effective strategy is to discuss beliefs and misperceptions of sex and sexual pressure.
6. **Teach communication skills.** For example, providing information about and practicing the skills of communication, such as negotiation and refusal, are critical in effective sexuality education.

7. **Include activities that are interactive.** Such methodologies include games, simulations, small group discussions, role-playing, and written exercises that will personalize the experience for participants.
8. **Reflect the age, sexual experience, and culture of the young people in the program.** For college age students, programs should emphasize avoiding unprotected sex, stressing abstinence, and the cultural norms experienced by students who are having sex.
9. **Last longer than several hours.** Programs that last longer than 14 hours are shown to have the greatest impact on sexual behavior.
10. **Carefully select leaders and train them.** Those who provide trainings should have been trained from six hours to three days in content information and teaching strategies.

A challenge in implementing these programs on college campuses are that they are achieved most easily with a captive audience in a curriculum-based setting. However, colleges should work to implement high-yield strategies for effective sexuality education as much as possible as they are research-based solutions that will foster healthier sexual activity. Clearly, significant challenges and roadblocks exist in finding ways to provide the depth of experiences that impact sexual decision making and behavior.

Regardless of the imperfections of the Trojan study, the company has triggered a valuable debate on college and university campuses about the best way to disseminate information and resources to promote the sexual health of their student body. At its core, this study is urging colleges and universities to maximize access to sexuality information and resources. Students would be well-advised to closely examine the study and question their own institution on ways in which the sexual well-being of their student body can be best supported. Combining Trojan's areas of examination with the National Campaign to Prevent Teen Pregnancy's ten qualities for effective sexuality education will enhance the sexual health of college students.

References

Bruckner, H., & Bearman, P. (2005). After the promise: The STD consequences of adolescent virginity pledges. *Journal of Adolescent Health, 36,* 271–278.

Bruno, M. (2006, September 19). New survey points to disparity of access to information about sexual health on college campuses nationwide: Yale tops list as most sexually healthy on Trojan Sexual Health Report Card. Edelman.

Hedgepeth, E. and Helmich, J. (1996). *Teaching about sexuality and HIV: Principles and methods for effective education.* New York: New York University Press.

Kaiser Family Foundation (2006, September). Sexual health statistics for teenagers and young adults in the United States. . . .

Klein, M. (2006). *America's war on sex: The attack on law, lust and liberty.* Westport, CT: Praeger.

National Campaign to Prevent Teen Pregnancy (2003, September). Science says: Characteristics of effective curriculum-based programs.

New Mexico AIDS Education and Training Center (2006, August 11). Fact sheet 156: Treatment after exposure to HIV. . . .

Van Vranken, M. (2004, November). About sexually transmitted diseases (STDs). . . .

A Different Sort of Measure

Fishermen and marketing agents have more in common than you'd imagine. Among other things, they both have the same objective—to get attention. Even as a fisherman knows he needs to draw a fish to his bait to have a successful day, a marketing director knows he needs to get his company's logo in the public spotlight to keep afloat. It doesn't matter how much money the fisherman spent on his equipment or how much money fueled the marketing director's ad campaign. At the end of the day, if the fisherman's cooler is empty or if the marketing director's promotion doesn't attract anyone's attention, they've both failed.

A lousy fisherman will just skewer a worm with a hook and cast it out into the middle of the lake, hoping a fish will notice it. In much the same way, a mediocre marketing director will buy advertising space in a newspaper, commercial time on a television channel or a billboard on a freeway, and hope that draws attention to his company. On the other hand, an expert fisherman will know his prey. He will bait his hook with a mayfly—the most beautiful of all aquatic insects, and he won't just stand on the lakeshore, waiting for the fish to come to his bait; he will cast it where he knows the fish will find it. In the same way, an expert marketing director won't flippantly spend his company's money on methods that may or may not attract attention. He will entice the public's attention with bait that is too irresistible to pass up.

Marketing directors work with a different sort of bait, of course. Instead of a lure fashioned to look like a tasty bug, they often use news releases—concisely written documents intended to "tip off" the media about something newsworthy the company is doing. Instead of a plump rainbow trout, the marketing director is fishing for the media's attention. He knows that if he can produce a news release that catches the media's interest, he will catch the public's attention. His company will score free an article in the local newspaper and perhaps a 45-second feature on the local evening news. If the marketing director did his job right, he'll be able to catch multiple media outlets with the same news release, just like his fisherman colleague catches many fish with the same bait. Even as fishermen have their tall tales and legends, future marketing prodigies will spin folklore about the Trojan Sexual Health Report—the news release that hooked a thousand newspapers.

It's important to understand the genesis of this whole chain of events was a simple news release. It's the reason the tidal wave of hastily written,

An original article for this volume. Copyright © 2006 by Jens Alan Dana. Reprinted by permission.

anonymous blogs swept through the Internet, one of which sarcastically stated, "[Brigham Young University's] sex education policy: don't talk about it and they won't do it." It's why idealistic, ill-informed freshman rifled off letters to BYU's campus newspaper, *The Daily Universe,* decrying "backward and utterly irresponsible university policies." It's what prompted news reporters around the country to shower a BYU spokeswoman's office with phone calls, demanding an explanation, and a good sound bite, for the so-called lack of on-campus sexual health services. Before all of this happened, there was a 12-page news release that Trojan, the condom manufacturer, disseminated to the media.

I first learned of the Trojan study when I unfolded a copy of Utah's *Desert Morning News* and a bolded, triple-stack, front-page headline jumped off the page at me 3-dimensional style, screaming, "Does BYU deserve F or A for sex health?" I reread the headline to make sure I understood it correctly, and then I laughed so hard the muscles on the back of my head cramped up. What's so funny is BYU is one of the largest, privately owned, religious universities in the nation that requires each of its students to adhere to a strict code of sexual abstinence while they are registered students. This policy of abstinence is an extension of the teachings of the university's owner and operator—The Church of Jesus Christ of Latter-day Saints. While this policy appears restrictive, and downright cruel, I should stress that each student who enrolls voluntarily commits to this standard. The majority of BYU students come from homes where we were taught sexual relations should be reserved until marriage. We are fully aware of the campus' abstinence policy before we come here; in fact, many of us came here because of it. My freshman year of college, I studied at a community college in Wyoming, and, by the end of the year, I was weary of ending dates by explaining that I wasn't turning down their advances because I didn't think they were attractive. When I came to BYU, it was refreshing to be among peers that shared my value; it was also great to no longer be known as "the guy that hasn't been laid yet" (it's amazing how quickly college gossip spreads, isn't it?).

While I'm not delusional enough to believe an abstinence-only policy means the BYU campus' collective sexual health is without blemish, I've always been confident enough that we have a clean bill of health, compared to other universities. Yet, Trojan challenged that belief by awarding our school seven straight goose eggs, which results in a solid 0.0 sexual health GPA and a 100th-place ranking—a place BYU is not used to being at when it comes to university rankings. After I finished the *Desert Morning News* article, I noticed the other local newspapers in Utah County also ran front-page stories based on the study. Later that day, I checked the Internet to see what other news organizations were covering the health report. A Google search for "Trojan Sexual Health Report" revealed more than 300,000 results. I found many college newspaper articles based on the report, but I was also amazed to see a large number of stories written by professional newspapers. On the blogosphere, the valiant bloggers were already dissecting the contents of several news articles based on the news release. One anonymous blogger said he hoped the ranking would awaken the university to the irresponsible nature of its policies regarding the treatment of sexual health topics on campus. He warned, "This stick-your-head-in-the-sand approach is going to come back to bite you in the butt." Again, the back of my head started to cramp. Once I'd rubbed the laugh-induced cramp out of my neck, I decided the serious tone of the blog posts and the news articles warranted an inspection of the actual health report. After all, I am a journalist. Besides, I might have laughed too quickly. I tracked-down a copy and reviewed the Trojan Sexual Health Report. For a moment, I was a fish, swimming through a cloudy lake. I spotted a flash of light. I swam up to it and circled it a few times. The scent emanating from the object nearly overpowered me, and I almost bit down on it. I almost swallowed the health report, hook, line and sinker. But then, I saw the hook.

From the various blogs on the Internet, as well as several letters to the editor, it seems people think the last-place finish meant BYU is a festering, decadent cesspool, a veritable cornucopia of every possible STD known to man. I must admit I too was misled by the perceived aura of credibility the newspaper articles radiated. The articles based on the study touted some very serious national statistics about the rate of STDs and a very credible company compiled the ranking system for Trojan. But after seeing the source of all this discussion, I realize Trojan Sexual Health Report is simply a news release cam-ouflaged as a credible sexual health report. It is a manifestation of the differing philosophies that BYU and Trojan brand condoms have when it comes to promoting sexual health. Moreover, the "health report" contains serious flaws in research methods and data analysis that undermine its conclusions.

Trojan's marketing director cleverly labeled the document a health report, but it is a news release in every sense of the word—and a good one, too. Whatever Trojan is paying their marketing staff isn't enough because this team clearly demonstrated an uncanny ability to bait the media. Upon first glance, the news release seems credible. It's a list comprising 100 different universities and colleges across the U.S., ranked according to their level of sexual health. According to the news release's methodology, Sperling's Best Places—an agency that specializes in data analysis—appraised each school based on several different criteria, including:

- The availability of sex health information on a university's Web site.
- The availability of condoms and contraception on campus.
- Provision of HIV and STD testing at student health centers.
- Sexual assault counseling and services.
- Whether or not the university newspaper publishes a sex advice columnist or not.
- The proliferation of sex discussions on campus.

The criteria seem fairly reasonable, but bear in mind who's sponsoring and contracting the health report—Trojan. If the underlying message of the news release were boiled down to its most basic substance, it would be "Supply more condoms to university students and the national rate of STDs and unwanted pregnancies will decrease." The news release even included a plug for Trojan brand condoms, "America's No. 1 condom." What more can be expected? Trojan is a commercial business that profits from the sale of condoms. It's similar to a news release *The Daily Universe* received December 2005 from The Princeton Review and Wrigley. The Princeton review cited high numbers of stressed college students during final examinations and recommended chewing gum to abate the problem. Surprise, surprise, they said chewing gum reduces stress. I don't contest Trojan's right to distribute material promoting their products, but to do so under the guise of intellectual or academic qualifications is dishonest, to say the least. In fact, for Trojan to be ranking universities based on availability of condoms is like putting the rooster in charge of guarding the henhouse, as one of my professors phrased it. If the ranking were a genuine research project, it would be heavily challenged and picked apart under peer review. The fact that a company that has a demonstrated interest in the report's conclusions sired this study undermines it credibility because it neglects to include other solutions to help reduce the national rate of STDs.

It is a disappointment, but not a surprise, that the Trojan news release didn't list abstinence as a solution to the STD pandemic. It's not in their business' interests to promote alternatives that would compromise their sales promotion. Besides, since they ranked both BYU and Notre Dame at the bottom of the report card, they appear to believe abstinence-only policies must be at the root of the spike of STD rates. It's not an argument I'm unfamiliar with. Critics often assume the abstinence-only policy is a shabby attempt to address the spread of STDs and unwanted pregnancies without broaching the subject of sex. Teaching abstinence only worsens the problem, they claim, because it propagates ignorance about sexual health. Proponents of abstinence, they dispute, brainwash people to believe sex is "dirty," something to fear, something to sweep under the rug. Some critics punctuate their point by simplifying an abstinence talk into a satirical scenario:

"Son . . . uh, what do you know about abstinence?"
"Doesn't it mean don't have sex?"
"That's right. I'm glad we had this talk."

I concede critics' claims are not always untrue. In fact, I know several people who have grown up with a meager knowledge regarding sexual health because their parents were too reticent to talk about sex. The seven straight Fs the Trojan Health Report Card awarded BYU assume we, the college students, are a generation of young adults raised in a bubble, a throng of individuals who are void of any knowledge regarding sexual health. But, in Sperling's haste to assess our school, they failed to accurately depict the sexual health education we receive at BYU.

The news release's ranking system is severely flawed because Sperling representatives didn't contact a single administrator or student at BYU while they graded the university's sexual health services. They just surfed the BYU Web site to see what they could find on the issue. It's true the university's Web site doesn't dedicate a whole section to matters pertaining to sexual health, but that does not mean services aren't available on campus. The Women's Services and Resources Center frequently sponsors classes on healthy relationships, pornography addiction and seminars aimed to educate women on what to do if they are sexually assaulted. In addition, if Sperling researchers would have gone beyond the skim-only method, they would have discovered BYU's student health center does provide prescriptions for contraceptives and tests for HIV and STDs. These blunders and misrepresentations of fact show exactly how lackadaisically Sperling approached this study, but it also undercuts the study's authoritative statement that BYU students know little or nothing about sex.

We believe the subject of sex is a discussion that is too important to be left to a student to study on his or her own. Just because BYU students agree to practice strict abstinence doesn't mean we don't talk about sex or know nothing about it. I've enrolled in general requirement classes where we've discussed sexually transmitted diseases. I've sat through lectures where we've unabashedly discussed sexual intercourse. I know what a diaphragm is, and I know what a condom is. BYU students aren't as clueless as the 0.0 GPA implies. We understand the severity of becoming infected with a sexually transmitted disease. But more important than this, the religious climate of our school allows our discussions to transcend the mere physical consequences of sex. In an environment nurtured by understanding, we learn that the sexual relationship is one that encompasses a person's emotional and—dare I say it?—spiritual being. Contrary to critics' assumption, we don't think sex is filthy; we don't fear it; we don't sweep it under the rug. We believe that sex is the ultimate expression of love that should be reserved for one's spouse. Are our reasons primarily a matter of morality? Yes. But as time passes, our reasons are also becoming highly pragmatic as well. The policy of abstinence reaffirms our values, but it is also our way to curb the spread of STDs and unplanned pregnancies. According to Trojan's methodology, we are sexually unhealthy, but a less-subjective, more factual measure of sexual health proves otherwise.

If Trojan is correct in its assumptions, a school that ranks lower on its sexual health report should be more prone to a higher incidence of STDs and unwanted pregnancies. This trend should be manifest in credible, published statistics. Although it's difficult to procure numbers for the rate of STDs at BYU, we can examine the statistics of the Utah County Health Office, where the BYU Student Health Center, and a dozen other health centers, report their statistics annually. According to the Health Center, Utah County reported 94 people in 100,000 suffered from chlamydia in 2005, which is nearly a fourth of the national average. Health officials concede they saw a 50 percent increase in the number of chlamydia cases treated, but they attribute this increase to more efficient and acceptable testing methods, rather than a sudden outbreak. In addition to this low rate, the Utah Department of Health Web site stated Utah ranked 43rd with a gonorrhea rate of 28.8 cases per 100,000 people, compared with 113.5 cases per 100,000 nationwide. Also, the state of Utah ranked 37th for syphilis rates of .32 per 100,000. If Trojan factored these statistics into its ranking system, BYU would not have faired so poorly. Instead, Trojan opted not to include such statistics and chose rather to conduct biased research that would support their preconceived notions that those colleges with a higher visibility of sexual health services will naturally have a cleaner bill of health.

But we cannot be naïve enough to believe throwing condoms at the problem, and drilling young people over and over again on the dangers of unprotected sex, will effectually solve the problem.

I don't discredit Trojan's intentions for drafting the news release. STD prevention is a serious issue we need to address. As Trojan stated, 65 million Americans suffer from an STD and, by the end of the year, another 19 million more will be infected. This pernicious plague not only causes untold physical and emotional suffering to those infected individuals, it also costs millions of dollars to treat annually. Trojan's intent to generate much-needed discussion is well placed. They are to be applauded for devising a marketing ploy that attracted so much attention and generated so much public discussion. But they demonstrated inadequate research methods and exercised preferential treatment, endorsing a course of action that favors their commercial interests. In determining which schools were sexually healthier than other schools based on subjective measures, rather than hard statistics, their findings inaccurately reflected BYU students as an uneducated horde whose "antiquated standard" of abstinence is counterproductive because it propagates ignorance about sexual health. But we believe our commitment to abstinence doesn't inhibit our knowledge about sexual health; it enables us to discuss sex from a physical, emotional and spiritual perspective. A long time ago, abstinence was purely a matter of morality and tradition. But the sexual revolution mitigated the social mores concerning abstinence and downplayed the special nature of the sexual relationship. Sex became as casual as a handshake, and, as a consequence, the spread of STDs has become just as casual. Attempts to counter the tide of STDs have improved over the years, but for all the technological advances, there is still no prophylactic as effective as abstinence. Trojan probably thought if they included this in their news release, it would compromise the strength of their assertion. Unfortunately, they didn't realize shabby research methods and prejudiced conclusions already weakened their assertion.

POSTSCRIPT

Does the Availability of "Sexual Health Services" Make Some College Campuses Healthier Than Others?

It might be interesting to investigate how "sexually healthy" your college campus is, based on the criteria set forth in the Trojan report. (Take a look at the full list of rankings on the pages that follow.) If your university was ranked, do you agree with the report's assessment of your school? If your school was not ranked, how do you think it would fare? What is your university Web site like? Can you get accurate sexual information? The report mentioned Columbia University's Web site "Go Ask Alice!" as a model (see www.alice.columbia.edu). How would you rate this Web site? How about your school newspaper—is there a regular column for sexual advice or information?

How available are condoms or other contraceptives? Emergency contraception? If a student is worried about HIV or other sexually transmitted infections, can she or he get tested easily on campus? Is rape crisis counseling available? What types of counseling services are available? Does your college offer a "Sex Week" like Yale's or peer-counseling programs like those offered at many other universities?

Are these appropriate indicators of "sexual health"? What other indicators of sexual health would you identify? For students studying at religious institutions, that might prohibit such sexual services or require sexual abstinence of their students, what criteria do you think would be appropriate to measure sexual health? Should there be separate measurements based on the ideologies fostered by different school cultures?

Dr. Hall commented on studies of teens who pledge abstinence. This research examined high school–aged teens who make virginity pledges, and found that 88 percent of these teens fail to keep their pledge. Those who are more successful tend to delay sexual intercourse for about 18 months. Research on colleges that ask students to make an abstinence pledge in accordance with their policies has not yet been compiled. Do you think young adults would be more successful with abstinence pledges in college or less successful? Why? Would your expectation be any different if the student were entering a university such as Brigham Young, where the student knows the school's expectations regarding student sexuality? Should a university offer preventative sexual health services, and treatment services for college students who change their decisions and decide to have sexual intercourse?

What do you think of Trojan issuing the report? Is it all about marketing hype (i.e., to sell more condoms), as Jens Alan Dana charges, and does that diminish the credibility or significance of the report's findings? Finally, what did you think of Dr. Hall's advocacy for sexuality education at the collegiate level? How does his description of effective sexuality education programs compare with the sex ed courses that you might have had at your university or high school?

Suggested Readings

M. Bruno, "New Survey Points to Disparity of Access to Information about Sexual Health on College Campuses Nationwide: Yale Tops List as Most Sexually Healthy on Trojan Sexual Health Report Card," *Edelman* (September 2006).

N. Doyle, "Auburn Ranks Low in Sexual Health Survey," *The Auburn Plainsman* (September 26, 2006).

S. Duin, "Orange and Black, Their Condoms Wave," *The Oregonian* (September 28, 2006).

C. Macbeth, "University Earns a Clean Bill of Health," *Yale Daily News* (September 26, 2006).

A. Mohler, "The Corruption of the University," www.albertmohler.com (September 2006).

S. Rosenbloom, "Here's Your Syllabus, and Your Condom," *New York Times* (September 24, 2006).

M. Slevin, "Monitoring Sex at C.U.," *The Cornell Daily Sun* (October 11, 2006).

C. Zach, "CSU Ranks 23rd in Sex Knowledge," *The Rocky Mountain Collegian* (October 30, 2006).

Internet References . . .

Alliance for Marriage

Alliance for Marriage is a nonprofit research and education organization dedicated to promoting marriage and addressing the epidemic of fatherless families in the United States. It educates the public, the media, elected officials, and civil society leaders on the benefits of marriage for children, adults, and society.

http://www.allianceformarriage.org

Alternatives to Marriage Project

The Alternatives to Marriage Project advocates for equality and fairness for unmarried people, including people who choose not to marry, cannot marry, or live together before marriage.

http://www.unmarried.org

American Family Association

The American Family Association is a national nonprofit organization that advocates for "traditional family values" through activism aimed at media outlets and advertisers, including those on the Internet.

www.afa.net

Electronic Frontier Foundation

The Electronic Frontier Foundation works to educate the press, policymakers, and the general public about civil liberties issues related to technology.

http://www.eff.org.

Federal Communications Commission (FCC)

The FCC is a United States government agency charged with regulating interstate and international communications by radio, television, wire, satellite, and cable.

http://www.fcc.gov

The Alan Guttmacher Institute

The Alan Guttmacher Institute is a nonprofit organization focused on sexual and reproductive health research, policy analysis, and public education.

www.guttmacher.org

The Coalition Against Trafficking in Women–International

The Coalition Against Trafficking in Women is an international organization focused on ending sexual exploitation, including the sex trafficking of women and girls.

www.catwinternational.org

Sex and Society

*C*ompeting *philosophical forces drive concerns about human sexuality on a societal level. Some are primarily focused on the well-being of individuals (or groups of individuals) and their right to individual expression versus their protection from harm; others are mainly concerned with either maintaining or questioning established social norms; still others are engaged by the extent to which the law should impose on a citizen's privacy. This section examines six such questions that affect our social understanding of sexuality.*

- Should Children Have an HPV Vaccination before They Enroll in School?
- Should Libraries and Other Places That Provide Public Wi-Fi Restrict Sexual Content?
- Should the FCC Fine TV Stations That Broadcast Indecency?
- Should Prostitution Be Legalized?
- Should Society Support Cohabitation before Marriage?

ISSUE 9

Should Children Have an HPV Vaccination before They Enroll in School?

YES: Cynthia Dailard, from "The Public Health Promise and Potential Pitfalls of the World's First Cervical Cancer Vaccine," *The Guttmacher Report on Public Policy* (Winter 2006)

NO: Roni Rabin, from "A New Vaccine for Girls, but Should It Be Compulsory?" *New York Times* (July 18, 2006)

ISSUE SUMMARY

YES: Cynthia Dailard, a senior public policy associate for the Alan Guttmacher Institute, outlines the potential for a new vaccination to prevent the spread of the human papillomavirus (HPV), a sexually transmitted infection that causes genital warts and most cases of cervical cancer. Dailard explains and summarizes the views of experts who believe that widespread vaccinations of preadolescent girls will dramatically reduce the incidence of HPV in the United States and abroad, especially in developing nations.

NO: *New York Times* columnist Roni Rabin acknowledges the potential for the HPV vaccination, but contends that cervical cancer can be staved off more economically by encouraging girls and women to have routine Pap smears.

What is HPV? Many people who know about sexually transmitted infections (STI), like genital herpes, gonorrhea, and HIV, seem to be surprisingly unfamiliar with the term human papillomavirus (HPV). Yet HPV is one of the most common STIs in the United States! The acronym HPV includes more than 100 strains of viruses, about 30 of which can infect the genital area. The Centers for Disease Control (CDC) estimates that 20 million Americans are currently infected with HPV and that 6.2 million Americans are newly infected every year. The CDC further estimates that at least *half* of people who have intercourse will acquire HPV at some point in their lives. Some HPV infections can cause cervical cancer. Strains of HPV can sometimes cause genital warts.

Genital or anal cancers caused by HPV are possible but appear to be rare. Some recent studies have also shown a link between HPV and some mouth and throat cancers.

In June 2006, the United States Food and Drug Administration (FDA) approved a new cervical cancer vaccine called Gardasil. The decision was met with an enthusiastic response from health care providers around the world. The vaccine works by protecting against two strands of the HPV that are responsible for over 70 percent of all cervical cancers. In order to be most effective, women need to be vaccinated before they begin having sexual intercourse.

The introduction of the vaccine was not without controversy. Many public health officials were quick to praise the vaccine and encourage its use. Some even called for the mandatory vaccination of elementary school girls. Other groups voiced strong objections to the vaccine and mandatory vaccinations. Bridget Maher, spokesperson for the Family Research Council (FRC), a conservative Christian group, was quoted in *New Scientist,* and other sources, as saying, "Giving the HPV vaccine to young women could be potentially harmful, because they may see it as a license to engage in premarital sex." The FRC and other abstinence-until-marriage-promoting organizations stressed that sexual abstinence was the only effective way to prevent HPV and all other sexually transmitted infections.

The Religious Right's initial focus on the potential sexual "promiscuity" that vaccines might bring eventually yielded, as conservatives reframed the debate to be about the impact of *mandatory* vaccinations. They warned that compulsory vaccinations violated "parents' rights" to make decisions for their children, and explained that young people who did not have sex before marriage need not worry about HPV or any other infections.

Vaccine proponents countered that vaccinating girls against HPV would not make them more likely to engage in unprotected intercourse and that parents should be sure to discuss the risks of contracting other STIs with their children as part of a continuing dialogue about healthy sexuality.

Other angles of debate formed, with some commentators simply distrustful of vaccines, despite evidence and reassurance from the CDC that the "risks of serious disease from not vaccinating are far greater than the risks of serious reaction to a vaccination." And still others argued that maybe they needn't be mandatory because routine Pap smears already do a good job at detecting cancerous cells.

In the following essays, Cynthia Dailard, a senior public policy associate for the Alan Guttmacher Institute, presents the case for early vaccination, while acknowledging concerns that some may have. *New York Times* columnist Roni Rabin argues that mandatory vaccination against HPV is unnecessary, especially when considering that cervical cancer is generally detected and treated early through the practice of regular Pap smears.

YES

Cynthia Dailard

The Public Health Promise and Potential Pitfalls of the World's First Cervical Cancer Vaccine

After a decade in development, a cervical cancer vaccine appears poised to become available to American women later this year. Given the vaccine's demonstrated high level of effectiveness in preventing transmission of the two strains of human papillomavirus (HPV) responsible for most cases of cervical cancer, researchers believe that widespread vaccination has the potential to reduce cervical cancer deaths around the world by as much as two-thirds. The vaccine, therefore, holds the promise of being an enormous public health advance, both for women in the United States and for women in developing countries, who disproportionately bear the global burden of cervical cancer.

Because HPV is sexually transmitted, experts say the vaccine needs to be administered to as many young adolescent females as possible prior to sexual activity to achieve maximum effectiveness. Adolescents, however, are typically considered to be a difficult population to reach through immunization programs. For the HPV vaccine, moreover, the politics of teen sex are likely to exacerbate many of the practical challenges involved in achieving high vaccination rates—practical challenges that are magnified exponentially in developing countries, where the vaccine is needed most.

What the Science Says

Virtually all cases of cervical cancer are linked to HPV, an extremely common sexually transmitted infection (STI) that is typically asymptomatic and harmless; most people never know they are infected, and most infections typically resolve on their own. The infection is so common, in fact, that it is considered virtually a "marker" for sexual activity; according to a 1997 *American Journal of Medicine* article, nearly three in four Americans between the ages of 15 and 49 have been infected with HPV at some point in their life.

Of the 30 known types of HPV that are sexually transmitted, more than 13 types have the potential to lead to cervical cancer; two of these types, HPV 16 and 18, are associated with 70% of all cases of cervical cancer. In the United States, notwithstanding the prevalence of HPV infection, cervical cancer is relatively rare. This is largely due to the widespread availability of Pap tests, which can detect cervical cancer in its earliest and most treatable stages, as

From *The Guttmacher Report on Public Policy,* vol. 9, no. 1, Winter 2006, pp. 6–9. Copyright © 2006 by Alan Guttmacher Institute. Reprinted by permission.

well as precancerous changes of the cervix, which can be treated before cervical cancer sets in. Nonetheless, the American Cancer Society estimates that in 2006, almost 10,000 cases of invasive cervical cancer will occur in American women, resulting in 3,700 deaths. More than half of all U.S. women diagnosed with cervical cancer have not had a Pap test in the last three years. These women are disproportionately low-income women and women of color who lack access to basic health services.

In resource-poor developing countries, the incidence of cervical cancer is much higher, and the disease is far more lethal. Of the 225,000 annual deaths from cervical cancer globally, 80–85% occur to women in developing countries. Most of these deaths occur in Sub-Saharan Africa, South Asia and Latin America—where the public health infrastructure is extremely poor and basic preventive health services such as Pap smears are largely unavailable. Because women in these regions typically do not receive care until their disease is well advanced, it is usually fatal (related article, August 2003, page 4).

A cervical cancer vaccine would therefore represent an enormous step forward for women's health. There are actually two currently under development. Merck & Company filed an application for approval of its vaccine, Gardasil, with the federal Food and Drug Administration (FDA) in December; it expects an expedited decision—which is reserved for medications that treat unmet medical needs—from the agency in June. It has also submitted applications to regulatory agencies in Europe, Australia, Mexico, Brazil, Argentina, Taiwan and Singapore. GlaxoSmithKline will be seeking regulatory approval of its vaccine, Cervarix, in Europe in March 2006 and at the end of the year in the United States. Both vaccines target HPV 16 and 18, although Merck's vaccine also offers protection against two types of HPV that cause almost all cases of genital warts. A consortium of agencies funded by the Bill & Melinda Gates Foundation, and which includes Harvard University, the International Agency for Research on Cancer, PATH and the World Health Organization, is laying the groundwork for implementation of the vaccine in the developing world, expecting that it may be licensed in selected developing countries as early as 2007.

Targeting Teens

To become widely available in the United States, a vaccine must win the endorsement of the Advisory Committee on Immunization Practices (ACIP) in addition to FDA approval. Organized by the federal Centers for Disease Control and Prevention (CDC), ACIP is a 15-member panel authorized under federal law to recommend who should receive a vaccination, when and how often they should receive it, and the appropriate dosage. In deciding whether to recommend a vaccine, the committee must weigh a host of factors, including efficacy, benefits and risks, and cost-effectiveness. It also determines whether the vaccine should be available through the federal Vaccines for Children Program, which provides free vaccines to doctors serving eligible low-income children. Although ACIP's recommendations are not binding, they are followed closely by physicians and medical professional organizations, and ACIP's endorsement determines with virtual certainty whether a vaccine becomes the standard of care in this country. ACIP recommendations are also widely relied upon by insurers for setting reimbursement policy and by states for public funding purposes.

Perhaps the single most important decision for ACIP will be the optimal age for administering an HPV vaccine. While the typical American female has intercourse for the first time at age 17, 13% do so prior to age 15, according to the 2002 National Survey of Family Growth. Because HPV infection is so widespread, most cases of HPV are acquired soon after women become sexually active, with the peak incidence currently occurring at age 19. Merck's trials, moreover, found that the vaccine produced a stronger immunological response in adolescents aged 10–15 than in women aged 16–23. For these reasons, both Merck and GlaxoSmithKline are recommending that all girls receive their vaccines when they are 10–12 years old.

There are other practical reasons for targeting this age-group. In order to address the historical lack of emphasis on adolescent immunization, ACIP, the American Academy of Pediatrics, the American Association of Family Physicians and the American Medical Association in 1996 jointly identified ages 11–12 as the optimal time for adolescent immunizations. Currently, the federal Childhood and Adolescent Immunization Schedule recommends that every 11–12-year-old receive two vaccines (a new vaccine for bacterial meningitis and a combined booster for tetanus, diphtheria and whooping cough); it also recommends that they be assessed for "catch-up" shots at that time.

If the vaccine is recommended for preadolescent girls, acceptability among pediatricians and parents will be key to its success. Survey results released in October by researchers from the CDC and the University of California found that most pediatricians would be willing to administer the vaccine to their patients. And, several surveys of parents published in 2005 in the *Journal of Adolescent Health* and elsewhere suggest that parental acceptance of the vaccine will in fact be high. Many of those surveyed who initially expressed reservations about the vaccine changed their minds when educated about HPV and cervical cancer, suggesting the importance of counseling and education targeting parents during an adolescent health visit.

Finally, each state decides for itself whether a particular vaccine will be required in order for children to enroll in school, and they typically rely on ACIP recommendations in making this determination. According to a 2005 report on adolescent vaccination by the National Foundation for Infectious Diseases (NFID), school-based immunization requirements are by far the most effective means to ensure rapid and widespread use of childhood or adolescent vaccines. Adolescents are typically a hard-to-reach population for vaccine programs, and adding a vaccine to the list of those required for school enrollment boosts vaccination rates considerably—and far more effectively than guidelines recommending the vaccine for certain age-groups or high-risk populations. NFID also notes that timing an adolescent vaccination to middle school entry (ages 11–12) is important given that dropout rates begin to climb at age 13. Along these lines, younger dropouts are at particularly high risk of early sexual activity and poor sexual and reproductive health outcomes, suggesting an even greater imperative for a school-based requirement targeting 11–12-year-olds.

The Politics of Teen Sex

No sooner had Merck publicly announced the results of its long-term clinical trials in October 2005 than conservative activists began suggesting that inoculating young adolescents against HPV would encourage teenage sexual promiscuity. The heads of various "family values" groups publicly declared that they would not vaccinate their own children. Vaccination "sends the wrong message," asserted Tony Perkins of the Family Research Council (FRC). "Our concern is that this vaccine will be marketed to a segment of the population that should be getting a message about abstinence." This shot across the bow signaled that the cervical cancer vaccine could become the next battlefront in the social conservatives' crusade to advance an abstinence-only-unless-married agenda, and that leading activists would be working to ensure that it would meet the same regulatory fate as efforts to bring emergency contraception over the counter.

Yet, these same groups now appear to be softening their stance. A statement on the FRC website now says that "media reports suggesting that the Family Research Council opposes all development or distribution of such vaccines are false" and that it "welcomes the news that vaccines are in development." At the same time, the statement warns, "we will seek to ensure that there is full disclosure to the public of what these vaccines can and cannot achieve, their efficacy, and their risks (including side effects) and benefits. We believe that adults must be provided with sufficient information to make an informed, free choice whether to vaccinate either themselves or their children for HPV."

Whether the new FRC statement heralds a genuine change in posture on the part of social conservatives remains to be seen. A more likely scenario, perhaps, is that leaders of that movement have made a tactical decision not to oppose federal approval of the cervical cancer vaccine outright but, rather, to hold their fire for 50 state battles over whether the vaccine will be mandatory for middle and high school students. The public health ramifications of such a decision could still be significant. Because universal uptake of the vaccine will have the most impact on cervical cancer rates, efforts designed to prevent mandatory vaccination programs in the name of "parental control" may ultimately hinder the eradication of cervical cancer in the United States.

Beyond Politics

Beyond these political challenges, the impending roll-out of a cervical cancer vaccine raises some very serious practical challenges, as well as a range of longer-term scientific, logistical and policy questions that must be confronted over time (see box). One immediate challenge, for example, is successfully providing the vaccine's three required doses over a six-month period to adolescents, who, unlike infants and toddlers, do not typically make frequent, successive visits to a doctor's office or health care clinic. Moreover, the three-shot regimen is likely to be relatively expensive—somewhere in the vicinity of $100–150 per shot, according to newspaper reports. And since ongoing clinical trials to date have only demonstrated the vaccine's effectiveness for four years, it may be that booster shots will be needed—either later in adolescence or during adulthood.

If anything, the challenges in developing countries are more acute, and overcoming them may be far more difficult. These include raising awareness of the need for a vaccine where knowledge of HPV is very low; ensuring acceptability among parents, providers and policymakers in cultural and political contexts that are particularly sensitive to teenage sexuality; delivering a series of three injections to a population that often has minimal contact with health care facilities or providers; and ensuring that the vaccines are affordable in extremely-low-resource settings. While some global health experts, as in the United States, note the appeal of school-based vaccination programs as a means for reaching large numbers of adolescents, sizeable proportions particularly of female adolescents in many developing countries do not enroll in school or leave school prior to the recommended age of vaccination.

Despite these considerable challenges, one thing is certain: widespread vaccination against HPV in order to prevent cervical cancer would bring an enormous payoff to women, both in the United States and abroad. It can only be hoped that the politics will not be allowed to sabotage the promise first.

KEY SCIENTIFIC, LOGISTICAL AND POLICY QUESTIONS ABOUT THE CERVICAL CANCER VACCINE

- Should older women who are already sexually active receive "catch-up" vaccines at the start of any vaccination effort?
- Should males be vaccinated, both to prevent HPV transmission to women and to protect against HPV-related genital and anal cancers, as well as genital warts, in men?
- Could a therapeutic vaccine be developed to help those who are already infected with HPV or have a persistent infection?
- Could a vaccine be developed that targets additional cancer-causing types of HPV?
- Could the HPV vaccine be combined with other vaccinations for ease of administration, and would that help to institutionalize the adolescent health visit?
- Will uptake of the vaccine prompt professional medical organizations and public health entities to change their recommendations for Pap smears, and what might longer recommended intervals between Pap smears mean for women's health and health care–seeking behavior?
- Will the uninsured, the underinsured and those who rely on public programs for their care be able to access this relatively expensive vaccine, or will the vaccine simply widen the cervical cancer disparities that already exist?

Roni Rabin    **NO**

A New Vaccine for Girls, but Should It Be Compulsory?

Around the time report cards came home this spring, federal health officials approved another new vaccine to add to the ever-growing list of recommended childhood shots—this one for girls and women only, from 9 to 26, to protect them from genital warts and cervical cancer.

One of my own daughters, who just turned 9, would be a candidate for this vaccine, so I've been mulling this over. A shot that protects against cancer sounds like a great idea, at first. States may choose to make it mandatory, though the cost for them to do so would be prohibitive.

But let's think carefully before requiring young girls to get this vaccine, which protects against a sexually transmitted virus, in order to go to school. This isn't polio or measles, diseases that are easily transmitted through casual contact. Infection with this virus requires intimate contact, of the kind that doesn't occur in classrooms.

Besides, we already know how to prevent cervical cancer in this country, and we've done a darn good job of it. In the war against cancer, the battle against cervical cancer has been a success story.

Why, then, did federal health officials recommend the inoculation of about 30 million American girls and young women against the human papillomavirus, a sexually transmitted disease that in rare cases leads to cervical cancer?

Vaccine supporters say that some 3,700 American women die of cervical cancer each year, and close to 10,000 cases are diagnosed. Cervical cancer has a relatively high survival rate, but every death is tragic and treatment can rob women of their fertility.

Still, you have to see the numbers in context. Cervical cancer deaths have been dropping consistently in the United States—and have been for decades.

Cervical cancer has gone from being one of the top killers of American women to not even being on the top 10 list. This year cervical cancer will represent just 1 percent of the 679,510 new cancer cases and 1 percent of the 273,560 anticipated cancer deaths among American women. By contrast, some 40,970 women will die of breast cancer and 72,130 will die of lung cancer.

According to the American Cancer Society Web site, "Between 1955 and 1992, the number of cervical cancer deaths in the United States dropped by 74 percent." Think about it: 74 percent.

From *The New York Times*, 2006. Copyright © 2006 by The New York Times Company. Reprinted by permission via PARS International.

The number of cases diagnosed each year and the number of deaths per year have continued to drop, even though the population is growing.

From 1997 to 2003, the number of cervical cancers in the United States dropped by 4.5 percent each year, while the number of deaths dropped by 3.8 percent each year, according to a government Web site that tracks cancer trends, called SEER or Surveillance, Epidemiology and End Results. . . . This, while many other cancers are on the rise.

If current trends continue, by the time my 9-year-old daughter is 48, the median age when cervical cancer is diagnosed, there will be only a few thousand cases of the cancer in women, and about 1,000 deaths or fewer each year, even without the vaccine.

The secret weapon? Not so secret. It's the Pap smear. A simple, quick, relatively noninvasive test that's part and parcel of routine preventive health care for women. It provides early warnings of cellular changes in the cervix that are precursors for cancer and can be treated.

An American Cancer Society spokeswoman said that most American women who get cervical cancer these days are women who either had never had a Pap smear or had not followed the follow-up and frequency guidelines. So perhaps we could redirect the public money that would be spent on this vaccine—one of the most expensive ever, priced at $360 for the series of three shots—to make sure all women in the United States get preventive health care.

Because even if you have the new vaccine, which protects against only some of the viral strains that may bring on cervical cancer, you still need to continue getting Pap smears.

To be clear, I'm talking only about American women. Sadly, hundreds of thousands of women worldwide die of cervical cancer each year because they don't have access to Pap smears and the follow-up care required. For them, and for American women at high risk, the vaccine should be an option.

Black, Hispanic and some foreign-born women are at higher risk, though rates have dropped precipitously among blacks. Certain behavior—smoking, eating poorly, having multiple sexual partners and long-term use of the pill, for example—are also associated with an increased risk. But most people infected with the human papillomavirus clear it on their own.

Vaccine supporters, including the American Cancer Society, say the immunization will reduce abnormal Pap test results, and the stress, discomfort and cost of follow-up procedures and painful treatments. That's a strong argument for the vaccine.

But vaccines carry risks. In recent years, children have been bombarded with new immunizations, and we still don't know the full long-term implications. One vaccine, RotaShield, was removed from the market in 1999, just a year after being approved for infants.

Merck has tested the cervical cancer vaccine in clinical trials of more than 20,000 women (about half of them got the shot). The health of the subjects was followed for about three and a half years on average. But fewer than 1,200 girls under 16 got the shots, among them only about 100 9-year-olds, Merck officials said, and the younger girls have been followed for only 18 months.

Public health officials want to vaccinate girls early, before they become sexually active, even though it is not known how long the immunity will last.

But girls can also protect themselves from the human papillomavirus by using condoms; a recent study found that condoms cut infections by more than half. Condoms also protect against a far more insidious sexually transmitted virus, H.I.V.

So yes, by all means, let's keep stamping out cervical cancer. Let's make sure women and girls get Pap smears.

POSTSCRIPT

Should Children Have an HPV Vaccination before They Enroll in School?

Many sexually transmitted infections (STI) are treatable and curable. Trichomoniasis, for example, afflicts more than 7 million Americans every year, but these cases can be treated and cured. The same is true for chlamydia (nearly 3 million new cases annually), gonorrhea (700,000 new cases annually), and other infections that are *bacterial* or *parasitic*.

As noted in the Introduction, HPV is one of the most common STIs. It is a *viral* infection, which, like herpes and HIV, cannot be cured. However, most people who acquire HPV will eventually clear the infection on their own. When there are manifestations of HPV, such as genital warts, they can be treated and removed, though reoccurrence is possible.

The Centers for Disease Control says that most of the 20 million Americans who currently have HPV don't even know they are infected. The virus lives in the skin, or in the mucous membranes, usually causing no symptoms. The asymptomatic nature of HPV may aid its spread. Given the potential harm that HPV can cause, from genital warts to cancer, what is the best public health solution? What are the benefits of vaccinating young girls against HPV before they enroll in school? Should these vaccinations be mandatory? At what age to you think this vaccine should be given? Are routine Pap smears enough, as Rabin suggests?

Might vaccinating at an early age make teen girls more likely to have unprotected intercourse, as the Family Research Council suggested? What do you think of the argument that teens who are sexually abstinent have no need for the vaccination? What if they change their decisions and decide to have intercourse sooner than they had planned (or sooner than their parents had wished)? If they do wait to have intercourse until adulthood, what if their partner did not wait, and was exposed to HPV? Also, studies show that one in six women will be the victim of sexual assault and that 44 percent of victims are under the age of 18. Should teens be vaccinated to prevent infection caused by rape or a sexual assault?

And finally, what about the boys? The current vaccine is available for girls, but what about the exposure of males to HPV. Should the vaccination be available to young males to help further stave off the spread of this virus and its impact on everyone?

Suggested Readings

J. Cornblatt, "HPV Vaccine Is the Hot Shot on Campus," *Newsweek* (September 25, 2006).

J.T. Cox, "Epidemiology and Natural History of HPV," *Journal of Family Practice* (vol. 55, no. 11, November 2006).

A.F. Dempsey et al., "Factors That Are Associated with Parental Acceptance of Human Papillomavirus Vaccines: A Randomized Intervention Study of Written Information about HPV (Human Papillomavirus)" *Pediatrics* (vol. 117, no. 5, May 2006).

"Should HPV Vaccines Be Mandatory for All Adolescents?" *The Lancet* (October 7, 2006).

J. Hoffman, "Vaccinating Boys for Girls' Sake?" *The New York Times* (February 28, 2008).

S. London, "Frequent Male Condom Use Decreases Women's Risk of HPV Infection," *International Family Planning Perspectives* (vol. 32, no. 3, September 2006).

M.C. Mahoney, "Protecting Our Patients from HPV and HPV-Related Diseases: The Role of Vaccines," *Journal of Family Practice* (vol. 55, no. 11, November 2006).

L.E. Manhart et. al, "Human Papillomavirus Infection among Sexually Active Young Women in the United States: Implications for Developing a Vaccination Strategy," *Sexually Transmitted Diseases* (vol. 33, no. 8, August 2006).

P. Sprigg, "Pro-Family, Pro-Vaccine—But Keep It Voluntary," *Washington Post* (July 15, 2006).

K. Springen, "The Fast Track," *Newsweek* (August 20, 2008).

R. Stein, "A Vaccine Debate Once Focused on Sex Shifts as Boys Join the Target Market," *The Washington Post* (March 26, 2009).

ISSUE 10

Should Libraries and Other Places That Provide Public Wi-Fi Restrict the Sexual Content?

YES: American Family Association, from "Library Internet Filtering: Internet Porn in Public Libraries and Schools," http://www.afa.net/lif/schools.asp (2007)

NO: Donald Dyson and Brent Satterly, from "Hey, Uncle Sam. Let my Wi-Fi go!" an original essay written for this volume (2009)

ISSUE SUMMARY

YES: The American Family Association, an organization that advocates for "traditional family values," argues that library filtering software is essential to protect children from harm.

NO: Donald Dyson, Ph.D., and Brent Satterly, Ph.D., professors at Widener University, argue that filtering software limits free access to information and state that Wi-Fi should be unrestricted in all settings, including libraries.

Wi-Fi is a term often used to describe wireless local area networks (WLAN). Wi-Fi transmits and receives high frequency radio signals over distances of a few hundred feet. Free Wi-Fi seems to be available everywhere these days. It enables people to log onto the Internet using their laptop computers in local and university libraries (and often throughout campuses) and in many other public buildings. Free Wi-Fi is also offered in many private and corporate institutions. A colleague of ours reported once walking into a hotel and being dissatisfied with the rate he was quoted at the desk. Realizing he could get a better rate online, he went back to his car in the hotel parking lot, took out his laptop and used the hotel's own free Wi-Fi to book a better rate!

Wi-Fi has become a prolific source of Internet use. Large parts of this book were researched and written in coffee shops, restaurants, airports, and hotels that provide free Wi-Fi. Some institutions—both public and private—have taken steps to restrict access to sexual content in the Wi-Fi services their patrons receive. In Panera Bread restaurants, for instance, filters on the Wi-Fi service prevent diners from viewing erotic or sexual material online. Intentionally or not, the Panera Bread filters also restrict access to non-erotic material. For example, members of the American Association of Sexuality Educators, Counselors, and Therapists are blocked when they try to view the program for an academic conference housed at www.aasect.org. Employees of Planned Parenthood cannot check their email because reproductive choice content is likewise blocked at these restaurants. And teenagers cannot read articles written by other teenage editors at the educational portal www.sexetc.org. In fact, the development of parts of this book were delayed when filters at certain establishments providing Wi-Fi prevented the editors from finding biographies of some contributing authors whose Web sites were blocked because they are sex educators, sex researchers, or sex therapists.

What is the purpose of restricting Wi-Fi? Dennis Sarich, customer-comment coordinator for Panera Bread, explained that some content is restricted to "maintain the community tone and standards that Panera Bread is known for." Many would find it quite reasonable to restrict sexual imagery in establishments that serve many people with many different sets of values. However, some hotels—such as Radisson hotels—also restrict sexual content in their overnight guest rooms. In such cases, supporters of free speech wonder why hotels would have an interest in preventing their visitors from viewing erotic material in privacy.

The American Library Association (ALA) has been an outspoken critic of attempts to restrict online access in one place where Wi-Fi is commonly used—libraries. Some patrons wish libraries would install filtering software to ensure that sexual material cannot be viewed. What exactly should be blocked—if anything—is debatable, with some wanting only sexually explicit content blocked and others wanting more aggressive filters that would also block sexuality education related Web sites.

In the following essays, the American Family Association (AFA), a social conservative advocacy group, describes library filtering software as essential to protecting children from harm and severely criticizes the ALA for its efforts resisting filtering software. The AFA suggests steps for taking action at your local library to ensure that patrons cannot access sexual content. Don Dyson and Brent Satterly, professors at Widener University, argue that Wi-Fi should be unrestricted in all settings, including libraries.

YES

American Family Association

Library Internet Filtering:
Internet Porn in Public Libraries
and Schools

It is critically important for our children and communities that we free our local libraries from the grip of the American Library Association and make our libraries safe for our children! Make no mistake, the danger to our children is real!

Consider these sobering facts:

- A teenager molested a little boy in a library restroom after viewing Internet porn on the library's computer.
- Smut dealers used their local library to run a child pornography ring.
- A report entitled "Dangerous Access 2000," published by the Family Research Council, documents hundreds of incidents of library patrons accessing pornography in public libraries, including many involving children.

ALA Refuses to Keep Porn from Kids

But when begged for help to protect children, not only did the American Library Association turn a blind eye and a deaf ear, the organization further demanded that every library in the country provide children with totally unrestricted access to Internet porn!

For example, when asked about "blocking software" for library computers so children couldn't access Internet porn, Judith Krug, director of the ALA Office of Intellectual Freedom, said, "Blocking material leads to censorship. That goes for pornography and bestiality too. If you don't like it, don't look at it."

Another ALA spokesman, Richard Matthews, echoed Krug saying, "We recognize that minors have First Amendment rights, and any attempt to treat them differently from adults really infringes on those rights."

ALA Influence Felt Far and Wide

And to make things worse, the American Library Association wields significant power in our local libraries, giving it great influence over:

- The universities that train librarians.
- Job market requirements for most librarians.

From www.afa.net 2007. Copyright © 2007 by American Family Association. Reprinted by permission.

- Sizable portions of state monies for local libraries.
- Major book awards (especially children's). NOTE: The ALA awards both the Newbery and Caldecott Medals for excellence in children's books.
- Training of local library board trustees.
- Lobbying at both state and federal levels on legislation relevant to the ALA's agenda.

ALA Works to Undermine Protection of Kids

Based on their statements and policies about Internet filtering, it's clear that protecting children from harmful material is not part of the ALA's agenda. The sad truth is that unsupervised, curious eyes will seek out the forbidden. That's what children do. And that's why God calls on us, their parents and concerned adults, to protect them. A brief look at the ALA's record is proof:

- The ALA played a major role in convincing the Supreme Court to overturn the Communications Decency Act, which Congress passed to protect children from Internet pornography.
- The ALA sued to stop the enforcement of a federal law that would withhold federal funds from any library or school that does NOT filter Internet pornography from children.
- Not only does the pornography industry help fund the ALA, but ALA president Ann Symons has served on the Playboy Foundation's awards committee.
- Playboy executive Christie Hefner was a forum panelist at an ALA convention.
- The bottom line always comes down to this official policy statement of the American Library Association: "Libraries, acting within their mission and objectives, must support access to information on all subjects that serve the needs or interest of each user, regardless of the user's age or the content of the material." (See ALA's Article V of the Library Bill of Rights. . . .)

Something Can Be Done about Reckless Endangerment of Our Children

Children do NOT have a Constitutional right to access and view Internet pornography in our local libraries! Or anywhere for that matter.

The question that must be answered is why is a private organization with no legal standing and no authority having so much influence over our libraries and the policies that protect children from harm.

Here's the good news: the ALA truly has no legal authority over what goes on in your local library. The answer lies with the citizens. YOU and your fellow taxpayers own your local library, not the ALA.

If you want the ALA and its pornographic policies out of your community and your local library, GET INFORMED, GET INVOLVED and KICK THEM OUT!

If concerned citizens are armed with solid information and commitment, our local libraries can be rescued from the ALA.

Take note: this fight will not be easy. The people who run the ALA—the Krugs, Symonses, and Matthewses—are radicals of the 1960s. They will not give up their control of your library without a tough fight.

Nevertheless, for the sake of our children and our communities, we must fight to free our local libraries from the radical, immoral agenda of the American Library Association. No sacrifice and no expense is too great when it comes to safeguarding children.

This fight is a local fight. There is no way it can be conducted from some national headquarters. YOU must fight for your own school and public libraries—you and the members of your local community.

There are already over FIVE MILLION sexually explicit adult web sites on the Internet. And thousands more are added EVERY DAY! And the American Library Association wants our children to have totally unrestricted access to every single one of them! We cannot afford to put this fight off a single day.

You Can Do It One Step at a Time

Here are some steps and information that will help you begin the process of communicating to your local librarian and directors the need to install filtering on your local library's Internet computers. By following the recommended guidelines, you will be better prepared to:

- Address the current problem of Internet porn in your library.
- Articulate your position to the library, civic leaders, and local media.
- Persuade others to join and support your goal and purpose.

Pray

Ask God to direct and guide you through the entire process. You are going to face opposition by the ALA and others. Pray for wisdom and success in your efforts.

Research

1. Read and understand as much as possible the facts surrounding Internet filtering, your library's Internet use policies, your library board members and their terms of service and authority.
2. Learn how the library administration is structured. Who are the board of directors? How are they selected? Is the library part of a regional system under authority of a central board? Do other cities contribute to the library budget?
3. Request to look at the public complaint file. Are there any "red flags" that suggest a problem, i.e., patrons viewing pornography, children accessing inappropriate material. What was the library's response to the complaints?
4. Learn state and local laws concerning legislative measures that can be taken, such as placing a ballot issue that would mandate filtering

before the people during the next election. What is the librarian's liability for allowing children to access harmful material?

5. Prepare a list of friends, families and churches that you feel will support you in this project.

Action Steps

1. Write or visit your local librarian. Share your concerns about the dangers of Internet pornography in the local library. Ask the librarian to consider placing filtering devices on library computers. However, be aware that the American Library Association has policies that instruct librarians how to respond.

2. Write or call the chairman of the library board. Request to address the board at their next scheduled meeting. A day or two before the meeting, you may wish to notify the local media that you are concerned about pornography in the library. This will help take your message to others who will agree and join with you. Invite friends and supporters to attend meetings and to voice their support of filtering.

3. Contact your city and county officials. Ask them to publicly stand with you on the issue by proclamation or resolution.

4. Write letters to the editor. Recruit others to do the same.

5. Form a local coalition in favor of safer libraries. Discuss ways to reach the community with your message. Newsletters, church bulletin inserts and flyers are excellent tools. Start a petition drive to raise public awareness and to create a database of supporters.

6. If your local library fails to implement filtering, ask an attorney who supports your efforts to begin drafting a voter initiative for your group. The attorneys at the AFA Center for Law & Policy are available to assist in this effort as well.

7. **Order the "Excess Access" video,** documenting the dangers that ALA policies can yield. Excess Access scrutinizes the ALA and uses both drama and interviews with experts who have analyzed the growing power of the group.

**Donald Dyson and
Brent Satterly**

 **NO**

Hey, Uncle Sam. Let My Wi-Fi Go!

In March of 2008, the Pew Research Center released a report indicating that 62% of all Americans are members of what they referred to as "a wireless mobile population" (p. 1). This population of fast, connected, mobile users crosses generational and demographic lines of all types. And, as cell phones and PDAs become more sophisticated and as laptop computers and public Internet "hotspots" become more common, these numbers are likely to increase significantly in the next few years.

Within the context of this mobile population, Pew reports that 64% of Internet users have accessed the Internet from places outside of their homes or their workplaces, likely from settings such as libraries, hotel rooms, and public "hot spots." Looking further at this report, it can be seen that although younger users access information at higher rates, the use of laptops to access the Internet crosses generational lines. In fact of all Internet users, 70% of those between the ages of 18 and 29 have used a laptop to log on wirelessly, 53% of those between 30 and 49, 39% of those between 50 and 64 and 29% of those 65 and older. It is clear that wireless Internet access is a significant and growing cultural phenomenon.

Add to this the growing list of locations from which such wireless access can found. In addition to libraries and hotels, airports [and] coffeeshops, laundromats and a host of retail outlets are adding wireless access to their list of services in attempts to meet customer demands and to attract new customers.

This proliferation of access meets a challenging intersection when considered in light of the vast array of content available on the net. Specifically, it is sexually explicit or "objectionable" content that is most often the issue of debate.

Sex Panic and the Internet

We know that the open discussion of sex and sexuality is problematic for many of us for many reasons. They may be related to our personal beliefs, our spirituality, our individual moral codes or simply our embarrassment and shame. However, there is a greater phenomenon that is occurring to further complicate these discussions.

In his book *America's War on Sex* (2006), Dr. Marty Klein identifies a cultural phenomenon that has been growing in the United States for many years. Dubbed the "Sexual Disaster Industry (SDI)," this group has been working

An original essay written for this volume. Copyright © 2009 by Donald A. Dyson and Brent Satterly. Reprinted by permission of the authors.

behind the cultural scenes to create a culture of panic connected to sex and sexuality that has significantly threatened many of our freedoms. According to Klein, the SDI works through many outlets to overstate the statistics of sexual violence and sexual danger in an effort to generate fear and attention.

Consider the popularity of television shows that sensationalize the capture of sexual predators for a national audience, or the outrage of some morality groups about the abundance of pornography available on the Internet. These things and more generate a sense of fear related to sexuality and a mysterious and dangerous "sexual other."

It is precisely this sexual panic, then, that fuels the push for filters that "protect" us from this mysterious and dangerous sexual predator hiding within our laptops and threatening our children, our marriages, our families and our morality. These are the arguments for Internet filters and blocking software designed to prevent the average coffeeshop consumer from looming sexual dangers.

Internet Filters and Censorship

Internet filters are designed to complete an advanced view of the Internet content that a given user is attempting to access, search it for specific keywords or images, and prevent access to that content if the word or image is included in a list of "unacceptable" content. While most filter companies do not release the specifics of their filters, the concept is generally the same: the software package will prevent the surfer from having access to content that the software designers have deemed to be unacceptable.

This concept is not a new one in human history. Since before the printed word, censorship has played a role in human politics and interactions as some groups of people attempt to control access to content that it deems unacceptable for others. It is no surprise that this same experience, fueled by sex panic, has affected Internet access.

Consider the case of the Child Online Protection Act of 1998. Originally passed by Congress to levy criminal charges and impose civil penalties on people who put material the government deems "harmful to minors" on the Internet. Although immediately challenged by the ACLU and other organizations, and as a result never enforced, a ten-year legal battle ensued. In 2009, the Supreme Court upheld the injunction against enforcement, arguing that the law censored material that was protected by the First Amendment of the Constitution.

In a similar case involving the 2000 Children's Internet Protection Act, which required libraries receiving public funds to put filters on public computers, the Supreme Court ruled that the libraries *must* remove such filters if a patron asks that they be removed. This once again demonstrated that Internet content was protected by the first amendment.

Consider the argument so far. Wireless Internet use is growing across the nation for people of all ages. More wireless hotspots are being introduced to everyday life and technology is increasing mobile access to the World Wide Web. At the same time, the sexual disaster industry is generating increasing fear of sexual danger and the sexual other, increasing a public's panicked cry for "protection". As a result, attempts to censor Internet content arise in unconstitutional attempts to safeguard our communities. As a result, constitutionally protected content gets blocked and the freedoms Americans hold dear threatened.

What Else Is Threatened?

It is not only freedom that is being threatened. Recent reports indicate that a vast majority of Internet users are accessing health-related data through the Internet. The Pew Internet and American Life project reports that between 75 and 80% of Internet users have looked up health-related information. The popularity and ubiquity of webMD© and other health-related websites has transformed the medical landscape in many ways.

More specifically, more and more people have been accessing sexual health information through the World Wide Web as well. In 2003, it was estimated that one in ten Internet users accessed information related to sexual health. Among adolescents, estimates rise to over 25% of teens seeking information about sexual health issues such as birth control, HIV, AIDS, or STDs. In a culture that is often silent on healthy sexual expression, such access is at the very least a necessity and at times, lifesaving.

This access goes beyond the basics of health, however. For some gay, lesbian, bisexual, and transgender youth the Internet offers the only resource for accessing information about their experiences, their communities, and the specific health information that affects them.

Research has indicated that not only is access related to sexual health blocked by a vast number of Internet "safety" packages, but that information is blocked at higher rates when it relates to those individuals who identify as gay, lesbian, bisexual or transgender (GLBT) (Richardson, Hansen, Resnick, & Derry, 2002). As a result, health information is denied to individuals already dealing with societal discrimination.

Beyond the sexual health needs of the general public, such censorship also limits access to important websites for educators and other professionals. The columnist working on an article related to youth suicide is restricted from accessing websites related to GLBT youth. The therapist, seeking information on working with married couples and sexual dysfunction cannot access the websites of the American Association of Sexuality Educators, Counselors and Therapists (AASECT) or the Society for Sex Therapy and Research (SSTAR). The middle school administrator cannot gather information on gender-based bullying from the Sexuality Information and Education Council of the United States (SIECUS).

What is the Solution?

In the end, the sexual disaster industry wants Americans to believe that there is an uncontrollable avalanche of unwanted pornography in every wireless coffeeshop and a predator lurking in every laptop at every library across the nation. Aided by the sensationalism of media that seeks ratings and readership over reliability, the sexual panic grows and the fear intensifies. Even in the face of decreasing rates of online sexual solicitation (Mitchell, Wolak, & Finkelhor, 2007), the panic and push for filters increases.

The answers, however, do not lie in the increasing censorship of online content. The honest reality is that sexual predators have been problematic for generations and that pornography has been accessible to industrious and curious youth for at least that long as well. Well-meaning attempts to protect people from experiences with unwanted sexual material, in the end, silence honest discussions about sexuality and prevent the development of lifesaving skills in navigating an increasingly complex sexual world.

Instead of attempting to block sexuality from our lives, time and energy is far better spent in teaching people the critical thinking skills necessary to make sense of the myriad sexual images that bombard them everyday. Rather than generating disproportionate panic about online sexual predators, teach adolescents Internet safety skills. Take the time to educate young people about how to recognize and report unwanted and inappropriate sexual overtures. Rather than limiting the access to sexual health information, increase the dialogue about its importance to our overall well-being.

In your panic about sexuality, do not seek to over-protect the people. It only serves to weaken our ability to manage the realities of our world. Instead, seek to build critical thinking and thoughtful action that can help every American become responsible sexual citizens. Hey, Uncle Sam, let my Wi-Fi go!

POSTSCRIPT

Should Libraries and Other Places That Provide Public Wi-Fi Restrict the Sexual Content?

$\mathbf{A}$s with all articles in *Taking Sides,* it is important to read these articles critically and challenge statements that are presented as facts. The American Family Association opens its argument by describing several "sobering facts," including a boy who was said to be molested in a library after viewing porn, and "smut dealers" who ran a child pornography ring from the local library. It is important to observe that the AFA offers no sources for these allegations, and no further details that might enable the reader to verify these claims independently. The AFA also provides a set of "Action Steps" for readers to take in order to curtail the availability of pornography in libraries. Do these steps seem effective?

In their opposing article, Dyson and Satterly also present several situations but do so as hypothetical circumstances rather than facts. They describe a columnist who is blocked from researching GLBT suicide, a therapist who cannot access professional Web sites, and a middle school administrator who cannot access information on gender-based bullying. Do you think their depiction of the far-reaching effects of Wi-Fi restrictions is accurate? Why or why not?

Marty Klein, author of *America's War on Sex,* tells of another related controversy that came to light late in 2008 when several airlines introduced Wi-Fi to their passengers. For a fee, passengers could access the Internet during their flights. Most airlines offering this new service placed filters restricting access to sexual material. At first, American Airlines decided that such filters were not needed, choosing instead to rely on their passengers to exercise "good judgment." After public pressure, American Airlines changed its decision and decided to block sexual content. Much of the pressure came from the Association of Professional Flight Attendants, a union that did not want its members in the awkward position of having to ask passengers to curtail their online, in-flight viewing habits. The group said that they had received "a lot of complaints" from passengers seeing "inappropriate content" on others' computer screens, although specific examples could not be produced. Klein wonders which sites should be blocked—"my blog? Your blog? Sites relating to breast cancer gay rights, *The Daily Show?* "And what about the rest of what people do on their laptops?" (Klein, 2008).

What do *you* think about this issue? Have you ever seen someone viewing (or viewed for yourself) pornographic material in a public library? Have you ever been blocked from viewing sexually related information in a public space? How did this make you feel? Should libraries and other public and private institutions block access to sexual content? Should some establishments filter content, but not others? (i.e., should airlines restrict content because of the close proximity of patrons?) If establishments are to block sexual content, should they block other content that might be offensive, such as Web sites that provide hate speech or violent imagery? And should filters be the responsibility of the person owning the laptop or the entity providing the service?

Suggested Readings

S. Fox, "The Engaged E-patient population," *Pew Internet & American Life Project* (August 2008).

M. Klein, *America's War on Sex* (Santa Barbara, CA: Praeger Publishing, 2006).

M. Klein, "Porn on Planes: Another Urban Legend Fans Hysteria," *Sexual Intelligence* (October 26, 2008).

K. Mitchell, J. Wolak, and D. Finkelhor, "Trends in Youth Reports of Sexual Solicitations, Harassment and Unwanted Exposure to Pornography on the Internet," *Journal of Adolescent Health,* (vol. 40, no. 2, 2007).

M. Schlangenstein, "American Air Attendants Urge Filters to Bar Web Porn," *Bloomberg News* (September 10, 2008).

ISSUE 11

Should the FCC Fine TV Stations That Broadcast Indecency?

YES: Federal Communications Commission, from *FCC Consumer Facts: Obscene, Profane, and Indecent Broadcasts*, http://www.fcc.gov/eb/Orders/2001/fcc01090.doc (2001)

NO: Judith Levine, from "Is 'Indecency' Harmful to Minors?" an adaptation of an article from *Extra!* www.fair.org (October 2004)

ISSUE SUMMARY

YES: The Federal Communications Commission (FCC), a U.S. government agency charged with regulating the content of the broadcast airways, including television and radio, outlines what it defines as "indecent" broadcast material and describes its enforcement policy.

NO: Author Judith Levine traces the history of censorship in the United States, and argues that much of what the FCC has determined is "indecent" sexual speech is not, in fact, harmful to children.

In January 2004, about 100 million viewers tuned in to CBS to watch the New England Patriots defeat the Carolina Panthers in Superbowl XXXVIII. But talk at water coolers, breakfast tables, and classrooms around the country the next day had little to do with the heroics of quarterback Tom Brady, nor was it about Adam Vinatieri's 41-yard field goal with four seconds left. Instead, the nation was talking about performer Janet Jackson's breast. During the half-time performance, Jackson's breast was exposed by co-star Justin Timberlake, revealing a nearly bare breast with her nipple covered by a star-shaped pastie. The incident caused a national uproar. Nielson ratings estimated that about one in five children between the ages of 2 and 11 witnessed the event. (And those who did not see it live had ample time so see the incident ad infinitum in the news media coverage that followed.) It remained a feature news story for days and then weeks, as commentators and news analysts examined who was responsible and how severely they should be punished. CBS and Jackson apologized, Timberlake called it an unfortunate "wardrobe malfunction," and much of America wondered what effect the incident would have on children.

Meanwhile, the Federal Communications Commission (FCC) was not amused. The governmental agency charged with enforcing "indecency" violations reported having received more than a half million complaints. The FCC began holding hearings about increasing the monetary fines and proceeded to scrutinize the alleged violations of other performers and media outlets. When the FCC fined Clear Channel Communications $495,000 for sexual content aired in six Howard Stern shows, Clear Channel dropped Stern from all its radio outlets. The fine was significant as it marked a departure from the FCC's standard practice of fining. In this case, each "indecent" utterance was fined individually; previously, the FCC would fine an entire program the maximum $27,500, regardless of the number of violations on each show.

What is "indecent"? The FCC defines it as "language or material that, in context, depicts or describes, in terms patently offensive as measured by contemporary community broadcast standards for the broadcast medium, sexual or excretory organs or activities." Such material is protected as free speech by the First Amendment. However, the FCC is empowered to restrict the times of day that such material can be aired, under the premise that children need to be protected from indecency. Indecent material may not be aired between 6 A.M. and 10 P.M. Likewise, "profanity" may not be aired during these times. "Profane" material includes "personally reviling epithets naturally tending to provoke violent resentment or denoting language so grossly offensive to members of the public who actually hear it as to amount to a nuisance."

Still, the definitions of "indecency" and "profanity" are quite subjective and may require further clarification. The same is true for material that is "obscene," which may not be aired at all. In the following essays, the FCC elaborates on its definitions of indecency, profanity, and obscenity, giving case examples to illustrate its enforcement policy more clearly. In response, Judith Levine argues that the very premise of restricting indecent material is flawed, as there is no evidence that sexual speech harms children.

YES

Enforcement Policies Regarding Broadcast Indecency

I. Introduction

The Commission issues this Policy Statement to provide guidance to the broadcast industry regarding our case law and our enforcement policies with respect to broadcast indecency. This document is divided into five parts. Section I gives an overview of this document. Section II provides the statutory basis for indecency regulation and discusses the judicial history of such regulation. Section III describes the analytical approach the Commission uses in making indecency determinations. This section also presents a comparison of selected rulings intended to illustrate the various factors that have proved significant in resolving indecency complaints. The cited material refers only to broadcast indecency actions and does not include any discussion of case law concerning indecency enforcement actions in other services regulated by this agency such as cable, telephone, or amateur radio. Section IV describes the Commission's broadcast indecency enforcement process. Section V is the conclusion.

II. Statutory Basis/Judicial History

It is a violation of federal law to broadcast obscene or indecent programming. Specifically, Title 18 of the United States Code, Section 1464 (18 U.S.C. § 1464), prohibits the utterance of "any obscene, indecent, or profane language by means of radio communication." Congress has given the Federal Communications Commission the responsibility for administratively enforcing 18 U.S.C. § 1464. In doing so, the Commission may revoke a station license, impose a monetary forfeiture, or issue a warning for the broadcast of indecent material.

    The FCC's enforcement policy has been shaped by a number of judicial and legislative decisions. In particular, because the Supreme Court has determined that obscene speech is not entitled to First Amendment protection, obscene speech cannot be broadcast at any time. In contrast, indecent speech is protected by the First Amendment, and thus, the government must both identify a compelling interest for any regulation it may impose on indecent speech and choose the least restrictive means to further that interest. Even under this

From *FCC Consumer Facts: Obscene, Profane, and Indecent Broadcasts*, 2001. Published by the Federal Communications Commission.

restrictive standard, the courts have consistently upheld the Commission's authority to regulate indecent speech, albeit with certain limitations.

FCC v. Pacifica Foundation provides the judicial foundation for FCC indecency enforcement. In that case, the Supreme Court held that the government could constitutionally regulate indecent broadcasts. In addition, the Court quoted the Commission's definition of indecency with apparent approval. The definition, "language or material that, in context, depicts or describes, in terms patently offensive as measured by contemporary community standards for the broadcast medium, sexual or excretory activities or organs," has remained substantially unchanged since the time of the *Pacifica* decision. Moreover, the definition has been specifically upheld against constitutional challenges in the *Action for Children's Television (ACT)* cases in the D.C. Circuit Court of Appeals. Further, in *Reno v. ACLU,* the U.S. Supreme Court struck down an indecency standard for the Internet but did not question the constitutionality of our broadcast indecency standard. Rather, the Court recognized the "special justifications for regulation of the broadcast media that are not applicable to other speakers."

Although the D.C. Circuit approved the FCC's definition of indecency in the *ACT* cases, it also established several restrictive parameters on FCC enforcement. The court's decisions made clear that the FCC had to identify the compelling government interests that warranted regulation and also explain how the regulations were narrowly tailored to further those interests. In *ACT I,* the court rejected as inadequately supported the Commission's determination that it could reach and regulate indecent material aired as late as 11:00 P.M., and remanded the cases involved to the Commission for proceedings to ascertain the proper scope of the "safe harbor" period, that is, the time during which indecent speech may be legally broadcast. Before the Commission could comply with the court's remand order, however, Congress intervened and instructed the Commission to adopt rules that enforced the provisions on a "24 hour per day basis." The rule adopted to implement this legislative mandate was stayed and was ultimately vacated by the court in *ACT II* as unconstitutional. In 1992, responding to the decision in *ACT II,* Congress directed the Commission to adopt a new "safe harbor"—generally 12 midnight to 6:00 A.M., but 10:00 P.M. to 6:00 A.M. for certain noncommercial stations. The Commission implemented this statutory scheme in January 1993. Before this rule could become effective, however, the court stayed it pending judicial review. In 1995, the D.C. Circuit, *en banc,* held in *ACT III* that there was not a sufficient justification in the record to support a preferential "safe harbor" period for noncommercial stations and that the more restrictive midnight to 6:00 A.M. "safe harbor" for commercial stations was therefore unconstitutional. The court concluded, however, that the less restrictive 10:00 P.M. to 6:00 A.M. "safe harbor" had been justified as a properly tailored means of vindicating the government's compelling interest in the welfare of children and remanded the case to the Commission "with instructions to limit its ban on the broadcasting of indecent programs to the period from 6:00 A.M. to 10:00 P.M." The Commission implemented the court's instructions by appropriately conforming. These changes became effective on August 28, 1995.

Thus, outside the 10:00 P.M. to 6:00 A.M. safe harbor, the courts have approved regulation of broadcast indecency to further the compelling government interests in supporting parental supervision of children and more generally its concern for children's well being. The principles of enforcement articulated below are intended to further these interests.

III. Indecency Determinations

A. Analytical Approach

Indecency findings involve at least two fundamental determinations. First, the material alleged to be indecent must fall within the subject matter scope of our indecency definition—that is, the material must describe or depict sexual or excretory organs or activities.

Second, the broadcast must be *patently offensive* as measured by contemporary community standards for the broadcast medium. In applying the "community standards for the broadcast medium" criterion, the Commission has stated:

> *The determination as to whether certain programming is patently offensive is not a local one and does not encompass any particular geographic area. Rather, the standard is that of an average broadcast viewer or listener and not the sensibilities of any individual complainant.*

In determining whether material is patently offensive, the *full context* in which the material appeared is critically important. It is not sufficient, for example, to know that explicit sexual terms or descriptions were used, just as it is not sufficient to know only that no such terms or descriptions were used. Explicit language in the context of a *bona fide* newscast might not be patently offensive, while sexual innuendo that persists and is sufficiently clear to make the sexual meaning inescapable might be. Moreover, contextual determinations are necessarily highly fact-specific, making it difficult to catalog comprehensively all of the possible contextual factors that might exacerbate or mitigate the patent offensiveness of particular material. An analysis of Commission case law reveals that various factors have been consistently considered relevant in indecency determinations. By comparing cases with analogous analytical structures, but different outcomes, we hope to highlight how these factors are applied in varying circumstances and the impact of these variables on a finding of patent offensiveness.

B. Case Comparisons

The principal factors that have proved significant in our decisions to date are: (1) the *explicitness or graphic nature* of the description or depiction of sexual or excretory organs or activities; (2) whether the material *dwells on or repeats at length* descriptions of sexual or excretory organs or activities; (3) *whether the material appears to pander or is used to titillate,* or *whether the material appears to have been presented for its shock value.* In assessing all of the factors, and particularly the third factor, the overall context of the broadcast in which the disputed material appeared is critical. Each indecency case presents its own particular mix of these, and possibly other, factors, which must be balanced to ultimately determine whether the material is patently offensive and therefore indecent. No single factor generally provides the basis for an indecency finding. To illustrate the noted factors, however, and to provide a sense of the weight these considerations have carried in specific factual contexts, a comparison of cases has been organized to provide examples of decisions in which each of these factors has played a particularly significant role, whether exacerbating or mitigating, in the indecency determination made.

It should be noted that the brief descriptions and excerpts from broadcasts that are reproduced in this document are intended only as a research tool and should not be taken as a meaningful selection of words and phrases to be evaluated for indecency purposes without the fuller context that the tapes or transcripts provide. The excerpts from broadcasts used in this section have often been shortened or compressed. In order to make the excerpts more readable, however, we have frequently omitted any indication of these ellipses from the text. Moreover, in cases where material was included in a complaint but not specifically cited in the decision based on the complaint, we caution against relying on the omission as if it were of decisional significance. For example, if portions of a voluminous transcript are the object of an enforcement action, those portions not included are not necessarily deemed not indecent. The omissions may be the result of an editing process that attempted to highlight the most significant material within its context. No inference should be drawn regarding the material deleted.

1. Explicitness/Graphic Description Versus Indirectness/Implication
The more explicit or graphic the description or depiction, the greater the likelihood that the material will be considered patently offensive. Merely because the material consists of double entendre or innuendo, however, does not preclude an indecency finding if the sexual or excretory import is unmistakable.

Following are examples of decisions where the explicit/graphic nature of the description of sexual or excretory organs or activities played a central role in the determination that the broadcast was indecent.

WYSP(FM), Philadelphia, PA: "Howard Stern Show"

> *God, my testicles are like down to the floor . . . you could really have a party with these . . . Use them like Bocci balls.*
>
> *(As part of a discussion of lesbians) I mean to go around porking other girls with vibrating rubber products . . .*
>
> *Have you ever had sex with an animal? Well, don't knock it. I was sodomized by Lambchop.*

Indecent—Warning Issued. Excerpted material (only some of which is cited above) consisted of "vulgar and lewd references to the male genitals and to masturbation and sodomy broadcast in the context of . . . 'explicit references to masturbation, ejaculation, breast size, penis size, sexual intercourse, nudity, urination, oral–genital contact, erections, sodomy, bestiality, menstruation and testicles.'". . . .

KROQ(FM), Los Angeles, CA: "You Suck" Song

I know you're really proud cause you think you're well hung, but I think it's time you learn how to use your tongue. You say you want things to be even and you want things to be fair, but you're afraid to get your teeth caught in my pubic hair. If you're lying there expecting me to suck your dick, you're going to have to give me more than just a token lick. . . . Go down baby, you suck, lick it hard and move your tongue around. If you're worried about babies, you can lower your risk, by giving me that special cunnilingus kiss. . . . you can jiggle your tongue on my clit. Don't worry about making me have an orgasm. . . . You asshole, you shit. I know it's a real drag, to suck my cunt when I'm on the rag. . . . You tell me it's gross to suck my yeast infection. How do you think I feel when I gag on your erection.

Indecent—NAL Issued.   (graphically and explicitly describes sexual and excretory organs or activities).

. . . Less explicit material and material that relies principally on innuendo to convey a sexual or excretory meaning have also been cited by the Commission as actionably indecent where the sexual or excretory meaning was unmistakable. . . .

KGB-FM, San Diego, CA: "Candy Wrapper" Song

I whipped out my Whopper and whispered, Hey, Sweettart, how'd you like to Crunch on my Big Hunk for a Million Dollar Bar? Well, she immediately went down on my Tootsie Roll and you know, it was like pure Almond Joy. I couldn't help but grab her delicious Mounds, . . . this little Twix had the Red Hots. . . . as my Butterfinger went up her tight little Kit Kat, and she started to scream Oh, Henry! Oh, Henry! Soon she was fondling my Peter Paul, and Zagnuts and I knew it wouldn't be long before I blew my Milk Duds clear to Mars and gave her a taste of the old Milky Way. . . . I said, Look . . . why don't you just take my Whatchamacallit and slip it up your Bit-O-Honey. Oh, what a piece of Juicy Fruit she was too. She screamed Oh, Crackerjack. You're better than the Three Musketeers! as I rammed my Ding Dong up her Rocky Road and into her Peanut Butter Cup. Well, I was giving it to her Good'n Plenty, and all of a sudden, my Starburst. . . . she started to grow a bit Chunky and . . . Sure enough, nine months later, out popped a Baby Ruth.

Indecent—NAL Issued. ("While the passages arguably consist of double entendre and indirect references, the language used in each passage was understandable and clearly capable of a specific sexual meaning and, because of the context, the sexual import was inescapable."); ("notwithstanding the use of candy bar names to symbolize sexual activities, the titillating and pandering nature of the song makes any thought of candy bars peripheral at best"). . . .

KMEL(FM), San Francisco, CA: "Rick Chase Show"; "Blow Me" Song

Blow me, you hardly even know me, just set yourself below me and blow me, tonight. Hey, a handy would certainly be dandy, but it's not enough to slow slow me, hey, you gotta blow me allright. Hey, when you part your lips that way, I want you night and day, when you squeeze my balls so tight. I want to blow my load with all my might.

Indecent—NAL Issued. Commission found that the language dwelled on descriptions of sexual organs and activities, "was understandable and clearly capable of a specific sexual meaning and, because of the context, the sexual import was inescapable."

Compare the following case in which the material aired was deemed not to be actionably indecent.

WFBQ(FM)/WNDE(AM), Indianapolis, IN: "Elvis" and "Power, Power, Power"

As you know, you gotta stop the King, but you can't kill him . . . So you talk to Dick Nixon, man you get him on the phone and Dick suggests maybe getting like a mega-Dick to help out, but you know, you remember the time the King ate mega-Dick under the table at a 095 picnic . . . you think about getting mega-Hodgie, but that's no good because you know, the King was a karate dude . . .

Power! Power! Power! Thrust! Thrust! Thrust! First it was Big Foot, the monster car-crunching 4x4 pickup truck. Well, move over, Big Foot! Here comes the most massive power-packed monster ever! It's Big Peter! (Laughter) Big Peter with 40,000 Peterbilt horsepower under the hood. It's massive! Big Peter! Formerly the Big Dick's Dog Wiener Mobile. Big Peter features a 75-foot jacked-up monster body. See Big Peter crush and enter a Volvo. (Laughter) . . . strapped himself in the cockpit and put Big Peter through its paces. So look out Big Foot! Big Peter is coming! Oh my God! It's coming! Big Peter! (Laughter)

Not Indecent. The licensee provided a fuller transcript of the cited "Elvis" excerpt and explained the context in which it was aired, arguing that no sexual meaning was intended and that no such meaning would be reasonably understood from the material taken as a whole. The licensee also explained the regional humor of the Power, Power, Power excerpt and the context in which it was broadcast. The Mass Media Bureau held that the material was not indecent because the "surrounding contexts do not appear to provide a background against which a sexual import is inescapable."

In assessing explicitness, the Commission also looks to the audibility of the material as aired. If the material is difficult or impossible to understand, it may not be actionably indecent. However, difficulty in understanding part of the material or an attempt to obscure objectionable material will not preclude a finding of indecency where at least some of the material is recognizable or understandable.

KGB-FM, San Diego, CA: "Sit on My Face" Song

> *Sit on my face and tell me that you love me. I'll sit on your face and tell you I love you, too. I love to hear you moralize when I'm between your thighs. You blow me away. Sit on my face and let my lips embrace you. I'll sit on your face and then I'll love you (?) truly. Life can be fine, if we both sixty-nine. If we sit on our faces in all sorts of places and play till we're blown away.*

Indecent—NAL Issued.   The song was found to be actionably indecent despite English accent and "ambient noise" because the lyrics were sufficiently understandable.

WWKX(FM), Woonsocket, RI: "Real Deal Mike Neil Show"

> *Douche bag, hey what's up, fu(Bleep)ck head? . . . You his fuck (Bleep) ho or what? You his fuck (Bleep) bitch man, where you suck his dick every night? . . . Suck some di(Bleep)ck make some money for Howard and pay your pimp okay?*

Indecent—NAL Issued.   Material was found to be actionably indecent despite attempt to obscure objectionable language because "editing was ineffective and merely resulted in a "bleep" in the middle of clearly recognizable words (or in some cases a "bleep" after the word)." The Mass Media Bureau held that "[b]ecause the words were recognizable, notwithstanding the editing," they were indecent within the context used in this broadcast.

2. Dwelling/Repetition versus Fleeting Reference
Repetition of and persistent focus on sexual or excretory material have been cited consistently as factors that exacerbate the potential offensiveness of broadcasts. In contrast, where sexual or excretory references have been made once or have been passing or fleeting in nature, this characteristic has tended to weigh against a finding of indecency.

WXTB(FM), Clearwater, FL: "Bubba, The Love Sponge"

> *Could you take the phone and rub it on your Chia Pet? Oh, let me make sure nobody is around. Okay, hang on a second (Rubbing noise). Okay I did it. . . . Now that really your little beaver? That was mine. Your what? That was my little beaver? Oh I love when a girl says beaver. Will you say it again for me honey please? It was my little beaver. . . . Will you say, Bubba come get my beaver? Bubba, would come get my little beaver? . . . tell me that doesn't do something for you. That is pretty sexy. . . . bring the beaver. It will be with me. We got beaver chow. I can't wait, will you say it for me one more time? Say what? My little beaver or Bubba come get my little beaver? Okay, Bubba come get my beaver. Will you say, Bubba come hit my beaver? Will you say it? Bubba, come hit my beaver. That is pretty sexy, absolutely. Oh, my God, beaver.*

Indecent—NAL Issued.

WXTB(FM), Clearwater, FL: "Bubba, The Love Sponge"

Well, it was a nice big fart. I'm feeling very gaseous at this point but there, so far has been no enema reaction, as far as. There's been no, there's been no expelling? No expelling. But I feel mucus rising. . . . Can't go like. (Grunting sound) Pushing, all I keep doing is putting out little baby farts. . . . on the toilet ready to go. . . . Push it, strain it. It looks normal. Just average, average. Little rabbit one. Little rabbit pellets. I imagine maybe, we'll break loose. Push hard, Cowhead. I'm pushing, I got veins popping out of my forehead. Go ahead, those moles might pop right off. You can tell he's pushing. I'm out of breath. One more, last one. One big push.

Indecent—NAL Issued. The cited material dwells on excretory activities and the Commission found it to be patently offensive.

Compare the following cases where material was found not indecent because it was fleeting and isolated.

WYBB(FM), Folly Beach, SC: "The Morning Show"

The hell I did, I drove mother-fucker, oh. Oh.

Not Indecent. The "broadcast contained only a fleeting and isolated utterance which, within the context of live and spontaneous programming, does not warrant a Commission sanction."

KPRL(AM)/KDDB(FM), Paso Robles, CA: News Announcer Comment

Oops, fucked that one up.

Not Indecent. The "news announcer's use of single expletive" does not "warrant further Commission consideration in light of the isolated and accidental nature of the broadcast."

In contrast, even relatively fleeting references may be found indecent where other factors contribute to a finding of patent offensiveness. Examples of such factors illustrated by the following cases include broadcasting references to sexual activities with children and airing material that, although fleeting, is graphic or explicit.

3. . . . *Presented in a Pandering or Titillating Manner or for Shock Value*
The apparent purpose for which material is presented can substantially affect whether it is deemed to be patently offensive as aired. In adverse indecency findings, the Commission has often cited the pandering or titillating character of the material broadcast as an exacerbating factor. Presentation for the shock value of the language used has also been cited. As Justice Powell stated in his opinion in the Supreme Court's decision affirming the Commission's determination that the broadcast of a comedy routine was indecent, "[T]he language employed is, to most people, vulgar and offensive. It was chosen specifically for this quality, and it was repeated over and over as a sort of verbal shock

treatment." On the other hand, the manner and purpose of a presentation may well preclude an indecency determination even though other factors, such as explicitness, might weigh in favor of an indecency finding. In the following cases, the decisions looked to the manner of presentation as a factor supporting a finding of indecency.

KLOL(FM), Houston, TX: "Stevens & Pruett Show"

> *Sex survey lines are open. Today's question, it's a strange question and we hope we have a lot of strange answers. What makes your hiney parts tingle? When my husband gets down there and goes (lips noise). . . . I love oral sex. . . . Well, my boyfriend tried to put Hershey kisses inside of me and tried to lick it out and it took forever for him to do it.*

Indecent—NAL Issued.   Explicit description in a program that focused on sexual activities in a lewd, vulgar, pandering, and titillating manner.

WEBN(FM), Cincinnati, OH: "Bubba, The Love Sponge"

> *All I can say is, if you were listening to the program last night you heard Amy and Stacy . . . come in here, little lesbians that they are. Little University of Cincinnati ho's and basically that we could come over and watch them. We got over to the house. . . . They start making out a little bit. They go to bed. They get, they start, they're starting like a mutual 69 on the bed. Guido all of a sudden whips it out. . . . Rather than take care of each other . . . Guido is like knee deep with the butch bitch and all of a sudden here is the fem bitch looking at me. Hot. I get crazy. I hook up a little bit. Then Guido says, hey, I done got mine, how about we switching? So I went into the private bedroom with the butch bitch and then got another one.*

Indecent—NAL Issued.   . . . In determining whether broadcasts are presented in a pandering or titillating manner, the context of the broadcast is particularly critical. Thus, even where language is explicit, the matter is graphic, or where there is intense repetition of vulgar terms, the presentation may not be pandering or titillating, and the broadcast may not be found actionably indecent.

. . . WABC-TV, New York, NY: "Oprah Winfrey Show" (How to Make Romantic Relations with Your Mate Better)

> *Okay, for all you viewers out there with children watching, we're doing a show today on how to make romantic relations with your mate better. Otherwise known as s-e-x. . . . I'm very aware there are a number of children who are watching and so, we're going to do our best to keep this show rated "G" but just in case, you may want to send your kids to a different room. And we'll pause for a moment while you do that. . . . According to experts and recent sex surveys the biggest complaints married women have about sex are . . . their lovemaking is boring . . . American wives all across the country have confessed to using erotic aids to spice up their sex life and . . . thousands of women say they fantasize while having sex with their husbands. . . . And most women say they are faking it in the bedroom.*

> *[Quiz:] I like the way my partner looks in clothing. . . . I like the way my partner looks naked. . . . I like the way my partner's skin feels. . . . I like the way my partner tastes. . . .*
>
> *[Psychologist and panelists:] Do you know that you can experience orgasm, have you experienced that by yourself? No, I have not . . . Okay, one of the things that, well, you all know what I'm talking about. . . . You need to at least know how to make your body get satisfied by yourself. Because if you don't know how to do it, how is he going to figure it out? He doesn't have your body parts, he doesn't know.*

Not Indecent.   Subject matter alone does not render material indecent. Thus, while material may be offensive to some people, in context, it might not be actionably indecent.

. . . WSMC-FM, Collegedale, TN: "All Things Considered" [National Public Radio]

> *Mike Schuster has a report and a warning. The following story contains some very rough language. [Excerpt from wiretap of telephone conversation in which organized crime figure John Gotti uses "fuck" or "fucking" 10 times in 7 sentences (110 words).]*

Not Indecent.   Explicit language was integral part of a bona fide news story concerning organized crime; the material aired was part of a wiretap recording used as evidence in Gotti's widely reported trial. The Commission explained that it did "not find the use of such [coarse] words in a legitimate news report to have been gratuitous, pandering, titillating or otherwise "patently offensive" as that term is used in our indecency definition."

. . . Compare the following cases where licensees unsuccessfully claimed that, because of the context of the broadcasts (*i.e.,* alleged news stories), the broadcasts were not pandering.

KSD-FM, St. Louis, MO: "The Breakfast Club"

> *I've got this Jessica Hahn interview here in Playboy. I just want to read one little segment . . . the good part.*
>
> *"[Jim Bakker] has managed to completely undress me and he's sitting on my chest. He's really pushing himself, I mean the guy was forcing himself. He put his penis in my mouth . . . I'm crying, tears are coming, and he is letting go. The guy came in my mouth. My neck hurts, my throat hurts, my head feels like it's going to explode, but he's frustrated and determined, determined enough that within minutes he's inside me and he's on top and he's holding my arms. He's just into this, he's inside me now. Saying, when you help the shepherd, you're helping the sheep."*
>
> *(followed by air personality making sheep sounds) This was rape. Yeah, don't you ever come around here, Jim Bakker, or we're going to cut that thing off.*

Indecent—NAL Issued.   The broadcast contained excerpts from a *Playboy* magazine account of the alleged rape of Jessica Hahn by the Rev. Jim Bakker. The licensee explained the broadcast was newsworthy "banter by two on-air personalities reflecting public concern, criticism, and curiosity about a public figure whose reputedly notorious behavior was a widespread media issue at the time." Responding to the licensee's argument, the Mass Media Bureau stated that "although the program . . . arguably concerned an incident that was at the time 'in the news,' the particular material broadcast was not only exceptionally explicit and vulgar, it was . . . presented in a pandering manner. In short, the rendition of the details of the alleged rape was, in context, patently offensive."

. . . KSJO(FM), San Jose, California: Lamont & Tonelli Show

". . . she should go up and down the shaft about five times, licking and sucking and on the fifth swirl her tongue around the head before going back down. . . ."
　　"Show us how its done" (evidently the guest had some sort of a prop).
　　"Well, if this was a real penis, it would have a ****ridge, I would like (sic) around the ridge like this. . . ."
　　[laughter, comments such as 'oh yeah, baby'].

Indecent—NAL Issued.   The licensee claimed that the program was a clinical discussion of oral sex. The Enforcement Bureau rejected this argument on the grounds that the disc jockeys' comments on her material showed that the material was offered in a pandering and titillating manner. "The disc jockeys' invitation to have Dr. Terry use a prop on a radio program, and their laughter and statements (such as "oh yeah, baby") while she conducted that demonstration showed that the material was intended to be pandering and titillating as opposed to a clinical discussion of sex."

The absence of a pandering or titillating nature, however, will not necessarily prevent an indecency determination, as illustrated by the following case.

WIOD(AM), Miami, FL: "Penis Envy" Song

If I had a penis, . . . I'd stretch it and stroke it and shove it at smarties . . . I'd stuff it in turkeys on Thanksgiving day. . . . If I had a penis, I'd run to my mother, Comb out the hair and compare it to brother. I'd lance her, I'd knight her, my hands would indulge. Pants would seem tighter and buckle and bulge. (Refrain) A penis to plunder, a penis to push, 'Cause one in the hand is worth one in the bush. A penis to love me, a penis to share, To pick up and play with when nobody's there. . . . If I had a penis, . . . I'd force it on females, I'd pee like a fountain. If I had a penis, I'd still be a girl, but I'd make much more money and conquer the world.

Indecent—NAL Issued.   The Mass Media Bureau found the material to be patently offensive. In response to the licensee's assertion that this song was not pandering or titillating and therefore should not be considered indecent, the Bureau stated: "We believe . . . that it is not necessary to find that the material is pandering or titillating in order to find that its references to sexual activities and organs are patently offensive. (Citations omitted.) Moreover, humor is no more an absolute defense to indecency . . . than is music or any other one component of communication."

IV. Enforcement Process

The Commission does not independently monitor broadcasts for indecent material. Its enforcement actions are based on documented complaints of indecent broadcasting received from the public. Given the sensitive nature of these cases and the critical role of context in an indecency determination, it is important that the Commission be afforded as full a record as possible to evaluate allegations of indecent programming. In order for a complaint to be considered, our practice is that it must generally include: (1) a full or partial tape or transcript or significant excerpts of the program; (2) the date and time of the broadcast; and (3) the call sign of the station involved. Any tapes or other documentation of the programming supplied by the complainant, of necessity, become part of the Commission's records and cannot be returned. Documented complaints should be directed to the FCC, Investigations and Hearings Division, Enforcement Bureau, 445 Twelfth Street, S.W., Washington, D.C. 20554.

If a complaint does not contain the supporting material described above, or if it indicates that a broadcast occurred during "safe harbor" hours or the material cited does not fall within the subject matter scope of our indecency definition, it is usually dismissed by a letter to the complainant advising of the deficiency. In many of these cases, the station may not be aware that a complaint has been filed.

If, however, the staff determines that a documented complaint meets the subject matter requirements of the indecency definition and the material complained of was aired outside "safe harbor" hours, then the broadcast at issue is evaluated for patent offensiveness. Where the staff determines that the broadcast is not patently offensive, the complaint will be denied. If, however, the staff determines that further enforcement action might be warranted, the Enforcement Bureau, in conjunction with other Commission offices, examines the material and decides upon an appropriate disposition, which might include any of the following: (1) denial of the complaint by staff letter based upon a finding that the material, in context, is not patently offensive and therefore not indecent; (2) issuance of a Letter of Inquiry (LOI) to the licensee seeking further information concerning or an explanation of the circumstances surrounding the broadcast; (3) issuance of a Notice of Apparent Liability (NAL) for monetary forfeiture; and (4) formal referral of the case to the full Commission for its consideration and action. Generally, the last of these alternatives is taken in cases where issues beyond straightforward indecency violations may be involved or where the potential sanction for the indecent programming exceeds the Bureau's delegated forfeiture authority of $25,000.

Where an LOI is issued, the licensee's comments are generally sought concerning the allegedly indecent broadcast to assist in determining whether the material is actionable and whether a sanction is warranted. If it is determined that no further action is warranted, the licensee and the complainant will be so advised. Where a *preliminary* determination is made that the material was aired and was indecent, an NAL is issued. If the Commission previously determined that the broadcast of the same material was indecent, the subsequent broadcast constitutes egregious misconduct and a higher forfeiture amount is warranted.

The licensee is afforded an opportunity to respond to the NAL, a step which is required by statute. Once the Commission or its staff has considered any response by the licensee, it may order payment of a monetary penalty by issuing a Forfeiture Order. Alternatively, if the preliminary finding of violation in the NAL is successfully rebutted by the licensee, the NAL may be rescinded. If a Forfeiture Order is issued, the monetary penalty assessed may either be the same as specified in the NAL or it may be a lesser amount if the licensee has demonstrated that mitigating factors warrant a reduction in forfeiture.

A Forfeiture Order may be appealed by the licensee through the administrative process under several different provisions of the Commission's rules. The licensee also has the legal right to refuse to pay the fine. In such a case, the Commission may refer the matter to the U.S. Department of Justice, which can initiate a trial *de novo* in a U.S. District Court. The trial court may start anew to evaluate the allegations of indecency.

V. Conclusion

The Commission issues this Policy Statement to provide guidance to broadcast licensees regarding compliance with the Commission's indecency regulations. By summarizing the regulations and explaining the Commission's analytical approach to reviewing allegedly indecent material, the Commission provides a framework by which broadcast licensees can assess the legality of airing potentially indecent material. Numerous examples are provided in this document in an effort to assist broadcast licensees. However, this document is not intended to be an all-inclusive summary of every indecency finding issued by the Commission and it should not be relied upon as such. There are many additional cases that could have been cited. Further, as discussed above, the excerpts from broadcasts quoted in this document are intended only as a research tool. A complete understanding of the material, and the Commission's analysis thereof, requires review of the tapes or transcripts and the Commission's rulings thereon.

OBSCENE, PROFANE, AND INDECENT BROADCASTS: FCC CONSUMER FACTS

It's Against the Law

It is a violation of federal law to broadcast **obscene** programming at any time. It is also a violation of federal law to broadcast **indecent** or **profane** programming during certain hours. Congress has given the Federal Communications Commission (FCC) the responsibility for administratively enforcing the law that governs these types of broadcasts. The Commission may revoke a station license, impose a monetary forfeiture, or issue a warning, for the broadcast of obscene or indecent material.

Obscene Broadcasts Are Prohibited at All Times

Obscene speech is not protected by the First Amendment and cannot be broadcast at any time. To be obscene, material must meet a three-prong test:

- An average person, applying contemporary community standards, must find that the material, as a whole, appeals to the prurient interest;
- The material must depict or describe, in a patently offensive way, sexual conduct specifically defined by applicable law; and
- The material, taken as a whole, must lack serious literary, artistic, political, or scientific value.

Indecent Broadcast Restrictions

The FCC has defined broadcast indecency as "language or material that, in context, depicts or describes, in terms patently offensive as measured by contemporary community broadcast standards for the broadcast medium, sexual or excretory organs or activities." Indecent programming contains patently offensive sexual or excretory references that do not rise to the level of obscenity. As such, the courts have held that indecent material is protected by the First Amendment and cannot be banned entirely. It may, however, be restricted in order to avoid broadcast during times of the day when there is a reasonable risk that children may be in the audience.

Consistent with a federal statute and federal court decisions interpreting the indecency statute, the Commission adopted a rule pursuant to which broadcasts—both on television and radio—that fit within the indecency definition and that are aired between 6:00 A.M. and 10:00 P.M. are subject to indecency enforcement action.

Profane Broadcast Restrictions

The FCC has defined profanity as including language that "denot[es] certain of those personally reviling epithets naturally tending to provoke violent resentment or denoting language so grossly offensive to members of the public who actually hear it as to amount to a nuisance."

Like indecency, profane speech is prohibited on broadcast radio and television between the hours of 6 A.M. to 10 P.M.

Enforcement Procedures and Filing Complaints

Enforcement actions in this area are based on documented complaints received from the public about indecent, profane, or obscene broadcasting. The FCC's staff reviews each complaint to determine whether it has sufficient information to suggest that there has been a violation of the obscenity, profanity, or indecency laws. If it appears that a violation may have occurred, the staff will start an investigation by sending a letter of inquiry to the broadcast station. Otherwise, the complaint will be dismissed or denied.

Context

In making indecency and profanity determinations, context is key! The FCC staff must analyze what was actually said during the broadcast, the meaning of what was said, and the context in which it was stated. Accordingly, the FCC asks complainants to provide the following information:

- *Information regarding the details of what was actually said (or depicted) during the allegedly indecent, profane or obscene broadcast.* There is flexibility on how a complainant may provide this information. Complainant may submit a significant excerpt of the program describing what was actually said (or depicted) or a full or partial recording (e.g., tape) or transcript of the material.

    In whatever form the complainant decides provide the information, it must be sufficiently detailed so the FCC can determine the words and language actually used during the broadcast and the context of those words or language. Subject matter alone is not a determining factor of whether material is obscene, profane, or indecent. For example, stating only that the broadcast station "discussed sex" or had a "disgusting discussion of sex" during a program is not sufficient. Moreover, the FCC must know the context when analyzing whether specific, isolated words are indecent or profane. The FCC does not require complainants to provide recordings or transcripts in support of their complaints. Consequently, failure to provide a recording or transcript of a broadcast, in and of itself, will not lead to automatic dismissal or denial of a complaint.
- *The date and time of the broadcast.* Under federal law, if the FCC assesses a monetary forfeiture against a broadcast station for violation of a rule, it must specify the date the violation occurred. Accordingly, it is important that complainants provide the date the material in question was broadcast. A broadcaster's right to air indecent or profane speech is protected between the hours of 10 P.M. and 6 A.M. Consequently, the FCC must know the time of day that the material was broadcast.
- The call sign of the station involved.

Of necessity, any documentation you provide the FCC about your complaint becomes part of the FCC's records and may not be returned. Complaints containing this information should be directed to:

Federal Communications Commission

Enforcement Bureau

Investigations and Hearings Division

445 12th St., SW, Room 3-B443

Washington, DC 20554

You may also file a complaint electronically using the FCC Form 475 (complaint form) . . . or by e-mail. . . .

Judith Levine  **NO**

Is "Indecency" Harmful to Minors?

"**F**or more than 75 years . . . Congress has entrusted the FCC with protecting children from broadcast indecency," the Federal Communications Commission's chief enforcer David H. Solomon declared in April, 2004. "There's no question that the FCC is taking indecency enforcement very seriously these days."

No question indeed. Solomon was referring to the commission's new regulatory enthusiasm—some would call it a crusade—spearheaded by Chairman Michael Powell, seconded by President Bush, and toughened by two GOP bills to raise fines from the current maximum of $27,500 to as high as a half-million dollars; the laws would also revoke licenses after "three strikes." Solomon crowed about enlivening the definition of indecency—"language or material that, in context, depicts or describes, in terms patently offensive as measured by contemporary community standards for the broadcast medium, sexual or excretory organs or activities"—with a broader subset of "profanity." In addition to blasphemy (an already questionable concept in a secular nation), the commission would prohibit as profane any "personally reviling epithets naturally tending to provoke violent resentment" or language "so grossly offensive . . . as to amount to a nuisance." The "F-word," as the commission delicately refers to it, would hereafter be considered such a violently resentment-provoking nuisance.

And, oh yes, the FCC "remain[ed] strongly committed" to the First Amendment.

Powell had been itching to act. In January, 2003, his enforcers ruled that the Bono's exclamation on NBC's Golden Globe awards—"Fucking brilliant!"—was not profane. All year on Clear Channel radio, Bubba the Love Sponge nattered on about "waxing [his] carrot," Howard Stern discussed cum with porn stars.

But the last straw was half-time, Superbowl 2004. During a song-and-dance duet, a scripted bodice-rip by Justin Timberlake resulted in the momentary baring of Janet Jackson's right breast, bedecked with a sunburst-shaped "nipple shield." Organized conservatives predicted the end of civilization and helped mobilize a half-million complaints to CBS. Powell told the press of his cozy family "celebration" being ambushed by this "classless, crass, and deplorable stunt," and vowed to investigate. Rejecting Timberlake's claim of a "wardrobe malfunction," the FCC in July found the performance indecent—to the tune of $550,000 in fines against Viacom Inc., parent company to the 20 CBS affiliates that aired the show.

From *Extra!*, October 2004. Copyright © 2004 by Judith Levine. Reprinted by permission of the author.

While civil libertarians protested the supersized penalties and the ever-vaguer regulations, media companies sped to adopt failsafe policies. Scripts from *NYPD Blue to Masterpiece Theatre* were scrubbed, on-air personalities were muzzled and non-compliers canned. Clear Channel dumped Stern, and at Santa Monica-based KCRW-FM, Sandra Tsing Loh lost her $150-a-week job when the "F-word" slipped by un-bleeped during a commentary on knitting (the station later offered the position back, but Loh declined). The FCC praised such "voluntary action." Many producers called it scared s—less self-censorship.

The concept of indecency is inextricably linked to protecting children, which is why most sexual speech is prohibited on radio and commercial television between 6 A.M. and 10 P.M., when minors might be in the audience. According to veteran civil liberties attorney Marjorie Heins, laws are routinely passed and upheld in court based on the notion that witnessing sexual words and images is harmful to minors. Even among those who challenge the laws' free-speech infringements, few question this truism.

But there is no evidence that sexual speech harms children.

The idea that young (or female or feeble) minds are vulnerable to media-induced bad thoughts, which might lead to bad acts, might be called the founding principle of obscenity law. In 1868, an English anti-clerical pamphlet called "The Confessional Unmasked" was deemed punishably obscene because its text might "suggest to the minds of the young of either sex, and even to persons of more advanced years, thoughts of a most impure and libidinous character."

The worry that mobilizes the law, while neither pan-historic nor universal, is nonetheless old and enduring. In 1700, an English anti-masturbation treatise called *Onania, or the Heinous Sin of Self-Pollution, And All its Frightful Consequences, in Both Sexes Consider'd, &c* became a best-seller with such warnings as "*Dogs* in the Streets and *Bulls* in the Fields may do mischief to Debauch's Fancy's, and it is possible that either Sex may be put in mind of Lascivious Thoughts, by their own *Poultry.*"

In the late 19th century, while Anthony Comstock scoured daily newspapers for censorable "traps for the young," the New York Society for the Prevention of Cruelty to Children "kept a watchful eye upon the so-called Museums of the City," whose advertisements were "like magnets to curious children." According to one of the society's reports, a play featuring "depravity, stabbing, shooting, and blood-shedding" so traumatized a 10-year-old girl that she was found "wander[ing] aimlessly along Eighth Avenue as if incapable of ridding herself of the dread impressions that had filled her young mind."

By 1914, essayist Agnes Repellier was inveighing against a film and publishing industry "coining money" creating a generation hypersophisticated in sin. "[Children's] sources of knowledge are manifold, and astoundingly explicit," she wrote in *The Atlantic*. Perhaps the first to propose a movie-rating system, Repellier asked "the authorities" to bar children "from all shows dealing with prostitution." And in 1934, Dr. Ira S. Wile indicted "lurid movies, automobiles, speed, jazz, [and] literature tinged with pornography," among the causes of "The Sexual Problems of Adolescence."

After jazz came comic books, then rock 'n' roll, hip-hop, videogames, Internet porn—it's a miracle anyone has survived childhood with sufficient morality to protect the next generation from corruption.

In spite of all this hand-wringing, though, evidence of the harm of exposure to sexually explicit images or words in childhood is inconclusive, even nonexistent. The 1970 U.S. Commission on Obscenity and Pornography, the "Lockhart Commission," failed to find harm to children in viewing erotica, and even suggested such exposure could "facilitate much needed communication between parent and child over sexual matters."

In a survey of 3,200 elementary school kids in the 1970s (before MTV!), "the most productive responses were elicited with the instructions, 'Why children shouldn't be allowed to see R- and X-rated movies'; or 'What is in R- and X-rated movies that children are too young to know about?' Here, the children proceeded with aplomb to tell all that they knew but were not supposed to know," wrote the study's authors. The conclusion: Children are sexual, they know about sex, and this does not harm them. Their "innocence" is an adult fantasy.

Assembled to overturn the 1970 findings, the Reagan Administration's 1985 Commission on Pornography (the "Meese Commission") could not establish factual links between sexual explicit materials and antisocial behavior either. The lion's share of the testimony it heard concerned adult consumers, yet the commission pitched its pro-restriction recommendations to popular fears about children: "For children to be taught by these materials that sex is public, that sex is commercial, and that sex can be divorced from any degree of affection, love, commitment, or marriage," the report read, "is for us the wrong message at the wrong time."

Indeed, some research suggests that less exposure to sexual materials may be worse for children than more. Interviews of sex criminals including child molesters reveal that the children who eventually became rapists were usually less exposed to pornography than other kids. In general, according to Johns Hopkins University sexologist John Money, "the majority of patients with paraphilias"—deviant sexual fantasies and behaviors—"described a strict anti-sexual upbringing in which sex was either never mentioned or was actively repressed or defiled." On a less criminal note, students who attend sex ed classes in which a wide range of sexual topics are discussed do far better than those in abstinence-only classes in protecting themselves against pregnancy and disease and negotiating their sexual relationships.

So what about these fresh corrupting "indecencies"? Anecdotal evidence suggests the breast, the F-word, or anything Bubba says are not news to any child who isn't Amish. Eighth-graders interviewed after the Superbowl evinced only mild concern—for their younger siblings. "I thought the end was a little bit inappropriate," commented one girl, "being that kids of all ages were watching it."

And Bono's outburst? In a successful appeal of NBC's exoneration, Parents Television Coalition argued that the singer could "enlarge a child's vocabulary . . . in a manner that many, if not most, parents would find highly detrimental and objectionable."

To test this thesis, I googled "swearing and children." A hundred-fifty-five thousand hits proved PTC right on one claim: parents object to their kids' swearing. On the other, though, the evidence is shaky. Kent State psychologist Timothy Jay, an expert on cursing, told NPR that as soon as kids can speak, they start to cuss—because everyone around them does. Nevertheless, every online "expert" predicts parental surprise: "What a shock [when] a foul word escapes your little angel's lips!"

As with much objection to victimless crimes, a circular logic emerges. Kids curse, often in "inappropriate" settings like Grandma's house or kindergarten, to gain attention, to shock. This works (see above) because, well, cursing is inappropriate. Cursing is inappropriate because it is shocking and shocking because it is inappropriate.

Older kids curse to be like other kids, say the experts. Which came first, the kids cursing or the other kids cursing, is never clear. As for harms to children, the worst one mentioned is that cursing elicits punishment. Cursing is bad because it is shocking and shocking because bad; bad because inappropriate and inappropriate because bad; punishable because harmful and harmful because punished.

But cursing can be reined in with gentle discipline (aka punishment). Since it is a minor offense, mouth-washing with soap is not recommended. Adult cursing, on the other hand, is "highly detrimental" to children; thus, fines up to $500,000 are recommended.

When discussing sexual speech, child-development experts often invoke "age-appropriateness," a determination of high sensitivity, with miscalculations carrying grave consequences (Penelope Leach: "Although secrecy makes for dangerous ignorance, too much openness can turn on what is meant to stay turned off until later"). This leads to movie and TV ratings indicating that this film is okay for 13-year-olds but not 12-year-olds, that one for 17-year-olds but only when accompanied by an adult (who could be 18).

Given the gradual and idiosyncratic nature of children's maturation, the timing mechanism of a sexual education probably resembles a sundial more than the IBM Olympic stopwatch. Parents needn't worry so much. But efforts to delineate the boundary between child and adolescent, adolescent and adult, express an anxiety far greater than whether a breast that is appropriate at 10:30 P.M. is inappropriate at 9:30.

What scares us is that these boundaries, if they ever existed, are disappearing.

Philippe Ariès, founder of childhood history, famously proposed that before the 18th century, there was no such thing as childhood. At seven, a 17th century person might become a maid or shoemaker's apprentice; by 14 he could be a soldier, a king, or a parent; by 40, he'd likely be dead. The 18th century Romantics gave us the Innocent Child, uncorrupted by adult knowledge; the following century, the Victorians figured childhood innocence sexual in nature, even as the dangers and pleasures of the Industrial Revolution gave the lie to this wishful invention.

We have not left off trying to fortify the official wall between childhood and adulthood. Twentieth-century innovations from Freudian psychology to child labor laws laid heavy bricks in it. But in our century, globalized economies and proliferating communications technologies are kicking that wall down. Worldwide, children work in sweatshops, invest in stocks, commit crimes, join armies. Even "sheltered" children watch the same videos, listen to the same music, and surf the same Web sites as adults. They know about sex and they engage in sex.

While we locate them in a separate political category, a medical specialty, a market niche—and an FCC-patrolled time slot. But children in the 21st century may be more like adults than they have been since the 17th century.

It is unlikely the air will get less dense with information, or with sex— and no law, no Internet filter or vigilant parent can keep tabs on every pixel that passes before a child's eyes. All adults can do is help kids understand and negotiate the sexual world.

But the campaign against indecency is bigger than children. Parents Television Council and their allies in and outside government would like to Bowdlerize the public sphere entirely. So far, the courts have limited attempts, such as numerous online decency statutes, that would reduce all communications to a level appropriate to the Teletubbies.

Still, it is wrong to see censorship as bad for adults and good for children. Everyone can benefit from abundant accurate, realistic sexual information and diverse narratives and images of bodies and sex. In sex as in politics, only more speech can challenge bad speech. We won't all agree on what is bad, but it is time to wrest those definitions from the hands of radical moralists.

POSTSCRIPT

Should the FCC Fine TV Stations That Broadcast Indecency?

One year after the Janet Jackson "wardrobe malfunction," *The Onion* satirized the incident with its headline, "U.S. Children Still Traumatized One Year after Seeing Partially Exposed Breast on TV." The faux article included mock drawings by children, demonstrating their terror and trauma at seeing breasts and nipples. In its parody, *The Onion* is clearly making a statement that the effects of exposure to this type of "indecency was overstated. The fine was eventually overturned by a federal appeals court several years later.

All broadcast outlets are responsible for knowing the FCC's policies regarding obscenity, indecency, and profanity. Ironically, station managers who carefully read the FCC's own publication, with all its vivid case studies, could reasonably determine the document itself to be obscene, indecent, and profane. Indeed, portions of the FCC's Enforcement Policies were too obscene to include in this text, as they cited crude jokes about pedophilia, for example. One must wonder how professionals in radio and television respond when such an obscene document arrives in the mail from the FCC. On the other hand, explicit guidance is necessary for station managers to fully understand what may and may not be aired.

The examples cited in the FCC's Enforcement Policies may not always seem congruous. Further, some argue that the FCC has not been even-handed in its enforcement. On Veterans Day in November 2004, ABC aired the movie *Saving Private Ryan* in prime time, uncut with all its expletives and graphic violent war imagery. Sixty-six ABC affiliates refused to air the film, uncertain about whether the FCC would levy substantial fines for every single expletive uttered throughout the film, or whether it would regard the film's airing as a patriotic way to honor veterans of World War II. Ultimately, the FCC took no action against ABC or the affiliates who aired it, eventually issuing a statement declaring the film did not break decency standards. Had the FCC taken action on the airing of *Saving Private Ryan,* it could have only fined ABC based on its airing of expletives. No portion of the FCC policy restricts airing violent imagery. Thus, scenes in which soldiers are maimed are deemed acceptable for viewing.

Recently, debate over indecency stirred over the use of "fleeting expletives." These are expletives that are spoken casually but have no real association with the sexual or excretory meaning of the words. When the Philadelphia Phillies won the 2008 World Series, second baseman Chase Utley declared the team the "world fucking champions!" Other celebrities like Bono, Cher, and Nicole Ritchie have come under fire for their use of fleeting expletives on live TV.

In 2009, the U.S. Supreme Court ruled that the FCC could in fact fine television stations for airing fleeting expletives.

What is harmful to children? Is sexual speech and sexual imagery inherently harmful as the FCC policy suggests? Do you agree with Levine when she rejects the idea that sexual material is harmful to children? What do you make of the various cases cited by the FCC? Would you decide differently for any of those cases? Which ones? What other content, if any, do you believe should be restricted as "indecent" or as harmful to children? What penalties would you impose for stations that violate these restrictions?

Suggested Readings

E. Boehlert, "Indecency Wars," *Salon* (April 14, 2005).

J. Levine, *Harmful to Minors: The Perils of Protecting Children from Sex* (University of Minnesota Press, 2002).

J. Markon, "Supreme Court Takes Up Case of Use of Profanity on TV," *The Washington Post* (November 5, 2008).

A. O'Connor, "Court Throws Out Superbowl Fine," *The New York Times* (July 22, 2008).

Parents' Television Council, "Basic Cable Awash in Raunch," http://www.parentstv.org/PTC/publications/reports/2004cablestudy/main.asp (November 2004).

Parents' Television Council, "Basic Cable Awash in Raunch," http://www.parentstv.org/PTC/publications/reports/2004cablestudy/main.asp (November 2004).

R. Pugh, "Decency Advocate: ABC's Ryan Broadcast Flouted FCC Rules—What Now?," http://headlines.agapepress.org/archive/11/afa/172004b.asp (November 17, 2004).

F. Rich, "The Great Indecency Hoax," *New York Times* (November 28, 2004).

T. Shales, "Michael Powell Exposed! The FCC Chairman Has No Clothes," *Washington Post* (November 21, 2004).

United States Government Printing Office, *Can You Say That on TV? An Examination of the FCC's Enforcement with Respect to Broadcast Indecency: Hearing Before the Subcommittee on Teleco* (2004).

ISSUE 12

Should Prostitution Be Legalized?

YES: **Susan Milstein**, from "Want a Safer Community? Legalize Prostitution," an original essay written for this volume (2009)

NO: **Donna M. Hughes,** from "The Demand: Where Sex Trafficking Begins," text of a speech given at the conference *A Call to Action: Joining the Fight Against Trafficking in Persons,* Rome, Italy (2004)

ISSUE SUMMARY

YES: Susan A. Milstein, Ed.D., CHES, associate professor in the Health Department at Montgomery College and advisory board member for Men's Health Network, argues that while the legalization of prostitution will not stop all of the social problems associated with the institution, the benefits of legalization make it the best option.

NO: Donna M. Hughes, Ph.D., professor at the University of Rhode Island and leading international researcher on trafficking of women and children, counters that the criminalization of prostitution not only reduces demand, but also slows the spread of international sex trafficking.

Prostitution is often referred to as the "oldest profession in the world." Despite the fact that prostitution is illegal in many places around the world, both female and male prostitutes can be found in every city of every country on the earth. Prostitution, often referred to as "sex work," ranges from solicitation in outdoor settings like parks or the street, to brothels and high-end escort services, to the trafficking of unwilling individuals. There exists an ongoing debate about whether prostitution should be criminalized, decriminalized, or legalized.

It may be helpful when examining this issue to gain clarity about the distinction between criminalization, decriminalization, and legalization. Those who seek to end the practice through the criminalization of prostitution would take an abolitionist perspective, meaning that all aspects of prostitution would be illegal and punishable by law. The decriminalization of prostitution would remove any criminal penalties associated with the trade and allow prostitutes to operate in a similar manner to independent contractors or other independently licensed businesses. The third option, the legalization of prostitution, would call for state licensing and regulations, including the possibility of mandated testing for sexually transmitted infections. According to the U.S. Department of State Bureau of Democracy, Human Rights, and Labor, the legality of prostitution varies across the world, with it being illegal in many countries, legalized and regulated in others, while in some parts of the world the act of prostitution itself is legal, though other activities related to it are illegal, such as soliciting sex in a public place.

In the United States, prostitution is legal in two states: Nevada and Rhode Island. Though prostitution is technically legal in Rhode Island, operating a brothel and street prostitution are illegal (Rhode Island Law). On the other hand, Nevada, which legalized prostitution in 1971, has 25 legal brothels and about 225 licensed female prostitutes. Brothels in Nevada are allowed in counties that have fewer than 400,000 residents, which excludes the county where Las Vegas is located. However, research has indicated that 90% of prostitution in Nevada takes place in Las Vegas and Reno, where it is in fact illegal (Farley, 2007). Legalized brothels are highly regulated and state law requires that brothel prostitutes receive weekly tests for chlamydia and gonorrhea and monthly tests for HIV and syphilis (Nevada Law). Condom use is also required. In fact, research has shown that condom use is higher during sexual activity between a prostitute and a client, compared to sexual activity between a prostitute and a nonpaying sex partner. Such regulations exist as a public health measure to reduce the rates of sexually transmitted infections (STIs). Among prostitutes affiliated with Nevada brothels studied, there have been no cases of HIV infection, and the positive gonorrhea rate is about 1 percent. A 1998 study found that the prevalence of STIs among illegal street prostitutes in Australia, working outside of the legalized and regulated system was drastically higher (80 times greater) than their brothel counterparts.

The views expressed by many about prostitution may even depend on the context in which it takes place. Organizations such as the Coalition Against Trafficking in Women (CATW) consider prostitution to be sexual exploitation and focus on abolishing sex trafficking of women and girls. According to the U.S. Department of State (2004), "Where prostitution is legalized or tolerated, there is a greater demand for human trafficking victims and nearly always an increase in the number of women and children trafficked into commercial sex slavery. Of the estimated 600,000 to 800,000 people trafficked across international borders annually, 80 percent of victims are female, and up to 50 percent are minors."

Some sex worker activist organizations, such as Call Off Your Old Tired Ethics (COYOTE) and the North American Task Force on Prostitution, view prostitution as a choice and support the decriminalization of prostitution but oppose the regulations that come with legalization such as in Nevada.

In the following essays, Dr. Susan Milstein presents a rationale for legalizing prostitution, outlining the benefits of doing so, including financial and public health benefits, whereas Dr. Donna M. Hughes asserts that prostitution is a violation of human rights, leads to the dehumanization of women and children, and should not be legalized.

YES

Susan A. Milstein

Want a Safer Community?
Legalize Prostitution

Prostitution is a reality in the United States, regardless of its legal status. If it becomes legal, then outreach services, like drug and mental health counseling, can be provided. This will not only improve the prostitute's quality of life, it may encourage them to leave the profession. Legalization means that measures could be taken to protect prostitutes from becoming victims of rape and other forms of violence, while mandatory condom use, and STI and HIV testing, will help decrease disease transmission. There is also the benefit of the government being able to make money by imposing taxes. It's in society's best interest to make prostitution as safe as possible, which can be accomplished through legalization.

Legalize it, decriminalize it, or keep it illegal, the fact remains that prostitution is going to happen regardless of what the law says. Once we come to accept that as fact, the question then becomes, what is the best way to approach it?

So What Is Prostitution?

When you say "prostitute" people automatically get an image in their head. That image may be of a streetwalker, a call girl or a male escort. It may be of Heidi Fleiss or Deborah Jeane Palfrey, the DC Madam. It may even be of Elliott Spitzer. But what is prostitution? It's the exchange of sex for money. With this definition in mind, let's change how we look at prostitution. Instead of thinking of a streetwalker and pimp, imagine a woman who sleeps with a man in exchange for rent money and gifts. Is this prostitution? Some might say no, others might say yes.

Change the scenario again. Imagine a woman who is engaging in a specific behavior in exchange for money. Is that prostitution, or is it a job? It may be difficult to think of prostitution as just another job, but why? Is it because prostitution is seen as demeaning and degrading? What's the difference between working as a prostitute, and being locked into a Wal-Mart overnight and being forced to clean (Greenhouse, 2005)? It may be difficult to separate prostitution out from what may seem like other degrading and dehumanizing jobs simply because it involves sex. But if we can look past the sexual aspect, if we can stop looking at prostitution as being inherently immoral or unacceptable, if we can start to look at it as an industry, then we can start to see the benefits of legalizing it.

An original essay written for this volume by Susan Milstein. Copyright © 2009 by The McGraw-Hill Companies. Reprinted by permission.

Benefits of Legalizing Prostitution

There are multiple benefits to legalizing prostitution, the first of which is improving the health of the prostitute. If the United Sates were to legalize prostitution then there could be legislation that would mandate regular STI and HIV testing. This is currently how it works in Nevada, the only state in the US that has legalized prostitution. In addition to STI and HIV testing, using condoms for every sex act could also be made mandatory. Both of these types of mandates would help to prevent disease transmission among the prostitutes, their clients, and their clients' other sexual partners. But decreasing the risk of disease transmission, while important, is not the only health benefit of legalizing prostitution.

A study done in New York City found that the majority of prostitutes were addicted to drugs. Many continue to work as prostitutes as a way of making money so that they can feed their addiction. If prostitution were legalized, it would be easier to do drug outreach and education for the prostitutes. This might decrease the amount of drug use that is seen amongst prostitutes, and it may also help to decrease the number of people who are engaging in sex for money. Once sober, they may look to other professions for a steady source of income.

In addition to drug use, another problem facing many prostitutes is that of violence. Many prostitutes are raped by their clients. One study found that 80% of prostitutes had either been threatened with violence, or had been victims of violence. Violence, and threats of, may come from clients, pimps or the police. Currently, if a prostitute is raped or otherwise victimized, he or she has little to no legal recourse. But if prostitution were to be legalized, a sex worker who is raped would have the ability to go to the police and report it without fear of being arrested.

Legalizing prostitution may also make the work safer in that precautions can be put into place ahead of time to try and prevent violence from occurring. Many of these types of strategies have already been implemented in Nevada, where prostitution is legal in selected counties. Installing panic buttons in rooms may help to save a prostitute from harm if a client does get violent. Additionally, if violence occurs, the brothel owners can call the police without fear of being arrested.

A safer working environment, counseling services to help deal with drug use and being victims of violence, and reducing the disease transmission rates all create a safer environment for the prostitutes and their customers, but what about the community?

Benefits to the Community

What kind of community are we creating if we legalize prostitution? Perhaps we can create a safer one. If we pass legislation mandating STI and HIV testing, and condom use during each sex act, we can also pass legislation that restricts where prostitutes can work. Since men and women won't be out be on the street trying to attract customers, the streets will see fewer streetwalkers, and fewer people trolling for prostitutes. Combine this with a decrease in the amount of violence and drugs that surround the profession, and all of this is a benefit to the community. There is also the financial benefit.

If we require a prostitute to register so that we can monitor his or her STI and HIV testing, then that will create jobs. There will be a need for more people to work in the labs that will be doing the testing, as well as a need to staff an office that deals with regulation and record maintenance. Increases in social service programs, like crisis counseling and drug programs, will provide even more jobs. And if it's legalized, it can be taxed.

Sin taxes are taxes that are imposed on activities that are considered immoral, yet are still legal. These taxes may be imposed on drugs, like nicotine and alcohol, or on specific activities like gambling. With this kind of precedent, there is no reason why prostitution couldn't be legalized, and then taxed. The revenue generated by a prostitution tax could be used to help benefit a myriad of different government programs. This could in turn lead to an increase in the quality of life for thousands of US citizens.

Rethinking Prostitution in the US

Some may wonder why it is that Americans say they live in a free society, yet an individual does not have the right to decide to have consensual sex for money. If the country, outside of Nevada, is so anti-prostitution, why do we punish the sex worker, and not the person who is paying for sex? The majority of laws in the US actually trap a person in a life of prostitution. It may be that one way to decrease the number of people who work as prostitutes, is to legalize it.

When someone gets arrested for prostitution, they have a criminal record that will follow him or her. What jobs are available to someone who has been arrested for prostitution? If we don't make it a crime, a prostitute may be able to get the job training, health care, and mental and legal counseling that would enable them to leave the world of prostitution. Perhaps the answer is to change the way we deal with prostitution and arrest the people who are paying for sex, which is the law in Sweden. Or perhaps the US can do what many other countries are doing, and either decriminalize or legalize prostitution.

The fact is that the United States has already taken a step towards legalization. Depending on the population of the county, prostitution is legal in Nevada. Prostitutes must register to work, must use condoms for all sex acts, and must be tested for STIs and HIV on a regular basis. Some countries have chosen to decriminalize prostitution. Since changing the law in 2003, New Zealand has found no major increase in the number of prostitutes in the country, and there has been a positive change in the lives of many sex workers. Other countries, including England, Argentina, Canada, Germany, Greece, Scotland, and more than twenty others, have chosen to legalize prostitution (Procorn.org, 2008).

Bottom Line. . . . Prostitution Happens

Legalizing prostitution will not make the industry perfectly safe. False negatives can occur on STI and HIV tests, and condoms can break, which means disease transmission is always a possibility. Panic buttons and good working relationships with police won't guarantee a prostitute's safety. Make eighteen the minimum working age for a prostitute, and you will find people younger than that selling their bodies for sex, and others who are more than willing to pay for it. Legalization is not a cure for all the issues surrounding sex work in the US.

The bottom line is that regardless of the law, prostitution is going to happen. By legalizing it we can make it safer, for the prostitutes, the clients, their significant others, and society at large.

Donna M. Hughes  **NO**

The Demand: Where Sex Trafficking Begins

In light of shared moral responsibility to help the millions of people who are bought, sold, transported and held against their will in slave-like condition, a conference entitled "A Call to Action: Joining the Fight Against Trafficking in Persons" was held at the Pontifical Gregorian University in Rome on June 17, 2004. The event was part of the 20th anniversary celebration of full diplomatic relations between the United States and the Holy See, and their shared work to promote human dignity, liberty, justice, and peace. The following is the text of my speech.

The Trafficking Process: The Dynamics of Supply and Demand

The transnational sex trafficking of women and children is based on a balance between the supply of victims from sending countries and the demand for victims in receiving countries. Sending countries are those from which victims can be relatively easily recruited, usually with false promises of jobs. Receiving or destination countries are those with sex industries that create the demand for victims. Where prostitution is flourishing, pimps cannot recruit enough local women to fill up the brothels, so they have to bring in victims from other places.

Until recently, the supply side of trafficking and the conditions in sending countries have received most of the attention of researchers, NGOs, and policy makers, and little attention was paid to the demand side of trafficking.

The trafficking process begins with the demand for women to be used in prostitution. It begins when pimps place orders for women. Interviews I have done with pimps and police from organized crime units say that when pimps need new women and girls, they contact someone who can deliver them. This is what initiates the chain of events of sex trafficking.

The crucial factor in determining where trafficking will occur is the presence and activity of traffickers, pimps, and collaborating officials running criminal operations. Poverty, unemployment, and lack of opportunities are compelling factors that facilitate the ease with which traffickers recruit women, but they are not the cause of trafficking. Many regions of the world are poor and chaotic, but not every region becomes a center for the recruitment or

From speech given at *A Call to Action: Joining the Fight Against Trafficking in Persons* conference, Rome, Italy, 2004. Copyright © 2004 by Donna M. Hughes. Reprinted by permission.

exploitation of women and children. Trafficking occurs because criminals take advantage of poverty, unemployment, and a desire for better opportunities.

Corruption of government officials and police is necessary for trafficking and exploitation of large numbers of women and children. In sending countries, large-scale operations require the collaboration of officials to obtain travel documents and facilitate the exit of women from the country.

In destination countries, corruption is an enabler for prostitution and trafficking. The operation of brothels requires the collaboration of officials and police, who must be willing to ignore or work with pimps and traffickers. Prostitution operations depend on attracting men. Pimps and brothel owners have to advertise to men that women and children are available for commercial sex acts. Officials have to ignore this blatant advertising.

Components of the Demand

There are four components that make-up the demand: 1) the men who buy commercial sex acts, 2) the exploiters who make up the sex industry, 3) the states that are destination countries, and 4) the culture that tolerates or promotes sexual exploitation.

The Men

The men, the buyers of commercial sex acts, are the ultimate consumers of trafficked and prostituted women and children. They use them for entertainment, sexual gratification, and acts of violence. It is men who create the demand, and women and children who are the supply.

I recently completed a report for the TIP Office, U.S. Department of State on the demand side of sex trafficking that focuses on the men who purchase sex acts. Typically, when prostitution and sex trafficking are discussed, the focus is on the women. The men who purchase the sex acts are faceless and nameless.

Research on men who purchase sex acts has found that many of the assumptions we make about them are myths. Seldom are the men lonely or have sexually unsatisfying relationships. In fact, donna who purchase sex acts are more likely to have more sexual partners than those who do not purchase sex acts. They often report that they are satisfied with their wives or partners. They say that they are searching for more—sex acts that their wives will not do or excitement that comes with the hunt for a woman they can buy for a short time. They are seeking sex without relationship responsibilities. A significant number of men say that the sex and interaction with the prostitute were unrewarding and they did not get what they were seeking; yet they compulsively repeat the act of buying sex. Researchers conclude that men are purchasing sex acts to meet emotional needs, not physical needs.

Men who purchase sex acts do not respect women, nor do they want to respect women. They are seeking control and sex in contexts in which they are not required to be polite or nice, and where they can humiliate, degrade, and hurt the woman or child, if they want.

The Exploiters

The exploiters, including traffickers, pimps, brothel owners, organized crime members, and corrupt officials make-up what is known as the sex industry. They make money from the sale of sex as a commodity. Traffickers and organized crime groups are the perpetrators that have received most of the attention in discussions about the sex trafficking.

The State

By tolerating or legalizing prostitution, the state, at least passively, is contributing to the demand for victims. The more states regulate prostitution and derive tax revenue from it, the more actively they become part of the demand for victims.

If we consider that the demand is the driving force of trafficking, then it is important to analyze the destination countries' laws and policies. Officials in destination countries do not want to admit responsibility for the problem of sex trafficking or be held accountable for creating the demand. At this point to a great extent, the wealthier destination countries control the debate on how trafficking and prostitution will be addressed. Sending countries are usually poorer, less powerful, and more likely to be influenced by corrupt officials and/ or organized crime groups. They lack the power and the political will to insist that destination countries stop their demand for women for prostitution.

In destination countries, strategies are devised to protect the sex industries that generate hundreds of millions of dollars per year for the state where prostitution is legal, or for organized crime groups and corrupt officials where the sex industry is illegal.

In the destination countries, exploiters exert pressure on the lawmakers and officials to create conditions that allow them to operate. They use power and influence to shape laws and polices that maintain the flow of women to their sex industries. They do this through the normalization of prostitution and the corruption of civil society.

There has been a global movement to normalize and legalize the flow of foreign women into sex industries. It involves a shift from opposing the exploitation of women in prostitution to only opposing the worst violence and criminality. It involves redefining prostitution as "sex work," a form of labor for poor women, and redefining the transnational movement of women for prostitution as labor migration, called "migrant sex work." It involves legalizing prostitution, and changing the migration laws to allow a flow of women for prostitution from sending regions to sex industry centers. The normalization of prostitution is often recommended as a way to solve the problem of trafficking.

States protect their sex industries by preventing resistance to the flow of women to destination countries by silencing the voice of civil society. In many sending countries, civil society is weak and undeveloped. Governments of destination countries fund non-governmental organizations (NGOs) in sending countries to promote the destination country's views on prostitution and trafficking. Authentic voices of citizens who do not want their daughters and sisters to become "sex workers" in other countries are replaced by the voice of the destination country, which says that prostitution is good work for women. The result is a corruption of civil society.

In a number of countries, the largest anti-trafficking organizations are funded by states that have legalized prostitution. These funded NGOs often support legalized prostitution. They only speak about "forced prostitution" and movement of women by force, fraud, or coercion. They remain silence as thousands of victims leave their communities for "sex work" in destination countries. Effectively, these NGOs have abandoned the women and girls to the pimps and men who purchase sex acts.

When prostitution is illegal, but thriving, government officials often look jealously at the money being made by criminals, and think they are not getting their share. In countries that are considering the legalization of prostitution, the estimated amount of the future tax revenue is often used to argue for legalization.

Germany legalized brothels and prostitution in 2002. German lawmakers thought they were going to get hundreds of millions of euros in tax revenue. But the newly redefined "business owners" and "freelance staff" in brothels have not been turned into taxpayers. The Federal Audit Office estimates that the government has lost hundreds of millions of euros in unpaid tax revenue from the sex industry. Recently, lawmakers started to look for ways to increase collection of taxes from prostitutes. The state seems to be taking on the role of pimp by harassing prostitutes for not giving them enough money.

Although legalization has resulted in big legal profits for a few, other expected benefits have not materialized. Organized crime groups continue to traffic women and children and run illegal prostitution operations along side the legal businesses. Legalization has not reduced prostitution or trafficking; in fact, both activities increase as a result of men being able to legally buy sex acts and cities attracting foreign male sex tourists.

The promised benefits of legalization for women have not materialized in Germany or the Netherlands. In Germany, legalization was supposed to enable women to get health insurance and retirement benefits, and enable them to join unions, but few women have signed up for benefits or for unions. The reason has to do with the basic nature of prostitution. It is not work; it is not a job like any other. It is abuse and exploitation that women only engage in if forced to or when they have no other options. Even where prostitution is legal, a significant proportion of the women in brothels is trafficked. Women and children controlled by criminals cannot register with an authority or join a union. Women who are making a more or less free choice to be in prostitution do so out of immediate necessity—debt, unemployment, and poverty. They consider resorting to prostitution as a temporary means of making money, and assume as soon as a debt is paid or a certain sum of money is earned for poverty-stricken families, they will go home. They seldom tell friends or relatives how they earn money. They do not want to register with authorities and create a permanent record of being a prostitute.

The Culture

The culture, particular mass media, is playing a large role in normalizing prostitution by portraying prostitution as glamorous or a way to quickly make a lot of money. Within academia, "sex workers" are represented as being empowered, independent, liberated women.

To counter these harmful messages, there is an important role for churches to play in describing the harm of prostitution to women, children, families, and communities. In the United States, the Evangelical Christian churches are increasingly involved in the human rights struggle against sex trafficking and exploitation.

Unfortunately, in the battle against the global sex trade, the voice of moral authority that condemns all forms of sexual exploitation and abuse is being lost. Some churches are compromising on their mission and their vision. For example, in the Czech Republic, there is a government proposal to legalize and regulate prostitution, as a way to combat trafficking. Catholic Bishop Vaclav Maly, the Auxiliary Bishop of Prague, has made a statement in favor of legalization of prostitution. According to a *Radio Praha* report in April 2002, he has given up the moral battle saying, "The chances of eliminating it are practically nil. . . . Under those circumstances, it is better to keep it in check and under control by giving it a legal framework. This is not to say that I approve of brothels—but it seems to me that it would be better to have prostitution take place there—with medical checks-ups and prostitutes paying taxes. It would be the lesser of two evils."

More recently, Bishop Maly has been silent in the legalization debate in Czech Republic, but his original statement is posted on web sites supporting legalization, which gives the impression that the Catholic Church supports legalization. A voice of moral authority in support of human dignity and against the sexual exploitation and abuse of victims of prostitution and trafficking is needed in the Czech Republic. Bishop Maly could be this voice. He has a long history of supporting human rights. He was an original signer and spokesman for Charter 77, the petition calling for the communist government of Czechoslovakia to comply with international human rights agreements they had signed. He knows the importance of resisting abusive power and laws that enslave people instead of freeing them.

Faith communities, from the grassroots to the leadership, need to use their voice of authority to combat the increasing sexual exploitation of victims and its normalization.

Abolitionist Movement

There is a growing abolitionist movement around the world that seeks to provide assistance to victims and hold perpetrators accountable.

In Sweden, beginning in 1999, the purchasing of sexual services became a crime. The new law was passed as part of a new violence against women act that broadened the activities that qualified as criminal acts of violence. With this new approach, prostitution is considered to be one of the most serious expressions of the oppression of and discrimination against women." The focus of the law is on "the demand" or the behavior of the purchasers of sex acts not the women.

The U.S. government has adopted an abolitionist approach at the federal level. In 2003, President George W. Bush issued a National Security Presidential Directive. It was the first U.S. opinion on the link between prostitution and trafficking: "Prostitution and related activities, which are inherently harmful and dehumanizing, contribute to the phenomenon of trafficking in persons..." This policy statement is important because it connects trafficking to prostitution and states that prostitution is harmful. This policy goes against attempts to delink prostitution and trafficking and redefine prostitution as a form of work for women.

As a result of this abolitionist approach, more attention is being focused on the demand side of sex trafficking. Destination countries, particularly those that legalize prostitution, are coming under new scrutiny.

Conclusion

I believe that only by going to the root causes, which are corruption and the demand in destination countries, will we end the trafficking of women and children.

We need to urge all governments, NGOs, and faith communities to focus on reducing the demand for victims of sex trafficking and prostitution. All the components of the demand need to be penalized—the men who purchase sex acts, the traffickers, the pimps, and others who profit, states that fund deceptive messages and act as pimp, and the culture that lies about the nature of prostitution.

We could greatly reduce the number of victims, if the demand for them was penalized. If there were no men seeking to buy sex acts, no women and children would be bought and sold. If there were no brothels waiting for victims, no victims would be recruited. If there were no states that profited from the sex trade, there would be no regulations that facilitated the flow of women from poor towns to wealthier sex industry centers. If there were no false messages about prostitution, no women or girls would be deceived into thinking prostitution is a glamorous or legitimate job.

POSTSCRIPT

Should Prostitution Be Legalized?

The "oldest profession in the world" exists in most places of the world. What differs are the ways with which it is dealt in the communities where it occurs. These communities consider a variety of issues when trying to determine the legal state of prostitution.

Susan Milstein posits that if we are able to move beyond viewing prostitution as immoral or unacceptable, and begin seeing it as an industry, it is easier to understand the benefits of legalizing it. Milstein outlines the benefits of legalization, both to prostitutes themselves and to society. Legalization would lead to mandated STI and HIV testing, and condom use for all sex acts, dramatically reducing the spread of STIs among prostitutes and their nonpaying partners, as well as between clients and their partners. She also highlights other health benefits of legalized prostitution, namely the reduction of drug abuse and violence against prostitutes. Violence against prostitutes, such as rape, typically comes from their clients, pimps, or the police, and the criminal penalties associated with prostitution often leave the prostitute with no ability to report the violence or take legal recourse against it. Milstein suggests that legalization, as in Nevada, would decrease violence against prostitutes through the installation of panic buttons in rooms, and the ability to report violence without fear of arrest. Milstein also suggests that legalizing prostitution would facilitate more drug outreach and education for the prostitutes. Do you think that legalized prostitution would reduce violence against prostitutes and drug addiction among them? How would these protections work if prostitution were to occur outside of the confines of a brothel? How would a street prostitute be safe from violence, or access drug education and outreach? Are there ways to reduce violence and increase drug outreach and education to prostitutes without legalization?

Milstein also outlines the financial benefit of legalized prostitution, including taxation and job creation at STI testing labs. What do you think about this? Is it appropriate for communities to reap the financial benefits resulting from prostitution? Perhaps this question lends itself to the morality of prostitution. Donna M. Hughes disagrees with proponents of legalized prostitution who argue that prostitution is a sexual choice and people have the right to chose what they do with their bodies. Hughes argues that prostitution is demoralizing and that prostitutes, the majority of who are women, are not exerting personal choice but are rather being subjected to criminal assault and kidnapping that arises from the exploitation of people from communities devastated by economic strife. Who do you think is in control in these types of relationships? Are women (and men) simply choosing to express their sexuality in this manner? Are the clients seeking their services exploiting or dehumanizing prostitutes in any way? Do the social, economic, and policy imbalances between men and women in our society influence the context in which the women's choices are being made? Do you think there is a distinction between women who knowingly enter prostitution and those who are forced into it through human trafficking? Do the women who choose to enter prostitution really have a choice? Hughes also posits that women may be coerced into prostitution because they find they have no other options for employment. Does this also stem from societal imbalances? Should we simply accept the lack of other viable jobs for women as an argument for legalized prostitution, or should we strive to create additional opportunities for women and a society where there are less structural imbalances based on sex and gender?

It is evident that the arguments for and against the legalization of prostitution are varied. Where do you stand on the issue? Will legalizing prostitution reduce rates of STIs? Will it lower violence toward prostitutes? Will it financially benefit our communities? Does it represent a core human right to be able to choose how to express one's sexuality? Does prostitution as it exists around the world today represent free choice or coercion? Does it support a patriarchal society?

Suggested Readings

P.R. Abramson, S.D. Pinkerton, and M. Huppin, *Sexual Rights in America: The Ninth Amendment and the Pursuit of Happiness* (New York University Press: New York, 2003).

B.G. Brents and K. Hausbeck, "Violence and Legalized Brothel Prostitution in Nevada: Examining Safety, Risk and Prostitution Policy, *Journal of Interpersonal Violence* (vol. 20, no. 3, 2005).

S. Church, M. Henderson, M. Barnard, and G. Hart, "Violence by Clients towards Female Prostitutes in Different Work Settings: Questionnaire Survey," *British Medical Journal* (vol. 322, 2001).

M. Farley, *Prostitution and Trafficking in Nevada: Making the Connections* (San Francisco: Prostitution Research and Education, 2007).

S. Friess, "Brothels Ask to Be Taxed, but Official Sees a Catch," *The New York Times* (January 26, 2009).

ISSUE 13

Should Society Support Cohabitation before Marriage?

YES: Dorian Solot and Marshall Miller, from *Unmarried to Each Other: The Essential Guide to Living Together as an Unmarried Couple* (Marlowe & Company, 2002)

NO: David Popenoe and Barbara Dafoe Whitehead, from *Should We Live Together? What Young Adults Need to Know About Cohabitation Before Marriage: A Comprehensive Review of Research* (The National Marriage Project, 2001)

ISSUE SUMMARY

YES: Dorian Solot and Marshall Miller, founders of the Alternatives to Marriage Project (www.unmarried.org), describe some of the challenges faced by people who choose to live together without marrying and offer practical advice for couples who face discrimination.

NO: David Popenoe and Barbara Dafoe Whitehead, directors of the National Marriage Project (marriage.rutgers.edu), contend that living together before marriage is not a good way to prepare for marriage or avoid divorce. They maintain that cohabitation weakens the institution of marriage and poses serious risks for women and children.

What do Americans think of sexual relationships and living together before marriage? Attitudes have changed dramatically during the past generation. In a 1969 Gallup poll of American adults, two-thirds said it was morally wrong for a man and a woman to have sexual relations before marriage. A more recent (2001) poll revealed that only 38 percent of American adults share this opinion today. These two surveys focus on the sexual behavior of young people before marriage. When the question is broadened to examine how today's Americans feel about couples "living together," or cohabiting, 52 percent approve.

In practice, more than one-half of Americans live together before marrying. Many cohabiting couples will live together for a relatively short period of time, with most couples either breaking up or marrying within about 1½ years, though couples with children are more likely to stay together. In addition, the 2000 U.S. Census indicates that there are almost 4 million opposite-sex, unmarried households in the United States. (These households include both couples who have been married previously and those who have never been married.) Forty-one percent of these households have at least one child under the age of 18.

Like their married counterparts, infidelity is not common among the majority of cohabiting couples, though rates are slightly different. According to the U.S. chapter of the *International Encyclopedia of Sexuality* (Continuum, 2004), about 94 percent of married persons had sex only with their spouse during the last year, compared with 75 percent of cohabiting persons.

Despite the growing acceptance of cohabitation, couples who live together without marrying often face pressure from family and loved ones to "tie the knot." For some, marriage may be in their future plans; others may be perfectly happy with their decision not to marry; still other couples may be legally restricted from marrying only a few states permit same-sex couples to legally marry. Recognizing the pressures and discrimination some cohabiting couples may face, the Alternatives to Marriage Project advocates for the "equality and fairness for unmarried people, including people who choose not to marry, cannot marry, or live together before marriage."

The first essay that follows is from a chapter of *Unmarried to Each Other: The Essential Guide to Living Together as an Unmarried Couple,* a guide written by the organization's cofounders, Dorian Solot and Marshall Miller.

On the other side of the debate is the National Marriage Project, which expresses concern about the growing trend toward greater acceptance of cohabitation. The National Marriage Project provides "research and analysis on the state of marriage in America and to educate the public on the social, economic and cultural conditions affecting marital success and child well-being." The second essay, written by the National Project's co-directors, David Popenoe and Barbara Dafoe Whitehead, provides commentary and analysis of existing literature on cohabitation. It warns young people, especially young women, of the dangers of cohabitation to them and their children.

YES

Dorian Solot and
Marshall Miller

When Others Disagree: Surviving Pressure and Discrimination

We wish living together were easy. We wish all parents welcomed the news of their child's cohabitation with cries of, "How wonderful, darling! I'll bring over a lasagna so you won't have to worry about dinner while you unpack." We wish friends threw celebratory bashes, ministers blessed the new level of love and commitment, wise neighbors shared their insights about getting through hard times, and landlords cheerfully added another name to the lease.

Unfortunately, that's not the world in which we live. While an unmarried couple moving to the block generally isn't worthy of backyard gossip anymore, it's not unusual for partners to run into snags along the way. For gay, lesbian, bisexual, and transgender (GLBT) people, homophobia is often a bigger problem than marital status discrimination, though the two are closely linked. This chapter offers insights on some common challenges from the outside, and suggests practical ways to deal with those who predict catastrophe for your relationship, those who nudge you down the aisle, and those who discriminate against you. Although we can't guarantee the naysayers will help load furniture into your U-Haul for the big move, if you're lucky they might give you a friendly wave as you pull away.

Pressure Not To Live Together

There's no question acceptance of cohabitation has come a long way quickly. In a span of a few decades the act of sharing a home without sharing a marriage license has been transformed from scandalous to normal. Today it's something most people do before they marry. But despite how common it's become, living together still draws frowns, wrinkled brows, and even outright condemnation from some people. Nicole describes her parents as "rigid Catholics" and says they frequently tell her she's "living in sin." Her father warns her of eternal damnation, saying, "Your life on earth is so short, but eternity is so long."

> *Every holiday it's a nightmare filled with anxiety when we have to get together with my family, because my mother makes it so uncomfortable for the two of us. Even though we've been together for nine years, and I don't rely on her financially or anything, she makes it very, very uncomfortable. About*

From chapter 3 of *Unmarried to Each Other: The Essential Guide to Living Together as an Unmarried Couple.* Copyright © 2002 by Dorian Solot and Marshall Miller. Reprinted by permission of Marlowe & Co., a division of Avalon Publishing/Perseus Books Group LLC.

six months ago it all came to a head. She said that I wasn't welcome at her
house, so I don't go to her house anymore except at holidays.

This intense disapproval isn't because cohabiting partners store their tooth-brushes so close together, or because people believe that seeing your sweetheart's morning bedhead should be an experience only for married spouses. The real reason why there's opposition to unmarried people living together is this: cohabi-tors have sex. Of course, *lots* of unmarried people have sex, whether they live with their lovers or not. At least 70 percent of first-time brides and 83 percent of first-time grooms are not virgins on their wedding day—the percentages are even higher for younger generations—revealing exactly how much unmarried love-making is going on. Much of that sex involves far less love and commitment than is present in many cohabiting relationships. But the nose-wrinklers care about sex between cohabitors because there's no attempt to hide it, no polite, "We were just sitting here in the back room having a conversation. Really!" When romantically-involved unmarried people live together, everyone assumes they're having sex, and critics say they're flaunting it. That's where the arguments begin. . . .

The Arguments

Whether you're already living together or just talking about it, odds are you've crossed paths with some of the common arguments against cohabitation. Maybe your relatives are the number one anti-cohabiting campaigners in your

MOM ALWAYS KNOWS

Have you heard the joke about the cohabiting guy whose mother came to dinner? His mom had long been suspicious of the relationship between her son, John, and his roommate, Julie. When they had her over for dinner one night, John read his mother's mind, and volun-teered, "I know what you must be thinking, Mom, but I assure you, Julie and I are just roommates."

About a week later, Julie came to John and said, "Ever since your mother came to dinner, I haven't been able to find the beautiful silver gravy ladle. You don't suppose she took it, do you?" John said, "Well, I doubt it, but I'll write a letter just to be sure." So he sat down and wrote a letter:

"Dear Mother, I'm not saying you did take a gravy ladle from my house, and I'm not saying you did not take a gravy ladle from my house, but the fact remains that one has been missing ever since you were here for dinner. Love, John."

Several days later, John received a letter from his mother:

"Dear Son, I'm not saying that you do sleep with Julie, and I'm not saying that you do not sleep with Julie, but the fact remains that if she were sleeping in her own bed, she would have found the gravy ladle by now. Love, Mother."

life, or perhaps you've encountered a sermon in church or read some disturbing statistics about living together in the newspaper. Whatever the source, almost every line of argument fits into one of these categories: Living in Sin Arguments, Pseudo-Scientific Arguments, or Mars and Venus Arguments. Each one emphasizes a different concern and warrants a different response. Below are explanations about the problems with each kind of argument, and tips for how to respond.

Living In Sin Arguments: The Moral View Against Cohabitation

These are the classic arguments, the meat and potatoes, of why you shouldn't live with your partner. You've probably heard, "Cohabitors are living in sin. It's wrong," or "The Bible says you shouldn't cohabit," or "People who shack up are undermining family values." Those are just the polite versions. At their most hostile, these sometimes bring dire warnings of hellfire and eternal doom.

Words like these can be deeply hurtful, particularly when respected people of faith aim them at people of their own religion. Some cohabitors feel forced to choose between their faith and their relationship, even when the relationship is a good one. Anita says:

> I have been in so much turmoil about my perplexing situation. I am forty-nine-years-old and engaged to a wonderful man, but because of my past divorce I will lose all my medical benefits if I marry. I love this man with all my heart. I want to marry by my Christian beliefs, but I have a heart problem and limited funds, so I cannot afford to lose my health insurance. We live together, and we are happy. But I am so torn. I pray all the time for God to love me and not scorn me for what I am doing. I would love to have His blessing upon us without the legal marriage, and to know that we will still go to heaven.

Jacquie says that the Bible's messages are the only things that trouble her about being in an unmarried relationship.

> According to the scriptures, I'm in trouble. The book of Deuteronomy says that my former husband is my husband until the day they throw dirt on me. In the church's eyes, we are wrong. In the African-American community, that is one of the biggest things that we struggle with.

Fortunately, there are many religious and ethical people who disagree with this moralistic view against cohabitation, and believe in supporting healthy, loving relationships regardless of marital status.

How To Respond to Living in Sin Arguments
Understand the Bible in today's context.   You might be surprised to realize that despite claims like, "Cohabitation is entirely contrary to God's law," there's nothing in the Judeo-Christian Bible that explicitly says cohabitation is

wrong. In fact, the Bible includes teachings about holy unmarried relationships that are valid alternatives to marriage, and poems in the Song of Songs that celebrate an unmarried relationship. Rabbi Arthur Waskow says of these, "I believe that the Song of Songs is our best guide from the ancient tradition as to how sexuality could express the joyful and pleasurable celebration of God."

While parts of the Bible do address "fornication," or sex between unmarried people, many religious leaders and scholars believe that some Biblical teachings are no longer applicable to today's world. Of the many mores mentioned and permitted in the Bible, most faith traditions—liberal, mainstream, fundamentalist, and evangelical alike—now condemn behaviors such as polygamy, slavery, and the treatment of women as property. Reverend Jim Maynard of American Baptists Concerned says, "Most hold that the Bible is inspired by God but written in the words of humans. It contains human perspectives and prejudice that reflect that time and place in which it was written. What is normal for one day and time is not always applicable to others." While the Bible can provide inspiration and guidance, many clergy agree that one need not interpret it literally to remain true to one's faith. It's the relationship between the two spouses (even legally unmarried ones) and God that ultimately matters, not the opinion of the minister or the cranky lady in the front pew.

Many Christian leaders have called for the church to stay focused on Jesus's message of love. For instance, in 2000 Dr. William Walsh, the Bishop of Killaloe in Ireland, publicly apologized for the Catholic Church's attitude towards cohabiting couples and said, "Christ did not condemn those who failed to meet the ideals of the church. . . . We must not condemn. We must not question the nature of that love that may not meet with our ideals. We must celebrate family, and all that is possible in family; the love between married spouses and between parents and children; the love of the unmarried mother and unmarried father and their children, and the struggle that being an unmarried mother and father can be in our society."

Help others respect your decision.   If the person who accuses you of "living in sin" is close to home—a parent or relative, member of your faith community, or someone else with whom you'll have an ongoing relationship—you can work to help him better understand and respect your decision to live together. It helps to know exactly what concerns him. If the values underlying your relationship are his primary care, he may soften if he realizes you share his values of commitment, honesty, love, and integrity. It might help him to understand what your relationship means to you, how your shared values are central to your love, and why you aren't or can't be married. Witnessing you put these values into practice over a period of years can be the most powerful way to earn the respect of these doubters. Few would remain judgmental of Anita, the woman above with a heart problem, if they understood her situation and saw the Christian values woven into her daily life.

Other objectors' opposition to living together stems from a deeply held moral or religious belief that opposes all unmarried sex and rigidly upholds heterosexual marriage as the only acceptable form of family. A friendly conversation is unlikely to transform one of these types into someone who supports your relationship. It might be possible, though, to come to respect each other's points of view, mutually understand that you've made different choices, and agree to disagree. Marshall experienced this "hate the sin, love the sinner" approach firsthand:

> Before his death at age ninety-one, my grandfather regularly attended Sunday services at his southern Virginia Baptist retirement home. One of his preacher's favorite pastimes was rallying against those who "live in sin." Although our living together had never seemed to concern my grandfather before he moved to the retirement home, over time this preacher's message caused him to decide that he no longer wanted to see or talk to Dorian and me because of the sin he felt we were committing. His silent treatment lasted for months, and while it hurt us, we were fortunate to have support from the rest of my family. After lots of conversations with my parents, he eventually came around, reaching out to us with the compromise, "I don't hate you, I just hate what you're doing." We were glad to have several months of positive reconnections before he passed away.

It's not easy, and sometimes not even possible, to reach this point with every family member. But it can be worth trying.

Live the kind of "family values" that matter.   Pundits and politicians who lament "declining family values" are usually talking about a narrow view of family. In the real world, family ties aren't based on whether you're legally married, have children, or are heterosexual. Unmarried partners can be a family unit, and part of each other's extended families. Connect with each other's extended families by going to visit them (especially for important occasions like reunions, graduations, performances, and significant birthdays and anniversaries), spending holidays together, planning opportunities for each other's relatives to meet each other, signing greeting cards together, staying connected by phone and email, and finding common interests or hobbies to explore with "in-laws" (some unmarried people jokingly call theirs "out-laws"). Joan said this kind of positive family relationship earned her and her male partner, Fran, a respectful tolerator, if not a supporter:

> Fran's dad is eighty-four and very opinionated. He's been a deacon in the Catholic Church. Considering how conventional and traditional his views are, it's amazed both of us that he has accepted me and accepted our relationship as well as he has. It's really been a pleasure. I think it's because he kind of likes me, and I like him. He's also very close to Fran, and I think it's really important to him to maintain Fran's love and goodwill and the closeness that they have. I think he would like it if Fran got married, but he doesn't make an issue of it.

The more your relationship fits into your family's culture, the easier it becomes for people to choose to forget about how you are different. Finding ways for each other's relatives to meet and connect is one of the most powerful ways we've found to strengthen ties. Dorian describes one method we've used:

Marshall and I each have sisters who are much younger than we are. When we were in college they'd sometimes visit us, so we decided to create an annual "Sister Convergence" weekend. Starting when the girls were six, seven, and eight, they'd come every spring with teddy bears and sleeping bags in tow, eat piles of peanut butter and jelly sandwiches, teach us the sing-song hand-clapping games they'd learned on the playground, make embroidery-thread friendship bracelets they'd sell to our housemates, and surprise us with stealth tickling attacks. The hiding of the peanut butter jar's top became part of the annual tradition; back home they'd talk to us on the phone, giggling with glee when they heard we'd finally discovered where they stowed it behind a sofa cushion or deep in a sock drawer. They grew up knowing each other and looking forward to their weekends together. Even though they're not related, I think they feel like each other's extended families.

Create your own family.   Unfortunately, being connecting to extended family isn't an option for everyone. Many who have been rejected from or need to separate themselves from their family of origin find tremendous strength by forming an intentional family. These kinds of families can include your partner, close friends, or other people who play a significant role in your life. You might choose to share holidays or important events with them, and see them as a place to turn for support during difficult times.

Find a supportive faith community.   If you're a religious person, you may not have to settle for a faith community that condemns your relationship. You can tell a lot about a given church's stance on diverse families by looking at its approach to gay and lesbian issues. Some denominations and many individual churches, synagogues, and clergy have affirmed their support for GLBT people, and these are more likely to welcome all kinds of "non-traditional" relationships. Unitarian Universalists, Quakers, Reform and Reconstructionist Jews, and the United Church of Christ are particularly known for welcoming all people, regardless of their sexual orientation or marital status. . . .

Pseudo-Scientific Arguments: The "Scientific" View Against Cohabitation

In the 1980s and 1990s, when arguments based on morality ceased to pack the punch they once did, anti-cohabitation campaigners donned crisp white lab coats, re-tooling their messages for today's science-trusting public. The new arguments sound like, "Living together before marriage increases the risk of divorce," "Cohabitors are less committed to each other than married couples," and "Cohabiting couples experience more domestic violence than married ones." Gwen heard them from her mother:

I received a major backlash from both my parents in response to my choice to live with my boyfriend. My mother actually called and lectured to me extensively for forty minutes about the various kinds of research to substantiate her opinion that cohabiting relationships are very unhealthy.

Arguments like these can be confusing, since to many couples it makes intuitive sense to live together before tying the knot. The reality is, many of the statistics batted around in the media don't tell the whole story. It's not a coincidence the general public is becoming familiar with these semi-truths—some political groups have made them a central part of their anti-cohabitation campaigns. Yet most of the facts about cohabitation that are published in respected research journals and presented at academic conferences draw quite different conclusions.

How to Understand the Truth Behind Pseudo-Scientific Arguments

Understand the difference between "the average cohabitor" and your life.   You are not necessarily "average." With eleven million cohabitors in this country, it is nearly impossible to draw any meaningful conclusions about what we all have in common. Yet pseudo-scientific arguments do just that.

People live with a partner for incredibly varied reasons—if cohabitors were paint colors, we'd be a veritable rainbow. For sake of explanation, imagine that one kind of cohabitor, couples who live together as a step between dating and marriage, are red paint. Senior citizens who live together so they don't lose their pensions will be yellow paint, and unmarried couples of several decades' duration with no plans to marry are green. Low-income couples who would like to marry but want to be sure their future spouse can help them escape poverty are blue.

Anytime a researcher comes up with an average about cohabitors, she takes all the red, yellow, green, blue, and a bunch of other colors for all the other cohabitors, stirs them together, and come up with a oh-so-serious, scientifically accurate shade of—you guessed it—brown. As everyone focuses on this average number that's been produced—the muddy brown color—they forget that this average is utterly meaningless when it comes to understanding the red cohabitors, the yellow ones, or any of the others.

Cohabiting types that exist in large numbers affect the color of the whole pool when it's averaged. So since poor people, whom we colored blue, cohabit at higher rates than middle or upper-class ones, the average brown color will always have a blue tint. That means that certain characteristics about poor people, like the fact that they tend to have more health problems and higher rates of depression will make the average for *all* cohabitors look more depressed and unhealthy. But those tendencies aren't necessarily true for other cohabitors in the pool. Average cohabiting couples who plan to marry or are considering marriage have characteristics very similar to married people. Green cohabitors in very long-term relationships are statistically a small splash—their characteristics hardly show up in the average at all.

In short, because of the way some groups pull the average up or down, statistics about cohabitation often lead to distorted conclusions. Poor people who cohabit in large numbers make the average cohabitor income look low, but if you're making a good salary, that doesn't affect you. There are higher levels of alcoholism in the cohabitor population because people are less likely to marry partners with alcohol problems, but that doesn't mean that living together will drive you to drink. The quality of your relationship—not any statistical average—determines whether your union will be strong.

Realize there is no evidence that cohabitation causes divorce. It's true research finds that on average, cohabitors who later marry have a higher divorce rate than those who marry without living together first. But it's a misrepresentation to say that cohabitation *causes* divorce. Here's why. This research compares two groups of people, those who live together before they marry and those who don't. But people aren't randomly assigned to these different groups—they choose to live together or not because they're different kinds of people. Those who don't live together before marriage are a minority today, and they tend to be more conservative, with stronger religious beliefs and stronger opposition to divorce. Given this, it's no surprise that this group doesn't consider divorce an acceptable option. The difference between the two groups' divorce rates is likely attributable to the types of people in each group, not because the cohabitation ruins their relationships. As Sociologist Judith Seltzer writes, "Claims that individuals who cohabit before marriage hurt their chances of a good marriage pay too little attention to this evidence."

Given that many couples cohabit to test their compatibility before making a lifetime commitment to marriage, could cohabitation actually result in *lower* divorce rates? It's possible. The divorce rate has been falling slightly since its peak two decades ago. During that same time period, the cohabitation rate has skyrocketed. There's no way to know for certain how the changes in divorce and cohabitation affect each other—just because two things happen at the same time (correlation) doesn't prove that one caused the other (causation). Since some cohabitors live together to try out a relationship but then ultimately break up, it's likely these people successfully avoided a marriage that would have ended in divorce. Chances are good the divorce rate would be higher if not for cohabitation.

Cohabitation opponents make a lot of noise about divorce statistics because divorce is such a common fear. When you look at all the facts, whether you divorce ultimately may not have much to do with whether you live together. If you never marry, you don't need to worry about divorce, though the end of a long-term relationship has the same emotional impact. Chapter 4 is about what you can do to keep your relationship strong.

Know that commitment and marriage are not the same thing. As with most stereotypes, there's a grain of truth to the claim that cohabitors are less committed than married spouses. Dating couples are usually less committed than married ones, too. Since most people move through the stages from dating to living together to marriage, you'd expect average commitment levels to follow the same trends—lowest among dating couples, highest among married ones—and they do.

Of course there are some cohabitors who have no commitment to each other, just as there are married couples who aren't very committed and soon got divorced. Other cohabitors' levels of commitment easily match the most loving, stable married pairs. Some have plans to marry and just haven't done so yet, while others stay together for decades without a marriage license. In all murkiness of averages, there's no way to distinguish the couple who's owned a home together for thirty years from one who moved in together last week when one partner got evicted. Sure, scientists can come up with an average number to indicate commitment among cohabitors. But it won't tell you anything about your own relationship.

It's worth pondering how those scientists even come up with a number that equals commitment. It's a slippery concept to pin down using a survey— imagine trying to compare your commitment to your relationship to your friend's commitment to his using a numerical scale. One oft-cited study of cohabitors and married couples found a difference of 1.3 points on a twenty point scale of "commitment," and a finding that small isn't unusual. So the pundits are telling the truth when they say cohabitors on average aren't as committed as married people—but it sure isn't the whole truth.

The best way to win the argument over commitment is to prove your relationship can stand the test of time. As the years tick by and you weather some tough times, outsiders will realize you're in it for the long haul. Calling yours a "committed relationship" or describing yourselves as "life partners" if that describes you can help people understand.

Understand the "accumulation factor." Cohabitation opponents exaggerate every negative research conclusion about the subject while ignoring research that finds cohabitors are just like everyone else. One of the most alarming claims might be that cohabiting women are at higher risk of domestic violence than married ones. What's actually going on? First of all, there isn't much of a difference between married and cohabiting women on this characteristic. One British study that's often cited found that 2 percent of married women had experienced domestic assault in the previous year, compared with 3 percent of cohabiting women. Nonetheless, since any amount of domestic violence is unacceptable, even a 1 percent difference could be cause for concern.

A more recent study explores why that difference exists. It finds that if you track a group of new cohabitors over time, the ones with less violent relationships are more likely to marry. No surprise there. The couples still in the cohabitor pool after the non-violent couples marry—the ones who "accumulate"—are probably using excellent judgement by deciding not to make a lifetime commitment to a dangerous partner. But they affect the average for the whole pool, and make it look as if cohabitors have more abusive relationships. It's likely that a similar process clouds a great deal of the research that compares married to unmarried people.

Marriage isn't a shield that can protect anyone from abuse, and cohabitation isn't automatically a battleground. A non-violent partner is unlikely to turn aggressive because you've cohabited too long. An abusive partner is unlikely to be transformed if you get married, and in fact, marrying could put you at greater risk. Marital status is a poor way to predict whether any particular relationship will be safe.

Mars and Venus Arguments: The Gendered View Against Cohabitation

Mars and Venus Arguments assume that all men (from Mars) are looking for sex without responsibility, while all women (from Venus) are looking for husbands and babies soon after. Mars and Venus are believed to be in their own orbits, at risk for major problems when they interact or live together. Women are most often the targets of these kinds of arguments, but men aren't immune. Perhaps you've heard, "In cohabitation, men get to have sex without making a commitment," "Women are the ones who get hurt by living together," or, "He won't buy the cow if you give away the milk for free."

It's certainly possible to run into these kinds of problems if you and your partner haven't talked about what living together means to you. If one of you thinks it's a new level of commitment while the other thinks it's a way to split the rent check, you're headed for trouble. If one partner thinks you're practically engaged while the other sees the setup as a roommate "with benefits," there's conflict ahead. But if you're on the same page because you've had a few of those capital letter Relationship Talks, you're unlikely to be taken by surprise, whatever your gender. Don't be surprised if Mars is the one dreaming of hearth and home, while Venus is hesitant to get tied down—gender roles aren't what they used to be. Sebastian gets a kick out of reminding people of this:

> My friends and acquaintances will say to me, "Oh, how long have you guys been together?" I'll say, "Almost eight years." They're in shock, and of course the next question is, "Why don't you get married?," as if they're asking, what's wrong with you? And of course they immediately assume that Janna wants to get married and I don't, because I want to go sow my wild oats, afraid of commitment, guy problem, or whatever. It's actually kind of fun to pop their bubble, to explain the decision that we've made together. I enjoy seeing them try to take that in.

Despite all the stereotypes, many more women have serious hesitations about marrying than men. Among hundreds of long-term male-female unmarried couples we've talked to, it's nearly always the woman who feels strongly about not marrying. Women's preferences about marriage generally seem to "trump" their male partners, perhaps because they tend to have stronger feelings on the issue—if a woman wants to marry, she'll keep looking until she finds a man who consents, and Stacey is a typical example:

> I've been with my partner for fifteen years and we've lived together ever since my pregnancy and the birth of our daughter, who is now ten. My father always wanted to know why we didn't get married. He pestered me about it, refusing to accept that I didn't wish to be married—after all, he thought, all women want to get married. One day he finally asked my partner straight out why he didn't marry me. When my partner said he was more than willing to get married, but that I was the one refusing, I think my father just gave up.

How To Respond to Mars and Venus Arguments

Point out that it's a lot easier to have sex without commitment if you're not living together.   If you're feeling bold, try, "We were making love long before we made the commitment to move in together." People who truly want sex without commitment don't cohabit—they just find a casual relationship or one-night-stand. By comparison, most partners who move in together are already in an intimate, sexual relationship and want to *increase* their level of connection and commitment. We don't know anyone who decided to cohabit because they wanted sex without commitment. As Mark told us, "My girlfriend and I intend to marry but do not want to rush into it before we are truly ready. We decided to live together because we were spending all our time together, anyway—why rent two apartments when we could rent one? We saw living together as a commitment to each other."

Point out that humans are not cattle.   "Mom, I'm not a cow," ought to suffice. Many younger women have never even heard the warning that if they "give away the milk for free," their partner "won't buy the cow." The adage used to refer to women who "gave away" sex without holding out for marriage. The theory was that if the man could get sex without paying the price (marriage), he would never feel the need to say "I do." Women of older generations were probably surprised to read the recent discussion about the saying on the Alternatives to Marriage Project's online list:

> *Someone mentioned the old adage about the cow and men getting free milk. What is this supposed to mean? Isn't the woman getting "free milk," as well? After all, women do enjoy sex, too.*

> —Jessica

> *I've been saying that to my boyfriend for about fifteen years. I also told him that if he wanted to get married, he shouldn't have moved in with me. When I saw the phrase, I thought the woman was getting the free milk.*

> —Tori

Most women today recognize themselves as sexual beings with their own desires, who choose sexual relationships or not based on their own situation and values. It doesn't make sense to men today, either. More than eight in ten first-time grooms has had sex before he marries, yet there men stand at the altar, undeterred by all that "free milk."

Gendered double standards still exist. Women are still expected to guard sex, are labeled "sluts" if they're perceived to be having too much sex, and are targeted for warnings about "ruining their reputations." Men, on the other hand, are told they need to guard their money. Guys hear that if they're not careful, while he's busy enjoying sex with his live-in lover, she will max out his credit cards and expect a stream of expensive gifts until she finds the next guy to run off with. The best way to prevent being taken advantage of is to understand your partner thoroughly—whatever your gender or what you want to protect. Know whether each of you is responsible with money, what sex means to each partner, and what your expectations are about commitment and monogamy. If you're clear about what living together means for you, it'll be much easier to calm the fears provoked by Mars and Venus alarmists. . . .

David Popenoe and
Barbara Dafoe Whitehead

NO

Should We Live Together? What Young Adults Need to Know about Cohabitation Before Marriage: A Comprehensive Review of Recent Research

Executive Summary

Cohabitation is replacing marriage as the first living together experience for young men and women. When blushing brides walk down the aisle at the beginning of the new millennium, well over half have already lived together with a boyfriend.

For today's young adults, the first generation to come of age during the divorce revolution, living together seems like a good way to achieve some of the benefits of marriage and avoid the risk of divorce. Couples who live together can share expenses and learn more about each other. They can find out if their partner has what it takes to be married. If things don't work out, breaking up is easy to do. Cohabiting couples do not have to seek legal or religious permission to dissolve their union.

Not surprisingly, young adults favor cohabitation. According to surveys, most young people say it is a good idea to live with a person before marrying.

But a careful review of the available social science evidence suggests that living together is not a good way to prepare for marriage or to avoid divorce. What's more, it shows that the rise in cohabitation is not a positive family trend. Cohabiting unions tend to weaken the institution of marriage and pose special risks for women and children. Specifically, the research indicates that:

- Living together before marriage increases the risk of breaking up after marriage.
- Living together outside of marriage increases the risk of domestic violence for women, and the risk of physical and sexual abuse for children.

From *Should We Live Together? What Young Adults Need to Know About Cohabitation Before Marriage: A Comprehensive Review of Recent Research,* Second Edition. Copyright 2002 by the National Marriage Project at Rudgers University. Reprinted by permission of the National Marriage Project.

- Unmarried couples have lower levels of happiness and wellbeing than married couples.

Because this generation of young adults is so keenly aware of the fragility of marriage, it is especially important for them to know what contributes to marital success and what may threaten it. Yet many young people do not know the basic facts about cohabitation and its risks. Nor are parents, teachers, clergy and others who instruct the young in matters of sex, love and marriage well acquainted with the social science evidence. Therefore, one purpose of this paper is to report on the available research.

At the same time, we recognize the larger social and cultural trends that make cohabiting relationships attractive to many young adults today. Unmarried cohabitation is not likely to go away. Given this reality, the second purpose of this paper is to guide thinking on the question: "should we live together?" We offer four principles that may help. These principles may not be the last words on the subject but they are consistent with the available evidence and may help never-married young adults avoid painful losses in their love lives and achieve satisfying and long-lasting relationships and marriage.

1. **Consider not living together at all before marriage.** Cohabitation appears not to be helpful and may be harmful as a try-out for marriage. There is no evidence that if you decide to cohabit before marriage you will have a stronger marriage than those who don't live together, and some evidence to suggest that if you live together before marriage, you are more likely to break up after marriage. Cohabitation is probably least harmful (though not necessarily helpful) when it is prenuptial—when both partners are definitely planning to marry, have formally announced their engagement and have picked a wedding date.
2. **Do not make a habit of cohabiting.** Be aware of the dangers of multiple living together experiences, both for your own sense of wellbeing and for your chances of establishing a strong lifelong partnership. Contrary to popular wisdom, you do not learn to have better relationships from multiple failed cohabiting relationships. In fact, multiple cohabiting is a strong predictor of the failure of future relationships.
3. **Limit cohabitation to the shortest possible period of time.** The longer you live together with a partner, the more likely it is that the low-commitment ethic of cohabitation will take hold, the opposite of what is required for a successful marriage.
4. **Do not cohabit if children are involved.** Children need and should have parents who are committed to staying together over the long term. Cohabiting parents break up at a much higher rate than married parents and the effects of breakup can be devastating and often long lasting. Moreover, children living in cohabiting unions with stepfathers or mother's boyfriends are at higher risk of sexual abuse and physical violence, including lethal violence, than are children living with married biological parents.

Should We Live Together? What Young Adults Need to Know about Cohabitation Before Marriage: A Comprehensive Review of Recent Research

Living together before marriage is one of America's most significant and unexpected family trends. By simple definition, living together—or unmarried cohabitation—is the status of couples who are sexual partners, not married to each other, and sharing a household. By 2000, the total number of unmarried couples in America was almost four and three-quarters million, up from less than half a million in 1960. It is estimated that about a quarter of unmarried women between the ages of 25 and 39 are currently living with a partner and about half have lived at some time with an unmarried partner (the data are typically reported for women but not for men). Over half of all first marriages are now preceded by cohabitation, compared to virtually none earlier in the century.

What makes cohabitation so significant is not only its prevalence but also its widespread popular acceptance. In recent representative national surveys nearly 66% of high school senior boys and 61% of the girls indicated that they "agreed" or "mostly agreed" with the statement "it is usually a good idea for a couple to live together before getting married in order to find out whether they really get along." And three quarters of the students stated that "a man and a woman who live together without being married" are either "experimenting with a worthwhile alternative lifestyle" or "doing their own thing and not affecting anyone else."

Unlike divorce or unwed childbearing, the trend toward cohabitation has inspired virtually no public comment or criticism. It is hard to believe that across America, only thirty years ago, living together for unmarried, heterosexual couples was against the law. And it was considered immoral—living in sin—or at the very least highly improper. Women who provided sexual and housekeeping services to a man without the benefits of marriage were regarded as fools at best and morally loose at worst. A double standard existed, but cohabiting men were certainly not regarded with approbation.

Today, the old view of cohabitation seems yet another example of the repressive Victorian norms. The new view is that cohabitation represents a more progressive approach to intimate relationships. How much healthier women are to be free of social pressure to marry and stigma when they don't. How much better off people are today to be able to exercise choice in their sexual and domestic arrangements. How much better off marriage can be, and how many divorces can be avoided, when sexual relationships start with a trial period.

Surprisingly, much of the accumulating social science research suggests otherwise. What most cohabiting couples don't know, and what in fact few people know, are the conclusions of many recent studies on unmarried cohabitation and its implications for young people and for society. Living together before marriage may seem like a harmless or even a progressive family trend until one takes a careful look at the evidence.

How Living Together Before Marriage May Contribute to Marital Failure

The vast majority of young people today want to marry and have children. And many if not most see cohabitation as a way to test marital compatibility and improve the chances of long-lasting marriage. Their reasoning is as follows: Given the high levels of divorce, why be in a hurry to marry? Why not test marital compatibility by sharing a bed and a bathroom for a year or even longer? If it doesn't work out, one can simply move out. According to this reasoning, cohabitation weeds out unsuitable partners through a process of natural de-selection. Over time, perhaps after several living-together relationships, a person will eventually find a marriageable mate.

The social science evidence challenges the popular idea that cohabiting ensures greater marital compatibility and thereby promotes stronger and more enduring marriages. Cohabitation does not reduce the likelihood of eventual divorce; in fact, it is associated with a higher divorce risk. Although the association was stronger a decade or two ago and has diminished in the younger generations, virtually all research on the topic has determined that the chances of divorce ending a marriage preceded by cohabitation are significantly greater than for a marriage not preceded by cohabitation. A 1992 study of 3,300 cases, for example, based on the 1987 National Survey of Families and Households, found that in their marriages prior cohabitors "are estimated to have a hazard of dissolution that is about 46% higher than for noncohabitors." The authors of this study concluded, after reviewing all previous studies, that the enhanced risk of marital disruption following cohabitation "is beginning to take on the status of an empirical generalization."

More in question within the research community is why the striking statistical association between cohabitation and divorce should exist. Perhaps the most obvious explanation is that those people willing to cohabit are more unconventional than others and less committed to the institution of marriage. These are the same people, then, who more easily will leave a marriage if it becomes troublesome. By this explanation, cohabitation doesn't cause divorce but is merely associated with it because the same types of people are involved in both phenomena.

There is substantial empirical support for this position. Yet, in most studies, even when this "selection effect" is carefully controlled statistically, a negative effect of cohabitation on later marriage stability still remains. And no positive contribution of cohabitation to marriage has ever been found.

The reasons for a negative "cohabitation effect" are not fully understood. One may be that while marriages are held together largely by a strong ethic of commitment, cohabiting relationships by their very nature tend to undercut this ethic. Although cohabiting relationships are like marriages in many ways—shared dwelling, economic union (at least in part), sexual intimacy, often even children—they typically differ in the levels of commitment and autonomy involved. According to recent studies, cohabitants tend not to be as committed as married couples in their dedication to the continuation of the relationship and reluctance to terminate it, and they are more oriented toward their own personal autonomy. It is reasonable to speculate, based on these studies, that once this low-commitment, high-autonomy pattern of relating is learned, it becomes hard to unlearn. One study found, for example, that "living with a romantic partner prior to marriage was associated with more negative and less positive problem solving support and behavior during marriage." A reason for this, the authors suggest, is that because long-term commitment is less certain in cohabitation, "there may be less motivation for cohabiting partners to develop their conflict resolution and support skills."

The results of several studies suggest that cohabitation may change partners' attitudes toward the institution of marriage, contributing to either making marriage less likely, or if marriage takes place, less successful. A 1997 longitudinal study conducted by demographers at Pennsylvania State University concluded, for example, "cohabitation increased young people's acceptance of divorce, but other independent living experiences did not." And "the more months of exposure to cohabitation that young people experienced, the less enthusiastic they were toward marriage and childbearing."

Particularly problematic is serial cohabitation. One study determined that the effect of cohabitation on later marital instability is found only when one or both partners had previously cohabited with someone other than their spouse. A reason for this could be that the experience of dissolving one cohabiting relationship generates a greater willingness to dissolve later relationships. People's tolerance for unhappiness is diminished, and they will scrap a marriage that might otherwise be salvaged. This may be similar to the attitudinal effects of divorce; going through a divorce makes one more tolerant of divorce.

If the conclusions of these studies hold up under further investigation, they may contain the answer to the question of why premarital cohabitation should effect the stability of a later marriage. The act of cohabitation generates changes in people's attitudes toward marriage that make the stability of marriage less likely. Society wide, therefore, the growth of cohabitation will tend to further weaken marriage as an institution.

An important caveat must be inserted here. There is a growing understanding among researchers that different types and life-patterns of cohabitation must be distinguished clearly from each other. Cohabitation that is an immediate prelude to marriage, or prenuptial cohabitation—both partners plan to marry each other in the near future—is different from other forms. There is some evidence to support the proposition that living together for a short period of time with the person one intends to marry has no adverse effects on the subsequent marriage. Cohabitation in this case appears to be very similar to marriage; it merely takes place during the engagement period. This proposition would appear to be less true, however, when one or both of the partners has had prior experience with cohabitation, or brings children into the relationship.

Cohabitation as an Alternative to Marriage

According to the latest information available, 46% of all cohabitations in a given year can be classified as precursors to marriage. Most of the remainder can be considered some form of alternative to marriage, including trial

Percentage of High School Seniors Who "Agreed" or "Mostly Agreed" with the Statement That "It Is Usually a Good Idea for a Couple to Live Together before Getting Married in Order to Find Out Whether They Really Get Along," by Period, United States

	Boys	Girls
1976–1980	44.9	32.3
1981–1985	47.4	36.5
1986–1990	57.8	45.2
1991–1995	60.5	51.3
1996–2000	66.0	61.3

Source: Monitoring the Future 2000, and earlier surveys conducted by the Survey Research Center at the University of Michigan.

marriages, and their number is increasing. This should be of great national concern, not only for what the growth of cohabitation is doing to the institution of marriage but for what it is doing, or not doing, for the participants involved. In general, cohabiting relationships tend in many ways to be less satisfactory than marriage relationships.

Except perhaps for the short term prenuptial type of cohabitation, and probably also for the post-marriage cohabiting relationships of seniors and retired people who typically cohabit rather than marry for economic reasons, cohabitation and marriage relationships are qualitatively different. Cohabiting couples report lower levels of happiness, lower levels of sexual exclusivity and sexual satisfaction, and poorer relationships with their parents. One reason is that, as several sociologists not surprisingly concluded after a careful analysis, in unmarried cohabitation "levels of certainty about the relationship are lower than in marriage."

It is easy to understand, therefore, why cohabiting is inherently much less stable than marriage and why, especially in view of the fact that it is easier to terminate, the break-up rate of cohabitors is far higher than for married partners. After 5 to 7 years, 39% of all cohabiting couples have broken their relationship, 40% have married (although the marriage might not have lasted), and only 21% are still cohabiting.

Still not fully known by the public at large is the fact that married couples have substantial benefits over the unmarried in labor force productivity, physical and mental health, general happiness, and longevity. There is evidence that these benefits are diluted for couples who are not married but merely cohabiting. Among the probable reasons for the benefits of marriage, as summarized by University of Chicago demographer Linda Waite, are:

- *The long-term contract implicit in marriage.* This facilitates emotional investment in the relationship, including the close monitoring of each other's behavior. The longer time horizon also makes specialization more likely; working as a couple, individuals can develop those skills in which they excel, leaving others to their partner.

- *The greater sharing of economic and social resources by married couples.* In addition to economies of scale, this enables couples to act as a small insurance pool against life uncertainties, reducing each person's need to protect themselves from unexpected events.
- *The better connection of married couples to the larger community.* This includes other individuals and groups (such as in-laws) as well as social institutions such as churches and synagogues. These can be important sources of social and emotional support and material benefits.

In addition to missing out on many of the benefits of marriage, cohabitors may face more serious difficulties. Annual rates of depression among cohabiting couples are more than three times what they are among married couples. And women in cohabiting relationships are more likely than married women to suffer physical and sexual abuse. Some research has shown that aggression is at least twice as common among cohabitors as it is among married partners. Two studies, one in Canada and the other in the United States, found that women in cohabiting relationships are about nine times more likely to be killed by their partner than are women in marital relationships.

Again, the selection factor is undoubtedly strong in findings such as these. But the most careful statistical probing suggests that selection is not the only factor at work; the intrinsic nature of the cohabiting relationship also plays a role. As one scholar summed up the relevant research, "regardless of methodology. . . . cohabitors engage in more violence than spouses."

Why Cohabitation Is Harmful for Children

Of all the types of cohabitation, those involving children is by far the most problematic. In 2000, 41% of all unmarried-couple households included a child under eighteen, up from only 21% in 1987. For unmarried couples in the 25–34 age group the percentage with children is higher still, approaching half of all such households. By one recent estimate nearly half of all children today will spend some time in a cohabiting family before age 16.

One of the greatest problems for children living with a cohabiting couple is the high risk that the couple will break up. Fully three quarters of children born to cohabiting parents will see their parents split up before they reach age sixteen, whereas only about a third of children born to married parents face a similar fate. One reason is that marriage rates for cohabiting couples have been plummeting. In the last decade, the proportion of cohabiting mothers who go on to eventually marry the child's father declined from 57% to 44%.

Parental break up, as is now widely known, almost always entails a myriad of personal and social difficulties for children, some of which can be long lasting. For the children of a cohabiting couple these may come on top of a plethora of already existing problems. Several studies have found that children currently living with a mother and her unmarried partner have significantly more behavior problems and lower academic performance than children in intact families.

It is important to note that the great majority of children in unmarried-couple households were born not in the present union but in a previous union of one of the adult partners, usually the mother. This means that they are living with an unmarried "stepfather" or mother's boyfriend, with whom the economic and social relationships are often tenuous. For example, unlike children in stepfamilies, these children have few legal claims to child support or other sources of family income should the couple separate.

Child abuse has become a major national problem and has increased dramatically in recent years, by more than 10% a year according to one estimate. In the opinion of most researchers, this increase is related strongly to changing family forms. Surprisingly, the available American data do not enable us to distinguish the abuse that takes place in married-couple households from that in cohabiting-couple households. We do have abuse-prevalence studies that look at stepparent families (both married and unmarried) and mother's boyfriends (both cohabiting and dating). Both show far higher levels of child abuse than is found in intact families. In general, the evidence suggests that the most unsafe of all family environments for children is that in which the mother is living with someone other than the child's biological father. This is the environment for the majority of children in cohabiting couple households.

Part of the differences indicated above are due to differing income levels of the families involved. But this points up one of the other problems of cohabiting couples—their lower incomes. It is well known that children of single parents fare poorly economically when compared to the children of married parents. Not so well known is that cohabiting couples are economically more like single parents than like married couples. While the 1996 poverty rate for children living in married couple households was about 6%, it was 31% for children living in cohabiting households, much closer to the rate of 45% for children living in families headed by single mothers.

One of the most important social science findings of recent years is that marriage is a wealth enhancing institution. According to one study, childrearing, cohabiting couples have only about two-thirds of the income of married couples with children, mainly due to the fact that the average income of male cohabiting partners is only about half that of male married partners. The selection effect is surely at work here, with less well-off men and their partners choosing cohabitation over marriage. But it also is the case that men when they marry, especially those who then go on to have children, tend to become more responsible and productive. They earn more than their unmarried counterparts. An additional factor not to be overlooked is the private transfer of wealth among extended family members, which is considerably lower for cohabiting couples than for married couples. It is clear that family members are more willing to transfer wealth to "in-laws" than to mere boyfriends or girlfriends.

Who Cohabits and Why

Why has unmarried cohabitation become such a widespread practice throughout the modern world in such a short period of time? Demographic factors are surely involved. Puberty begins at an earlier age, as does the onset of sexual activity, and marriages take place at older ages mainly because of the longer time period spent getting educated and establishing careers. Thus there is an extended period of sexually active singlehood before first marriage. Also, our sustained material affluence enables many young people to live on their own for an extended time, apart from their parents. During those years of young adulthood, nonmarital cohabitation can be a cost-saver, a source of companionship, and an assurance of relatively safe sexual practice. For some, cohabitation is a prelude to marriage, for some, an alternative to it, and for yet others, simply an alternative to living alone.

More broadly, the rise of cohabitation in the advanced nations has been attributed to the sexual revolution, which has virtually revoked the stigma against cohabitation. In the past thirty years, with the advent of effective contraceptive technologies and widespread sexual permissiveness promoted by advertising and the organized entertainment industry, premarital sex has become widely accepted. In large segments of the population cohabitation no longer is associated with sin or social impropriety or pathology, nor are cohabiting couples subject to much, if any, disapproval.

Another important reason for cohabitation's growth is that the institution of marriage has changed dramatically, leading to an erosion of confidence in its stability. From a tradition strongly buttressed by economics, religion, and the law, marriage has become a more personalized relationship, what one wag has referred to as a mere "notarized date." People used to marry not just for love but also for family and economic considerations, and if love died during the course of a marriage, this was not considered sufficient reason to break up an established union. A divorce was legally difficult if not impossible to get, and people who divorced faced enormous social stigma.

In today's marriages love is all, and it is a love tied to self-fulfillment. Divorce is available to everyone, with little stigma attached. If either love or a sense of self-fulfillment disappear, the marriage is considered to be over and divorce is the logical outcome.

Fully aware of this new fragility of marriage, people are taking cautionary actions. The attitude is either try it out first and make sure that it will work, or try to minimize the damage of breakup by settling for a weaker form of union, one that avoids a marriage license and, if need be, an eventual divorce.

The growth of cohabitation is also associated with the rise of feminism. Traditional marriage, both in law and in practice, typically involved male leadership. For some women, cohabitation seemingly avoids the legacy of patriarchy and at the same time provides more personal autonomy and equality in the relationship. Moreover, women's shift into the labor force and their growing economic independence make marriage less necessary and, for some, less desirable.

Underlying all of these trends is the broad cultural shift from a more religious society where marriage was considered the bedrock of civilization and people were imbued with a strong sense of social conformity and tradition, to a more secular society focused on individual autonomy and self invention. This cultural rejection of traditional institutional and moral authority, evident in all of the advanced, Western societies, often has had "freedom of choice" as its theme and the acceptance of "alternative lifestyles" as its message.

In general, cohabitation is a phenomenon that began among the young in the lower classes and then moved up to the middle classes. Cohabitation in America—especially cohabitation as an alternative to marriage—is more common among Blacks, Puerto Ricans, and disadvantaged white women. One reason for this is that male income and employment are lower among minorities and the lower classes, and male economic status remains an important determinant as to whether or not a man feels ready to marry, and a woman wants to marry him. Cohabitation is also more common among those who are less religious than their peers. Indeed, some evidence suggests that the act of cohabitation actually diminishes religious participation, where- as marriage tends to increase it.

People who cohabit are much more likely to come from broken homes. Among young adults, those who experienced parental divorce, fatherlessness, or high levels of marital discord during childhood are more likely to form cohabiting unions than children who grew up in families with married parents who got along. They are also more likely to enter living-together relationships at younger ages. For young people who have already suffered the losses associated with parental divorce, cohabitation may provide an early escape from family turmoil, although unfortunately it increases the likelihood of new losses and turmoil. For these people, cohabitation often recapitulates the childhood experience of coming together and splitting apart with the additional possibility of more violent conflict. Finally, cohabitation is a much more likely experience for those who themselves have been divorced.

Conclusion

Despite its widespread acceptance by the young, the remarkable growth of unmarried cohabitation in recent years does not appear to be in children's or the society's best interest. The evidence suggests that it has weakened marriage and the intact, two-parent family and thereby damaged our social wellbeing, especially that of women and children. We can not go back in history, but it seems time to establish some guidelines for the practice of cohabitation and to seriously question the further institutionalization of this new family form.

In place of institutionalizing cohabitation, in our opinion, we should be trying to revitalize marriage—not along classic male-dominant lines but along modern egalitarian lines. Particularly helpful in this regard would be educating young people about marriage from the early school years onward, getting them to make the wisest choices in their lifetime mates, and stressing the importance of long-term commitment to marriages. Such an educational venture could build on the fact that a huge majority of our nation's young people still express the strong desire to be in a long-term monogamous marriage.

These ideas are offered to the American public and especially to society's leaders in the spirit of generating a discussion. Our conclusions are tentative, and certainly not the last word on the subject. There is an obvious need for more research on cohabitation, and the findings of new research, of course, could alter our thinking. What is most important now, in our view, is a national debate on a topic that heretofore has been overlooked. Indeed, few issues seem more critical for the future of marriage and for generations to come.

POSTSCRIPT

Should Society Support Cohabitation before Marriage?

There is a common misperception that premarital sex is a cultural phenomenon that was introduced to American society during the sexual revolution of the 1960s and 1970s. Sexologist Robert T. Francoeur dispels this myth by commenting on the prevalence of premarital sex dating back to colonial American times. As an example, Francoeur describes the courtship ritual of "bundling," which helped frontier farmers know that a bride-to-be was fertile and could produce children to work the farm: A courting couple was permitted to sleep together, fully dressed, in a small bed in the corner of a small, often single-room log cabin or sod house. A bundling board between the couple or a bundling bag for the woman was not an insurmountable obstacle to sexual intercourse. When the prospective bride became pregnant, the marriage was announced. This is but one example of historically positive and functional attitudes toward premarital sexual intercourse in the United States.

Other countries have experienced growing trends in relationship patterns that contrast with the U.S. rise in cohabitation. In Sweden and other Scandinavian countries, for example, a concept called "LAT" (living alone together) has become increasingly popular. Adult couples who "LAT" maintain a committed interpersonal relationship but also maintain separate households. In Italy, mammoni (literally, "mama's boys") are adult men who continue to live at home with their parents. While calling a man a "mama's boy" may be an insult in American culture, it is not so in Italy, where more and more men are avoiding marriage into their later adult years, regardless of whether they are involved in a committed relationship. Not surprisingly, this growing trend has resulted in a drastic lowering of the Italian birth rate.

In the United States, why would a couple want to choose cohabitation before marriage, or as a relationship option instead of marriage? The following reasons have been identified:

- Some couples are not legally allowed to marry because they are members of the same sex, and some heterosexual couples avoid marriage in objection to an institution that is not legally available to all.
- Some couples believe that one's intimate relationship does not require the endorsement of government or religion.
- Some people are troubled by the divorce rate, or have experienced a divorce themselves, and wish to avoid the risk (or stigma) of divorce.
- Some people believe that a relationship does not need to be a lifelong commitment.

- Some people are not sure if their current partner is the one they would select for a lifetime commitment. They might try cohabitation as a precursor to marriage.
- Some people feel their relationship is working fine without marriage.
- Some people might lose financial benefits if they decide to marry (such as from the pension of a prior spouse).
- Some people are uncomfortable with marriage's historical view toward women as property.

Some opponents of cohabitation before marriage are concerned primarily about the sexual aspect of these relationships; namely, they believe that sexual intercourse before marriage is impermissible. However, sexual and marital trends indicate that most young people begin having intercourse in their mid-to-late teens, about *seven to nine* years before they marry. Is it better for young people to begin having sex later, or consider marrying earlier? Are the main issues the timing of sex and the marital decision, or the health and happiness of the couple?

Suggested Readings

S. Avni, "Unwedded Bliss," *Salon* (January 10, 2003).

R. T. Francoeur, "Challenging Common Religious/Social Myths of Sex, Marriage, and Family," *Journal of Sex Education and Therapy* (vol. 26, no. 4, 2001).

R. Harmanci, "New Data—and Views—on Living Together, *San Francisco Chronicle* (February 1, 2009).

T. Ihara, R. Warner, and F. Hertz, *Living Together: A Legal Guide for Unmarried Couples* (Nolo Press, 2001).

J. Marks, "Living in Sin, In Sickness and in Health? An Investigation of Cohabitation, Marriage, and Health," (Dissertation, North Carolina State University, 2009).

K. Musick, "Cohabitation, whether Nonmarital Childbearing, and the Marriage Process," *Demographic Research* (vol. 16, Article 9, 2006).

D. Popenoe and B. Dafoe Whitehead, *Ten Important Research Findings on Marriage and Choosing a Marriage Partner: Helpful Facts for Young Adults* (National Marriage Project, Rutgers University, 2004).

Y. Roberts, "Don't Bother with 'I Do'," *Guardian* (June 12, 2007).

D. Solot and M. Miller, "Ten Problems (Plus One Bonus Problem) with the National Marriage Project's Cohabitation Report," *A Report of the Alternatives to Marriage Project* (2001).

K. Williams, et al., "For Better or For Worse? The Consequences of Marriage and Cohabitation for Single Mothers," *Social Forces* (vol. 86, no. 4, 2008).

Internet References . . .

Emergency Contraception Web Site

Operated by the Office of Population Research at Princeton University and the Association of Reproductive Health Professionals, this Web site provides accurate information about emergency contraception derived from the medical literature and a directory of local clinicians willing to provide emergency contraceptives.

http://www.not-2-late.com

Food and Drug Administration (FDA)

The FDA is a government body overseen by the U.S. Department of Health and Human Services. Among its many responsibilities is to promote and protect public health by helping safe and effective products reach the market in a timely way.

http://www.fda.gov

Religious Coalition for Reproductive Choice (RCRC)

The RCRC is a network of clergy and leaders from mainstream religions working to ensure reproductive choice to all, including underserved populations, through education and advocacy.

www.rcrc.org

Planned Parenthood Federation of America

Planned Parenthood Federation of America, Inc., is the world's largest and most trusted voluntary reproductive health care organization and provider of sexuality education.

www.plannedparenthood.org

National Right to Life Committee (NRLC)

The NRLC is an organization that works toward legislative goals opposing abortion, provides information, and advocates for the right-to-life movement.

www.nrlc.org

Center for Genetics and Society

The Center for Genetics and Society is a nonprofit information and public affairs organization working to encourage responsible uses and effective societal governance of the new human genetic and reproductive technologies.

www.genetics-and-society.org

RESOLVE: The National Infertility Association

RESOLVE: The National Infertility Association provides education, advocacy, and support related to infertility.

http://www.resolve.org

Reproductive Choices

*S*ome *of the most contentious modern debates involve reproduction: Should abortion be legal and accessible? Should abortion be restricted at some stages of embryonic or fetal development? Should parents be encouraged to space the births of their children? Is the use of contraception a moral decision for people who do not wish to become parents? Should schools teach about contraception? Should people avoid sex that does not result in the possibility of pregnancy? If so, does this include sex between two males or two females? Does it mean all oral, anal, or touching sex is illicit? Does it mean no sex should take place when a woman is beyond menopause, or if one or both partners are infertile? In this section, we examine four contemporary issues that involve reproductive choice.*

- Should Pharmacists Have the Right to Refuse Contraceptive Prescriptions?

- Is Abortion Immoral?

- Should There Be Restrictions on the Number of Embryos Transferred during In-Vitro Fertilization?

- Should Parents Be Allowed to Select the Sex of Their Baby?

ISSUE 14

Should Pharmacists Have the Right to Refuse Contraceptive Prescriptions?

YES: Eileen P. Kelly, from "Morally Objectionable Work Assignments: Catholic Social Teaching and Public Policy Perspectives," The Catholic Social Science Review (vol. 12, 2007)

NO: National Women's Law Center, from "Pharmacy Refusals 101" (July 2009)

ISSUE SUMMARY

YES: Eileen Kelly, a professor of Management at Ithaca College, argues that conscience clauses are necessary to protect the religious liberty and rights of pharmacists and others in the workplace.

NO: The National Women's Law Center, a national organization that works to promote issues that impact the lives of women and girls, highlight laws and public opinion while stressing that free and unrestricted access to contraception is in the best interest of women's health.

$\mathbf{A}$fter the Supreme Court's 1973 decision on Roe v. Wade that legalized abortion, the Church Amendment was passed. The amendment, deemed a "conscience clause," was seen as a way to protect health care providers from being required to take part in procedures they may object to, despite the legality of the service. Essentially the Church Amendment "prevents the government (as a condition of a federal grant) from requiring health care providers or institutions to perform or assist in abortion or sterilization procedures against their moral or religious convictions. It also prevents institutions receiving certain federal funds from taking action against personnel because of their participation, nonparticipation, or beliefs about abortion or sterilization" (Sonfield, 2005).

Over the years, additional federal conscience clauses have been enacted dealing not only with abortion services, but also education about abortion and training in abortion or sterilization procedures (Feder, 2006). Additionally, nearly all states have enacted their own conscience clauses Most states allow individuals the right to refuse to participate in abortion services. Others protect objectors from participating in sterilization and contraceptive services as well (Sonfield, 2005). More recently, more attention has been given to the impact these clauses have in allowing pharmacists to refuse to fill prescriptions for birth control based on their beliefs. State laws differ on how much protection is provided for pharmacists. In some cases, the pharmacist must offer to transfer the prescription to a willing pharmacy. In other states, there is no such requirement (Sonfield, 2008).

How far should conscience clauses be allowed to reach? Is pharmacy refusal without a referral to another pharmacy acceptable? Or should pharmacists who oppose contraception be forced to refer a customer to a pharmacist that does not share their values? Is part of being a doctor or pharmacist providing the best services and information available regardless of belief? If a medication is approved by the Food and Drug Administration (FDA), should licensed pharmacists, trained and licensed to dispense these medications, be able to pick and choose which prescriptions they fill?

Across the country, several "pro-life" pharmacies have opened. These pharmacies refuse to stock condoms, hormonal birth control, or emergency contraception (Stein, 2008). Is this an acceptable compromise? Should such pharmacies be required to inform potential customers that they do not stock such items by posting the information on the door?

Supporters of the conscience clauses stress that they are simply living their ethics and that they should not be punished for their religious beliefs. Opponents warn that such laws interfere with women's access to health care and that refusal to fill a prescription can be used as an attempt to shame and humiliate.

In her essay, "Morally Objectionable Work Assignments: Catholic Social Teaching and Public Policy Perspectives," Eileen Kelly argues that conscience clauses are a necessary protection of civil rights. The National Women's Law Center, in a document entitled "Pharmacy Refusals 101," zeros in on the effects of such refusals on women's health and what can be done to prevent them.

References

J. Feder, "The History and Effect of Abortion Conscience Clause Laws," accessed at https://www.policyarchive.org/bitstream/handle/10207/3696/RS21428_20060227.pdf?sequence=2 (2006).

A. Sonfield, "Rights vs. Responsibilities: Professional Standards and Provider Refusals," *The Guttmacher Report on Public Policy* (vol. 8, no. 3, August 2005), accessed at http://www.guttmacher.org/pubs/tgr/08/3/gr080307.html

A. Sonfield, "Provider Refusal and Access to Reproductive Health Services: Approaching a New Balance," *Guttmacher Policy Review* (vol. 11, no. 2, Spring 2008), accessed at http://www.guttmacher.org/pubs/gpr/11/2/gpr110202.html

R. Stein, "Pro-Life Drugstores Market Beliefs. *The Washington Post,* accessed at http://www.washingtonpost.com/wp-dyn/content/article/2008/06/15/AR2008061502180.html?sid=ST2008082103218 (2008)

YES

Eileen P. Kelly

Morally Objectionable Work Assignments: Catholic Social Teaching and Public Policy Perspectives

This article examines the increasing problem of health care employees other than physicians and nurses, especially pharmacists, facing discipline or termination for refusing to engage in immoral practices such as dispensing contraceptives. The article considers the limitations of current anti-discrimination statutes in protecting such employees, and believes that "conscience laws"—which so far only a minority of states have enacted, but many are considering—afford the best possibility for protection.

In Ohio, a pharmacist is fired for refusing to fill a prescription for birth control pills. In Wisconsin, another pharmacist faces a similar fate plus sanctions from the state licensing board for refusing to fill a prescription for emergency contraceptives. In Illinois, an emergency medical technician is terminated for refusing to drive a woman to an abortion clinic. In each instance, the employee is placed in the untenable position of having to choose between providing services that are contrary to their deeply held religious beliefs or facing discipline and discharge for refusing to do so.

In the last several years, there has been a notable increase in the number of incidences of employees placed in such nightmarish dilemmas. Not coincidentally, most of the employees receiving media scrutiny are health care workers, particularly pharmacists. While doctors and nurses have long had the right to refuse morally objectionable work under state statutes, pharmacists and other health care workers have not. The statutory right of refusal has only recently been extended by a minority of states to other categories of health care employees.

Catholic Social Teaching

A vigorous and contentious national debate is now occurring over whether health care professionals have the right to withhold services for procedures they find morally objectionable. Advances in medical technology, coupled with the overall decline in morality in society, make the outcome of this debate critical for

From *Catholic Social Science Review*, Vol. 12, 2007, pp. 425–430. Copyright © 2007 by Society of Catholic Social Scientists. Reprinted by permission.

society's long term welfare. Morally objectionable procedures and practices that were unthought-of in previous generations are now commonplace and either legally sanctioned or conceivably will be in the not too distant future.

Embryonic stem cell research, euthanasia, physician assisted suicide, abortion, abortifacients, artificial birth control, sterilization and artificial insemination are just a few of the procedures and practices that contribute to the "culture of death" enveloping society. The Catholic Church has consistently upheld the value and dignity of each human life and taught that life must be unequivocally protected in all its various stages. John Paul II persuasively articulated the gospel of life in *Evangelium Vitae*. In doing so, he underscored long-standing Church teaching. As the *Catechism* notes, abortion has been condemned by the Church since the first century.

Rational employees do not accept jobs or undertake professions that are opposed to their religious beliefs. In short, no morally upright person is going to voluntarily work for Don Corleone or become an abortionist. More commonly, employees enter into employment relationships that subsequently force them to make choices in morally compromising situations. In extreme scenarios, the employee may be compelled to leave a job to maintain his or her moral integrity. What is particularly pernicious with the current moral crisis facing the health care professions is that most employees enter into those professions with the understanding that they are embarking on a noble and moral career to help others. In most instances, the employee invests a great deal of time and expense getting an education for his or her profession. Increasingly, Catholic health care workers are now being confronted with having to choose between their jobs or their religious beliefs. In some cases, they may even have to leave their profession.

Existing public policy is somewhat muddled in both protecting and encroaching on the employee's right to refuse morally objectionable work. While there is some legal protection for an employee's right of refusal, that protection is very limited. Employees who refuse to perform morally objectionable work have essentially two legal avenues of recourse open to them. First, they can seek protection under existing federal and state discrimination laws. Second, if they live in a state with a "conscience law" covering their particular job, they can seek protection under it. On the other hand, there is a movement afoot to pass state statutes requiring certain health care providers to provide morally objectionable services.

Anti-Discrimination Statutes

Title VII of the Civil Rights Act of 1964 makes it illegal for a non-sectarian employer to discriminate against an applicant or employee on the basis of religion. All fifty states have similar prohibitions in their respective state anti-discrimination laws, as well as some municipalities. In addition to prohibiting employers from discriminating on the basis of religion, Title VII and related statutes require that the employer reasonably accommodate the religious beliefs and practices of their employees to the extent that it does not create an undue hardship on the business. There are essentially three common types of accommodations that employees seek. The first is accommodation for religious observances or practices, such as asking time off for Sabbath observance. The second is grooming and dress code accommodation, such as a Muslim woman asking to wear a hijab. The third and most contentious is accommodation for conscientious objections to assigned work which is in opposition to an employee's religious beliefs, such as a pharmacist requesting not to dispense emergency contraceptives.

Notably, the employer's duty to accommodate the religious beliefs and practices of their employees is not an absolute one. Rather, the employer has only a duty to reasonably accommodate an employee's request to the extent that it does not create an undue hardship on the business. Unlike disability cases, the Supreme Court ruled in *TWA v. Hardison*, 432 U.S. 63 (1973) that the obligation to accommodate religious beliefs and practices is a *de minimis* one. The Supreme Court held in *Ansonia Board of Education v. Philbrook*, 55 USLW 4019 (1996) that once the employer offers any reasonable accommodation, they have met their statutory burden. Notably, that accommodation need not be the most optimal one or the employee's preferred one. The determination of undue hardship is at issue only when the employer claims that it is unable to offer any reasonable accommodation without such hardship. The definition of undue hardship is essentially any accommodation that would be unduly costly, extensive, substantial, disruptive, or that would fundamentally alter the nature or operation of the business. Factors that would be taken into account in assessing undue hardship would be the nature of the business, the cost of the accommodation, the nature of the job needing accommodation, and the effect of the accommodation on the employer's operations. No bright line rule exists to determine precisely what constitutes an undue hardship. Rather the determination is made on a case-by-case basis contingent upon the particular factual scenario of each situation.

The limited nature of an employer's *de minimis* legal obligation to accommodate an employee's religious beliefs and practices has serious implications for employees requesting to refrain from morally objectionable work assignments. In many instances, an employer could readily demonstrate undue hardship. For example, a pharmacist may request reasonable accommodation for his or her religious beliefs by being allowed not to fill customer prescriptions for emergency contraceptives. The employer can readily demonstrate undue hardship if the pharmacy normally has only one pharmacist on duty. It is impossible to foresee when a customer may appear at the counter with a prescription for emergency contraceptives. Thus only three practical accommodations could be made. First, the pharmacy could hire another pharmacist to be on site with the conscientious objector pharmacist. This obviously would entail extra expense. Second, the customer could be directed by the objecting pharmacist to another pharmacy. Third, the objecting pharmacist could direct the customer to return when a non-objecting pharmacist is on duty. The latter two alternatives would both entail possible lost revenue, customer alienation, bad publicity and lawsuits. Thus the employer could readily meet its *de minimis* obligation and demonstrate that it would create an undue hardship to accommodate the pharmacist with religious objections.

Because the bar is set so low for an employer to meet its duty of reasonable accommodation for religious beliefs and practices, existing federal and state anti-discrimination statutes provide inadequate legal protection for employees with moral and religious objections to assigned work. More often than not, such employees would find themselves disciplined or discharged with scant legal recourse. Because of this inadequate statutory protection, many observers believe that conscience laws are needed to provide more substantive protection to employees.

Conscience Laws

Conscience laws are laws that grant an employee a statutory right to refuse to perform work or provide services that violate their religious or moral beliefs (see: Dennis Rambaud, "Prescription Contraceptives and the Pharmacist's Right to Refuse: Examining the Efficacy of Conscience Laws," *Cardozo Public Law, Policy and Ethics Journal* (2006), 195–231). Conscience laws are also referred to as conscience clauses or right of refusal clauses. Conscience laws first appeared in the aftermath of *Roe v. Wade, 410 U.S. 113* (1973) when state laws were passed which permitted doctors and other direct providers of health care services the statutory right to refuse to provide or participate in abortions. In general, conscience laws would prevent an employer from taking coercive, adverse or discriminatory action against an employee who refuses to perform assigned work for reasons of conscience. Depending on the particular text of the statute, conscience clauses may additionally protect the worker from civil liability and from adverse action by licensing boards.

More recent conscience clauses have focused on pharmacists, although some have broader coverage. The impetus for the flurry in state legislative action was the FDA approval of the morning-after pill. In the wake of that approval, pharmacists who refused to dispense the drug on moral grounds increasingly faced discipline, discharge and confrontations with state licensing boards. The current status of state conscience laws and pending bills is constantly in flux as more legislatures consider such laws. According to the National Conference of State Legislatures at the time of this writing, Arkansas, Georgia, Mississippi and South Dakota have passed statutes which permit a pharmacist to refuse to dispense emergency contraception because of moral convictions. Four other states (Colorado, Florida, Maine and Tennessee) enacted conscience clauses that are broader in nature and do not specifically mention pharmacists. California has enacted a more restrictive conscience clause which permits a pharmacist to refuse to fill a prescription only if the employer approves the refusal and the customer can still have the prescription filled in a timely manner (see: National Conference of State Legislatures, "Pharmacist Conscience Clauses: Laws and Legislation," [October 2006] . . .). At least 18 states are contemplating some 36 bills with varying scope and protection. Among those, nine states are considering conscience clauses that cover a broad array of health care workers. A few states are even considering bills that would permit insurance companies to opt out of providing coverage for morally objectionable services (see: Rob Stein, "Health Workers' Choice Debated," *Washington Post* [January 30, 2006], A01).

Needless to say, the surfeit of proposed state protective legislation has created an outcry among pro-choice and Planned Parenthood proponents. Some of this backlash is being translated into state law. In Illinois for example, the governor passed an emergency rule that requires a pharmacist to fill prescriptions for FDA-approved contraception. Several Illinois pharmacists have been fired for refusing to fill such prescriptions.

On the federal level in 2004, President Bush signed into law the Weldon Amendment which bars federal funding of any government program that subjects any institutional or individual health care provider to discrimination on the basis that the health care provider does not provide, pay for, provide coverage of, or refer for abortions. The U.S. Conference of Catholic Bishops has gone on record supporting the amendment. The State of California has filed a lawsuit challenging the constitutionality of the amendment.

Conscience laws seek to provide a balance between protecting workers compelled to choose between their livelihood and their religious beliefs and the public welfare. Whether American society will support this compromise or instead insist on forcing compliance by employees with moral objections to work assignments remains to be played out in the legal system.

Pharmacy Refusals 101

Prescription Contraception is Basic Health Care for Women

- Family planning is central to good health care for women. Access to contraception is critical to preventing unintended pregnancies and to enabling women to control the timing and spacing of their pregnancies. Contraceptive use in the United States is virtually universal among women of reproductive age. A woman who wants only two children must use contraception for roughly three decades of her life. Also, women rely on prescription contraceptives for a range of medical purposes in addition to birth control, such as regulation of cycles and endometriosis.
- Emergency contraception (EC), also known as the morning after pill, is an FDA-approved form of contraception. EC is an extremely time-sensitive drug that is most effective if used within the first 12 to 24 hours following birth control failure, unprotected sex, or sexual assault. EC has great potential to prevent unintended pregnancies. Currently, it is available without a prescription for individuals 18 and older and by prescription for women 17 and younger. In March 2009, however, a court ordered the FDA to make EC available to 17-year-olds without a prescription, and the FDA has begun the process to do so.

Refusals to Dispense Contraception are Increasing

- Increasing reports of pharmacist refusals to fill prescriptions for birth control—or provide EC to individuals who do not require a prescription—have been attracting media attention. Reports of pharmacist refusals have surfaced in at least twenty-four states across the nation, including: AZ, CA, DC, GA, IL, LA, MA, MI, MN, MO, MT, NH, NY, NC, OH, OK, OR, RI, TN, TX, VA, WA, WV, WI.
- These refusals to dispense prescription contraceptives or provide EC are based on personal beliefs, not on legitimate medical or professional concerns. The same pharmacists who refuse to dispense contraceptives because of their personal beliefs often refuse to transfer a woman's prescription to another pharmacist or to refer her to another

From www.nwlc.net, July 2009. Copyright © 2009 by National Women's Law Center. Reprinted by permission.

pharmacy. These refusals can have devastating consequences for women's health.

- Despite the FDA's decision to make EC available without a prescription to certain individuals, refusals based on personal beliefs are still a problem. Under the FDA's conditions, EC is kept behind the counter, so even women who do not need a prescription must interact with pharmacists or other pharmacy staff who may have strong personal beliefs against providing the drug. Since non-prescription EC arrived in pharmacies, there have been a number of refusal incidents.
- Some examples of refusals in the pharmacy:
  - October 2008: A "pro-life" pharmacy refusing to stock or dispense contraception opened in **Chantilly, Virginia**. Staff at the pharmacy will not provide referrals or help individuals find contraception elsewhere.
  - May 2007: In **Great Falls, Montana**, a 49-year-old woman who used birth control to treat a medical condition went to her local pharmacy to fill her latest prescription. She was given a slip of paper informing her that the pharmacy would no longer fill any prescriptions for birth control. When she called back to inquire about the policy change, the owner of the pharmacy told her that birth control was "dangerous" for women.
  - January 2007: In **Columbus, Ohio**, a 23-year-old mother went to her local Wal-Mart because she had read that Wal-Mart was stocking EC in all its pharmacies. When she asked for non-prescription EC, the pharmacist on staff "shook his head and laughed." She was told that even though the store stocked EC, no one on staff would give it to her. She had to drive 45 miles to find another pharmacy that would provide her with EC.
  - December 2006: In **Seattle, Washington**, a 25-year-old woman went to her local Rite-Aid to get non-prescription EC after she and her fiancé experienced a birth control failure. The pharmacist told her that although the pharmacy had EC in stock, he would not give it to her because he thought it was wrong. The woman had to repeatedly insist that the pharmacist find her another pharmacy in the area that would provide her with EC before he would do so.
  - January 2006: In **Northern California**, a married mother of a newborn baby experienced a birth control failure with her husband. Her physician called in a prescription for EC on her behalf the next morning. However, the pharmacist on duty not only refused to dispense the drug, which was in stock, but also refused to enter the prescription into the pharmacy's computer so that it could be transferred elsewhere. By refusing, the pharmacist jeopardized the young mother's ability to obtain the drug in time for it to be effective.
  - January 2005: In **Milwaukee, Wisconsin**, a mother of six went to her local Walgreens with a prescription for emergency contraception. The pharmacist refused to fill the prescription and berated the mother in the pharmacy's crowded waiting area, shouting "You're a murderer! I will not help you kill this baby. I will not have the blood on my hands." The mother left the pharmacy mortified and never had her prescription filled. She subsequently became pregnant and had an abortion.

- April 2004: In North **Richland Hills, Texas,** 32-year-old Julee Lacey, a mother of two who had relied on birth control pills for years, went to her local CVS for her regular prescription refill. The pharmacist refused to refill her prescription because of his personal beliefs. Outraged, Ms. Lacey summoned her husband to the store, where he was told that the pharmacist would not fill the prescription because oral contraceptives are "not right" and "cause cancer."
- January 2004: In **Denton, Texas,** a rape survivor seeking EC was turned away from an Eckerd pharmacy by three pharmacists, who refused to fill the time-sensitive prescription due to their religious beliefs. The pharmacists' refusal put the survivor in danger of becoming pregnant due to the rape.

The Legal Landscape: What Governs the Practice of Pharmacy?

- The laws governing pharmacists vary from state to state. Pharmacists must abide by state laws and regulations, which are written by the state legislature and the state Pharmacy Board.
- The laws and regulations in most states do not specifically speak to the issue of pharmacist refusals based on personal beliefs. States that provide general guidance about when pharmacists may refuse to dispense tend to limit the reasons for such a refusal to professional or medical considerations—such as potentially harmful contraindication, interactions with other drugs, improper dosage, and suspected drug abuse or misuse—as opposed to personal judgments.
- Many pharmacist associations that have considered this issue, including the American Pharmacists Association, have issued policies requiring that pharmacists ensure patient access to legally prescribed medications—for example by either filling valid prescriptions or transferring them to another pharmacist who can. Although such policies are not legally binding, they encourage pharmacists to meet consumers' needs.

Legislative and Administrative Responses to Pharmacist Refusals
Prohibiting or Limiting Refusals

- **Eight states**—CA, IL, ME, MA, NV, NJ, WA, WI—explicitly require pharmacists or pharmacies to ensure that valid prescriptions are filled.
- **In seven states**—AL, DE, NY, NC, OR, PA, TX—pharmacy boards have issued policy statements that prohibit pharmacists from obstructing patient access to medication or from refusing to transfer prescriptions to another pharmacy.
- Legislators in the Austin (TX) City Council unanimously passed a measure to require Walgreens, the city's pharmaceutical contractor, to fill all prescriptions "without discrimination or delay" for patients enrolled in its medical assistance program.

Permitting Refusals

- **Five states**—AR, AZ, GA, MS, and SD—have laws or regulations that allow refusals based on pharmacists' personal beliefs without patient protections.

Public Opinion

- According to surveys, the public is overwhelmingly opposed to allowing pharmacists to refuse to provide contraception based on their personal beliefs.
  - A national survey of Republicans and Independent voters conducted in September and October 2008 on behalf of the National Women's Law Center and the YWCA found that 51% *strongly* favor legislation that requires pharmacies to ensure that patients get contraception at their pharmacy of choice, even if a particular pharmacist has a moral objection to contraceptives and refuses to provide it. That includes 42% of Republicans and 62% of Independents.
  - In a national opinion survey released in July 2007, which was conducted for the National Women's Law Center and Planned Parenthood Federation of America by Peter D. Hart Research Associates, 71% of voters said that pharmacists should not be allowed to refuse to fill prescriptions on moral or religious grounds, including majorities of every voter demographic such as Republicans (56%), Catholics (73%), and evangelical Christians (53%). Even more respondents (73% overall) supported requiring pharmacies to dispense contraception to patients without discrimination or delay.
  - A poll conducted in May 2007 by Lake Research Partners found that 82% of adults and registered voters believed that "pharmacies should be required to dispense birth control to patients without discrimination or delay."
  - An August 2006 poll conducted by the Pew Research Center on People and the Press found that 80% of Americans believe that pharmacists should not be able to refuse to sell birth control based on their religious beliefs. This was true across party lines and religious affiliations. Particularly notable was the poll's finding that "No political or religious groups express majority support for this type of conscience clause."
  - A November 2004 CBS / *New York Times* poll showed that public opinion disfavoring pharmacist refusals was strong regardless of party affiliation. Seventy-eight percent of Americans believe that pharmacist refusals should not be permitted, including 85% of Democrat respondents and 70% of Republican respondents.

How to Respond to a Pharmacist's Refusal

- File a complaint with your state's pharmacy board to get sanctions against the pharmacist or pharmacy.
- Communicate your story to the press.

- Ask the state pharmacy board or legislature to put in place policies that will ensure every consumer's right to access legal pharmaceuticals.
- Alert the pharmacy's corporate headquarters; some pharmacies have policies that protect women's right to receive contraception in store, without discrimination or delay.
- Get EC *today*, before you need it!

POSTSCRIPT

Should Pharmacists Have the Right to Refuse Contraceptive Prescriptions?

Imagine, for a moment, that you (or your partner or friend) have just received a prescription for hormonal contraceptives. You take the prescription to your local pharmacy and hand it to the pharmacist on duty. Now imagine that the pharmacist hands the slip of paper back to you, stating that he or she will not fill your prescription because doing so would violate his or her religious or ethical beliefs. When you ask the pharmacist to call the other local pharmacy, which is about a 30-minute drive across town, he or she again refuses, citing that this is a right under state law. How would you feel?

Now, picture yourself as a pharmacist in another state. Your religious beliefs are such that you feel any attempt to prevent pregnancy goes against God's will. However, you fear that refusing to fill prescriptions for contraception could cost you your job. You like your job and your short commute, which allows you to spend more time with your family. If you lost your job, you would have to try your luck with another pharmacy, and there would be no guarantee that they would support your religious beliefs either. How would you feel if your manager insisted you fill prescriptions for birth control, or risk being fired?

In the final days of his second term as president, George W. Bush expanded the reach of federal conscience clauses through the Provider Refusal Rule. Supporters, including the United States Conference of Catholic Bishops and the group Pharmacists for Life, praised the president for protecting the religious freedom of those who work in the health care fields, from surgeons to ambulance drivers. Opponents, including the American Medical Association and Planned Parenthood, stressed that ideology should not trump patient care. At the time of this writing, President Obama is said to be considering reversal of the Bush policy.

The two essays selected for this issue present a compelling contrast between the rights of employees and the rights of patients. Both provide examples of scenarios with minor citations. Are these types of examples useful or does the lack of clear citation damage their effectiveness? Kelly presents her side from the perspective of Catholic social teaching. It is important, however, to understand that followers of particular religions are not completely homogeneous in their beliefs and practices. While Christian organizations like the U.S. Conference of Catholic Bishops and the Christian Medical and Dental Association support broadening the reach of conscience clauses, other religious organizations like Catholics for Choice and the The United Methodist General Board of Church and Society have encouraged President Obama to reverse Bush's expansion of the clause. Similarly, not all who support the expansion of the "right of refusal" are religiously identified.

The National Women's Law Center provides a set of statistics showing widespread opposition to pharmacists' refusal of contraception. Were any of the statistics surprising? Why or why not? The group also provides a set of steps to take if a prescription is refused. Would you feel comfortable taking any of these steps? How are these steps similar or different to those presented by the American Family Association in Issue 10?

Where do you stand on this issue? Most people agree that freedom of religion is a valuable part of our democratic society. But does that freedom have limits? And what about other medications? If a pharmacist's religion adheres to the belief that antidepressants are not the best way to treat depression, should the pharmacist be allowed the right of refusal? Why do you think much of the controversy over pharmacist refusals have focused on contraception and not other medications? The Provider Refusal Rule also covers other health care workers—should pharmacy technicians be allowed to refrain from ordering contraceptives during their routine inventory checks? Should an EMT be allowed to refuse to drive the ambulance to the hospital if he or she fears an abortion may be necessary in order to save the patient's life?

Suggested Readings

H. Clinton & C. Richards, "Blocking Care for Women," *New York Times* (September 18, 2008).

G. Cook, "The Battle Over Birth Control," *Salon* (April 27, 2005).

J. Feder, "The History and Effect of Abortion Conscience Clause Laws," accessed at https://www.policyarchive.org/bitstream/handle/10207/3696/RS21428_20060227.pdf?sequence=2 (2006)

A. Sonfield, "Rights vs. Responsibilities: Professional Standards and Provider Refusals," *The Guttmacher Report on Public Policy* (vol. 8, no. 3, August 2005), accessed at http://www.guttmacher.org/pubs/tgr/08/3/gr080307.html

A. Sonfield, "Provider Refusal and Access to Reproductive Health Services: Approaching a New Balance," *Guttmacher Policy Review* (vol. 11, no. 2, Spring 2008), accessed at http://www.guttmacher.org/pubs/gpr/11/2/gpr110202.html

R. Stein, "Pro-Life Drugstores Market Beliefs," *The Washington Post,* accessed at http://www.washingtonpost.com/wp-dyn/content/article/2008/06/15/AR2008061502180.html?sid=ST2008082103218

ISSUE 15

Is Abortion Immoral?

YES: Douglas Groothuis, from "Why I am Pro-Life: A Short, Non-sectarian Argument," adapted from http://theconstructivecurmudgeon .blogspot.com/2009/03/why-i-am-pro-life-short-nonsectarian.html (2009)

NO: Jennifer Webster, from "Choosing Abortion is Choosing Life," an original essay written for this volume (2009)

ISSUE SUMMARY

YES: Douglas Groothuis, author and professor of philosophy at Denver Seminary, draws on the philosophical tradition to present his moral argument against abortion.

NO: Jennifer Webster, projects coordinator for the Network for Reproductive Options, asserts that the choice of abortion is a multi-factoral decision that always expresses a moral consideration.

Women have abortions for a variety of reasons. Financial concerns, health issues, relationship problems, family responsibilities, and the desire to attend or remain in school or pursue a career path are but a few (Finer et al., 2005). Abortions have been practiced all around the world and throughout history (Jones & Lopez, 2006). Until the onset of modern surgical techniques, folk methods such as ingesting plant compounds (Riddle, 1992) or inserting chemicals or sharp objects into the vagina or uterus were used to induce abortion (Jones & Lopez, 2006). Information about contraception and abortion was passed from woman to woman through generations of oral history, thanks in part to religious and legal prohibitions against transmitting written instructions or information (Riddle, 1992).

Discussions about abortion are often framed as a matter of "rights," in other words, a woman's right to reproductive autonomy versus the right of the unborn to be born. The right to an abortion is essentially determined by the laws in one's area. In the United States, Comstock Laws formalized the illegal status of abortion in 1873. During the late 1960s and early 1970s, several states began to loosen their restrictions (Jones & Lopez, 2006). The year 1973 brought the cases of *Roe v. Wade* and *Doe v. Bolton*, which legalized abortion on the federal level. They established the "trimester framework," essentially legalizing first trimester abortions on demand, allowing states to regulate second trimester procedures with regard to the mother's health, and allowing states to prohibit abortion during the third trimester, unless the mother's health is at risk (Hatcher et al., 2007).

As the legality of abortion changed over time, individual states enacted legislation to restrict access to abortion. In many states, anti-abortion advocates have imparted restrictions on abortion rights through an array of tactics including restricting federal funding for abortion, enacting waiting periods, and requiring counseling for those seeking abortions (Hatcher et al., 2007). The Supreme Court upheld the "Partial-Birth Abortion Ban Act of 2003" in 2007, which made dilation and extraction procedures illegal without regard for a woman's health (Hatcher et al., 2007).

According to the Guttmacher Institute (2008), about 40 percent of unintended pregnancies are terminated. About one-third of women will have had an abortion by the age of 45. The number of abortions in 2005 was 1.21 million, down from 1.31 million in 2000. The number of abortions per 1,000 women ages 15–44, per year, has fallen from 29.3 in the early 1980s to 19.4 in 2005. Fifty percent of abortions are obtained by women over age 25. Thirty-three percent are obtained by women between the ages of 20 and 24. Teenagers account for 17 percent of abortions. Almost 90 percent of abortions occur during the first 12 weeks of pregnancy (Guttmacher, 2008)

For many, the decision of whether to have an abortion, or to support or deny access to abortion procedures, has little to do with law or statistics. Certainly, laws can make accessing an abortion provider easier or more difficult, but abortions still take place in countries where abortion is illegal. For many, the question often boils down to morality. And our concepts of morality are often based on our worldviews (Lakoff, 2002). For people with different worldviews, it can be hard to see eye to eye on any number of issues. Is abortion immoral? If your worldview holds that abortion kills an innocent life, the answer is probably always "yes." If your worldview emphasizes the well-being and autonomy of women, the answer may often be "no." And many people have much more complex and nuanced beliefs that are based on a variety of factors that do not allow for an easy answer to the question "Is abortion a moral or immoral decision?"

In the following essays, Douglas Groothuis, professor of philosophy at Denver Seminary, presents the reasons he finds abortion immoral, whereas Jennifer Webster, projects coordinator for the Network for Reproductive Options, asserts that choosing abortion is always a moral decision.

References

Alan Guttmacher Institute, *Facts on Induced Abortion in the United States* (July 2008), accessed November 26, 2008, at http://www.guttmacher.org/pubs/fb_induced_abortion.html

L. Finer et al., "Reasons U.S. Women Have Abortions: Quantitative and Qualitative Perspectives, *Perspectives on Sexual and Reproductive Health* (vol. 37, 2005).

R. Hatcher et al., eds., *Contraceptive Technology*, 19th ed. (New York: Ardent Media, 2007).

R. Jones and K. Lopez, *Human Reproductive Biology*. (Boston: Academic Press, 2006).

G. Lakoff, *Moral Politics: How Liberals and Conservatives Think* (Chicago: University of Chicago Press, 2002).

J. Riddle, *Contraception and Abortion from the Ancient World to the Renaissance* (Cambridge, MA: Harvard University Press, 1992).

YES

Douglas Groothuis

Why I Am Pro-life:
A Short, Nonsectarian Argument

Abortion is the intentional killing of a human fetus by chemical and/or surgical means. It should not be confused with miscarriage (which involves no human intention) or contraception (which uses various technologies to prohibit sperm and egg from producing a fertilized ovum after sexual inter-course). Miscarriages are natural (if sad) occurrences, which raise no deep moral issues regarding human conduct—unless the woman was careless in her pregnancy. Contraception is officially opposed by Roman Catholics and some other Christians, but I take it to be in a moral category entirely separate from abortion (since it does not involve the killing of a fetus); therefore, it will not be addressed here.[1]

Rather than taking up the legal reasoning and history of abortion in America (especially concerning Roe vs. Wade), this essay makes a simple, straightforward moral argument against abortion. Sadly, real arguments (reasoned defenses of a thesis or claim) are too rarely made on this issue. Instead, propaganda is exchanged. Given that the Obama administration is the most pro-abortion administration in the history of the United States, some clear moral reasoning is called for at this time.

The first premise of the argument is that human beings have unique and incomparable value in the world. Christians and Jews believe this is the case because we are made in God's image and likeness. But anyone who holds that humans are special and worthy of unique moral consideration can grant this thesis (even if their worldview does not ultimately support it). Of course, those like Peter Singer who do not grant humans any special status will not be moved by this.[2] We cannot help that. Many true and justified beliefs (concerning human beings and other matters) are denied by otherwise intelligent people.

Second, the *burden of proof* should always be on the one taking a human life and the *benefit of doubt* should always be given to the human life. This is not to say that human life should never be taken. In an often cruel and unfair world, sometimes life-taking is necessary, as many people will grant. Cases include self-defense, the prosecution of a just war, and capital punishment. Yet all unnecessary and intentional life-taking is murder, a deeply evil and repugnant offense against human beings. (This would also be acknowledged by those, such as absolute pacifists, who believe that it is never justifiable to take a human life.)

An original essay written for this volume. Copyright © 2009 by Douglas Groothuis. Reprinted by permission.

Third, abortion nearly always takes a human life intentionally and gratuitously and is, therefore, morally unjustified, deeply evil, and repugnant—given what we have said about human beings. The fetus is, without question, a *human being*. Biologically, an entity joins its parents' species at conception. Like produces like: apes procreate apes, rabbits procreate rabbits, and humans procreate humans. If the fetus is not human, what else could it possibly be? Could it be an ape or a rabbit? Of course not.

Some philosophers, such as Mary Anne Warren, have tried to drive a wedge between *personhood* and *humanity*. That is, there may be persons who are not human (such as God, angels, ETs—if they exist), and there may be humans that are not persons (fetuses or those who lose certain functions after having possessed them). While it is true that there may be persons who are not humans, it does not logically follow that there are humans who are not persons. The fetus is best regarded as a person with potential, not a potential person or nonperson.[3]

When we separate personhood from humanity, we make personhood an achievement based on the possession of certain qualities. But what are these person-constituting qualities? Some say a basic level of consciousness; others assert viability outside the womb; still others say a sense of self-interest (which probably does not obtain until after birth). All of these criteria would take away humanity from those in comas or other physically compromised situations.[4] Humans can lose levels of consciousness through injuries, and even infants are not viable without intense and sustained human support. Moreover, who are we to say just what qualities make for membership in the moral community of persons?[5] The stakes are very high in this question. If we are wrong in our identification of what qualities are sufficient for personhood and we allow a person to be killed, we have allowed the wrongful killing of nothing less than a person. Therefore, I argue that personhood should be viewed as a substance or essence that is given at conception. The fetus is not a lifeless *mechanism* that only becomes what it is after several parts are put together—as is the case with a watch or an automobile. Rather, the fetus is a living human *organism,* whose future unfolds from within itself according to internal principles. For example, the fertilized ovum contains a complete genetic code that is distinct from that of the mother or father. But this is not a mere inert blueprint (which is separable from the building it describes); this is a living blueprint that becomes what its human nature demands.

Yet even if one is not sure when personhood becomes a reality, one should err on the side of being conservative simply because so much is at stake. That is, if one aborts a fetus who is already a person, one commits a deep moral wrong by wrongfully killing an innocent human life. Just as we do not shoot target practice when we are told there may be children playing behind the targets, we should not abortion fetuses if they may be persons with the right not to be killed. As I have argued, it cannot be disputed that abortion kills a living, human being.

Many argue that outside considerations experienced by the mother should overrule the moral value of the human embryo. If a woman does not want a pregnancy, she may abort. But these quality of life considerations always involve issues of lesser moral weight than that of the conservation and protection of a unique human life (which considers the sanctity or innate and intrinsic value of a human life).[6] An unwanted pregnancy is difficult, but the answer is not to kill a human being in order to end that pregnancy. Moreover, a baby can be put up for adoption and bring joy to others. There are many others who do want the child and would give him or her great love and support. Furthermore, it is not uncommon for women to experience deep regrets after aborting their offspring.

The only exemption to giving priority to the life of the fetus would be if there were a real threat to the life of the mother were the pregnancy to continue. In this case, the fetus functions as a kind of intruder that threatens the woman's life. To abort the pregnancy would be tragic but allowable in this imperfect world. Some mothers will nonetheless choose to continue the pregnancy to their own risk, but this is not morally required. It should be noted that these life-threatening situations are extremely rare.

This pro-life argument does not rely on any uniquely religious assumptions, although some religious people will find it compelling. I take it to be an item of natural law (what can be known about morality by virtue of being human) that human life has unique value. A case can be made against abortion by using the Bible (only the Hebrew Bible or both the Hebrew Bible and New Testament combined) as the main moral source, but I have not given that argument here.[7] Rather, this essay has given an argument on the basis of generally agreed upon moral principles. If the argument is to be refuted, one or more of those principles or the reasoning employed needs to be refuted.

Although at the beginning of this essay I claimed I would not take up the legal reasoning related to abortion, one simple point follows from my argument. In nearly every case, abortion should be illegal simply because the Constitution requires that innocent human life be protected from killing.[8] Anti-abortion laws are not an intrusion of the state into the family any more than laws against murdering one's parents are an intrusion into the family.

Notes

1. See Scott Rae, *Moral Choices,* 3rd ed. (Grand Rapids, MI: Zondervan, 2009), 288–291.

2. For an exposition and critique of Singer's thought, see Gordon R. Preece, ed., *Rethinking Peter Singer* (Downers Grove, IL: InterVarsity Press, 2002).

3. See Clifford Bajema, *Abortion and the Meaning of Personhood* (Grand Rapids, MI: Baker Books, 1974). This book is on line. . . .

4. On the dangerous implications of his perspective, see Francis A. Schaeffer and C. Everett Koop, *Whatever Happened to the Human Race?*, revised ed. (Wheaton, IL: Crossway Books, 1983).

5. For a developed philosophical and legal case for including the unborn in the moral community of human beings, see Francis Beckwith, *Defending Life: A Moral and Legal Case Against Abortion Choice* (Cambridge University Press, 2007); and Robert P. George and Christopher Tollefsen, *Embryo: A Defense of Human Life* (New York: Doubleday, 2008).

6. On the distinction between a quality of life ethic and a sanctity of life ethic, see Ronald Reagan, "Abortion and the Conscience of a Nation." . . . This was originally an article in the Spring 1983 issue of *The Human Life Review*.
7. See Rae, 129133.
8. See Beckwith, Chapter 2.

Jennifer Webster  **NO**

Choosing Abortion
Is Choosing Life

I think it is a measure of how well the anti-abortion movement has been able to influence thinking and discussion of abortion in this country that when I sat down to write this essay I found myself confounded and conflicted on what I see as a fairly straightforward question. Can abortion be moral? Yes. Absolutely, without question, choosing an abortion is always a moral decision.

I say this and immediately I hear all the objections of the anti-abortion movement, what about the rights of the innocent baby, abortion is murder, women shouldn't be allowed to use abortion as birth control. Even I, who ought to know better, hear these voices and feel compelled to answer them. For nearly four decades we have allowed those most vehemently opposed to abortion to control the public debate and claim the moral high ground on abortion.

Women have abortions for lots of reasons.

- A senior in college has an abortion after one night celebrating with her boyfriend.
- A woman raped by her brother-in-law chooses to have an abortion, contrary to her Catholic upbringing, because she knows that this baby will cause her to re-live the the horror of the attack she suffered every day that she is pregnant and perhaps for the rest of her life.
- A young woman just moved to a new city with her husband who is finishing his master's degree and is overwhelmed by the needs of her 10-month-old baby; she chooses an abortion because she knows her son will suffer if she has a second baby so soon.
- A mother of three who lost her job, pregnant by the man who is divorcing her, chooses an abortion to enable her to care for the three kids she has.
- A woman trying to get out of an abusive relationship gets an abortion because she doesn't want to be tied to her abuser for the rest of her life and doesn't feel she is emotionally capable of caring for his child.

These are just a handful of stories that women seeking abortions tell everyday. They are by no means the only stories. Often a woman simply knows she does not have the emotional, social, or material resources to nurture and care for a child.

An original essay written for this volume. Copyright © 2009 by Jennifer Webster. Reprinted by permission.

According to a study by the Guttmacher Institute,[1] approximately 3 million US women become pregnant unintentionally every year. Nearly half of those women were using some form of birth control and of those 3 million pregnancies, about 1.3 million will end with an abortion. Among women choosing abortion, 60% are already mothers. By far, the most common reason women give for terminating pregnancies is they feel that now is not a good time for them to have a baby, because, for whatever reason, they are not able to provide for a child the way that child needs and deserves to be provided for. Women choose to have abortions because they want to be good mothers. Women who choose to have an abortion are making a moral decision for their own welfare and for the welfare of their children and family. As one young woman put it, "Choosing an abortion, for me, was choosing life. It was the first time I acted as if my life mattered."[2]

One reason abortion is not seen as a moral decision in our society is the historical discounting of women as moral agents. It is only recently that women have been recognized as capable of thinking, reasoning and making moral decisions. Take the story of a young married woman in the 1940s. She and her husband decided to postpone having children because of their limited income, need to finish school and no desire to live with their parents. They use a diaphragm to prevent conception, but it fails and she becomes pregnant. Her doctor tells her he can recommend someone who will perform a safe, although illegal, abortion but she must first get written permission from her husband and her father.[3] Is it even possible to imagine a medical procedure for which a man would need to get permission from his wife and mother?

There is a lot of complexity in the decision to terminate a pregnancy (as there is in virtually every moral decision we face in our lives). Abortion is the only moral deliberation that we, as a society, reduce to the black and white question of whose life is valued. It is only because women are the primary moral agents in abortion decisions that we allow it to be seen in such absolute terms.

When we collectively deliberate on the morality of any issue, we have to look at all the factors. The only way to look at abortion as an immoral decision is to see the unborn fetus as having an absolute right to life and to discount or erase the life of the woman faced with the decision. If you look at the preceding stories of women who have chosen abortion, who can say that those women made the wrong choice? Do those women deserve to be punished? No, those women made brave decisions to protect their welfare and to improve the welfare of their families. Women who choose abortions are making a moral decision by choosing to protect the lives of the already-born.

There are vast social and economic inequities in our society that impact on women's reproductive decision-making. Women living at or below the Federal Poverty Level are four times more likely to get an abortion than women who live at 300% above the Federal Poverty Level. Women in certain communities of color are more likely to choose to terminate a pregnancy, probably because they are more likely to be living in poverty. These women also tend to have less access to contraception, health care and educational opportunities. This lack of access is part of a larger system of social and economic inequality that abortion opponents rarely, if ever address. By ignoring a woman's life and circumstances, we erase her history, her autonomy and her right to self-determination.

In a society filled with racism, sexism, poverty, war and violence, in a country where half a million children live in foster care, four children die every day from abuse and 28 million children live in poverty[4], we have much more pressing moral concerns than the question of when life begins and the rights of fetuses. It is the height of arrogance, or perhaps just misplaced priorities, to question the morality of abortion decisions, when so many members of our communities don't enjoy access to their basic human rights.

What is truly immoral and unjust are the attempts by courts and legislatures to restrict women's access to abortion. Everything from requiring parental notification/consent, mandatory waiting periods, mandated counseling with medically inaccurate information are all attempts to restrict abortion access and disproportionately impact young women, women of color and low-income women.

These attempts at restricting women's access to abortion are particularly troublesome in light of a 2007 study by the Guttmacher Institute[5]. The study found that abortion rates were lowest in the countries in which abortion was the most accessible. In countries where abortion is legal, free and available, such as the Netherlands, abortion rates are among the lowest in the world. Likewise, in countries as diverse as Peru, the Philippines or Uganda, where abortion is illegal, abortion rates are only slightly higher than the United States. The countries with the lowest abortion rates were also the countries in which contraception is readily available and sexuality education is comprehensive and evidence-based, two things that the anti-abortion movement also generally opposes.

The Guttmacher study clearly indicates that the best way to reduce the number of abortions performed was to reduce the need for abortion. The history of abortion in the US vividly illustrates that restricting access to abortion does little to stop abortions. Despite this overwhelming evidence, the anti-abortion movement continues to seek to restrict women's access to abortion, which raises a lot of questions about the motivations and true purpose of the anti-abortion movement.

The abortion debate in the United States is a tiring one. For decades now, both sides have argued for their position and given little ground. Life is pitted against Choice and there seems to be no way to move forward. What gets lost in this endless debate is the reality of women's lives. The decision of what to do with an unintended pregnancy is a morally complex one and women faced with the decision weigh their responsibilities carefully to examine what they have to offer to a new child. The issue is not so much a woman's right to choose to have an abortion, as a woman's right to choose her life.

Until women are seen as equal to men, with full complement of human rights, discussing the morality of abortion is specious. If we truly believed in women's autonomy, moral authority and right to self-determination, if we believed that only women can rightly make the decisions that will shape their lives, then we would recognize abortion for what it is: a safe medical procedure that is sometimes necessary for some women. If we lived in a society that valued women and women's lives this debate would go away. We would all work to prevent unintended pregnancy, to support women and the children they choose to have, recognizing that a woman's fundamental right to choose her own life is the first step to creating a morally just society.

Notes

1. Heather Boonstra, Rachel Benson Gold, Cory Richards and Lawrence Finer, *Abortion in Women's Lives* (Guttmacher Institute, 2006).

2. Anne Eggebroten, *Abortion: My Choice, God's Grace, Christian Women Tell Their Stories* (New Paradigm Books, 1994, p. 32).

3. From Helen Forelle, *If Men Got Pregnant, Abortion Would Be a Sacrament* (Canton, SD: Tesseract Publications, 1991).

4. Child Welfare Information Gateway. . . .

5. "Induced Abortion: Rates and Trends Worldwide," a study by the Guttmacher Institute and the World Health Organization authored by Gilda Sedgh, Stanley Hensha, Susheela Singh, Elisabeth Aahman and Iqbal Shah, published in *The Lancet,* October 13, 2007.

POSTSCRIPT

Is Abortion Immoral?

Recent years have seen a shift in attitudes toward abortion. A 2009 Gallup poll found that 51 percent of Americans considered themselves "pro-life" on abortion, compared with 42 percent who described themselves as "pro-choice." This poll marked the first time that a majority of Americans have taken a "pro-life" position since the Gallup poll began asking the question in 1995. Why do you think there has been a shift in attitudes? How would you define the terms "pro-life" and "pro-choice"? How do these terms differ with alternate descriptors, such as "pro-abortion," "anti-abortion," and "anti-choice"? It is interesting to note that further polling by the Gallup group found that 53 percent of people said that abortion should be legal under certain circumstances. Under what circumstances, if any, do you think abortion should be legal?

Early in Groothuis's essay, he describes President Barack Obama's administration as "the most pro-abortion administration in the history of the United States." Early in his first term, Obama rescinded the "global gag-rule," enacted by President George W. Bush, which restricted federal funding for abortion-related services (including providing information) in other countries. Despite this, Obama has stated publicly that he would "like to reduce the number of unwanted pregnancies that result in women feeling compelled to get an abortion or at least considering getting an abortion." Secretary of State Hillary Clinton has stated repeatedly that she believes abortion should be "safe, legal, and rare."

This wording—"safe, legal, and rare"—concerns people on both sides of the abortion debate. Ardent pro-choice advocates question why abortions should "rarely" occur? If they are both legal and safe, why should their frequency matter? Pro-life activists assert abortion can never be "safe" because they say that abortion harms innocent life and therefore should never be legal.

Groothuis presents three premises to advance his opposition to abortion. Do you agree with his logic? Groothius did make an exception for allowing abortion if the mother's life is at risk because of the child's birth (which he posits is a rarity). But what if the child's birth would keep the mother and her other children in poverty? Could staying in poverty be seen as immoral when you have other children to care for? Webster presents a variety of scenarios in which women may seek an abortion. Do you feel that abortion could be an appropriate decision in each of these situations? Is it more or less of a moral decision for a senior in college who "has an abortion after one night celebrating with her boyfriend" or for "a woman raped by her brother-in-law?" Or are they equally moral decisions?

To what extent does either description of morality—Groothuis's or Webster's—represent your own? What nuances, exceptions, or other reasons help to establish your own viewpoints on abortion? Finally, in a speech given at Notre Dame in 2009, President Obama called for a continued dialogue about abortion that includes "open hearts, open minds, and fair-minded words." What was the president saying about the history of the public discourse on abortion? In what ways have Americans' hearts and minds been closed, or their words unfair? How well do Groothuis and Webster succeed at responding to the president's invitation for civil dialogue?

Suggested Readings

Alan Guttmacher Institute, *Facts on Induced Abortion in the United States,* accessed November 26, 2008, at http://www.guttmacher.org/pubs/fb_induced_abortion.html

J. Baumgardner and T. Todras-Whitehill, *Abortion and Life* (New York: Akashic Books, 2008).

D. Marquis, "Why Abortion Is Immoral," *The Journal of Philosophy* (vol. 86, no. 4, 2009).

A. Sanger, *Beyond Choice: Reproductive Freedom in the 21st Century* (New York: Public Affairs, 2004).

S. Wicklund and A. Kessleheim, *This Common Secret: My Journey as an Abortion Doctor.* (New York: Public Affairs, 2008).

J. Williams, "Obama Urges Dialogue, Not Demonization, on Abortion," *Boston Globe* (May 18, 2009).

ISSUE 16

Should There Be Restrictions on the Number of Embryos Transferred during In-Vitro Fertilization?

YES: Charalambos Siristatidis and Mark Hamilton, from "Single Embryo Transfer," *Obstetrics, Gynecology, & Reproductive Medicine* (June 2007)

NO: William Saletan, from "Crocktuplets: Hijacking the Octuplets Backlash to Restrict IVF." Accessed May 01, 2009, at http://www.slate.com/id/2212876/

ISSUE SUMMARY

YES: Charalambos Siristatidis, an obstetrician, and Mark Hamilton, a gynecologist, advocate for restrictions on the number of embryos implanted during in-vitro fertilization, presenting evidence for the reduction of risk to mother and child.

NO: William Saletan, national correspondent for slate.com and author acknowledges the inherent risk of multiple embryo transfer but argues that any attempts to legislate the practice must consider women's reproductive autonomy.

A variety of assisted reproduction technologies (ART) have helped millions of women become pregnant and give birth. In 2005, the Centers for Disease Control reported that 1 percent of all live births in the U.S. were born as a result of ART (Wright, 2008). Over the past 30 years, in vitro fertilization (IVF) has become a popular choice for those who have had trouble becoming pregnant through traditional means. IVF is a procedure that allows egg cells to be surgically removed and fertilized by sperm cells in a laboratory. The fertilized egg cells are then transferred into the woman's uterus in hopes of a full-term pregnancy and birth occurring (CDC, 2008).

In the United States, fertility clinics have typically transferred more than one fertilized embryo in order to increase the chances of success. Because of this, between 35 and 42 percent of pregnancies through IVF result in multiple births (Jones, 2006). Although some expecting parents see this as an added bonus, or even wish for twins, many medical experts warn that the increased risks (to both mother and child) involved in multiple births make the implantation of more than one embryo too risky to be considered ethical. Multiple births through IVF have a higher risk of being premature, having lower birth weights, and having disabilities (Jones, 2006). Several European countries have implemented laws restricting the number of embryos that can be implanted per IVF cycle. The United Kingdom's Human Fertilisation and Embryology Authority encourages Single Embryo Transfer (SET), though, as in the United States, this is only a guideline.

In early 2009, headlines were made when 32-year-old Californian Nadya Suleman gave birth to octouplets born as a result of in vitro fertilization (IVF). Initially, the births were seen as a miracle of science. The fact that all eight were born and appeared in good condition brought accolades for the delivery team (46 doctors and nurses in all). The media speculated about which diaper company would step up to provide free products, as had been the trend with other recent multiple births. The good will quickly turned to criticism, however, as more information emerged. It was revealed that Suleman, dubbed "Octomom" by the media, was already the mother of six children, all produced via IVF. She was also unemployed and living with her mother. Critics from across the political and media spectrum weighed in on whether she was "fit" to be a mother. Television talking heads wondered where she got the money for the procedure and how she could afford to care for 14 children.

The births sparked controversy on both the medical and social fronts. The implantation of six embryos by Suleman's clinic was considered by many to be outright dangerous, and raised eyebrows and voices in the medical community. The fertility clinic that performed Suleman's IVF came under scrutiny. The American Society for Reproductive Medicine recommends that the number of embryos transferred should depend on the age of the patient. According to the guidelines, the transfer of one embryo is ideal, and no more than two should be transferred under normal circumstances for women under the age of 35. For women over 40, the maximum number of embryos to be transferred should be five. Though these guidelines are from a respected organization, they are not law.

From an efficiency and safety standpoint, the guidelines make sense. A recent study found that implanting more than two embryos did not increase the pregnancy rate, only the incidence of multiple births (Templeton & Morris, 1998). Two additional studies found that single embryo implantation resulted in higher pregnancy rates than double embryo implantation (Fiddelers et al., 2009; Veleva et al., 2009). So why not follow those guidelines? In Suleman's case, she said that she could not imagine leaving embryos frozen, nor having them donated to infertile couples. Her concerns and actions raise the related ethical question of what is to be done with frozen embryos.

In the aftermath of the "Octomom" controversy, questions and criticism came from politicians, child welfare advocates, and mental health professionals alike.

In the following selection, Siristatidis and Hamilton present evidence for the reduction of risk to mother and child through the practice of single embryo transfer. William Saletan challenges the introduction of legislation that supposedly protects women's health through outlawing multiple embryo transfer but in reality restricts their reproductive options.

YES

**Charalambos Siristatidis
and Mark Hamilton**

Single Embryo Transfer

Abstract

Multiple pregnancies present significant problems for mothers and babies. The incidence of twin pregnancies has increased dramatically in the last 30 years, linked to the development of assisted reproductive technologies including *in vitro* fertilisation (IVF). The occurrence of multiple pregnancies after IVF is directly related to the number of embryos replaced during treatment. Policies to reduce the number of multiple pregnancies through limiting the numbers of embryos transferred have been successfully introduced in some parts of Europe. Anxieties that pregnancy rates would decline significantly after introduction of a policy of single embryo transfer have not been realised, particularly when the pregnancies derived from the transfer of additional cryopreserved embryos are taken into consideration. Obstacles to the introduction of such a policy in the UK relate to the commissioning arrangements for IVF and the competitive commercial environment in which IVF is provided. Continued high multiple pregnancy rates are not acceptable. IVF children should be given the best chance possible of safe delivery, at term, as singletons.

Introduction

One in seven couples has infertility problems. For many, the only effective treatment is *in vitro* fertilisation (IVF). Each year in the UK, over 40,000 such treatment cycles are undertaken, resulting in the birth of more than 10,000 babies. Many of the babies born arise from multiple pregnancies. More than half of all twin pregnancies in the UK result from fertility treatment. The observed secular trends in the incidence of multiple pregnancies over the last 25 years are thus a direct consequence of the increased use of IVF in infertility care.

The Burden of Multiple Pregnancy

The number of twin births in the UK has risen dramatically over the last 30 years, from just under 6000 in 1975 to over 9000 in 2004. Multiple pregnancies pose major risks for both women and children. Obstetric complications such as haemorrhage, pre-eclampsia, diabetes and pre-term delivery are common. Neonatal consequences are often profound, with significantly increased

From *Obstetrics, Gynaecology and Reproductive Medicine,* 17(6), June 2007, pp. 192–194.
Copyright © 2007 by Elsevier Health Sciences. Reprinted by permission via Rightslink.

risks of death and cerebral palsy. The long-term consequences of extremely pre-term birth may impose a major health burden on the child, and the costs incurred through such birth complications can be extremely high. In addition, there are often health and social consequences for the families concerned.

Risk Reduction

The link between the number of embryos transferred to the uterus during IVF and the likelihood of multiple pregnancy is irrefutable. In 2001, the Human Fertilisation and Embryology Authority (HFEA), the regulator of treatment centres in the UK, limited the number of embryos allowed to be transferred, other than in exceptional circumstances, to two. This policy was toughened in 2004, allowing no exceptions below the age of 40 years. The consequence of this has been a massive reduction in the incidence of triplet pregnancies but little effect on the number of twins. Further restrictions on embryo transfer practice merit consideration. Intuitively, since most twin pregnancies in IVF are dizygotic, a unilateral move to elective single embryo transfer (eSET) for all patients would virtually abolish the problem. Inevitably, matters are not as simple as this because patients, many of whom are funding their treatment themselves, are concerned to have the maximum chance of a pregnancy, and restriction of embryo transfer numbers might prejudice the one opportunity they have to conceive. Furthermore, it is likely that not all patients have the same prospect of successful treatment and thus, when considering restrictive embryo transfer policies, it is necessary to identify the patients in whom the chance of pregnancy is greatest and the embryos with the highest chance of implantation.

Experience of Single Embryo Transfer

To date, single embryo transfer is widely practiced only in Scandinavia, Holland and Belgium. Randomised controlled trial evidence suggests that the pregnancy rates per cycle after eSET are lower than in double embryo transfer (DET) cycles. These trials have been conducted in patients deemed to have a good prognosis regarding the woman's age and the number and quality of available embryos. Analyses, as summarised in a recent Cochrane review, suggest that, compared with eSET, DET in fresh IVF/intracytoplasmic sperm injection cycles leads to a higher live birth rate (OR 1.94, 95% CI 1.47–2.55; $p < 0.00001$). The multiple pregnancy rate, however, was significantly higher in women who underwent DET (OR 23.55, 95% CI 8.00–69.29; $p < 0.00001$). These and other trials have also examined the influence on overall pregnancy rates if the use of any additional cryopreserved embryos derived from the same ovary stimulation cycle is taken into account. The difference in pregnancy rate is eliminated when pregnancies following a subsequent frozen/thawed transfer cycle are added.

It can be deduced from these data that the introduction of a single embryo transfer policy involving fresh followed by frozen single embryo transfers, in patients with a good prognosis, can virtually abolish the risk of multiple pregnancy while maintaining a live birth rate similar to that achieved by transferring two fresh embryos.

Defining the good-prognosis patient is a requirement for a successful eSET policy. Further research in this area will be required, but at present studies take into account the age of the woman (usually <36 years), previous failed IVF attempts (usually first cycle), basal follicle-stimulating horome (<10 IU/l) and number of good-quality embryos available (usually at least two).

The experience in Sweden merits particular attention. Persuaded by the trial evidence, a national policy has evolved based on the principle that only one embryo should be replaced, apart from in exceptional circumstances. In practice, 70% of all IVF cycles are now eSET cycles. Importantly, perhaps as embryological expertise has increased, pregnancy rates have been maintained and the twin rate resulting from treatment has decreased from 25% in 1999 to 5% in 2004.

The Patient's Perspective

While the cumulative pregnancy rates achieved through eSET policies match those of DET, the need for additional cycles of care is not attractive to patients. More embryo transfers cost more money, and entail more time off work and more trips to hospital. The emotional strain caused by extra cycles associated with disappointment is an issue. For many patients, the experience of a failed cycle is akin to bereavement. Additional exposure to risk of failure may be interpreted by some as compounding their anguish. Clinics need therefore to strike a balance between a desire to maximise the chance of conception for the patient and minimising the risk of multiple pregnancy. Both aspirations have the intention of maximising the chance of a safe live birth of a healthy child.

Embryo Selection

The future success of single embryo transfer policies will be influenced by our ability to improve culture conditions for embryos, and the development of techniques to determine with confidence the best embryo to select for transfer; that is, the embryo with the greatest potential for implantation. At present, embryo selection is determined on morphological grounds, which is a relatively crude technique in terms of predicting the genetic competence of individual embryos. Research into more sophisticated techniques such as biochemical and genetic screening may prove fruitful. Extended culture to the blastocyst stage may be a useful method of determining the embryo with the maximum implantation potential.

Commissioning Care

An examination of the way in which IVF is commissioned in countries where eSET has become the norm is informative. In Belgium, a reimbursement system has been introduced that links the funding of six IVF cycles for a patient to the compulsory use of eSET in the patient's first cycle. Further eSET is required if the patient's age and available embryo quality are favourable. In contrast, no legislative proscription on IVF care has been imposed in Sweden, Denmark or Norway, yet the sector, perhaps through peer pressure, has largely moved to eSET as the default position. Experience in the UK suggests that proscription rather than appeal to clinical sensibility is more likely to result in a change in practice. Implementation in full of the guideline on the assessment and treatment for people with fertility problems issued by the National Institute for Clinical Excellence in 2004, in which three cycles of treatment were recommended, including transfer of fresh and all frozen embryos per cycle, would help to facilitate a change in practice. The way in which IVF data is presented to the public, both by the regulatory authority and by clinics, could also make a difference. Outcome per cycle, as currently used, tends to be a disincentive to good clinical practice rather than a more responsible description of cumulative pregnancy rates. The HFEA, and the infertility sector itself, has a major role to play in changing the mind-set of patients and clinics regarding how embryo transfer is conducted. In a commercially driven marketplace derived from inadequate state funding of IVF, this is a significant challenge.

Conclusions

The evidence base linking the practice of multiple embryo transfer and the consequent establishment of pregnancies at high risk of serious complications is irrefutable. The health benefits to children, the reduction in distress for families and the enormous cost savings for society that would be achieved through a reduction in the need for immediate and long-term health care for affected children make an overwhelming case for change in this area of clinical practice. Modification of embryo transfer practice through careful patient and embryo selection can significantly reduce the risk of such hazards.

To quote a recent important document from the HFEA: "The fertility sector has for too long been responsible for the creation of children with complex needs. IVF children deserve the best possible chance to be born at full term and as healthy singletons. The only way this can be achieved is by making eSET the norm."

Practice Points

- Twin pregnancies carry much higher obstetric risks for women
- Multiple birth is the single biggest risk to the health and welfare of children born after IVF
- Modification of embryo transfer practice through careful patient and embryo selection can significantly reduce the risk of such hazards

William Saletan  **NO**

Crocktuplets: Hijacking the Octuplets Backlash to Restrict IVF

No more octuplets! That's the rallying cry for Georgia Senate Bill 169, which faces a committee hearing Thursday morning. The bill's lead sponsor, state senator Ralph Hudgens, says he believes in "less government," "more personal responsibility," and "greater individual freedoms." Supposedly, that's what galls him about Nadya Suleman, the now-infamous woman who had six kids and, through in vitro fertilization, just gave birth to eight more. "Nadya Suleman is going to cost the state of California millions of dollars over the years; the taxpayers are going to have to fund the 14 children she has," Hudgens told the *Wall Street Journal.* "I don't want that to happen in Georgia." Georgia Right to Life, which helped Hudgens draft his bill, puts a gentler spin on it. The Suleman case shows that "the fertility industry needs governmental oversight," the group argued in a press release two weeks ago. Its president explained that S.B. 169 "is written to help reduce the attendant harm that could come to the mother and her children through the creation and implantation of more embryos than is medically recommended." The release was titled "Georgia Right to Life Introduces Legislation to Protect the Mother and Child."

So which rationale should we believe? The one about protecting taxpayers or the one about protecting women?

Neither. Never trust the press release. Always read the bill.

S.B. 169 does limit the number of embryos you can implant in an IVF patient to two or three, depending on whether the patient is younger or older than 40. But it also does several things that have nothing to do with saving tax money or protecting women from the risks of carrying multiple fetuses. It forbids the sale of eggs or sperm, bans therapeutic human cloning, and prohibits any stem-cell research involving the destruction of leftover embryos.

"This bill would limit the number of embryos transferred in any given cycle to the same number that are fertilized," says the Georgia Right to Life press release. But that's not what the bill says. Here's the actual text of the legislation:

> In the interest of reducing the risk of complications for both the mother and the transferred in vitro human embryos, including the risk of preterm birth associated with higher-order multiple gestations, a person or entity performing in vitro fertilization shall limit the number of in vitro human embryos created in a single cycle to the number to be transferred in that cycle.

From *Slate*, by William Saletan, March 2009. Copyright © 2009 by Slate Group and Washingtonpost.Newsweek Interactive Company, LLC. Reprinted by permission. All rights reserved.

In other words, if you're 39, your doctor is forbidden to fertilize more than two of your eggs per treatment cycle. Take all the hormones you can stand, make all the eggs you want, but you get two shots at creating a viable embryo, and that's it.

How does this restriction "protect the mother" and "reduce the risk of complications" for her? It doesn't. If you wanted to protect the woman, you might limit the number of embryos that could be transferred to her womb, not the number that can be created in the dish. In fact, by limiting the number that can be created, you increase her risk of complications. The fewer eggs you fertilize, the lower your chances of producing an embryo healthy enough to be transferred and carried to term. That means a higher failure rate, which in turn means that women will have to undergo more treatment cycles, with the corresponding risks of ovarian hyperstimulation and advancing maternal age.

So why limit the number of embryos created per cycle? Because the bill's chief purpose isn't really to help women. It's to establish legal rights for embryos. That's why it bans cloning and embryo-destructive stem-cell research. And if the woman and her husband get into a legal battle over what to do with their embryos, guess which of them has the final say? Neither. According to the bill's text, "the judicial standard for resolving such disputes shall be the best interest of the in vitro human embryo."

From the standpoint of respecting embryos, this is all wonderful stuff. But it doesn't serve the health interests of women seeking IVF, and it certainly doesn't protect taxpayers. "A living in vitro human embryo is a biological human being who is not the property of any person or entity," the bill declares. "The fertility physician and the medical facility that employs the physician owe a high duty of care to the living in vitro human embryo." Guess who's going to foot the bill for that "high duty of care"? With half a million embryos already frozen and thousands more accumulating every year, a declaration of medical rights for embryos would be one of the biggest entitlement programs in history.

Oh, and if you like what Suleman did, you'll love S.B. 169. By requiring doctors to "limit the number of in vitro human embryos created in a single cycle to the number to be transferred," the bill logically requires them to transfer every embryo created. That's exactly what Suleman did. She loved her babies too much to leave any of them behind. Enough with the opportunism about the octuplets. Respecting embryos is a noble idea. But it won't be safer for women, and it won't come cheap.

POSTSCRIPT

Should There Be Restrictions on the Number of Embryos Transferred during In-Vitro Fertilization?

Siristatidis and Hamilton state the benefits of single embryo transfer. Although guidelines are in place that recommend this practice, do you feel that laws should be created in order to reduce multiple transfers? Saletan does not disagree with the health benefits of single embryo transfer. However, he feels that much of the legislation currently being discussed is intended to restrict women's reproductive freedom more than protect their health. Is there a way to legislate IVF without infringing on a woman's reproductive autonomy? Is there a line that should be drawn between the desires of the patient and concern for their safety? Should couples who undergo fertility treatments have restrictions placed on the number of children they can ultimately have?

Is any attempt to reduce the options available unfair to women and hopeful couples? Should women be allowed total reproductive freedom concerning their bodies and embryos? Does placing restrictions on what can be done with embryos place the legal status of other reproductive choices at risk? If the sex of a child can be selected through a medical procedure (see Issue 17 in this edition) should doctors or patients also be allowed to use procedures that would influence the number of children? Is it acceptable for parents to seek out ART in order to have multiple children in one cycle (as in the desire for "IVF twins")?

And what, as many commentators asked, about the welfare of the children after their release from the hospital? Should single mothers who undergo fertility treatments like IVF be held to a different set of rules than couples? Should parents who opt to have more than one embryo transferred be required to undergo background screenings? These kinds of questions may make reproductive rights advocates nervous. They see the possibility of restrictions a form of modern day eugenics. In the early 1900s, the eugenics movement pushed for reduced reproduction among groups, including the poor, minorities, and the disabled, who were thought to possess negative hereditary traits. Should the government have a say in who gets to be a mother? Or how many children she can give birth to at once? And upon what criteria would the mother or couple be judged? Should there be different rules if the mother is singe? Married? In a same sex marriage or relationship? Wealthy or poor? Suffering from depression? Developmentally disabled? Is legislation that limits an individual's right or ability to reproduce a form of eugenics? Should the lambasting of media pundits who have criticized Nadya Suleman for her decision impact the reproductive freedom of others?

Suggested Readings

Centers for Disease Control, "2006 Assisted Reproductive Technology (ART) Report: Commonly Asked Questions," accessed at http://www.cdc.gov/ART/ART2006/faq.htm (2008).

A. Fiddelers et al. "Cost-effectiveness of Seven IVF Strategies: Results of a Markov Decision-Analytic Model," *Human Reproduction,* Advance Access, published online on March 24, 2009.

R. Jones and K. Lopez, K., *Human Reproductive Biology* (Burlington, MA: Academic Press, 2006).

Z. Veleva et al., "Elective Single Embryo Transfer with Cryopreservation Improves the Outcome and Diminishes the Costs of IVF/ICSI," *Human Reproduction,* Advance Access, published online on March 24, 2009.

V.C. Wright et al., "Assisted Reproductive Technology Surveillance— United States, 2005," accessed at http://www.cdc.gov/mmwr/preview/mmwrhtml/ss5705a1.htm (2008).

ISSUE 17

Should Parents Be Allowed to Select the Sex of Their Baby?

YES: John A. Robertson, from "Extending Preimplantation Genetic Diagnosis: Medical and Non-medical Uses," *Journal of Medical Ethics* (vol. 29, 2003)

NO: Marcy Darnovsky, from "Revisiting Sex Selection: The Growing Popularity of New Sex Selection Methods Revives an Old Debate," http://www.gene-watch.org/genewatch/articles/17-1darnovsky. html (January–February 2004)

ISSUE SUMMARY

YES: Law professor John A. Robertson argues that preimplantation genetic diagnosis (PGD), a new technique that allows parents-to-be to determine the gender of their embryo before implantation in the uterus, should be permissible. Robertson argues that it is not sexist to want a baby of a particular gender and that the practice should not be restricted.

NO: Marcy Darnovsky, associate director of the Center for Genetics and Society, argues that by allowing PGD for sex selection, governments are starting down a slippery slope that could create an era of consumer eugenics.

The practice of selecting the sex of a child is nothing new. Historically, couples who wanted a child of a specific gender might abandon an unwanted child of the other gender in the wilderness, leave the baby on the doorstep of a church or orphanage, or kill the unwanted baby. Although these practices still continue in some societies today, sex selection has also changed in significant ways. The development of ultrasound technology, for example, allows expecting parents to determine the gender of the baby before it is born, and some couples might consider abortion if the child is not the desired sex. Parents might feel additional pressure to make this decision in countries like China, which has a "one child" policy, whereby additional children receive no governmental support—a critical consideration in a communist nation that also places higher value on male infants than females.

For many Americans, the idea of sex selection by abandonment, abortion, or infanticide would be considered unethical, if not appalling. But in other areas of the world, the practice is carried out routinely to help parents meet strong cultural preferences to produce a male child. Such actions are based in the entrenched sexism of these male-dominated societies.

A seemingly more ethical technique that sorted sperm before conception has offered about a 50–85 percent effectiveness rate at predetermining sex for the past 30 years. More recently a new development in medical technology known as preimplantation genetic diagnosis (PGD), previously used to screen embryos for markers that may signal diseases like cystic fibrosis, now allows people using in vitro fertilization to select the sex of an embryo, with 99.9 percent accuracy, before it is implanted in the uterus. To many satisfied customers, this has provided the opportunity to "balance" a family, by adding a child of the other sex or evening out the number of male and female children. In some cases, first-time parents simply desire a child of one sex or the other.

While the use of PGD for medical reasons, such as screening for Down syndrome, in an embryo are generally seen as acceptable, there is less consensus concerning its use for nonmedical reasons, including sex selection. Is wanting to choose the sex of your child sexist? Does it reflect or perpetuate a gender bias in society? If selecting the sex of your unborn child is possible and legal, what about predetermination of other characteristics, such as eye color? Height? Musical ability? Sexual orientation?

In the following selections, John A. Robertson, professor at the University of Texas School of Law, argues that using PGD for sex selection in certain instances is not inherently sexist, and that it—and perhaps other nonmedical types of PGD should not be regulated based on the fear of what could possibly happen at some future time. Marcy Darnovsky, associate director of the Center for Genetics and Society, argues that by allowing PGD for sex selection, governments are starting down a slippery slope that could create an era of consumer eugenics.

YES

John A. Robertson

Extending Preimplantation Genetic Diagnosis: Medical and Non-Medical Uses

PGD and Its Prevalence

PGD has been available since 1990 for testing of aneuploidy in low prognosis in vitro fertilisation (IVF) patients, and for single gene and X linked diseases in at risk couples. One cell (blastomere) is removed from a cleaving embryo and tested for the genetic or chromosomal condition of concern. Some programmes analyse polar bodies extruded from oocytes during meiosis, rather than blastomeres.[1] Cells are then either karyotyped to identify chromosomal abnormalities, or analysed for single gene mutations and linked markers.

Physicians have performed more than 3000 clinical cycles of PGD since 1990, with more than 700 children born as a result. The overall pregnancy rate of 24% is comparable to assisted reproductive practices which do not involve embryo or polar body biopsy.[1] Four centres (Chicago, Livingston (New Jersey), Bologna, and Brussels) accounted for nearly all the reported cases. More than 40 centres worldwide offer the procedure, however, including other centres in the United States and Europe, four centres in London and centres in the eastern Mediterranean, Southeast Asia, and Australia.

More than two-thirds of PGD has occurred to screen out embryos with chromosomal abnormalities in older IVF patients and in patients with a history of miscarriage. About 1000 cycles have involved single gene mutational analysis.[1] Mutational analysis requires additional skills beyond karyotyping for aneuploidies, including the ability to conduct the multiplex polymerase chain reaction (PCR) of the gene of interest and related markers.

Several new indications for PGD single gene mutational analysis have recently been reported. New uses include PGD to detect mutations for susceptibility to cancer and for late onset disorders such as Alzheimer's disease.[2,3] In addition, parents with children needing hematopoietic stem cell transplants have used PGD to ensure that their next child is free of disease and a good tissue match for an existing child.[4] Some persons are also requesting PGD for gender selection for both first and later born children, and others have speculated that selection of embryos for a variety of non-medical traits is likely in the future.

PGD is ethically controversial because it involves the screening and likely destruction of embryos, and the selection of offspring on the basis of expected

From *Journal of Medical Ethics*, vol. 29, 2003, pp. 213(4). Copyright © 2003 by Institute of Medical Ethics. Reprinted by permission of BMJ Publishing Group.

traits. While persons holding right to life views will probably object to PGD for any reason, those who view the early embryo as too rudimentary in development to have rights or interests see no principled objection to all PGD. They may disagree, however, over whether particular reasons for PGD show sufficient respect for embryos and potential offspring to justify intentional creation and selection of embryos. Donation of unwanted embryos to infertile couples reduces this problem somewhat, but there are too few such couples to accept all unwanted embryos, and in any event, the issue of selecting offspring traits remains.

Although ethical commentary frequently mentions PGD as a harbinger of a reproductive future of widespread genetic selection and alteration of prospective offspring, its actual impact is likely to be quite limited.[5,6] Even with increasing use the penetrance of PGD into reproductive practice is likely to remain a very small percentage of the 150,000 plus cycles of IVF performed annually throughout the world. Screening for susceptibility and late onset diseases is limited by the few diseases for which single gene predispositions are known. Relatively few parents will face the need to conceive another child to provide an existing child with matched stem cells. Nor are non-medical uses of PGD, other than for gender, likely to be practically feasible for at least a decade or more. Despite the limited reach of PGD, the ethical, legal, and policy issues that new uses raise, deserve attention.

New Medical Uses

New uses of PGD may be grouped into medical and non-medical categories. New medical uses include not only screening for rare Mendelian diseases, but also for susceptibility conditions, late onset diseases, and HLA matching for existing children.

Embryo screening for susceptibility and late onset conditions are logical extensions of screening for serious Mendelian diseases. For example, using PGD to screen out embryos carrying the p53 or BRCA1&2 mutations prevent the birth of children who would face a greatly increased lifetime risk of cancer, and hence require close monitoring, prophylactic surgery, or other preventive measures. PGD for highly penetrant adult disorders such as Alzheimer's or Huntington's disease prevents the birth of a child who will be healthy for many years, but who in her late 30s or early 40s will experience the onset of progressive neurological disease leading to an early death.

Although these indications do not involve diseases that manifest themselves in infancy or childhood, the conditions in question lead to substantial health problems for offspring in their thirties or forties.[7] Avoiding the birth of children with those conditions thus reflects the desire of parents to have offspring with good prospects for an average life span. If PGD is accepted to exclude offspring with early onset genetic diseases, it should be accepted for later onset conditions as well.

PGD for adult onset disorders does mean that a healthy child might then be born to a person with those conditions who is likely to die or become incompetent while the child is dependent on her.[8] But that risk has been tolerated in other cases of assisted reproduction, such as intrauterine insemination with sperm of a man who is HIV positive, IVF for women with cystic fibrosis, and use of gametes stored prior to cancer therapy. As long as competent caregivers will be available for the child, the likely death or disability of a parent does not justify condemning or stopping this use, anymore than that reproduction by men going off to war should be discouraged.

A third new medical indication—HLA matching to an existing child—enables a couple to have their next child serve as a matched hematopoietic stem cell donor for an existing sick child. It may also ensure that the new child does not also suffer from that same disease. The availability of PGD, however, should not hinge on that fact, as the Human Fertilisation and Embryology Authority, in the UK, now requires.[9] A couple that would coitally conceive a child to be a tissue donor should be free to use PGD to make sure that that child will be a suitable match, regardless of whether that child is also at risk for genetic disease. Parents who choose PGD for this purpose are likely to value the new child for its own sake, and not only for the stem cells that it will make available. They do not use the new child as a "mere means" simply because they have selected HLA matched embryos for transfer.[10, 11]

Non-Medical Uses of PGD

More ethically troubling has been the prospect of using PGD to screen embryos for genes that do not relate to the health of resulting children or others in the family. Many popular accounts of PGD assume that it will eventually be used to select for such non-medical traits as intelligence, height, sexual orientation, beauty, hair and eye colour, memory, and other factors.[5, 6] Because the genetic basis of those traits is unknown, and in any case is likely to involve many different genes, they may not be subject to easy mutational analysis, as Mendelian disease or susceptibility conditions are. Aside from gender, which is identifiable through karyotyping, it is unrealistic to think that non-medical screening for other traits, with the possible exception of perfect pitch, will occur anytime soon.

Still, it is useful to consider the methodology that ethical assessment of non-medical uses of PGD, if available, should follow. The relevant questions would be whether the proposed use serves valid reproductive or rearing interests; whether those interests are sufficient to justify creating and destroying embryos; whether selecting for a trait will harm resulting children; whether it will stigmatise existing persons, and whether it will create other social harms.

To analyse how these factors interact, I discuss PGD for sex selection and for children with perfect pitch. Similar issues would arise with PGD for sexual orientation, for hair and eye color, and for intelligence, size, and memory.

PGD for Gender Selection

The use of medical technology to select the sex of offspring is highly controversial because of the bias against females which it usually reflects or expresses, and the resulting social disruptions which it might cause. PGD for gender selection faces the additional problem of appearing to be a relatively weak reason for creating and selecting embryos for discard or transfer.

The greatest social effects of gender selection arise when the gender of the first child is chosen. Selection for first children will overwhelmingly favour males, particularly if one child per family population policies apply. If carried out on a large scale, it could lead to great disparities in the sex ratio of the population, as has occurred in China and India through the use of ultrasound screening and abortion.[12, 13] PGD, however, is too expensive and inaccessible to be used on a wide scale for sex selection purposes. Allowing it to be used for the first child is only marginally likely to contribute to societal sex ratio imbalances. But its use is likely to reflect cultural notions of male privilege and may reinforce entrenched sexism toward women.

The use of PGD to choose a gender opposite to that of an existing child or children is much less susceptible to a charge of sexism. Here a couple seeks variety or "balance" in the gender of offspring because of the different rearing experiences that come with rearing children of different genders. Psychologists now recognise many biologically based differences between male and female children, including different patterns of aggression, learning, and spatial recognition, as well as hormonal differences.[14, 15] It may not be sexist in itself to wish to have a child or children of each gender, particularly if one has two or more children of the same gender.

Some feminists, however, would argue that any attention to the gender of offspring is inherently sexist, particularly when social attitudes and expectations play such an important role in constructing sex role expectations and behaviours.[16] Other feminists find the choice of a child with a gender different from existing children to be morally defensible as long as "the intention and consequences of the practice are not sexist", which is plausibly the case when gender variety in children is sought.[17] Desiring the different rearing experiences with boys and girls does not mean that the parents, who have already had children of one gender, are sexists or likely to value unfairly one or the other gender.[18]

Based on this analysis the case is weak for allowing PGD for the first child, but may be acceptable for gender variety in a family. With regard to the first child, facilitating preferences for male firstborns carries a high risk of promoting sexist social mores. It may also strike many persons as too trivial a concern to meet shared notions of the special respect due preimplantation embryos. A proponent of gender selection, however, might argue that cultural preferences for firstborn males should be tolerated, unless a clearer case of harm has been shown. If PGD is not permitted, pregnancy and abortion might occur instead.

The case for PGD for gender variety is stronger because the risk of sexism is lessened. A couple would be selecting the gender of a second or subsequent children for variety in rearing experiences, and not out of a belief that one gender is privileged over another. Gender selection in that case would occur without running the risks of fostering sexism and hurting women.[18]

The question still arises whether the desire for gender variety in children, even if not sexist, is a strong enough reason to justify creating and discarding embryos. The answer depends on how strong an interest that is. No one has yet marshalled the evidence showing that the need or desire for gender variety in children is substantial and important, or whether many parents would refrain from having another child if PGD for gender variety were not possible. More evidence of the strength and prevalence of this need would help in reaching a conclusion. If that case is made, then PGD for gender variety might be acceptable as well.[19]

The ethics committee of the American Society of Reproductive Medicine (ASRM) has struggled with these issues in a series of recent opinions. It initially addressed the issue of PGD for gender selection generally, and found that it "should be discouraged" for couples not going through IVF, and "not encouraged" for couples who were, but made no distinction between PGD for gender selection of first and later children.[20] Subsequently, it found that preconception gender selection would be acceptable for purposes of gender variety but not for the first child.[18]

Perceiving these two positions to be inconsistent, a doctor who wanted to offer PGD for gender selection inquired of the ethics committee why preconception methods for gender variety, which lacked 100% certainty, were acceptable but PGD, which guaranteed that certainty, was not. Focusing only on the sexism and gender discrimination issue, the chair of the ethics committee, in a widely publicised letter, found that PGD for gender balancing would be acceptable.[21] When the full committee reconsidered the matter, it concluded that it had not yet received enough evidence that the need for gender variety was so important in families that it justified creating and discarding embryos for that purpose.[19] In the future if such evidence was forthcoming then PGD for gender variety might also be acceptable.

What might constitute such evidence? One source would be families with two or more children of one gender who very much would like to have another child but only if they could be sure that it would be a child of the gender opposite of existing children. Given the legitimacy of wanting to raise children of both genders, reasonable persons might find that this need outweighs the symbolic costs of creating and discarding embryos for that purpose.

Another instance would be a case in which a couple has had a girl, but now wants a boy in order to meet cultural norms of having a male heir or a male to perform funeral rituals or play other cultural roles. An IVF programme in India is now providing PGD to select male offspring as the second child of couples who have already had a daughter.[22] Because of the importance of a male heir in India, those couples might well consider having an abortion if pregnant with a female fetus (even though illegal in India for that purpose). In that setting PGD for gender selection for gender variety appears to be justified.

PGD for Perfect Pitch

Perfect or "absolute" pitch is the ability to identify and recall musical notes from memory.[23] Although not all great or successful musicians have perfect pitch, a large number of them do. Experts disagree over whether perfect pitch is solely inborn or may also be developed by early training, though most agree that a person either has it or does not. It also runs in families, apparently in an autosomal dominant pattern.[23] The gene or genes coding for this capacity have not, however, been mapped, much less sequenced. Because genes for perfect pitch may also relate to the genetic basis for language or other cognitive abilities, research to find that gene may be forthcoming.

Once the gene for perfect pitch or its linked markers are identified, it would be feasible to screen embryos for those alleles, and transfer only those embryos that test positive. The prevalence of those genes is quite low (perhaps three in 100) in the population, but high in certain families.[23] Thus only persons from those families who have a strong interest in the musical ability of their children would be potential candidates for PGD for perfect pitch. Many of them are likely to take their chances with coital conception and exposure of the child to music at an early age. Some couples, however, may be willing to undergo IVF and PGD to ensure musical ability in their child. Should their request be accepted or denied?

As noted, the answer to this question depends on the importance of the reproductive choice being asserted, the burdens of the selection procedure, its impact on offspring, and its implications for deselected groups and society generally. The strongest case for the parents is if they persuasively asserted that they would not reproduce unless they could select that trait, and they have a plausible explanation for that position. Although the preference might appear odd to some, it might also be quite understandable in highly musical families, particularly ones in which some members already have perfect pitch. Parents clearly have the right to instill or develop a child's musical ability after birth. They might reasonably argue that they should have that right before birth as well.

If so, then creating and discarding embryos for this purpose should also be acceptable. If embryos are too rudimentary in development to have inherent rights or interests, then no moral duty is violated by creating and destroying them.[24] Some persons might think that doing so for trivial or unimportant reasons debases the inherent dignity of all human life, but having a child with perfect pitch will not seem trivial to parents seeking this technique. Ultimately, the judgment of triviality or importance of the choice within a broad spectrum rests with the couple. If they have a strong enough preference to seek PGD for this purpose and that preference rationally relates to understandable reproductive goals, then they have demonstrated its great importance to them. Only in cases unsupported by a reasonable explanation of the need—for example, perhaps creating embryos to pick eye or hair colour, should a person's individual assessment of the importance of creating embryos be condemned or rejected.

A third relevant factor is whether musical trait selection is consistent with respect for the resulting child. Parents who are willing to undergo the costs and burdens of IVF and PGD to have a child with perfect pitch may be so overly invested in the child having a musical career that they will prevent it from developing its own personality and identity. Parents, however, are free to instill and develop musical ability once the child is born, just as they are entitled to instill particular religious views. It is difficult to say that they cross an impermissible moral line of risk to the welfare of their prospective child in screening embryos for this purpose. Parents are still obligated to provide their child with the basic education and care necessary for any life plan. Wanting a child to have perfect pitch is not inconsistent with parents also wanting their child to be well rounded and equipped for life in other contexts.

A fourth factor, impact on deselected groups, is much less likely to be an issue in the case of perfect pitch because there is no stigma or negative association tied to persons without that trait. Persons without perfect pitch suffer no stigma or opprobrium by the couple's choice or public acceptance of it, as is arguably the case with embryo selection on grounds of gender, sexual orientation, intelligence, strength, size, or other traits. Nor is PGD for perfect pitch likely to perpetuate unfair class advantages, as selection for intelligence, strength, size, or beauty might.

A final factor is the larger societal impact of permitting embryo screening for a non-medical condition such as perfect pitch. A valid concern is that such a practice might then legitimise embryo screening for other traits as well, thus moving us toward a future in which children are primarily valued according to the attractiveness of their expected characteristics. But that threat is too hypothetical to justify limiting what are otherwise valid exercises of parental choice. It is highly unlikely that many traits would be controlled by genes that could be easily tested in embryos. Gender is determined by the chromosome, and the gene for pefect pitch, if ever found, would be a rare exception to the multifactorial complexity of such traits. Screening embryos for perfect pitch, if otherwise acceptable, should not be stopped simply because of speculation about what might be possible several decades from now.

PGD for Other Non-Medical Traits

The discussion of PGD for perfect pitch illustrates the issues that would arise if single gene analysis became possible for other traits, such as sexual orientation, hair or eye colour, or height, intelligence, size, strength, and memory. In each case the ethical assessment depends on an evaluation of the importance of the choice to the parents and whether that choice plausibly falls within societal understandings of parental needs and choice in reproducing and raising children. If so, it should usually be a sufficient reason to create and screen embryos. The effect on resulting offspring would also be of key moral importance. Whether selection carries a public or social message about the worth of existing groups should also be addressed.

Applying this methodology might show that some instances of non-medical selection are justified, as we have seen with embryo selection for gender variety and perhaps for having a child with perfect pitch. The acceptability of PGD to select other non-medical traits will depend on a careful analysis of the relevant ethical factors, and social acceptance of much greater parental rights to control the genes of offspring than now exists.

Conclusion

Although new indications are emerging for PGD, it is likely to remain a small part of reproductive practice for some time to come. Most new indications serve legitimate medical purposes, such as screening for single gene mutations for late onset disorders or susceptibility to cancer. There is also ethical support for using PGD to assure that a child is an HLA match with an existing child.

More controversial is the use of PGD to select gender or other non-medical traits. As with medical uses, the acceptability of non-medical screening will depend upon the interests served and the effects of using PGD for those purposes. Speculations about potential future non-medical uses should not restrict new uses of PGD which are otherwise ethically acceptable.

References

1. International Working Group on Preimplantation Genetics. Preimplantation genetic diagnosis: experience of 3000 clinical cycles. Report of the 11th annual meeting, May 15, 2001. *Reprod Biomedicine Online* 2001;3:49–53.

2. Verlinsky Y, Rechitsky S, Verlinsky O, et al. Preimplantation diagnosis of P53 tumor suppressor gene mutations. *Reprod Biomedicine Online* 2001;2:102–5.

3. Verlinsky Y, Rechitsky S, Schoolcraft W, et al. Preimplantation diagnosis for fanconi anemia combined with HLA matching. *JAMA* 2001;285:3130–3.

4. Verlinsky Y, Rechitsky S, Verlinsky O, et al. Preimplantation diagnosis for early-onset alzheimer's disease caused by V717L mutation. *JAMA* 2002;283:1018–21.

5. Fukuyama F. *Our postmodern future: consequences of the biotechnology revolution.* New York: Farrar, Strauss, & Giroux, 2002.

6. Stock G. *Redesigning humans: our inevitable genetic future.* New York: Houghton Mifflin, 2002.

7. Simpson JL. Celebrating preimplantation genetic diagnosis of p53 mutations in Li-Fraumeni syndrome. *Reprod Biomedicine Online* 2001;3:2–3.

8. Towner D, Loewy RS. Ethics of preimplantation diagnosis for a woman destined to develop early-onset alzheimer disease. *JAMA* 2002;283:1038–40.

9. Human Fertilisation and Embryology Authority. Opinion of the ethics committee. Ethical issues in the creation and selection of preimplantation embryos to produce tissue donors. London: HFEA, 2001 Nov 22.

10. Pennings G, Schots S, Liebaers I. Ethical considerations on preimplantation genetic diagnosis for HLA typing to match a future child as a donor of haematopoietic stem cells to a sibling. *Hum Reprod* 2002;17:534–8.

11. Robertson JA, Kahn J, Wagner J. Conception to obtain hematopoietic stem cells. *Hastings Cent Rep* 2002;32:34–40.

12. Sen A. More than 100 million women are missing. *New York Review of Books* 1990;37:61–8.

13. Eckholm E. Desire for sons drives use of prenatal scans in China. *The New York Times* 2002 Jun 21: A3.

14. Jaccoby EE, Jacklin CN. *The psychology of sex differences.* Palo Alto: Stanford University Press, 1974.

15. Robertson JA. Preconception gender selection. *Am J Bioeth* 2001;1:2–9.

16. Grubb A, Walsh P. Gender-vending II. *Dispatches* 1994;1:1–3.

17. Mahowald MB. *Genes, women, equality.* New York: Oxford University Press, 2000: 121.

18. American Society of Reproductive Medicine, Ethics Committee. Preconception gender selection for nonmedical reasons. *Fertil Steril* 2001;75:861–4.

19. Robertson JA. Sex selection for gender variety by preimplantation genetic diagnosis. *Fert Steril* 2002;78:463.

20. American Society of Reproductive Medicine, Ethics Committee. Sex selection and preimplantation genetic diagnosis. *Fertil Steril* 1999;72:595–8.

21. Kolata G. Society approves embryo selection. *The New York Times* 2001 Sept 26: A14.

22. Malpani A, Malpani A, Modi D. Preimplantation sex selection for family balancing in India. *Hum Reprod* 2002;17:11–12.

23. Blakeslee S. Perfect pitch: the key may lie in the genes. *The New York Times* 1990 Nov 30: 1.

24. American Society of Reproductive Medicine, Ethics Committee. Ethical considerations of assisted reproductive technologies. *Fertil Steril* 1994; 62(suppl):32–7S.

Marcy Darnovsky

Revisiting Sex Selection: The Growing Popularity of New Sex Selection Methods Revives an Old Debate

In the United States and a few other prosperous, technologically advanced nations, methods of sex selection that are less intrusive or more reliable than older practices are now coming into use. Unlike prenatal testing, these procedures generally are applied either before an embryo is implanted in a woman's body, or before an egg is fertilized. They do not require aborting a fetus of the "wrong" sex.

These pre-pregnancy sex selection methods are being rapidly commercialized—not, as before, with medical claims, but as a means of satisfying parental desires. For the assisted reproduction industry, social sex selection may be a business path toward a vastly expanded market. People who have no infertility or medical problems, but who can afford expensive out-of-pocket procedures, are an enticing new target.

For the first time, some fertility clinics are openly advertising sex selection for social reasons. Several times each month, for example, the *New York Times'* Sunday Styles section carries an ad from the Virginia-based Genetics & IVF (in-vitro fertilization) Institute, touting its patented sperm sorting method. Beside a smiling baby, its boldface headline asks, "Do You Want To Choose the Gender Of Your Next Baby?"

Recent trends in consumer culture may warm prospective parents to such offers. We have become increasingly accepting of—if not enthusiastic about—"enhancements" of appearance (think face-lifts, collagen and Botox injections, and surgery to reshape women's feet for stiletto heels) and adjustments of behavior (anti-depressants, Viagra, and the like). These drugs and procedures were initially developed for therapeutic uses, but are now being marketed and normalized in disturbing ways. When considering questions of right and wrong, of liberty and justice, it is well to remember that the state is not the only coercive force we encounter.

This constellation of technological, economic, cultural, and ideological developments has revived the issue of sex selection, relatively dormant for

From http://www.gene-watch.org/genewatch/articles/17-1darnovsky.html, January/February 2004.
Copyright © 2004 by Council for Responsible Genetics. Reprinted by permission.

more than a decade. The concerns that have always accompanied sex selection debates are being reassessed and updated. These include the prospect that selection could reinforce misogyny, sexism, and gender stereotypes; undermine the well-being of children by treating them as commodities and subjecting them to excessive parental expectations or disappointment; skew sex ratios in local populations; further the commercialization of reproduction; and open the door to a high-tech consumer eugenics.

Sex Selection Debates in the United States

Sex selection is not a new issue for U.S. feminists. In the 1980s and early 1990s, it was widely discussed and debated, especially by feminist bioethicists. This was the period when choosing a boy or girl was accomplished by undergoing prenatal diagnostic tests to determine the sex of a fetus, and then terminating the pregnancy if the fetus was of the undesired sex.

Ultrasound scanning and amniocentesis, which had been developed during the 1970s to detect, and usually to abort, fetuses with Down's syndrome and other conditions, were on their way to becoming routine in wealthier parts of the world. Soon they were also being openly promoted as tools for enabling sex-selective abortions in South and East Asian countries where the cultural preference for sons is pervasive. Opposition in these countries, especially strong in India, mounted in the early 1980s and remains vibrant today.

Throughout the 1980s and early 1990s, feminists and others in the U.S. who addressed the issue of sex selection were—almost universally—deeply uneasy about it. Not all opposed it equally, but none were enthusiastic or even supportive.

Some, like Helen Bequaert Holmes, pointed out that the deliberate selection of the traits of future generations is a form of eugenics.[1] Many deplored the practice as a symptom of a sexist society, in effect if not always in intent. In a book-length treatment of these concerns, published in 1985, philosopher Mary Anne Warren asked whether the practice should be considered an aspect of what she dubbed 'gendercide'—"no less a moral atrocity than genocide"— and published an entire book on the topic in 1985.[2]

But there was also broad consensus among feminists that any effort to limit sex-selective abortions, especially in the U.S., would threaten reproductive rights. Warren, despite her misgivings, argued that choosing the sex of one's child was sexist only if its intent or consequence was discrimination against women. She concluded that "there is great danger that the legal prohibition of sex selection would endanger other aspects of women's reproductive freedom," and considered even moral suasion against the practice to be unwarranted and counterproductive.

By the mid-1990s, the discussion had reached an impasse. No one liked sex selection, but few were willing to actively oppose it. Sex selection largely faded as an issue of concern for U.S. feminists, especially outside the circles of an increasingly professionalized bioethics discourse.

Separating Sex Selection from Abortion Politics

The new technologies of sex selection (and, perhaps, their potential profits) have prompted some bioethicists to argue in favor of allowing parents to choose their offspring's sex. As in past debates on other assisted reproductive procedures, they frame their advocacy in terms of "choice," "liberty," and "rights." John Robertson, a lawyer and bioethicist close to the fertility industry, is one of the leading proponents of this approach. In a lead article of the Winter 2001 issue of *American Journal of Bioethics,* Robertson wrote, "The risk that exercising rights of procreative liberty would hurt offspring or women—or contribute to sexism generally—is too speculative and uncertain to justify infringement of those rights."[3]

Robertson's claims are based on a world view that gives great weight to individual preferences and liberties, and little to social justice and the common good. As political scientist Diane Paul writes in a commentary on Robertson's recent defense of "preconception gender selection," "If you begin with libertarian premises, you will inevitably end up having to accept uses of reprogenetic technology that are even more worrisome" than sex selection.[4]

Definitions of procreative liberty like Robertson's are expansive—indeed, they often seem limitless. They are incapable, for example, of making a distinction between terminating an unwanted pregnancy—that is, deciding whether and when to bear children—and selecting the qualities and traits of a future child. However, sex selection and abortion are different matters, especially when a pregnancy is not involved.

Since new sex selection technologies are used before pregnancy, political discussions and policy initiatives which address them need not directly affect women's rights or access to abortion. In fact, many countries already prohibit "non-medical" sex selection, with no adverse impact on the availability or legality of abortion. One such nation is the United Kingdom, where, in November, 2003, after a comprehensive reconsideration of the issue, their Human Fertilization and Embryology Authority recommended that sex selection for social reasons continue to be prohibited, and that the Authority's purview be expanded to include regulation of sperm sorting technologies as well as other sex selection procedures. Even in the United States, where abortion rights are imminently threatened, the emergence of pre-pregnancy technologies should make it far easier than before, when sex determination meant selective abortion, to consider sex selection apart from abortion politics.

Eugenics: Is the Slope Becoming More Slippery?

When Mary Anne Warren considered sex selection in 1985, she summarily dismissed concerns of its contribution to a new eugenics as "implausible" on the grounds that "[t]here is at present no highly powerful interest group which is committed to the development and use of immoral forms of human genetic engineering."[5]

However, less than two decades later, a disturbing number of highly powerful figures are in fact committed to the development and use of a form of human genetic engineering that huge majorities here and abroad consider immoral—inheritable genetic modification, or manipulating the genes passed on to our children. These scientists, bioethicists, biotech entrepreneurs, and libertarians are actively advocating a new market-based, high-tech eugenics.

Princeton University molecular biologist Lee Silver, for example, positively anticipates the emergence of genetic castes and human sub-species. "[T]he GenRich class and the Natural class will become . . . entirely separate species," he writes, "with no ability to cross-breed, and with as much romantic interest in each other as a current human would have for a chimpanzee."[6] Nobel laureate James Watson promotes redesigning the genes of our children with statements such as, "People say it would be terrible if we made all girls pretty. I think it would be great."[7]

Silver's and Watson's remarks (and all too many similar ones) refer to technologies that are being used routinely in lab animals, but have not been applied to human beings. However, pre-implantation genetic diagnosis (PGD), the most common new sex selection method, is very much related to these technologies. It was introduced in 1990 as a way to identify and discard embryos affected by serious genetic conditions, and thus prevent the birth of children with particular traits. Though PGD is touted as a medical tool, disability advocates have pointed out that many people who have the conditions it targets live full and satisfying lives. PGD, they say, is already a eugenic technology.

In recent years, PGD has begun to be used to screen for more and more genetic attributes—late-onset conditions, tissue types suitable for matching those of a future child's sick sibling, and sex. Advocacy of even greater permissiveness in the use of PGD is beginning to pepper the professional literature. Bioethicist Edgar Dahl recently published an essay arguing that if a "safe and reliable genetic test" for sexual orientation were to become available, "parents should clearly be allowed" to use it, as long as they are permitted to select for homosexual as well as heterosexual children.[8] Bioethicist Julian Savulescu even baits disability advocates with the argument that we "should allow people deliberately to create disabled children."[9]

Concern about consumer eugenics and the commodification of children looms large for critics of social sex selection. As part of a recent campaign aimed at the Human Fertilization and Embryology Authority, the UK-based bioethics group Human Genetics Alert writes, "If we allow sex selection it will be impossible to oppose 'choice' of any other characteristics, such as appearance, height, intelligence, et cetera. The door to 'designer babies' will not have been opened a crack—it will have been thrown wide open."[10]

Another British NGO, Gene Watch UK [*no relation to* GeneWatch *magazine—ed.*] puts it this way: Allowing sex selection "would represent a significant shift towards treating children as commodities and [subjecting] the selection of a child's genetic make-up . . . to parental choice, exercised through paying a commercial company to provide this 'service'."[11]

Some researchers, bioethicists, and fertility practitioners have publicly opposed such uses of PGD, and expressed alarm at what the new push for social sex selection seems to portend. In September, 2001, Robertson, then acting chair of the Ethics Committee of the American Society for Reproductive Medicine (ASRM), issued an opinion that overturned the organization's opposition to PGD for social sex selection. The *New York Times* reported that this "stunned many leading fertility specialists." One fertility doctor asked, "What's the next step? . . . As we learn more about genetics, do we reject kids who do not have superior intelligence or who don't have the right color hair or eyes?"[12]

In the US, several women's organizations and other NGOs drafted a letter, signed by nearly a hundred groups and individuals, urging the ASRM not to loosen its recommendations on sex selection. Several months later, the ASRM affirmed its opposition to the use of PGD for "non-medical" sex selection. (The organization does not oppose sperm selection to select the sex of a child for "family balancing.") The spread of social sex selection and the ASRM episode were described in an *Atlantic Monthly* article titled "Jack or Jill? The era of consumer-driven eugenics has begun." Author Margaret Talbot concluded,

> [I]f we allow people to select a child's sex, then there really is no barrier to picking embryos—or, ultimately, genetically programming children—based on any whim, any faddish notion of what constitutes superior stock. . . . A world in which people (wealthy people, anyway) can custom-design human beings unhampered by law or social sanction is not a dystopian sci-fi fantasy any longer but a realistic scenario. It is not a world most of us would want to live in.[13]

A Transnational Issue and a Preference for Girls

In 1992, Nobel Prize-winning economist Amartya Sen estimated the number of "missing women" worldwide, lost to neglect, infanticide, and sex-specific abortions, at one hundred million. Similarly shocking figures were confirmed by others.

Many in the global North are distressed by the pervasiveness and persistence of sex-selective abortions in South and East Asia, and believe bans on sex selection procedures may be warranted there. At the same time, some of these people believe sex selection in countries without strong traditions of son preference may not be so bad.

This double standard rests on shaky grounds. The increased use and acceptance of sex selection in the U.S. would legitimize its practice in other countries, while undermining opposition by human rights and women's rights groups there. Even *Fortune* recognized this dynamic. "It is hard to overstate the outrage and indignation that MicroSort [a sperm sorting method] prompts in people who spend their lives trying to improve women's lot overseas," it noted in 2001.[14]

In addition, there are also large numbers of South Asians living in European and North American countries, and sex selection ads in *India Abroad* and the North American edition of *Indian Express* have specifically targeted them.[15] South Asian feminists in these communities fear that sex selection could take new hold among immigrants who retain a preference for sons. They decry the numerous ways it reinforces and exacerbates misogyny, including violence against women who fail to give birth to boys. If these practices are unacceptable—indeed, often illegal—in South Asia (and elsewhere), should they be allowed among Asian communities in the West?

In contrast to sex selection in South and East Asia, however, a preference for girls may be emerging in North America and Europe. Anecdotal evidence—based on reports from companies offering various methods for sex control and on perusal of the "Gender Determination" message board . . ., which has over a quarter million postings—tends to confirm that of North Americans trying to determine the sex of their next child, many are women who want daughters.

That North Americans may not use new technologies to produce huge numbers of "extra" boys does not, however, mean that sex selection and sexism are unrelated. One study, by Roberta Steinbacher at Cleveland State University, found that 81% of women and 94% of men who say they would use sex selection would want their firstborn to be a boy. Steinbacher notes that the research literature on birth order is clear: firstborns are more aggressive and higher-achieving than their siblings. "We'll be creating a nation of little sisters," she says.[16]

Observers of sex selection point to another discriminatory impact: its potential for reinforcing gender stereotyping. Parents who invest large amounts of money and effort in order to "get a girl" are likely to have a particular kind of girl in mind. As a mother of one of the first MicroSort babies recalled, "I wanted to have someone to play Barbies with and to go shopping with; I wanted the little girl with long hair and pink fingernails."[17]

There are many reasons people may wish for a daughter instead of a son, or a boy rather than a girl. In a sympathetic account, *New York Times* reporter and feminist Lisa Belkin described some of the motivations of U.S. women who are "going for the girl."

"They speak of Barbies and ballet and butterfly barrettes," she writes, but "they also describe the desire to rear strong young women. Some want to recreate their relationships with their own mothers; a few want to do better by their daughters than their mothers did by them. They want their sons to have sisters, so that they learn to respect women. They want their husbands to have little girls. But many of them want a daughter simply because they always thought they would have one."[18]

Wishes and Consequences

Compelling though some of these longings may be, sex selection cannot be completely understood or appropriately confronted by evaluating the rightness or wrongness of parental desires. The preferences of prospective parents are obviously relevant in child-bearing matters, but so are the well-being of future children, and the social consequences of technologies—especially those that are already being aggressively marketed.

Wishing for a girl, or for a boy, is cause for neither shame nor condemnation. But as legal scholar Dorothy Roberts points out, it is important to "scrutinize the legal and political context which helps to both create and give meaning to individuals' motivations."[19]

If wishes, choices, and preferences are to be appropriately balanced with social justice and the common good, they cannot be unthinkingly transformed into protected liberties, much less codified rights. Isolated from social consequences, both wishes and liberties are at best naïve.

Notes

1. Humber and Almeder, eds. "Sex Preselection: Eugenics for Everyone?" *Biomedical Ethics Reviews,* 1985

2. Mary Ann Warren. *Gendercide: The Implications of Sex Selection.* Rowman & Littlefield, 1985

3. John A. Robertson. "Preconception Gender Selection," *American Journal of Bioethics,* Winter 2001

4. Dian Paul. "Where Libertarian Premises Lead," *American Journal of Bioethics,* Winter 2001

5. Mary Ann Warren. *Gendercide: The Implications of Sex Selection.* Rowman & Littlefield, 1985

6. Lee Silver. *Remaking Eden.* Avon, 1997

7. Shaoni Bhattacharya. "Stupidity should be cured, says DNA discoverer," *New Scientist,* February 28, 2003 . . .

8. Edgar Dahl. "Ethical Issues in New Uses of Preimplantation Genetic Diagnosis," *Human Reproduction,* Vol. 18 No. 7

9. Julian Savunescu, from the title of a November 25, 2003 presentation in London. . . .

10. "The Case Against Sex Selection," December 2002 . . .

11. "GeneWatch UK Submission to the HFEA Consultation on Sex Selection," January 2003

12. Gina Kolata. "Fertility Ethics Authority Approves Sex Selection," *The New York Times,* September 28, 2001

13. Margaret Talbot. "Jack or Jill? The era of consumer-driven eugenics has begun," *The Atlantic Monthly,* March 2002

14. Meredith Wadman. "So You Want A Girl?," *Fortune,* February 2001

15. Susan Sachs. "Clinics' Pitch to Indian Émigrés," *New York Times,* August 15, 2001

16. Lisa Belkin. "Getting the Girl," *The New York Times Magazine,* July 25, 1999

17. "Choosing Your Baby's Gender," . . . November 7, 2002

18. Belkin.

19. Dorothy Roberts, *Killing the Black Body: Race, Reproduction, and the Meaning of Liberty,* New York: Vintage Books, 1997, p. 286

POSTSCRIPT

Should Parents Be Allowed to Select the Sex of Their Baby?

Imagine yourself in the position of being able to choose the sex of your future children. What would be the benefits of having a daughter as opposed to a son, or vice versa? How much of these benefits rest on your expectations of your future child's personality? Are these traits inherently tied to their sex or gender?

Now imagine the way your future child looks. How tall is s/he? What color eyes does s/he have? Hair color? Is your child athletic? Artistic? Intelligent? In the near future, it may be possible to make your "dream family" come true, for around $18,000 per child. If you had the economic means, would you? Why or why not?

Is there something about yourself that you consider unique? Is it a physical ability or talent, or even a physical feature that sets you apart from the crowd? Did it come from your mother or father—or is it distinctive from all of your family members? Now imagine that your parents told you that they wanted you to have this feature so bad that they "selected" it while you were still an embryo. Would you feel any less unique? What if they simply said they wanted you to be a certain sex? Would that change the way you feel about yourself? Would you feel different about a friend whose athletic talent was thanks in part to their parents' design, rather than nature's (though both would require discipline and hard work to cultivate)?

Do you consider it acceptable to use PGD (or other prenatal techniques) to predetermine the characteristics of your baby? Is it acceptable to screen for hereditary debilitating conditions and diseases? What did you make of Darnovsky claim that allowing PGD for sex selection could pave the way for "designer babies"?

Robertson challenged the "slippery slope" argument by stating, "Speculations about potential future non-medical uses should not restrict new uses of PGD which are otherwise ethically acceptable." Do you agree? Is genetic sex selection medically ethical? Is preferring a child of one sex inherently sexist? If genetic markers are found for musical ability, intelligence, sexual orientation, or any other trait, will companies begin to offer the selection or deselection of these traits to potential parents and customers? Should these types of procedures be regulated or restricted even if they do not yet exist?

Suggested Readings

A. R. Fahrenkrog. "A Comparison of International Regulation of Preimplantation Genetic Diagnosis and a Regulatory Suggestion for the United States," *Transnational Law & Contemporary Problems* (vol. 15, no. 2, Spring 2006).

D. Grady, "Girl or Boy? As Fertility Technology Advances, So Does an Ethical Debate," *New York Times* (February 6, 2007).

L. Harris, "Choosy Moms Choose Their Babies' Sex?" *Salon* (February 26, 2009).

M. Healy, "Fertility's New Frontier," *Los Angeles Times* (July 21, 2003).

S. Matthew Liao, "The Ethics of Using Genetic Engineering for Sex Selection," *Journal of Medical Ethics* (vol. 31, no. 2, February 2005).

B. Trivedi, "Boy or Girl? Embryo Tests Give Parents the Choice," *New Scientist* (September 30, 2006).

Internet References . . .

National Center for Transgender Equality

The National Center for Transgender Equality is a nonprofit organization founded in 2003 that advocates for public policy, and provides training and education to transpeople and their allies.

www.nctequality.org

Human Rights Campaign

The Human Rights Campaign is America's largest gay and lesbian organization. It seeks to increase public understanding through innovative education and communication strategies.

www.hrc.org

National Organization for Marriage

The National Organization for Marriage is a nonprofit organization that opposes same-sex marriage by serving as a national resource for state and local marriage initiatives.

www.nationformarriage.org

Gender and Sexual Orientation

*T*he Lesbian, Gay, Bisexual, and Transgender (LGBT) community has made strides toward acceptance and more equitable treatment under the law in the last few decades. Although this progress has been welcomed by many, a strong backlash against these gains has emerged as well. The legalization of same-sex marriage is seen as a "wedge issue" in American politics. Questions of transgender inclusion and rights divide some within the most politically liberal circles. In this section, we examine three contemporary issues that involve issues of gender identity and sexual orientation.

- Is "Gender Identity Disorder" an Appropriate Psychiatric Diagnosis?
- Should Corporations Ensure Equal Rights for their Lesbian, Gay, Bisexual, and Transgender Employees?
- Should Same-Sex Marriage Be Legal?

ISSUE 18

Is "Gender Identity Disorder" an Appropriate Psychiatric Diagnosis?

YES: Mercedes Allen, from "Destigmatization Versus Coverage and Access: The Medical Model of Transsexuality" at http://dentedbluemercedes .wordpress.com/2008/04/05/destigmatization-versus-coverage-and-access-the-medical-model-of-transsexuality/ (2008)

NO: Kelley Winters, from GID Reform Advocates, "Issues of GID Diagnosis for Transsexual Women and Men" from http://www .gidreform.org/GID30285a.pdf (2007)

ISSUE SUMMARY

YES: Mercedes Allen, educator, trainer, and founder of AlbertaTrans. org, recognizes the bias in the DSM's classification of Gender Identity Disorder as a mental disorder, but argues that changes run the risk of leaving the trans community at risk of losing medical care and treatment.

NO: Kelley Winters, Ph.D, writer and founder of GID Reform Advocates, argues the inclusion of Gender Identity Disorder in the DSM adds to the stigma faced by transpersons and that reclassification is necessary in order to adequately address the population's health care needs.

Gender identity can be a difficult concept to describe. Many people have probably never given much thought to questions of how they feel about themselves in terms of maleness or femaleness. It is assumed that most people have a gender identity that is congruent with their anatomical sex. While some men may feel more (or less) masculine than others, the majority strongly *identify* as male. The same could be said for most women—regardless of how feminine they feel (or don't feel), the majority *identify* as women. If asked, most women would probably say they feel like a woman. Most men simply feel like a man. But what does it mean to "feel" like a woman or a man? What is it to "feel" feminine or masculine? Is there only one type of femininity? One style of masculinity?

And what about those who feel that their gender identity, their feeling of maleness or femaleness, doesn't match their birth sex? For those whose gender does not match societal expectations for a person of their anatomical sex, gender identity can be hard to ignore. Their gender identities do not fit the binary gender system that is firmly in place in American society. Because of this, a diagnosis of Gender Identity Disorder (GID) has been applied to those who identify as transgender or transsexual. This diagnosis can be found in the Diagnostic and Statistical Manual of Mental Disorders, commonly referred to as the DSM, published by the American Psychiatric Association.

In 2012, an updated, fifth edition of the DSM will be published (Melby, 2009). Over the years, new editions have been greatly anticipated to see what changes occur. With each edition, new disorders have been identified, adding to the list of mental illnesses. Diagnostic criteria for others have been refined and some behaviors, once defined as disordered, have been removed because they no longer meet the criteria for diagnosis as a mental illness. An example of this is homosexuality. In the DSM-II, published in 1968, homosexuality was considered a mental illness. The 1973 publication of the DSM-III did not list homosexuality as a disorder. This declassification erased some of the stigma associated with same-sex attraction and provided a boost to the gay rights movement in the United States (Melby, 2009).

As the release of the DSM-V draws closer, experts from various fields, appointed to an array of work groups, are holding meetings to discuss what should be added, revised, or removed. For those interested in the field of human sexuality, much attention is being given to the status of GID. There has even been controversy over those appointed to the Sexual and Gender Identity Disorders Work Group (National Gay and Lesbian Task Force, 2008). The changes made to the upcoming DSM-V concerning GID, or the lack thereof, could have great impact on the lives of transgender individuals.

In an essay entitled *Destigmatization Versus Coverage and Access: The Medical Model of Transsexuality,* Mercedes Allen argues that the removal of Gender Identity Disorder from the DSM would put access to mental health care, hormonal treatments, and surgeries needed by some transsexual individuals at risk of being denied. Kelly Winters, in an essay called *Issues of GID Diagnosis for Transsexual Women and Men,* argues that the inclusion of GID in the DSM only serves to stigmatize the transgender and transsexual community, while failing to promote hormonal or surgical treatments as medical necessities.

References

T. Melby, "Creating the DSM-V," *Contemporary Sexuality* (vol. 43, no. 3) (2009).

National Gay and Lesbian Task Force, "Task Force Questions Critical Appointments to APA's Committee on Sexual and Gender Identity Disorders," accessed at http://www.thetaskforce.org/press/releases/PR_052808 (2008).

YES

Mercedes Allen

Destigmatization Versus Coverage and Access: The Medical Model of Transsexuality

In recent years, the GLB community has been more receptive to (and even energized in) assisting the transgender community, but regularly asks what its needs are. One that is often touted is the "complete depathologization of Trans identities" (quoting from a press release for an October 7, 2007, demonstration in Barcelona, Spain) by removing "Gender Identity Disorder" (GID) from medical classification. The reasoning generally flows in a logic chain stating that with homosexuality removed from the Diagnostic and Statistical Manual (DSM, the "bible" of the medical community) in 1974, gay and lesbian rights were able to follow as a consequence—and with similar removal, we should be able to do the same. Living in an area where GRS (genital reassignment surgery) is covered under provincial Health Care, however, provides a unique perspective on this issue. And with Presidential candidates proposing models for national health care in the U.S., it would obviously be easier to establish GRS coverage for transsexuals at the ground floor, rather than fight for it later. So it is important to note, from this "other side of the coin," how delisting GID could do far more harm than good.

Granted, there are concerns about the current classification as a "mental disorder," and certainly as a transgender person myself, it's quite unnerving that my diagnosis of GID puts me in the same range of classification as things such as schizophrenia or even pedophilia. And when the emotional argument of "mental unfitness" can lead to ostracism, discrimination in the workplace or the loss of custody and/or visitation rights of children, there are some very serious things at stake. But when the lobbies are calling for a reclassification— or more dramatically a total declassification—of GID, one would expect that they had a better medical and social model to propose. They don't.

Basic Access to Services

The argument for complete declassification is a great concern, because unlike homosexuals, transgender people—especially transsexuals—do have medical needs and issues related to their journey. Genital reassignment surgery (GRS), mastectomies and hysterectomies for transmen, tracheal shave, facial hair

From http://dentedbluemercedes.wordpress.com/. Copyright © 2008 by (Anne) Mercedes Allen. Reprinted by permission.

removal and breast augmentation for transwomen . . . there are clear medical applications that some require, even to the point of being at risk of suicide from the distress of not having these things available (which is an important point to keep in mind for those in our own communities who assume that GRS is cosmetic surgery and not worthy of health care funding). And we need to use caution about taking psychiatry out of the equation: GID really does affect us psychologically, and we do benefit from having a central source of guidance through the process that keeps this in mind, however flawed and gated the process otherwise might be.

Declassification of GID would essentially relegate transsexuality to a strictly cosmetic issue. Without being able to demonstrate that GID is a real medical condition via a listing in the Diagnostic and Statistical Manual (DSM), convincing a doctor that it is necessary to treat us, provide referrals or even provide a carry letter that will enable us to use a washroom appropriate to our gender presentation could prove to be very difficult, if not impossible. Access to care is difficult enough *even with* the DSM-IV recommending the transition process—imagine the barriers that would be there without it weighing in on that! And with cases regarding the refusal of medical services already before review or recently faced in California, Ontario and elsewhere, the availability of services could grow overwhelmingly scarce.

A Model of Medical Coverage

And then there is health care coverage, which often causes a lot of issues of itself, usually of the "not with my tax money" variety. But no one just wakes up out of the blue and decides that alienating themselves from the rest of the world by having a "sex change" is a good idea. Science is developing a greater understanding that physical sex and psychological gender can, in fact, be made misaligned, causing a person to be like a stranger in their own body. In extreme cases (transsexuals), this often makes it impossible to function emotionally, socially, sexually, or to develop any kind of career—and often makes one constantly borderline suicidal. The medical community currently recognizes this with the existing medical classification, which is why GRS surgery is the recognized treatment, and why it (GRS, that is, and usually not things like breast augmentation) is funded by some existing health plans.

Canada provides an interesting model on this, as the nation has universal health care, and several provinces fund GRS with some limitations (British Columbia, Newfoundland, Saskatchewan and Quebec fund vaginaplasty, hysterectomy and breast reduction for FTMs, Alberta funds those plus phalloplasty, and Manitoba funds 60% of GRS-related costs). Funding may be restored in Ontario and gained in Nova Scotia, pending some ongoing activism.

This exists specifically because it is classified as a medical issue, and is treated according to the recommendations of WPATH. There are some idiosyncracies, of course—a diagnosis of Intersex, for example, overrides a diagnosis of GID, and if someone is diagnosed as IS, the treatment is different (namely, GRS is not covered). Phalloplasty and metoidioplasty (FTM surgeries) are not covered in several areas because they are considered "experimental." Some provinces insist on treatment only in publically-funded hospitals, resulting in the rather unusual situation of Quebec sending patients to the U.S. or overseas, even though one of the top-rated (but privately-owned) GRS clinics in the world is located in Montreal. And many provinces direct transsexuals to the notoriously restrictive and obstacle-laden Clarke Institute (CAMH in Toronto) for treatment. Waiting lists can be long, and only a select few GID-certified psychiatrists are able to be a primary signature on letters authorizing surgery and funding. Still, the funding provides opportunity that many non-Canadian transsexuals would leap at within a moment, if they could.

Future Considerations

This possibility, remote as it may seem, is also out there for future American transsexuals. Both Democratic Presidential nominees have discussed developing a national health care program. The time is now for the trans, gay/lesbian/bisexual and allied communities to lobby insurance companies to develop policies that cover GRS. The time is now to lobby companies to seek out group policies for their employees with such coverage, and with more emphasis than the HRC's impossibly easy Corporate Equality Index (CEI), in which providing mastectomies for breast cancer patients qualifies as "transgender-related surgeries." The more prevalent health care coverage is for transgender persons when a national program is developed, the more effective the argument is that a national program should include it. Certainly, it will be much harder to lobby to have it specifically added later.

   This possibility, remote as it may seem, exists because of the current classification. Even some existing coverage of and access to hormone treatment is called into question in a declassification scenario. And certainly, where coverage is not available, it is the impoverished, disenfranchised and marginalized of our community—who quite often have more to worry about than the stigma of mental illness—who lose the most.

   So a total declassification is actually not what's best for the transgender community. Too, if anyone had been thinking that proclaiming that "transsexuality is not a mental disorder" would magically change the way that society thinks about transfolk, then they are spectacularly and embarrassingly wrong.

The Question of Reclassification

At some point in the future, I expect that we will find more biological bases for GID, and that transgender people will perhaps become a smaller part of the larger intersex community (rather than the other way around). Recent studies in genetics have demonstrated some difference in chromosomal structure in male brains versus female brains, and the UCLA scientists who conducted the study have also proposed that their findings demonstrate gender dysphoria as a biological characteristic. Other studies into endocrine disrupting chemicals (EDCs) could open new discoveries related to variance in gender correlation. A reassessment of GID is almost certainly something that will be on the medical community's table at some point in the future, but it definitely needs to be in the DSM somewhere. But for now, GID is not something that can be determined by a blood test or an ultrasound, and is not easy to verifiably place with biological conditions. The science is not there; the evidence and solutions are not yet at hand.

This is why reclassification is not yet feasible. It's difficult to convince scientific and medical professionals to move a diagnosis when the current model is workable in their eyes (even if not perfect), while the alternatives are not yet proven, cannot be demonstrated as more valid than the current listing, and no modified treatment system has been devised or proposed. Any move of the diagnosis is not likely to be very far from the current listing, and from the literature I've seen, I doubt that those in the community who advocate to changing or dropping the current classification would be happy with that. For some, even listing it as a "physical disability" could constitute an "unwanted stigma." I have heard one WPATH doctor suggest the term "Body Morphology Disorder"—for many, I suspect, this would still be too "negative."

"Unnecessary Mutilation"

That's not to say that complacency is an answer. In the face of conservative reluctance and new activism on the left by the likes of Julie Bindel, claiming that GRS is "unnecessary mutilation," we need to demonstrate the necessity of treatments, in order to ensure that any change would be an improvement on the existing model, rather than a scrapping of it. This is, of course, something that affects a small portion of the transgender community in the full umbrella stretch of the term, but the need for those at the extreme on the spectrum is profound—not simply a question of quality of life, but often one of living at all—or at least a question of being able to function. If and when a reclassification occurs, it will need to be this sense of necessity that will determine the shape of what will be written into any revision.

The solution isn't to destroy the existing medical model by changing or eliminating the current classification of "Gender Dysphoria." Collecting data, demonstrating needs, fighting for inclusion in existing health plans, examining verifiable and repeatable statistics on transgender suicide and success rates and other information relevant to the medical front is where medical-related activism should be focused, for the moment.

 **NO**

GID Reform Advocates

Issues of GID Diagnosis for Transsexual Women and Men

Gender Identity Disorder in Adolescents or Adults, 302.85

Section: Sexual and Gender Identity Disorders
Subsection: Gender Identity Disorders

"Gender Identity Disorder" (GID) is a diagnostic category in the *Diagnostic and Statistical Manual of Mental Disorders* (DSM), published by the American Psychiatric Association (APA, 1994). The DSM is regarded as the medical and social definition of mental disorder throughout North America and strongly influences the *The International Statistical Classification of Diseases and Related Health Problems* (ICD) published by the World Health Organization. GID currently includes a broad array of gender variant adults and children who may or may not be transsexual and may or may not be distressed or impaired. GID literally implies a *"disordered"* gender identity.

Thirty-four years after the American Psychiatric Association (APA) voted to delete homosexuality as a mental disorder, the diagnostic categories of "gender identity disorder" and "transvestic fetishism" in the *Diagnostic and Statistical Manual of Mental Disorders* continue to raise questions of consistency, validity, and fairness. Recent revisions of the DSM have made these diagnostic categories increasingly ambiguous, conflicted and overinclusive. They reinforce false, negative stereotypes of gender variant people and at the same time fail to legitimize the medical necessity of sex reassignment surgeries (SRS) and procedures for transsexual women and men who urgently need them. The result is that a widening segment of gender non-conforming youth and adults are potentially subject to diagnosis of psychosexual disorder, stigma and loss of civil liberty.

A Question of Legitimacy

The very name, Gender Identity Disorder, suggests that cross-gender identity is itself disordered or deficient. It implies that gender identities held by diagnosable people are not legitimate, in the sense that more ordinary gender identities are, but represent perversion, delusion or immature development. This message

From http://www.gidreform.org/GID30285a.pdf, 2007, pp. 1–5 (refs. omitted). Copyright © 2007 by Kelley Winters. Reprinted by permission.

is reinforced in the diagnostic criteria and supporting text that emphasize difference from cultural norms over distress for those born in incongruent bodies or forced to live in wrong gender roles.

Under the premise of "disordered" gender identity, self-identified trans-women and trans-men lose any rightful claim to acceptance as women and men, but are reduced to mentally ill men and women respectively.

DIAGNOSTIC CRITERIA (APA 2000, P 581)

A. A strong and persistent cross-gender identification (not merely a desire for any perceived cultural advantages of being the other sex). In adolescents and adults, the disturbance is manifested by symptoms such as a stated desire to be the other sex, frequent passing as the other sex, desire to live or be treated as the other sex, or the conviction that he or she has the typical feelings and reactions of the other sex.

B. Persistent discomfort with his or her sex or sense of inappropriateness in the gender role of that sex. In adolescents and adults, the disturbance is manifested by symptoms such as preoccupation with getting rid of primary and secondary sex characteristics (e.g., request for hormones, surgery, or other procedures to physically alter sexual characteristics to simulate the other sex) or belief that he or she was born the wrong sex.

C. The disturbance is not concurrent with a physical intersex condition.

D. The disturbance causes clinically significant distress or impairment in social, occupational, or other important areas of functioning.

Specify if (for sexually mature individuals) Sexually Attracted to Males, . . . Females, . . . Both, . . . Neither.

Maligning Terminology

Of the disrespectful language faced by gender variant people in North America, none is more damaging or hurtful than that which disregards their experienced gender identities, denies the affirmed gender roles of those who have transitioned full time and relegates them to their assigned birth sex. Throughout the diagnostic criteria and supporting text, the affirmed gender identities and social role for transsexual individuals is termed "other sex." In the supporting text, subjects are offensively labeled by birth sex and not their experienced affirmed gender. Transsexual women are repeatedly termed "males," and "he." For example,

> For some <u>males</u> . . . , the individual's sexual activity with a woman is accompanied by the fantasy of being lesbian lovers or that <u>his</u> partner is a man and <u>he</u> is a woman. (APA, 2000, p. 577, emphasis noted by underline)

Perhaps most disturbing, the term "autogynephilia" was introduced in the supporting text of the DSM-IV-TR to demean lesbian transsexual women:

> Adult <u>males</u> who are sexually attracted to females, . . . usually report a history of erotic arousal associated with the thought or image of one-self as a woman (termed *autogynephilia*). (p. 578, emphasis noted by underline)

The implication is that all lesbian transsexual women are incapable of genuine affection for other female partners but are instead obsessed with narcissistic paraphilia. The fact that most ordinary natal women possess images of themselves as women within their erotic relationships and fantasies is conspicuously overlooked in the supporting text.

Medically Necessary Treatment of Gender Dysphoria

Gender Dysphoria is defined in the DSM-IV-TR as:

> A persistent aversion toward some or all of those physical characteristics or social roles that connote one's own biological sex (APA, 2000, p. 823).

The focus of medical treatment described by the current World Professional Association for Transgender Health Standards of Care is on relieving the distress of gender dysphoria and not on attempting to change one's gender identity (WPATH, 2001). Yet, the DSM-IV-TR emphasizes cross-gender identity and expression rather than the distress of gender dysphoria as the basis for mental disorder. While criterion B of Gender Identity Disorder may imply gender dysphoria, it is not limited to ego-dystonic subjects suffering distress with their born sex or its associated role. Ego-syntonic subjects who do not need medical treatment may also be ambiguously implicated. In failing to distinguish gender diversity from gender distress, the APA has undermined the medical necessity of sex reassignment procedures for transsexuals who need them. It is little wonder that the province of Ontario and virtually all insurers and HMOs in the U.S. and have denied or dropped coverage for sex reassignment surgery (SRS) procedures. Since gender dysphoria is not explicitly classified as a treatable medical condition, surgeries that relieve its distress are easily dismissed as "cosmetic" by insurers, governments and employers.

The transgender community and civil rights advocates have long been polarized by fear that access to SRS procedures would be lost if the GID classification were revised. In truth, however, transsexuals are poorly served by a diagnosis that stigmatizes them unconditionally as mentally deficient and at the same time fails to establish the medical necessity of procedures proven to relieve their distress.

Overinclusive Diagnosis

Distress and impairment became central to the definition of mental disorder in the DSM-IV (1994, p. xxi), where a generic clinical significance criterion was added to most diagnostic categories, including criterion D of Gender Identity Disorder. Ironically, while the scope of mental disorder was narrowed in the DSM-IV, Gender Identity Disorder was broadened from the classification of Transsexualism in prior DSM revisions and combined with Gender Identity Disorder of Adolescence or Adulthood, Nontranssexual Type (GIDAANT) from the DSM-III-R (1987, pp. 74–77).

Unfortunately, no specific definition of distress and impairment is given in the GID diagnosis. The supporting text in the DSM-IV-TR lists relationship difficulties and impaired function at work or school as examples of distress and disability (2000, p. 577) with no reference to the role of societal prejudice as the cause. Prostitution, HIV risk, suicide attempts and substance abuse are described as associated features of GID, when they are in truth consequences of discrimination and undeserved shame. The DSM does not acknowledge the existence of many healthy, well-adjusted transsexual or gender variant people or differentiate them from those who could benefit from medical treatment. These are left to the interpretation of the reader. Tolerant clinicians may infer that transgender identity or expression is not inherently impairing, but that societal intolerance and prejudice are to blame for the distress and internalized shame that transpeople often suffer (Brown, 1995). Intolerant clinicians are free to infer the opposite: that cross-gender identity or expression by definition constitutes impairment, regardless of the individual's happiness or well-being. Therefore, the GID diagnosis is not limited to ego-dystonic subjects; it makes no distinction between the distress of gender dysphoria and that caused by prejudice and discrimination. Moreover, the current DSM has no clear exit clause for transitioned or post-operative transsexuals, however well adjusted. It lists postsurgical complications as "associated physical examination findings" of GID (2000, p. 579).

Pathologization of Ordinary Behaviors

Conflicting and ambiguous language in the DSM serves to confuse cultural nonconformity with mental illness and pathologize ordinary behaviors as symptomatic. The Introduction to the DSM-IV-TR (2000, p. xxxi) states:

> Neither deviant behavior ... nor conflicts that are primarily between the individual and society are mental disorders unless the deviance or conflict is a symptom of dysfunction...

However, it is contradicted in the Gender Identity Disorder section (p. 580):

> Gender Identity Disorder can be distinguished from simple nonconformity to stereotypical sex role behavior by the extent and pervasiveness of the cross-gender wishes, interests, and activities.

The second statement implies that one may deviate from social expectation without a diagnostic label, but not too much. Conflicting language in the DSM serves the agendas of intolerant relatives and employers and their medical expert witnesses who seek to deny transgender individuals their civil liberties, children and jobs.

In the supporting text of the Gender Identity Disorder diagnosis, behaviors that would be ordinary or even exemplary for ordinary women and men are presented as symptomatic of mental disorder on a presumption of incongruence with born genitalia. These include passing, living and a desire to be treated as ordinary members of the preferred gender. For example, shaving legs for adolescent biological males is described as symptomatic, even though it is common among males involved in certain athletics. Adopting ordinary behaviors, dress and mannerisms of the preferred gender is described as a manifestation of preoccupation for adults. It is not clear how these behaviors can be pathological for one group of people and not for another.

POSTSCRIPT

Is "Gender Identity Disorder" an Appropriate Psychiatric Diagnosis?

It is important to realize that, while both Allen and Winters take opposing sides to the question presented, both oppose the labeling of transgender or transsexual individuals as mentally ill. To a certain extent, the debate over the inclusion, reclassification, or exclusion of GID in the upcoming edition of the DSM exemplifies the phrase "You're damned if you do, you're damned if you don't." To remove GID from the DSM would in all likelihood help to reduce some of the stigma attached to transsexuality. However, many transsexual individuals need a diagnosable condition in order to receive adequate coverage for medical care. Could there possibly be a "correct" answer in this situation?

Allen's essay, which acknowledges the stigma attached to the label of mental disorder and notes the possible benefits of re- or declassification of GID, focuses on the issue of access to medical care. The point is made that declassification would impact transgender and transsexual individuals in much different ways than the declassification of homosexuality affected gay men and lesbians. Unlike other sexual minorities, "transgender people—especially transsexuals—do have medical needs and issues related to their journey," Allen states. What would be the risks of removing GID from the upcoming DSM? Why would some transgender advocates argue for its continued inclusion? Allen also mentions the impact of nationalized health care on the GID debate. How would the discussion be different if the United States implemented health care coverage for all citizens?

Winters focuses on deconstructing the current diagnosis of GID. Despite recent revisions, she states, the diagnostic criteria are "increasingly ambiguous, conflicted and overinclusive." After reading the most recent DSM criteria for GID, included in her essay, would you agree? Fears that a revised classification would endanger medical care for the transgender community are essentially moot, states Winters, given the fact that the current diagnosis "fails to establish the medical necessity of procedures proven to relieve their distress." With the criteria put in place by the DSM, Winters argues, many insurers are already refusing to cover treatments, dismissing surgeries as "cosmetic" in nature, rather than necessary for treatment.

Do you feel that total declassification is the correct step to take? Or would a revision of the current classification be more appropriate? What if these changes resulted in the denial of access to medical care for transgender or transsexual individuals? Is there a middle ground that reduces stigma while maintaining access to medical treatment?

Suggested Readings

P.T. Cohen-Kettenis, "The Treatment of Adolescent Transsexuals," *Journal of Sexual Medicine* (vol. 5, no. 8, 2008).

R. Ehrbar, "Clinical Judgment in the Diagnosis of Gender Identity Disorder in Children," *Journal of Sex and Marital Therapy* (vol. 34, no. 5, 2008).

K. Hausman, "Controversy Continues to Grow over DSM's GID Diagnosis," *Psychiatric News* (vol. 38, no. 14, 2003). Accessed at http://pn.psychiatryonline.org/cgi/content/full/38/14/25.

ISSUE 19

Should Corporations Ensure Equal Rights for Their Lesbian, Gay, Bisexual, and Transgender Employees?

YES: **David M. Hall**, from *Allies at Work* (Out & Equal Workplace Advocates, 2009)

NO: **Glen E. Lavy**, from "Behind the Rhetoric: The Social Goals of GLBT Advocacy in Corporate America," Corporate Resource Council at http://www.corporateresourcecouncil.org/white_papers/Behind_The_Rhetoric.pdf (2002)

ISSUE SUMMARY

YES: David Hall outlines, from a chapter in his book *Allies at Work: Creating a Lesbian, Gay, Bisexual and Transgender Friendly Works Environment*, the need for corporations to work as allies in establishing equal rights for LGBT employees.

NO: Glen E. Lavy suggests, on behalf of the Corporate Resource Council, that by offering equal rights to LGBT employees, corporations are doing much more than that—they are actually signing on to support broader social changes sought by LGBT individuals.

$\mathbf{E}$ven when not required to do so by law, many corporations have decided that there are sound business reasons to promote diversity and provide support for lesbian, gay, bisexual, and transgender (LGBT) employees through nondiscrimination policies and extending benefits to domestic partners. This should come as no surprise, as federal protections prohibit workplace discrimination against marginalized populations since the 1960s.

The Civil Rights Act of 1964 prohibits employment discrimination based on race, color, religion, sex, or national origin. Subsequent federal laws have been enacted to prohibit employment discrimination based on age (1967) and disability (1990). Despite these movements, there are currently no federal protections from discrimination based on sexual orientation and gender identity. The Employment Non-Discrimination Act (ENDA), which would prohibit workplace discrimination on the basis of sexual orientation or gender identity, has not yet passed in Congress. Until ENDA passes through both the House and Senate, LGBT employees are left at the mercy of state laws or workplace policies. Only 20 states have laws that prohibit discrimination based on sexual orientation, with only 12 of them offering protections based on gender identity. Discrimination on the basis of sexual orientation is legal in 30 states, and discrimination on the basis of gender identity is legal in 38 states.

Despite the lack of federal protection against employee discrimination based on sexual orientation and gender identity, support for LGBT equal rights in the workplaces themselves has been growing steadily in the last decade. Several companies, including many Fortune 500 businesses have become proactive in incorporating equal rights for their LGBT employees. Such equal rights include implementing policies that prohibit discrimination based on sexual orientation and/or gender identity, having LGBT Employee Resource Groups (ERGs), and extending benefits to domestic partners. As of 2009, 85 percent of the Fortune 500 businesses have policies that offer protections based on sexual orientation, compared with 51 percent in 2000, and 35 percent (176) of Fortune 500 businesses have policies that offer protections based on gender identity, compared to only three businesses in 2000. Fifty-seven percent of the Fortune 500 businesses extend benefits to domestic partners (including health, family medical leave, and retirement benefits). Also, in 2009, 259 of the Fortune 500 businesses received a 100 percent score on the Human Rights Campaign's Corporate Equality Index, which measures the level of equitable support for LGBT employees. This represents a 33 percent increase since 2008, and only 13 companies received this score in 2002 (HRC, 2009).

The issue of workplace equality is occurring amidst other recent and growing movements for LGBT equality. More public figures, including politicians, celebrities, and even religious leaders, are coming out, which helps raise awareness about diverse sexual orientations and gender identities. Many schools have Gay–Straight Alliances, which are supportive and safe places for students of all sexual orientations to discuss issues related to sexual orientations and work to end homophobia. In 2003, the United States Supreme Court overturned sodomy laws, many of which were specific to same-sex partners. By January 2010, Connecticut, Iowa, Massachusetts, Vermont, Maine, and New Hampshire will offer full marriage rights to same-sex partners; eight other states offer either full or limited marriage rights to same-sex partners (either referred to as civil unions, or domestic partnerships); and two states recognize same-sex marriages performed in other states. Despite such advances, there are still many obstacles for LGBT individuals to overcome. Instances of hate crimes based on sexual orientation and gender identity prevail—college student Matthew Shepard was killed for being gay in 1998, and 39 percent of LGBT students report being verbally or physically assaulted, often with a weapon (GLSEN, 2003).

In the following essays, David Hall outlines, from a chapter in his book *Allies at Work: Creating a Lesbian, Gay, Bisexual and Transgender Friendly Works Environment,* the need for corporations to work as allies in establishing equal rights for LGBT employees. Glen E. Lavy suggests, on behalf of the Corporate Resource Council, that by offering equal rights to LGBT employees, corporations are doing much more than that—they are actually signing on to support broader social changes sought by LGBT individuals.

YES

David M. Hall

Excerpts from *Allies at Work*

Workplace equality is a cause that takes courage, passion, tenacity and patience. Equity for lesbian, gay, bisexual and transgender people is often referred to in the national media as part of a culture war. While it is not a literal war, the use of a violent metaphor reflects the reality that people truly get hurt and become proverbial casualties in this struggle. In many instances, lesbian, gay, bisexual and transgender individuals stand up, sometimes at great personal risk, because they can no longer remain silent. Allies have a responsibility to stand with them. Corporations that support their workers find that doing so is in their economic best interest. This book will examine how we develop that awareness and effectively build ally support and advocacy.

Federal & State Law, ENDA and Public Debate

The Employment Non-Discrimination Act (ENDA) would make it illegal to fire someone due to his or her sexual orientation.[1] Many people are under the mistaken impression that such discrimination is already illegal, because many Americans like to think that our laws reflect our nation's commitment to equality. However, those working for lesbian, gay, bisexual and transgender equity see clearly that a decidedly different reality is reflected in our federal laws. Sadly, it is a worldview, sometimes connected to a moral code, that says to those who are lesbian, gay, bisexual and transgender that their identities are unworthy of protection from discrimination and that their families are unworthy of equality.

Indeed, there is currently no federal protection from discrimination based on sexual orientation. The lack of federal protections carries dangerous implications, suggesting at the very least that extending non-discrimination in the workplace to lesbian, gay, bisexual and transgender individuals is unnecessary. At worst, the lack of federal protection further perpetuates bigotry and discrimination, fostering an atmosphere in which companies have the right to fire individuals just for being lesbian, gay, bisexual or transgender. If your boss were, for example, a member of the American Family Association or sympathetic to the group's ideas, then merely disclosing that you are lesbian, gay, bisexual and transgender could cost you your job, and in many parts of the country you would have little recourse.

From *Allies at Work: Creating a Lesbian, Gay, Bisexual and Transgender Inclusive Work Environment*, 2009 (excerpts). Copyright © 2009 by David M. Hall. Reprinted by permission of Out & Equal Workplace Advocates.

As proposed in 2008, the Employment Non-Discrimination Act passed by the U.S. House of Representatives (but not taken up in the Senate in 2008) excluded protection from discrimination based on gender identity.[2] This omission illustrates the sad reality that transgender individuals face even more resistance and obstacles than lesbian, gay and bisexual individuals do. It also raises important issues regarding the degree to which we are cohesively working for equality for all lesbian, gay, bisexual and transgender employees. Omitting protections related to gender identity at the federal level has implications for the workplace, signaling to transgender employees that they are unworthy of the same protections that would be extended to gay employees. Furthermore, many incidents of workplace bullying related to sexual orientation are directed at gender nonconformity. This creates a significant link between protection based on gender identity and working towards establishing a workplace free from bullying and harassment.

With a threat of a filibuster in the Senate and an expected veto from President George W. Bush, the Employment Non-Discrimination Act had little chance of becoming law during the Bush administration. ENDA's slow progress suggests that lesbian, gay, bisexual and transgender individuals enjoy limited public support, because they were unable to gather the necessary votes on Capitol Hill or persuade President Bush to rethink his position. However, to a great extent, public opinion and corporate practice at that time ran counter to government policy. ENDA is now expected to be passed by the House and Senate and signed into law by President Barack Obama.

Cultural conservatives benefit from the fact that most people apparently pay little attention, if any, to this battle. Survey results show that 60% of heterosexual adults thought that federal law already protected people from being fired due to sexual orientation. After learning that it is legal to fire someone for being gay or lesbian, 64% said that they believed that to be unfair. In this case, as in many others, there is a gap between public will and political leadership.[3] Those who oppose equality for lesbian, gay, bisexual and transgender individuals are typically vociferous and passionate. They have been successful in creating the impression that they represent a significant mass of voters, although they actually constitute a powerful fringe group.

Public opinion regarding transgender employees reveals a higher level of resistance by the general public to transgender rights. In a 2007 national survey of 2,868 adult respondents, 67% of all heterosexuals surveyed believed that transgender employees should be evaluated based on their work performance rather than for being transgender. In this same survey, 79% of heterosexual respondents said that lesbian, gay or bisexual employees should be judged based on their work performance rather than their sexual orientation.[4] The twelve-point difference in the findings illustrates the sad reality that those surveyed were more supportive of lesbian, gay, and bisexual employees than of transgender workers.

Without federal protection, lesbian, gay, bisexual and transgender individuals must look to state laws or workplace policies that provide them with protections from discrimination. Currently, 20 states prohibit discrimination based on sexual orientation and 12 of those states also prohibit discrimination based on gender identity.[5] At the time of this writing, states that provide protection based on sexual orientation and gender identity are California, Colorado, Illinois, Iowa, Maine, Minnesota, New Jersey, New Mexico, Oregon, Rhode Island, Vermont, and Washington. States that provide only protection based on sexual orientation are Connecticut, Hawaii, Maryland, Massachusetts, Nevada, New Hampshire, New York, and Wisconsin. As *Allies at Work* goes to press, the other 30 states offer no protection.

If you work for a company that provides job security for lesbian, gay, bisexual and transgender individuals, you are still likely to experience discrimination in the distribution of benefits. Millions of lesbian, gay, bisexual and transgender individuals are denied health care benefits that the spouses of heterosexual employees enjoy. As a result, domestic partner benefits are critically important; 76% of lesbian, gay, bisexual and transgender adults rate it as extremely or very important that their company offer equal health benefits to all employees.

However, even well-intentioned employers cannot easily offer health benefits that are exactly equal. Married heterosexual employees may enjoy spousal benefits in terms of health insurance and other benefits, and these employees are not taxed for the cost of their family benefits, which ultimately amounts to additional compensation. However, lesbian and gay employees are taxed for their domestic partner benefits, because the Internal Revenue Service deems domestic partner benefits to be reportable income.[6] For example, if domestic partner benefits total $20,000 per year for someone in the 25% tax bracket, that person has to pay an additional $5,000 in taxes on what the IRS identifies as additional income. In contrast, married employees do not pay taxes on family benefits. As a result of federal law, heterosexual privilege results in more disposable income for heterosexuals, even in companies that have more equitable policies. Even if your company has equitable policies in place, your lesbian, gay, bisexual and transgender colleagues experience discrimination every time that they receive a paycheck.

The national media regularly reports about the controversy related to same-sex marriage. While a number of states have recently passed laws and state constitutional amendments banning same-sex marriage, a growing number of heterosexual adults believe in extending many of the same rights and benefits of marriage to gay and lesbian couples. For example, 49% of heterosexuals believe that all employees should enjoy the same benefits on the job regardless of sexual orientation. Furthermore, 64% of heterosexuals believe that Family and Medical Leave should apply equally to heterosexual and gay employees. 56% of heterosexuals believe that gay and lesbian employees should receive the same family assistance as heterosexual employees when being transferred.[7] It is evident that there's a disconnect between public opinion and corporate policy and practice at this time.

Corporate Matters

The general public has been far more supportive of lesbian, gay, bisexual and transgender individual rights than has the typical elected official. The positions taken by America's corporate leaders also merit examination. Corporations are increasingly demonstrating their support for lesbian, gay, bisexual and transgender employees. This support is the result of courage, hard work, personal risk and advocacy by those who are lesbian, gay, bisexual and transgender, along with their allies. We can see these gains within prominent corporations.

Here's a case in point. Until 1996, Procter & Gamble would not permit the formation of a lesbian, gay, bisexual and transgender Employee Resource Group. In 1998, children of same-sex parents were not even allowed to attend a company-sponsored family function at a local amusement park.[8] Employees received a clear message that if they were lesbian, gay, bisexual or transgender, they'd better leave that identity at home. At work, each of these individuals needed to spend energy into hiding details about their lives. Former Proctor & Gamble employee Heidi Green, now Co-chair of Out & Equal, San Francisco Bay Area, remembers the situation vividly: "That fear of revealing who I was, particularly at work. I had a boss who suspected I was a lesbian, and I tried to hide it. I was one of those people who didn't use pronouns and thought no one could tell. And the thing I realized was that it was so disruptive of my work that I was thinking more about *that* than I was about work. And that frustrated me a lot." Procter & Gamble, like many other Fortune 500 companies, eventually realized that their policies were counter-productive and at odds with their goals of fostering an efficient, productive workforce and also becoming an employer-of-choice. Heidi decided to begin reaching out to her co-workers. They formed an Employee Resource Group, GABLE, with support from the company and from people involved in ERGs at Nestle and Disney.

In 2004, Procter & Gamble donated $10,000 for a ballot initiative in Cincinnati that would help ensure equal protection for lesbian, gay, bisexual and transgender individuals. The corporation supported this measure despite the fact that some conservative groups opposing homosexuality organized a boycott of the company's products.[9] By 2009, Procter & Gamble received an 95% rating on the Human Rights Campaign's Corporate Equality Index, a rating that means many of the company's policies are inclusive of lesbian, gay, bisexual and transgender people.[10] Within one decade, the workplace environment progressed from adversarial to one of advocacy.

Procter & Gamble's growth had parallels in other parts of corporate America. When Out & Equal was formed in 1998, according to the organization's founder Selisse Berry, "5% of companies were voluntarily putting sexual orientation in their EEO policies. No one was talking about gender identity and expression. Now 98% of the world's largest employers put sexual orientation in their EEO policies, and 40% have gender identity and expression."[11]

Not long ago, negative views of lesbian, gay, bisexual and transgender individuals permeated most corporations. Mike Syers, a 42-year-old partner at Ernst & Young, said that when he was a young man, he lost his best friend when Mike disclosed his sexual orientation. As a result, during the early stages of his career, Mike never came out at work. Reflecting on opportunities for career advancement, he noted, "I really didn't think there was a long-term career opportunity for me. Being a gay man, I didn't see gay partners."[12] Corporations have to restructure not just their definition of equity, but also their definition of family in order to compete in a 21st Century global economy. They are doing so despite the fact that the federal and state governments are too often working to turn back the clock in American society.

Hiring and Retaining Top Talent

Heyward Bell, chief diversity officer for Raytheon, explains, "Over the next ten years we're going to need anywhere from 30,000 to 40,000 new employees. We can't afford to turn our back on the talent pool."[13] Ed Offshack, a chemical engineer and gay activist at Procter & Gamble, connects corporate support for lesbian, gay, bisexual and transgender employees with the demands that drive business, including the need to develop the most talented staff: "It's a logic-based community."[14] Many corporations support lesbian, gay, bisexual and transgender workers in order to meet company goals of growing as a business and increasing profits.

The corporation and the employee have a common goal: a financial one. It is estimated that nearly 40% of employee compensation is met through the benefits package.[15] If a company's competitor offers domestic partner benefits, then there is pressure to offer the same benefits just to attract and retain the most talented workforce possible. It can cost a company six figures to lose a high-level executive or manager to a competitor. Demonstrating leadership regarding lesbian, gay, bisexual and transgender equality maximizes a corporation's competitive position in the market.

While there has been improvement, supporting lesbian, gay, bisexual and transgender employees is not without controversy. Walgreens, for example, donated $100,000 to the 2006 Gay Games. A Walgreens store manager quit in protest, and the company's chief executive received 250,000 protesting emails, most of them organized by the American Family Association. One individual email read, "Make no mistake: The 'Gay Games' was conceived as a way to build acceptance for homosexuality in the name of sport—a perversion of the athletic ideal." Walgreens, despite the protest, felt that it was important to send a message to their lesbian, gay, bisexual and transgender customers and employees that they were supportive. The company did not waiver in their support for the Gay Games.

Of course, companies do not like controversy. Corporations are entering into a contentious social and political area primarily because it is in their best economic interest to do so. Corporate philanthropy, salary and benefits are business decisions, aimed in part at helping the company position itself as an employer-of-choice. Executives have a responsibility to address the bottom line and maximize profits, which includes having the most talented, productive workforce possible.

Joe Solmonese, President of the Human Rights Campaign, notes that corporations have adjusted their policies and culture to remain competitive: "More businesses than ever before have recognized the value of a diverse and dedicated workforce. More importantly, these employers understand that discrimination against GLBT workers will ultimately hurt their ability to compete in the global marketplace."[16]

In 2009, the Human Rights Campaign gave 259 United States businesses a score of 100% on the Corporate Equality Index, an HRC-originated tool that measures the degree to which a company offers equitable support for lesbian, gay, bisexual and transgender employees. Perfect scores for 259 companies are equivalent to a 33% increase over the previous year. As recently as 2002, only 13 companies qualified for the 100% score. Today, 9 million American workers are employed at a company that has earned a perfect score on the Human Rights Campaign Corporate Equality Index.[17] It is important to note that not only have the number of perfect scores increased, but the criteria to obtain a perfect score has become increasingly rigorous.*

Many companies are working to improve or maintain their Corporate Equality Index rating. Perhaps even more important is that the higher a company is ranked by *Fortune* magazine, the higher their Corporate Equality Index ranking is likely to be. For example, among *Fortune*'s top 10 companies:

- 90% prohibit discrimination based on sexual orientation.
- 50% prohibit discrimination based on gender identity.
- 80% offer domestic partner health benefits.[18]

The hateful statements by Westboro Baptist Church and the American Family Association quoted at the start of this chapter clearly show the active campaign being waged against social and legal equity for lesbian, gay, bisexual and transgender individuals. At the same time, corporations are working for every possible competitive advantage. As companies do so, an increasing number of them have determined that it's good business to be lesbian, gay, bisexual and transgender-friendly.

Hewlett-Packard has paid attention to this market sector and is credited with being one of the nation's first major corporations to establish an Employee Resource Group and adopt EEO policies prohibiting discrimination on the basis of sexual orientation. "A couple of years ago, as we tried to begin cracking the code for marketing to lesbians, gays, bisexuals and transgender people, we realized we did not have any approved gay or lesbian images in the HP library," says Greg Nika, a global Program Manager with the company. "Within HP, all of the images that we use have to be in an approved image library. So our previous chief marketing officer worked with our corporate office, and they did a gay and lesbian photo shoot. Now we have lifestyle images of gay and lesbian couples, groups of gay and lesbian people and gay and lesbian couples with kids in different home settings, both using HP products and in general day-to-day activities. We also have an internal pride logo that is brand compliant, and we have a corporate team that is really starting to come to us proactively when they get opportunities to the market to the [gay and lesbian] community. . . . We have a lot more work to do, but we have all the building blocks in place."[19]

---

*It is also critical to note that there is much debate among lesbian, gay, bisexual and transgender workers as to whether the Corporate Equality Index criterion is rigorous enough, particularly concerning gender identity and expression. The Corporate Equality Index is continuously reevaluated and revised to reflect more rigorous criteria for obtaining a perfect score.

Eleven computer hardware and office equipment companies, including Hewlett-Packard, received a 100% rating and the designation "Best Place to Work for LGBT Equality" on the 2009 HRC Corporate Equality Index. "Now what you see is business people looking at not only how to make their work environments more equitable, but how to take that equity to drive performance," says Adam Wolf, a District Manager at Hewlett-Packard. "A lot of our competitors and a lot of our business partners are moving the bar up. . . . There's always a goal to reach, and it just keeps us motivated because we want everyone one to feel so comfortable and so accepted at work that they can really come and be their authentic selves."[20]

Allies' Surveyed on an Inclusive Work Environment

Let's examine how heterosexual coworkers, our allies and potential allies, view diversity and inclusion based on sexual orientation and gender identity.

An overwhelming majority of heterosexuals, 88%, would feel either positive or indifferent if they learned that a co-worker is lesbian or gay. In contrast, 12% would feel negatively about the person.[21] While the results show high rates of acceptance or at least indifference, the 12% number is understandably intimidating for lesbian, gay, bisexual and transgender individuals. A person who possesses negative feelings could be a direct supervisor or even the CEO. The risk of coming out on the job increases significantly if there is little or no support network in the workplace. Allies are critical in creating and fostering this support network, and they can do so without risking the personal backlash or rejection so often experienced by lesbian, gay, bisexual and transgender individuals.

In opinion polls, a large majority of heterosexuals report positive or indifferent feelings toward gay coworkers, but the work environment continues to be hostile and even harassing for some lesbian, gay, bisexual and transgender individuals. For example, 51% of lesbian and gay workers have heard anti-gay comments at work, and 15% report having been harassed by their coworkers.[22] For lesbian, gay, bisexual and transgender workers, this too often results in a complicated division between work and personal life. While a solid majority of the American workforce is accepting of lesbian, gay, bisexual and transgender individuals, the small, rejecting minority can have an adverse impact on one's work-life and livelihood.

Lesbian, gay, bisexual and transgender employees understandably fear discrimination. In the United States military, for example, it is policy to fire lesbian and gay patriots who have risked their lives for America. The Pentagon fires two lesbian, gay, bisexual and transgender people every day and even fired 58 Arabic translators, professionals who are scarce and sorely needed by the U.S. military in Iraq and Afghanistan.[23] More than 12,000 enlisted men and women have been discharged from the military since the 1994 enactment of the policy, "Don't Ask, Don't Tell." Randy Foster, a former Navy Air Force Captain, lied about being gay while serving in the United States military. Eventually tired of hiding his identity, he left the military for the private sector.

The skills that he developed in the military building observation satellites now benefit his new employer, IBM. He explained his decision to leave the military: "Come hell or high water, I wanted to live one life. The only thing I have to hide now are national security secrets, and those are good secrets."[24]

Companies that create non-discrimination policies find wide support from their employees; 67% of lesbian, gay, bisexual and transgender adults consider it extremely or very important that they have a written non-discrimination policy inclusive of sexual orientation.[25] Without such a policy, employees are understandably hesitant to come out of the closet, and this situation leaves them less likely to contribute their highest level of productivity.

For most, coming out is a multi-faceted and ongoing process. Individuals often come out of the closet in stages, related to trust and intimacy that they have developed with those around them. Those who are openly gay are most likely to come out to their friends (92%). Additional groups, listed in descending order, include their parents (78%), grandparents or cousins (68%), and acquaintances or causal friends (68%). The lowest comfort level measured in this study involved coming out to colleagues at work (66%). While it is encouraging to see that a majority of self-identified lesbian, gay, bisexual and transgender employees are out at work, almost one-third who are out to friends are not out at work.

The implication is that there is significant work necessary to ensure greater comfort and equity at work. Indeed, lesbian, gay, bisexual and transgender individuals have a long list of good reasons for not coming out. For example, 54% cite concern about becoming a victim of a hate crime. Rejection by families is a concern for 39% of individuals surveyed, and rejection by friends is a concern for 32%. Over one-quarter of lesbian, gay, bisexual and transgender individuals fear losing their jobs.[26] It is reasonable to assume that most of those who reported fearing job loss are located in states and workplaces that lack nondiscrimination policies inclusive of sexual orientation and gender identity.

Mark Shields of the Human Rights Campaign's Coming Out Project notes that 70% of heterosexuals now know someone who is lesbian, gay, bisexual or transgender. This shows that today it is more common to self-disclose one's sexual orientation or gender identity. Shields' comments are a reminder that changing corporate culture is a process and there is a need for a company to progress in adjusting its work culture: "For most people, coming out or opening up to someone starts with a conversation. And for those interested in fostering strong, deep relationships with their friends and family, living openly often allows for closer relationships with the people they care about most."[27]

People who are out to friends and family are often ready to acknowledge their sexual orientation the work world. In 2007, 64% of gay employees were comfortable introducing their significant other to their coworkers, while in 2002, only 50% were comfortable doing so. When it comes to putting a picture of a significant other on an office desk or wall, 54% of gay employees were comfortable doing so in 2007. Only 34% were comfortable doing so in 2002. It is encouraging that this research demonstrates an increased level of comfort. However, the levels of discomfort are unacceptably high when one considers that it is the expected norm for heterosexual employees to not just display pictures but also refer to or discuss their families and relationships.

However, family matters can sometimes be a prompt for lesbian, gay, bisexual and transgender individuals to disclose their orientation. For example, Mike Syers, the business partner at Ernst & Young who was reluctant to come out because he knew no other gay executives, decided to self-disclose when he and his partner adopted a daughter. This change in his family impelled him to come out: "I will never, ever let her think that her family is something to be ashamed of." When he disclosed his sexual orientation to a colleague, she was accepting and seemingly unfazed.[28]

Sadly, not every lesbian, gay, bisexual and transgender individual receives a positive or neutral response when coming out to co-workers. Individual reluctance to disclose sexual orientation or gender identity/expression at work may often relate to messages and values in the larger society regarding lesbian, gay, bisexual and transgender people. The reality is that openly sharing that one is lesbian, gay, bisexual, or transgender can lead to facing not just tension but even perfectly legal discrimination.

The reality is that the challenges for creating true workplace equity are considerable. In fact, establishing equity is so very difficult that in many companies, you may find more failed attempts than success stories. It can be infuriating to fight for simple fairness and lose. Keep in mind that working for change has never been easy. Consider that it took over 70 years after the Seneca Falls Women's Rights Convention for American women to win the right to vote—a civil right that African American women and men in many Southern states had to continue to fight to establish till the 1960's.

Those who work to create change in their corporate culture sometimes do so at great risk. They may be seen as agitators, and this can impact their career trajectory. At a minimum, they are focusing on changing business operations in a way that will cause discomfort for a number of colleagues. This points to the importance of establishing policy, the company framework that supports managers and employees in their conversations, work situations or struggles with prejudiced or antagonistic colleagues. While it may be uncomfortable to take on the responsibilities of reform, it is important to remember that any significant changes in American society—from the birth of this nation through the present—have required taking risks. In fact, our history books dedicate little space to those who approach life perfunctorily.

Today's advocates already benefit from the hard work carried out by of the first wave of reform, pioneers who risked so much more. Our efforts to create and improve workplace inclusion are almost expected by many large corporations, due to the work, policy and successful models already established.

Additionally, for those who have been active in any cause, there are few feelings more elating than creating meaningful change that move us toward equity. The satisfaction and meaning derived from helping to form a community, or even a world, that more closely reflects our humanity can be among our life's most important accomplishments. More employers each day recognize the impact of such efforts on diversity and inclusion. These victories themselves inspire further hard work to address the next objective in creating an equitable workplace environment.

Neil Walton, a senior finance manager at Frito Lay, a company which has courted lesbian, gay, bisexual and transgender customers through advertising campaigns, corporate giving and other programs, gives this overview of his company's progress over the last decade: "We've come light-years since we originally announced domestic partner benefits. It's not even thought of anymore as being a big issue at all. And I think that it's just like knocking down dominoes: you start and you push that one thing down, and then something else comes along, and the next thing. We certainly have policies in place. There's no doubt about that. And the questions have come up. . . . 'Okay, we're there on the policies, but how do we change the culture? How do we keep doing that?' And that's something you do day by day, that's not something you do like knocking down a domino. You change one heart and one mind, one person at a time."[29]

"People understanding diversity, especially LGBT diversity, has to do with the human connection," says Marcelo Roman, an IBM executive who leads the company's global learning delivery outsourcing services in 68 countries. "We announced domestic partner benefits in 2005 for all of the countries where IBM does business, including Latin America. To accomplish that, we had to find allies in those countries. We found country general managers and other executives that we were able to connect with through some personal stories, and they became our ambassadors, they became our allies. And the country general managers are so committed that they're saying, 'What can I do to make sure that the people in my organization feel okay to come out?'

"So telling the story and making that human connection between an LGBT employee and an ally or a decision maker or a human resources executive makes a tremendous difference. . . . The human connection is very, very important for us to drive any of our initiatives forward."[30]

Those who are reading this book already possess enough passion to educate themselves on this issue. The next step is establishing the path toward equity. That requires ongoing education and advocacy. It requires a level of energy, understanding, and patience that on some days will be difficult if not nearly impossible to find. On other days, it will come quite easily. However, one day this era will be written about as history. It is up to us to decide on which side of history we will stand. Much has already been accomplished by pioneering gay and transgender employees who risked their own jobs and incomes to advocate for equality. They have dedicated so much, because more was at stake than just improving their own individual workplace experiences. For many of us, work is an essential part of who we are. Lesbian, gay, bisexual and transgender individuals who are in the closet often surround themselves within walls of isolation as a form of protection from the bigotry and hatred that exists in the mainstream.

Our work for lesbian, gay, bisexual and transgender workplace equity improves people's life experience by allowing them to take down the barriers that protect, isolate and limit them in the workforce. We are creating a workplace that reflects our humanity, the belief that every individual should feel a valued member of the team. An atmosphere of respect for diversity is what we owe to those who dedicate so very much to a company's advancement. Dedication to workplace equity for all employees safeguards the efficacy and livelihood of our loved ones and colleagues while strengthening our companies, community and nation.

Notes

1. Human Rights Campaign (2007, Nov. 7). "U.S. House takes historic steps by passing the Employment Non-Discrimination Act."
2. Planet Out (2008, April 2). "Senator Kennedy lobbies for ENDA protection without trans protections."
3. Out & Equal (2007, Sept. 11). "Significant majority of all adult Americans believe it is unfair that federal law allows employers to fire someone because they are gay or lesbian."
4. Ibid.
5. Human Rights Camapign (2008, March 31). "Statewide employment laws and policies."
6. National Lesbian & Gay Journalists Association (2008). "Domestic partner benefits overview."
7. Ibid.
8. Gunther, M. (2006, Nov. 30). "Queer Inc." *CNNMoney.*
9. Musback, Tom (2004, Sept. 17). "Anti-gay groups boycott Procter & Gamble." *PlanetOut Network.*
10. Human Rights Campaign (2009). *Corporate equality index: a report on lesbian, gay, bisexual and transgender equality in corporate America.*
11. Berry, Selisse (2008, May 30). Personal interview.
12. Gunther, M. (2006, Nov. 30). "Queer Inc." *CNNMoney.*
13. Ibid.
14. Ibid.
15. Out & Equal (2007, Sept.). "Understanding the lesbian, gay, bisexual and transgender perspective in the workplace."
16. Human Rights Campaign (2007, Sept. 17). "New report finds unprecedented growth in employer policies for lesbian, gay, bisexual and transgender workers."
17. Human Rights Campaign (2009). Corporate equality index: a report on lesbian, gay, bisexual and transgender equality in corporate America; Human Rights Campaign (2009, Sept. 2). "Number of companies with top rating for lesbian, gay, bisexual, and transgender jumps by one-third."
18. Human Rights Campaign (2007, Aug. 25). "GLBT equality at the Fortune 500."
19. Nika, Greg (2008). Out & Equal 2008 Summit interviews.
20. Wolf, Adam (2008. Out & Equal 2008 Summit interviews.
21. Out & Equal (2007, Sept. 11). "Significant Majority of all adult Americans believe it is unfair that federal law allows employers to fire someone because they are gay or lesbian."

22. Ibid.

23. Servicemembers Legal Defense Network (2006, Dec. 13). "Latest news."

24. Gunther, M. (2006, Nov. 30). "Queer Inc." *CNNMoney.*

25. Out & Equal (2007, Sept. 11). "Significant majority of all adult Americans believe it is unfair that federal law allows employers to fire someone because they are gay or lesbian."

26. Out & Equal (2006, Oct. 10). "In the lesbian, gay, bisexual, and transgender workplace."

27. Ibid.

28. Gunther, M. (2006, Nov. 30). "Queer Inc." *CNNMoney.*

29. Walton, Neil (2008). Out & Equal 2008 Summit interviews.

30. Roman, Marcelo (2008). Out & Equal 2008 Summit interviews.

Glen E. Lavy
 **NO**

Behind the Rhetoric: The Social Goals of GLBT Advocacy in Corporate America

GLBT Social Goals

GLBT advocates have clearly spelled out social goals in their publications. A strategy published in the book *After the Ball* (1989), written by two gay activists, included the following elements:

- Begin portraying gays "as victims in need of protection so that straights will be inclined by reflex to adopt the role of protector";
- Present gays in the media as "wholesome and admirable by straight standards, and . . . indistinguishable from the straights we'd like to reach";
- Desensitize people to gay issues by inundating the media with GLBT messages;
- Convert people to the belief that gayness is good. "Conversion" means "conversion of the average American's emotions, mind, and will, through a planned psychological attack, in the form of propaganda fed to the nation via the media."

Admitting that a media campaign portraying gays as "icons of normality" would be false, the advocates' response is that "it makes no difference that the ads are lies."

Traditional marriage and family values are obstacles to GLBT social goals. Thus, many GLBT advocates are pursuing same-sex "marriage" not because they value the traditional concept, but because they want to change it. They intend to "fight for same-sex marriage and its benefits and then, once granted, redefine the institution of marriage completely . . . and radically alter an archaic institution that as it now stands keeps us down."

Corporate policies and civil statutes granting same-sex couples the same status and rights as married spouses will inevitably lead to same-sex marriage. Such changes in the Netherlands led to a law making it "illegal for any employer and for any provider of goods or services, to distinguish between married and unmarried couples," and ultimately to the "small step" of legalizing same-sex marriage.

From Corporate Resource Council *White Papers,* 2002, pp. i–ii, 1–12. Copyright © 2002 by Glen E. Lavy. Reprinted by permission of the author.

Corporate Advocacy

GLBT advocates also have published a plan for accomplishing social goals through corporations. Advocates say that corporations are important to their social goals because corporate leaders "can often wield even more power than state and local officials in creating significant changes that affect their employees' lives. They can enact new policies with the approval of a few board members rather than thousands or even millions of voters." The steps within corporate America include:

- Establish a GLBT employee resource group;
- Demand that the corporation include sexual orientation in its EEO policy;
- Use the sexual orientation policy as leverage to obtain domestic partner benefits because, advocates argue, without domestic partner benefits "a company that otherwise purports to be fair is violating its own non-discrimination policy";
- Demand corporate support for GLBT organizations or events, such as Gay Pride events;
- Silence or punish opposition within the corporation. For example:
  a. It is now a violation of many corporate policies to express a moral or religious objection to gay sex;
  b. Employees at major corporations have been fired for expressing opposition to gay sex;
- Leverage corporate acceptance of same-sex relationships to promote legislation requiring such acceptance by society in general.

A corporation should be cautious about adopting any policy changes specifically directed toward GLBT employees unless the corporation is willing to support the entire spectrum of social changes being sought. GLBT employees, like all other employees, can be adequately protected by corporate policies that promote treating all employees with dignity and respect.

Introduction

Gay, lesbian, bisexual and transgendered persons ("GLBT") constitute a very small but influential percentage of the population. The most reliable surveys estimate that from 1–2% of Americans consider themselves to be GLBT.[1] Yet this relatively small group of people has created a powerful political movement by adopting the rhetoric of the civil rights movement of the 1960's. Over the past ten years GLBT advocates have:

1. Obtained special civil rights protection for sexual orientation in 12 states and numerous localities;[2]
2. Succeeded in enacting ordinances in San Francisco, Los Angeles, Seattle and other localities that require all city contractors (3,087 as of October 2001) to provide domestic partner benefits;[3]
3. Created an extensive network for pursuing social goals through corporations;[4]

4. Held hundreds of Gay Pride events funded by corporate dollars; and
5. Nearly one third of the Fortune 500 companies to provide domestic partner benefits.[5]

What the GLBT advocates say they want is nothing less than what has been described as a "gay revolution" in American culture.[6] They demand civil rights protection for sexual orientation. They seek to extend the legal and social status of traditional marriage to same-sex unions. They insist that corporations and society in general treat GLBT relationships as healthy, normal and equal to heterosexual relationships. An employer's adoption of a domestic partner benefit policy is an especially important step, GLBT advocates say, because such a policy acknowledges that "all of its employees are equal, and therefore their relationships are also equal."[7]

GLBT advocates often persuade corporations to establish domestic partner benefit programs by focusing on a few complaints or needs. But GLBT literature suggests they have much broader goals than reformation of corporate culture.

I. The Quest for a Society without Sexual Limitations

Advocates for GLBT rights have been working publicly and behind the scenes to achieve full parity with heterosexuality for more than two decades. Much of the advocacy of GLBT rights involves challenges to traditional views of morality and sexuality.

Gay authors Marshall Kirk and Hunter Madsen articulated an elaborate strategy for achieving acceptance of gay sexuality in *After the Ball: How America Will Conquer its Fear & Hatred of Gays in the 90's,* which laid "vital groundwork for the next stage of the gay revolution."[8] Notwithstanding opposition from more militant activists, the authors recommended that "In any campaign to win over the public, gays must be portrayed as victims in need of protection so that straights will be inclined by reflex to adopt the role of protector."[9] This "victim imagery" was to be portrayed in a media campaign designed to present gays as no different from heterosexuals: "Persons featured in the media campaign should be wholesome and admirable by straight standards, and completely unexceptional in appearance; in a word, they should be indistinguishable from the straights we'd like to reach."[10] Kirk and Madsen recognized that ads featuring gays as "icon[s] of normality . . . are lies; that that is *not* how all gays actually look; that gays know it, and bigots know it."[11] Their response to this likely objection to the media campaign of "normality" was:

> Yes, of course—we know it, too. But it makes no difference that the ads are lies; not to us, because we're using them to ethically good effect, to counter negative stereotypes that are every bit as much lies, and far more wicked ones; not to bigots, because the ads will have their effect on them whether they believe them or not.[12]

Kirk and Madsen proposed exposing straight people to gay messages until the straights are desensitized: "to desensitize straights to gays and gayness, inundate them in a continuous flood of gay-related advertising, presented in the least offensive fashion possible. If straights can't shut off the shower, they may at least eventually get used to being wet."[13] The purpose of desensitization is simply part of a strategy leading up to "conversion," which literally involves changing the hearts and minds of the American people. The authors warn readers not to confuse conversion with subversion, which "has a nasty ring" to it. But they acknowledge the subversive nature of the strategy:

> Yet, ironically, by Conversion we actually mean something far more profoundly threatening to the American Way of Life, without which no truly sweeping social change can occur. *We mean conversion of the average American's emotions, mind, and will, through a planned psychological attack, in the form of propaganda fed to the nation via the media.* We mean 'subverting' the mechanism of prejudice to our own ends–using the very processes that made America hate us to turn their hatred into warm regard–whether they like it or not.[14]

Most American GLBT advocates distance themselves from the least accepted element of the GLBT community, the North American Man/Boy Love Association (NAMBLA), which militantly advocates pederasty (molesting a child of the same sex). Avoidance of NAMBLA is consistent with the strategy promoted by Kirk and Madsen in *After the Ball*:

> When you're very different, and people hate you for it,[15] this is what you do: *first,* you get your foot in the door, by being as *similar* as possible; then, and only then–when your one little difference is finally accepted–can you start dragging in your other peculiarities, one by one. **You hammer in the wedge narrow end first.** As the saying goes, Allow the camel's nose beneath your tent, and the whole body will soon follow.
>
> By the same token, allowing advocates of legalized "love" between men and boys to participate in gay pride marches is, from the standpoint of public relations, an unalloyed disaster. . . .[16]

The authors made it clear that by publicly conveying an image of gays as normal, they do not intend to permanently disassociate themselves from the more "exotic elements of the gay community":

> Our ultimate objective is to expand straight tolerance so much that even gays who look unconventional can feel safe and accepted. But like it or not, by the very nature of the psychological mechanism, desensitization works gradually or not at all. For the moment, therefore, unconventional-looking gays are encouraged to live their lives as usual, but out of the limelight. . . . In time, as hostilities subside and stereotypes weaken, we see no reason why more and more diversity should not be introduced into the projected image [of gays]. This would be healthy for society as well as for gays.[17]

GLBT advocates have not always been so reluctant to be open about their goal of eliminating all sexual mores. At a 1972 conference of the National Coalition of Gay Organizations, the participants adopted a "Gay Rights Plat-form" demanding a number of social changes. One of them was: "Repeal of all laws governing the age of sexual consent." Although most advocates do not currently highlight it, that goal has not changed. NAMBLA spokesman David Thorstad affirmed the continuing existence of the goal when he stated that "The ultimate goal of the gay liberation movement is the achievement of sexual freedom for all–not just equal rights for 'lesbians and gay men,' but also freedom of sexual expression for young people and children."[18] GLBT advocates have succeeded in having the age of sexual consent lowered to 14 in Ontario, Canada, and to 12 in Holland.[19]

One GLBT advocate who has publicly expressed support for legalization of adult-child sex is lesbian author Pat Califia. Two essays in the book *Public Sex: The Culture of Radical Sex* are entitled "The Age of Consent: The Great Kiddy-Porn Panic of '77" and "The Aftermath of the Great Kiddy-Porn Panic of '77."[20]

Califia advises that advocates of unrestrained sexuality, including adult-child sex, join organizations "like the American Civil Liberties Union, Californians Against Censorship Together, Feminists for Free Expression, the National Coalition Against Censorship, the National Campaign for Free-dom of Expression, Planned Parenthood Federation of America, or Coyote [because t]hese groups are fighting for your sexual freedom."[21]

Society's longstanding embrace of traditional marriage interferes with the goal of complete sexual freedom. GLBT advocates consider marriage to be "the last legal bastion of *compulsory* heterosexuality."[22] So they intend to reinvent marriage:

> Initially, it seems unlikely that married gay couples would be just like married straight couples. For example, same-sex couples are less likely to follow the traditional breadwinner-housekeeper division in their households. Nor would the gay and lesbian culture cease to be distinctive. One feature of our experience has been an empha-sis on "families we choose," anthropologist Kath Weston's felicitous phrase. Such families are *fluid alliances independent of the ties imposed by blood and by law*. Often estranged from blood kin, openly gay people are more prone to rely on current as well as former lovers, close friends, and neighbors as their social and emotional support system. Include children in this fluid network and the complexity becomes more pronounced. Because same-sex couples cannot have children through their own efforts, a third party must be involved: a former different-sex spouse, a sperm donor, a surrogate mother, a parent or agency offering a child for adoption. The family of choice can and often does include a relationship with this third party. Gay and lesbian couples are pioneering novel family configurations, and gay marriage would not seriously obstruct the creation of the larger families we choose.[23]

One advocate has observed that "marriage for gays is not an end in and of itself so much as a means to impel a general redefinition of masculinity and femininity."[24] Michelangelo Signorile advises gays and lesbians:

> to fight for same-sex marriage and its benefits and then, once granted, redefine the institution of marriage completely, to demand the right to marry not as a way of adhering to society's moral codes but rather to debunk a myth and radically alter an archaic institution that as it now stands keeps us down. The most subversive action lesbians and gay men can undertake—and one that would perhaps benefit all of society—is to transform the notion of "family" entirely.[25]

Thomas Stoddard, a former president of the Lambda Legal Defense and Education Fund (Lambda),[26] likewise sees GLBT marriage as inherently transforming the institution:

> enlarging the concept [of marriage] to embrace same-sex couples would necessarily transform it into something new. . . . Extending the right to marry to gay people–that is, abolishing the traditional gender requirements of marriage–can be one of the means, perhaps the principal one, through which the institution divests itself of the sexist trappings of the past.[27]

Some GLBT advocates think that opening marriage to gays and lesbians does not go far enough in reordering society. Paula Ettelbrick, director of the Family Policy Program at the National Gay and Lesbian Task Force Policy Institute and a former legal director of Lambda, is one:

> Being queer is more than setting up house, sleeping with a person of the same gender, and seeking state approval for doing so. . . . Being queer means pushing the parameters of sex, sexuality, and family, and in the process, transforming the very fabric of society. . . . As a lesbian, I am fundamentally different from non-lesbian women. . . . In arguing for the right to legal marriage, lesbians and gay men would be forced to claim that we are just like heterosexual couples, have the same goals and purposes, and vow to structure our lives similarly. . . . We must keep our eyes on the goals of providing true alternatives to marriage and of radically reordering society's views of family.[28]

Even though Ettelbrick views marriage, no matter how broadly defined, as a hindrance to her social goals, she supports the idea of undermining traditional marriage by making it available to gays and lesbians.[29]

When a society provides special protection for sexual orientation and mandates that domestic partners receive the same economic benefits as spouses, there is little reason to refuse to allow same-sex marriage. Netherlands writer Kees Waaldijk argues that the legalization of same-sex marriage in the Netherlands is simply a "small step" that inexorably follows from the prior changes in Dutch law: the decriminalization of gay sex, the granting to cohabiting couples (heterosexual and homosexual) a growing number of legal rights and duties similar to those of married couples, and ultimately the passing of a law making it "illegal for any employer and for any provider of goods or services, to distinguish between married and unmarried couples . . . ."[30] Waaldijk concludes that in view of all the prior changes, which occurred in incremental steps, "what to mankind, and to all its representatives at this conference, may seem a giant step–the opening up of the institution of marriage to same-sex couples–will, for the Dutch, only be another small change law."[31] GLBT rights advocates are seeking the same social and legal status that they have obtained in the Netherlands.

II. Corporate America's Role in Furthering GLBT Social Goals[32]

GLBT advocates have concluded that corporate leaders "can often wield even more power than state and local officials in creating significant changes that affect their employees' lives. They can enact new policies with the approval of a few board members rather than thousands or even millions of voters."[33] Thus, advocates focus a significant part of their efforts for social reform on corporations.

The strategy for pursuing GLBT goals through corporate America is well established, and much of it is described in detail in the *Domestic Partnership Organizing Manual for Employee Benefits.*[34] The steps are:

1. Form an employee resource group;
2. Use the employee resource group to lobby for the inclusion of sexual orientation in the company's non-discrimination policy;
3. Demand domestic partner benefits on the ground that failing to provide them is a violation of the sexual orientation non-discrimination policy;
4. Demand corporate support of GLBT organizations to demonstrate publicly that the corporation truly supports its GLBT employees;
5. Upon obtaining full corporate support for GLBT issues, silence or punish opposition.
6. Leverage corporate acceptance of same-sex relationships to promote legislation requiring such acceptance by society in general.

A. Employee Groups

The first step in effecting change in a corporation is to create a GLBT employee resource group:

> Before starting to work on specific issues in the workplace, it is important to form an employee organization to identify needs, operate with [a] common cause, and link employees who are interested in working for change. Even if it is not possible to form an official group of GLBT employees, it is valuable [to] create an informal, unofficial group from which the organizing efforts can be launched. . . .[35]

Once organized, the GLBT employee group is "a useful vehicle for creating change within the workplace . . . ."[36]

B. Sexual Orientation Policy

The second step in the GLBT program for corporations is to establish a sexual orientation policy.[37] Although sometimes presented as an urgently needed policy to stop workplace discrimination, the *Manual* simply presents this step as a precursor to a domestic partnership policy:

> Before attempting to get DP [domestic partner] benefits from your employer, it is imperative that the company's non-discrimination policy include sexual orientation. This is for two reasons:
>
> 1. A common rationale for establishing DP benefits is that the failure to do so is contradictory to a non-discrimination clause that includes sexual orientation (and/or marital status). Hence, a sexual orientation non-discrimination clause is an important tool in trying to get DP benefits.
> 2. Also, without a sexual orientation non-discrimination clause, GLBT employees will be reluctant to come out in support of DP benefits for fear that they will be fired or otherwise discriminated against.[38]

The *Manual* emphasizes that a sexual orientation clause is important even where state or local law prohibits discrimination on the basis of sexual orientation, because a corporate policy is easier to enforce.[39]

C. Domestic Partner Benefits

Upon implementation of a sexual orientation non-discrimination policy, GLBT advocates are ready to lobby for domestic partner (DP) benefits.[40] After obtaining a sexual orientation policy, GLBT advocates argue that the corporation *must* give DP benefits to avoid violating the policy. The Human Rights Campaign (HRC), a gay civil rights organization in Washington, D.C., argues that "DP benefits are a logical extension of an employer's commitment to provide a workplace free of sexual orientation discrimination."[41] Therefore, the HRC asserts, *"By not making employee benefits available on equal terms, regardless of marital status or sexual orientation, a company that otherwise purports to be fair is violating its own non-discrimination policy."*[42]

Advocates also attempt to leverage competitors' DP benefits policies to persuade their employers to adopt such benefits. In describing what should be included in proposals about DP benefits, the *Manual* advises advocates to "Talk about other employers in your company's industry or region which offer DP benefits . . . ."[43] However, advocates do not inform corporations that most of the companies with DP benefits have adopted them in order to continue doing business with San Francisco.[44] In a June 15, 2001, press release, HRC boasted that "Some 76 percent of all employers known to be offering DP benefits in 1999 could be attributed to the enactment of the San Francisco law . . . ."[45] As of October 2001, less than 1,200 employers nationwide had adopted domestic partner benefits without being required to do so by local ordinances.[46]

The quest for DP benefits may proceed in one step or two, depending upon a corporation's amenability to providing such benefits. If an employer is reluctant to incur the cost of DP benefits, advocates may accept only "soft benefits" as an initial step.[47] However, employers should be aware that agreeing to a policy of soft benefits does not settle the issue: "Acquiring soft benefits is an important step toward full and equal treatment, but companies should carefully consider the repercussions and implications of ruling out the extension of comprehensive benefits."[48]

GLBT advocates generally will not be satisfied until companies "extend the same benefits to domestic partners as they extend to spouses."[49]

One of the arguments advanced on behalf of DP benefits is that the cost is low because not many employees will take advantage of them.[50] At General Motors, for example, only 166 workers out of 1,330,000–.01%—had chosen the benefit as of 2001.[51] Such limited participation, especially in light of the enormous effort required to establish and administer the benefit, suggests that GLBT advocacy of DP benefits is driven more by a desire for social change than a true need for workplace benefits or protections. This conclusion is borne out by the *Manual* itself:

> In many regards, the workplace is the leading edge of change for the GLBT community. Company CEOs and executives can often wield even more power than state and local officials in creating significant changes that affect their employees' lives. They can enact new policies with the approval of a few board members rather than thousands or even millions of voters. . . . Through the enactment of DP benefits, employers send the message that all employees, including GLBT workers, are valued and accepted as equal, which paves the way for more employees to come out of the closet and fully contribute to their work and their community. *DP benefits are not the final step in the GLBT quest for equality,* but they are integral to its achievement. *Equal protection for our relationships, whether through marriage or DP benefits, is a key goal for millions of GLBT people.*[52]

The political nature of the quest for DP benefits is further demonstrated by Lambda's support of a federal lawsuit in Chicago. An unmarried woman who had been living with the same man for over twenty years sued the Chicago Board of Education for giving DP benefits to same-sex couples only. She claimed that the limitation of DP benefits to same-sex couples only violated her equal protection rights. The federal court dismissed her claims. On appeal, Lambda filed an amicus curiae brief on behalf of the plaintiff, and argued that the School Board should not give benefits to same-sex partners only. The Court of Appeals found Lambda's support for the appeal "surprising" because the plaintiff's success would likely have resulted in termination of the benefits for gays and lesbians (*Irizarry v. Board of Ed.,* 251 F.3d 604, 609 (7th Cir. 2001)). The Court described Lambda's position as follows:

> . . . Lambda is concerned with the fact that state and national policy encourages (heterosexual) marriage in all sorts of ways that domestic-partner health benefits cannot begin to equalize. Lambda wants to knock marriage off its perch by requiring the board of education to treat unmarried heterosexual couples as well as it treats married ones, so that marriage will lose some of its luster.
>
> This is further evidence of the essentially symbolic or political rather than practical significance of the board's policy. Lambda is not jeopardizing a substantial benefit for homosexuals because very few of them want or will seek the benefit. . . (*ibid.*).

It is clear that obtaining DP benefits is simply a step toward the ultimate goal of changing cultural views about human sexuality. What is not quite so clear is the precise nature of the subsequent steps.[53] Some of those steps are at least vaguely identified in GLBT publications, while other steps may be primarily discernible from events at corporations that have adopted the requested GLBT policies.

D. Corporate Support of GLBT Advocacy

One of the goals that the Human Rights Campaign recommends for GLBT employee groups is to persuade corporations to provide public support for GLBT issues:

> [After] achieving full domestic partner benefits for same-sex spouses[, another goal might be] winning public demonstration by the organiza-tion that it supports all employees, regardless of orientation. (This might take the form of allowing the group to march with the company's banner at a gay pride [event] or it might entail a corporate contribution to a gay non-profit group).[54]

A similar goal was stated in the materials for a conference on organizing for GLBT advocacy in the workplace, Out & Equal Leadership Summit 2000 (Out & Equal). In response to the question, "What Do Gay Employees Want?," one item was "Public support of issues important to them."[55]

The success that GLBT employee groups have had with the goal of public, corporate support is shown by the level of financial assistance that companies like Ford Motor Company and United Airlines have given to GLBT causes. Ford is a sponsor of the Out & Equal conferences; it sponsors a "Gay History and Culture Display" in its offices for "Lesbian and Gay History Month" in October; it provides new vehicles for certain "Gay Pride" events; and it regularly funds groups such as the Policy Group of the NGLTF, Lambda, and other GLBT advocacy groups.[56] United provides similar funding for GLBT causes. Indeed, in 2000, United agreed to give Lambda up to $300,000 worth of free flights for all Lambda staff, round-trip tickets to be used as prizes at Lambda events, and special offers for new Lambda members.[57] Many other Fortune 500 corporations are also providing significant support for GLBT organizations. As additional corporations adopt GLBT friendly policies, they too will be asked to provide public support for GLBT causes.

E. Silence or Punish Opposition

After obtaining full corporate support for GLBT rights, advocates are ready to move forward with efforts to silence opposition, or to punish anyone who dares express opposition. GLBT advocates do not believe that opponents of gay sex have the right to express themselves as part of the recognition of diversity–only opinions supportive of GLBT relationships are permitted.[58]

The compulsion to express only thoughts that are supportive of or neutral toward GLBT relationships is at least implicit in "zero-tolerance" policies like the ones in effect at US Airways and United Airlines. On February 27, 2001, US Airways mailed to its employees a brochure entitled *Employee respect in the workplace: US Airways Zero Tolerance Program,* which included "sexual orientation" as a protected category. The non-discrimination policy includes the following:

> Discriminatory or harassing conduct in any form (speech, writing, gestures, pictures, drawings, cartoons, etc.) will not be tolerated at US Airways. Violation of US Airways' non-discrimination policy may result in disciplinary action, up to and including immediate dismissal (*ibid.*).

United has posted its zero-tolerance policy on its Web site for employment policies: "United has a zero-tolerance policy on harassment and discrimination in any form–whether verbal, visual, physical or otherwise. It is United's express policy to forbid harassment and discrimination based on . . . sexual orientation."[59] A seminar at the 2000 Out & Equal conference similarly asserted that GLBT employees want a "[s]afe work environment, free of disrespectful behaviors" and for corporations to "[c]learly communicate intolerance for disrespectful behavior . . . [and to] [t]alk about gay, lesbian, bisexual friends and relatives and current events in [a] positive way."[60]

These statements about zero-tolerance or intolerance for disrespectful behavior would not have such a militant note if it were not for the assumption behind GLBT rights advocacy: that there can be no legitimate opposition–moral, religious or otherwise–to gay sex or GLBT relationships.[61] Because of this presupposition, *all* opposition to gay sex or GLBT relationships is assumed to be disrespectful, harassing or discriminatory, and the result of homophobia.

Homophobia is defined as the "irrational fear of, aversion to, or discrimination against homosexuality or homosexuals."[62] The operative term in this definition is "irrational." However, the Gay and Lesbian Medical Association describes the "legal and religious proscription" of gay sex as "external homophobia."[63] In *After the Ball,* the authors use the term "homohatred" to describe opposition to GLBT relationships that does not involve actual fear.[64] Some GLBT advocates refer to "negative attitudes" or "dislike of homosexuality" as homophobic.[65] If "negative attitudes" toward GLBT relationships and "dislike of homosexuality" are impermissible, then any statement that directly or indirectly says that gay sex is immoral or that GLBT persons can change would be deemed at least disrespectful.[66] Therefore, no one may express opposition to gay sex or GLBT relationships in a workplace with a "zero tolerance" policy, and any expression of opposition is likely to be suppressed by the mere existence of a sexual orientation policy.

GLBT advocates have made great strides in silencing opposition at AT&T and Xerox through the Safe Space® programs.[67] AT&T's "Safe Space Program is designed to provide a non-threatening way for managers and employees to make a statement that homophobia and hostility will not be tolerated in the workplace."[68] Displaying an AT&T Safe Space® "magnet shows gay co-workers that they can feel safe with you and shows *unsupportive co-workers* that you won't tolerate bigotry or discrimination."[69] Since any opposition to GLBT relationships is assumed to constitute "bigotry," no one is free to express a religious or other moral belief that gay sex is improper. Xerox, which uses the "Safe Space®" name and logo with the permission of LEAGUE at AT&T, has a theme of "Promoting Diversity One Cubicle at a Time" on its Safe Space® poster.[70] In its diversity training, Xerox makes it clear that persons who oppose homosexual conduct must change their minds and support GLBT relationships if they wish to succeed at Xerox.[71] *Diversity of opinion is intolerable.* Indeed, AT&T boldly states, "Diversity is not about tolerance."[72]

GLBT activists have also succeeded in punishing opposition. At Hewlett Packard's plant in Boise, Idaho, an employee with a twenty-one year record of meeting or exceeding expectations was fired for refusing to remove Bible verses about gay sex from his cubicle. The employee allegedly posted the Bible verses in response to a poster near his cubicle that he perceived to be promoting GLBT relationships. In a January 12, 1999 letter to the Idaho Human Rights Commission, Hewlett Packard admitted that the reason for firing the employee was "His overt opposition to HP's Diversity Advertising Campaign . . . ."[73] That opposition consisted of "posting Bible quotes on the overhead bin in his cubicle. The contents of his posters was a clear objection to HP's diversity policy."[74] Hewlett Packard further stated that the employee "also knew that HP would allow him to *make the choice between his personal values or HP Company values.*"[75] In other words, the employee could remain at Hewlett Packard if he were willing to refrain from expressing his religious beliefs about GLBT relationships.

Similarly, an employee of Trilogy Software, Inc. in Austin, Texas was fired for referring to "the lies of homosexuality" in his personal page in the company's on-line phone book. The terminated employee's supervisor informed him that he was being terminated because his reference to "the lies of homosexuality" was offensive to other employees.[76] Trilogy did not offer to retain the employee if he removed the "offending" statement–in fact, the employee was terminated after removing it.

On April 30, 2001, an Eastman Kodak employee received an anonymous e-mail that he assumed was from a co-worker. Thinking that he was responding to a discouraged co-worker, the employee encouraged the e-mail sender to "Be concerned . . . about the job and do your best to try and improve it also." He further expressed his belief that God was judging Kodak for "promoting the gay and lesbian lifestyle at our workplace . . . ." He suggested that the e-mail sender "Pray for the company and the new leadership that God will forgive this company for promoting the . . . alternative lifestyle . . . ." Unfortunately for the employee, he also sent a copy of the e-mail to everyone in his building.[77]

A termination memorandum dated May 4, 2001, informed the employee that "The content of the note was in direct violation of our Fair Treatment/Rules of Conduct and the Kodak Values. This action also constitutes inappropriate use of Company property." The employee alleges that even though he had worked for Eastman Kodak for over 16 years, and had recently received an excellent employee review, no one asked him why he sent the note or whether he knew it would be distributed to so many people.

These terminations of employees who refuse to remain silent about their moral opposition to gay sex or GLBT relationships are not incidental. GLBT advocates have said that they are determined to "do whatever must be done" to force people to treat GLBT relationships as equal to heterosexual ones, or to at least silence all adversaries.[78] The tenor of the "zero tolerance" policies at corporations such as United makes the intent to punish opposition unmistakable. Rather than making the workplace safe for all employees, such policies cause division and uncertainty.[79] *Rather than enabling corporations to retain productive employees, such policies may result in the loss of such employees.* Indeed, highly qualified employees have resigned from corporations such as American Airlines and Xerox because of the companies' promotion of GLBT relationships.[80]

F. Use Corporate Policies as Leverage against Governmental Entities

With the growth in numbers of corporations providing domestic partner benefits, GLBT rights advocates are increasingly pointing to private companies as the example that governmental entities should follow. U.S. Representative Barney Frank of Massachusetts argued on April 16, 2001, that a federal DP benefits bill should be enacted because "[i]t's time for the federal government to follow the lead of many private sector employers and recognize that providing benefits to domestic partners is not just the fair thing to do, it's good business."[81] An editorial in the *Arizona Republic* cited the number of colleges, governmental agencies and private companies, including sixteen of Arizona's thirty-two largest employers, who offer domestic partner benefits as a justification for adopting domestic partner benefits in Scottsdale: "Clearly, this is an idea whose time has come."[82] As with employees who point to other corporations as the reason their corporation should give domestic partner benefits, these proponents of domestic partner benefits fail to acknowledge that the vast majority of corporations with domestic partner benefits adopted them because of the San Francisco ordinance.[83]

Some courts have found the example of private companies and the alleged need for governmental entities to compete for employees persuasive in rejecting challenges to a city's authority to provide DP benefits. The court in *Devlin v. City of Philadelphia,* No 1631, First Judicial Dist. of Penn., slip op. 9 (Oct. 5, 2000), rejected a challenge to Philadelphia's power to adopt a DP law, in part, on the ground that "[p]rohibiting the extension of such benefits may in-fact place the City of Philadelphia at a competitive disadvantage with private employers who allow for such benefits." The court in *Crawford v. City of Chicago,* 304 Ill. App. 3d 818, 829, 710 N.E.2d 91, 99 (Ct. App. 1999), likewise referred to the fact that "Many private employers now offer insurance and other benefits to cohabiting same-sex couples" in support of its decision to reject a challenge to Chicago's authority to grant DP benefits. Thus, GLBT advocates are succeeding in their efforts to use the precedent of private employers as a reason for public employers to provide DP benefits.

Conclusion

Corporate leaders should not assume that overtures by GLBT employees requesting changes in corporate policies are merely independent actions driven by the needs of individual employees. While some employees may genuinely desire changes for themselves, the quest for GLBT-oriented corporate policies is part of a comprehensive agenda for social change. Unless a corporation is willing to support the entire spectrum of social changes sought by GLBT rights advocates, it should refuse all requests for corporate policy changes specifically directed toward GLBT employees. GLBT employees, like all other employees, can be adequately protected by corporate policies that promote treating all employees with dignity and respect.

Endnotes

1. GLBT advocates often proclaim that 10% of the population is homosexual. The 10% figure is based upon studies and publications by Dr. Alfred C. Kinsey. However, Dr. Kinsey's methodology was defective. He used data gathered from interviews with felons, including sex offenders; volunteers who were coached to give answers that skewed the results; and the sexual stimulation of boys ages 2 months to 15 years old. (Judith A. Reisman, *Kinsey: Crimes & Consequences,* The Institute for Media Education, Inc.: Arlington, Va., 1998; Wardell B. Pomeroy, *Dr. Kinsey and the Institute for Sex Research,* Harper & Row: New York, 1972, pp. 97–137.) In contrast, a 1993 report from the Alan Guttmacher Institute found that only 1.1% of 3,321 men surveyed considered themselves to be exclusively homosexual, and only 2.3% had engaged in sex with another man in the prior ten years. (John O.G. Billy, et al., *Family Planning Perspectives,* Alan Guttmacher Institute, March/April 1993.) *Sex in America: A Definitive Survey* reported that of 3,432 respondents, "about 1.4 percent of women said they thought of themselves as homosexual or bisexual and about 2.8% of the men identified themselves in this way." (Robert T. Michael, et al., Warner Books: New York, 1995, p. 176.) An article published in *Pediatrics* likewise reported that of 34,706 adolescents surveyed (grades 7-12), 1.1% said that they were bisexual or predominantly homosexual. (Gary Remafedi, et al., abstract, "Demography of Sexual Orientation in Adolescents," *Pediatrics,* Vol. 89, 1992, pp. 714–721.) No survey using random sampling techniques has duplicated Kinsey's results.

2. Human Rights Campaign (HRC), *Discrimination in the Workplace,* www.hrc .org/worknet/nd/index.asp.

3. *HRC, The State of the Workplace 2001,* pp. 18-19, www.hrc.org/worknet/ publica-tions/state_work-place/2001/sow2001.pdf.

4. For example, see the Web sites of the Human Rights Campaign at www .hrc.org/worknet/dp/index.asp, and the National Gay and Lesbian Task Force Web site at www.ngltf.org/downloads/dp/dp_99.pdf.

5. HRC Worknet, *Discrimination in the Workplace,* www.hrc.org/worknet/dp/ index.asp.

6. Marshall Kirk and Hunter Madsen, *After the Ball: How America Will Conquer its Fear & Hatred of Gays in the 90's,* Penguin Books: New York, 1990, paper-back edition, back cover.

7. Sally Kohn, *The Domestic Partnership Organizing Manual for employee bene-fits* ("Manual"), p. 26, The Policy Institute of the National Gay and Lesbian Task Force, 1999, www.ngltf.org/downloads/dp/dp_99.pdf.

8. *After the Ball,* back cover, paperback edition.

9. *ibid.,* p. 183. Many homosexuals objected to portraying homosexuals as victims (*Ibid,* pp. 185–86). Nevertheless, Kirk and Madsen argued that homosexuals "must deploy the special powers of the weak, including the play for sympathy and tolerance" (*ibid.*).

10. *Ibid.,* p. 183.

11. *Ibid.,* p. 154 (emphasis original).

12. *Ibid.*

13. *Ibid.,* p. 149.

14. *Ibid.,* pp. 153–54 (emphasis added).

15. Kirk and Madsen consider any opposition to GLBT relationships to be the result of fear or hatred (*ibid.,* p. xxv).

16. Ibid., p. 146 (emphasis original). The authors are critical of NAMBLA for interfering with efforts to portray gays as just like everyone else. However, while they hint that opposition to pederasty may be valid, they do not explicitly condemn the practice (*ibid.,* pp. 146–47).

17. *Ibid.,* pp. 186–87.

18. David Thorstad, "Man/Boy Love and the American Gay Movement," in "Male Intergenerational Intimacy: Historical, Socio-Psychological, and Legal Perspectives," *Journal of Homosexuality,* Vol. 20, Nos. 1/2, 1990, p. 255.

19. F. York & R. Knight, *Homosexual Activists Work to Lower the Age of Sexual Consent,* pp. 5–6, a Family Research Council publication.

20. Pat Califia, *Public Sex: The Culture of Radical Sex,* Cleis Press: San Francisco, 1994.

21. Book review of *Public Sex,* one of "Forty-two Things You Can Do to Make the Future Safe for Sex," www.amazon.com/exec/obidos/tg/stores/detail/ books/1573440965/reviews/102-69145823557749#15734409655101.

22. William N. Eskridge, Jr., *The Case for Same-Sex Marriage,* The Free Press: New York, 1996, p. 65.

23. *Ibid.,* p. 81 (emphasis added, footnotes omitted).

24. *Ibid.,* p. 61.

25. Michelangelo Signorile, "Bridal Wave," *Out,* December/January 1994, p. 161.

26. Lambda's Web site describes it as "a national organization committed to achieving full recognition of the civil rights of lesbians, gay men, and people with HIV/AIDS through impact litigation, education, and public policy work. Lambda carries out its legal work principally through test cases selected for the likelihood of their success in establishing positive legal precedents that will affect lesbians, gay men, and people with HIV/AIDS" (www.lambdalegal.org/cgi-bin/pages/about).

27. Thomas Stoddard, "Why Gay People Should Seek the Right to Marry," in *Lesbians, Gay Men & the Law,* W.B. Rubenstein, ed., The New Press: New York, 1993, p. 401.

28. Paula Ettelbrick, "Since When is Marriage a Path to Liberation?", Rubenstein, pp. 401–405.

29. *Ibid.*

30. Kees Waaldijk, "The 'Law of Small Change': How the Road to Same-Sex Marriage Got Paved in the Netherlands," a paper presented to the Conference on National, European, and International Law, King's College, University of London, July 1–3, 1999, pp. 3–4.

31. *Ibid.,* p. 5.

32. GLBT advocates often ridicule the notion of a "GLBT agenda." Yet, in *After the Ball,* the authors unabashedly refer to their "agenda for change" (*After the Ball,* pp. 106, 379).

33. *Manual,* p. 1. The *Manual,* published by the National Gay and Lesbian Task Force (NGLTF), is available on the NGLTF Web site at www.ngltf.org/downloads/dp/dp_99.pdf. NGLTF describes itself as an organization that is "building a powerful political movement" to effect social change (www.ngltf.org/about/work.htm).

34. *Ibid.*

35. *Ibid.,* p. 17.

36. *Ibid.,* p. 18.

37. For unions, which are already organized, sexual orientation policies are "The First Step" (Pride at Work, AFL-CIO, "Domestic Partner Benefits & Union Bargaining," www.prideatwork.org/tools.html).

38. *Manual,* p.18.

39. *Ibid.* The *Manual* explicitly refers to internal enforcement, but corporate sexual orientation policies are also enforced through litigation (Lambda Legal Defense & Ed. Fund, "Sexual Orientation Discrimination in Employment: A Guide to Remedies," p. 22, www.lambdalegal.org).

40. GLBT advocates argue that DP benefits are about "fair treatment of all employees . . . about fairness in the work place for everyone" (*Manual,* p. 1). However, if an employer provides domestic partner benefits, unmarried employees without dependants and without a domestic partner will continue to receive fewer benefits than married employees or employees with domestic partners who perform the same work for the same salary. Since such employees account for approximately one third of the work force–far more than domestic partners—it is questionable whether domestic partner benefits provide more "fairness in the workplace for everyone." In fact, "fairness" in insurance benefits simply means that a company

provides health insurance that enables an employee to provide and pay for health care for those to whom the employee has legal obligations. Domestic partners generally have no legal obligation to pay for their partners' health care. Moreover, domestic partnerships are neither legally nor socially equal to marriage, even in Vermont where civil unions are essentially the legal equivalent of marriage. Therefore, domestic partners are not situated similarly to married couples (Maggie Gallagher, *Why Supporting Marriage Makes Business Sense,* Corporate Resource Council 2002).

41. HRC WorkNet, *How to Achieve Domestic Partner Benefits in Your Workplace,* p. 2, www.hrc.org/worknet/dp/dptool.pdf.

42. *Ibid.,* p. 3 (emphasis added). The *Manual* asserts that "[i]ncreasingly, employers have realized that failing to provide equal benefits to employee's [sic] partners, regardless of sexual orientation, violates the nature of [sexual orientation] policies," (*Manual,* p. 9), and that "'[o]nce a company says no, we won't discriminate, then you have to say, my goodness, here we have some interesting discrimination in benefits. If they agree on the first point, then they absolutely have to look at the second'" (*ibid.,* p. 18, citation omitted). The irony of this line of argument is that in advocating sexual orientation policies, GLBT activists will assert that such a policy does "not require the company to offer equal benefits to partners of gay employees." Al Stamborski, "Guests add spice to Emerson's annual meeting," *The Post-Dispatch,* St. Louis, Mo., Feb. 7, 2001, p. 2.

43. *Manual,* p. 20.

44. In 1996 San Francisco passed an ordinance requiring all businesses that contract with the city to treat domestic partnerships the same as marriage for purposes of employee benefits. Other localities such as Seattle and Los Angeles have recently followed suit. As of October 2001, 3,087 of the 4,285 employers that provide domestic partner benefits are businesses who contract with these cities. HRC, *The State of the Workplace 2001,* p. 18, www.hrc.org/worknet/publi-cations/state_workplace/2001/sow2001.pdf.

45. HRC Press Release, "San Francisco's Pioneering Domestic Partner Benefits Law Upheld by Federal Appeals Court," June 15, 2001.

46. HRC, *The State of the Workplace 2001,* pp. 18–19.

47. "SOFT BENEFITS are lower cost, non-health benefits that may include, among other benefits: Bereavement and sick leave; Adoption assistance; Relocation benefits; Child resource and referral services; Access to employer recreational facilities; Participation in employee assistance programs; [and] Inclusion in employee discount policies" (*Manual,* p. 5). "HARD BENEFITS are generally insurance benefits that may include: Medical benefits; Dental and vision care; Dependent life insurance; Accidental death and dismemberment benefits; Tuition assistance; Long term care; Day care; [and] Flexible spending accounts" (*ibid.*). The AFL-CIO Manual describes soft benefits as "The Second Step," and hard benefits as "The Third Step" (AFL-CIO Manual, p. 2).

48. *Manual,* p. 6.

49. *Ibid.* In fact, GLBT advocates may ultimately demand more benefits than are generally given to heterosexuals and their spouses. Early in 2001 San Francisco decided to pay up to $50,000 each for sex-change operations for employees (*San Francisco To Pay for Sex Changes,* AP, 4/30/01). Avaya,

a spin-off company of Lucent Technologies, has provided such benefits for some time (Karyn-Siobhan Robinson, "Gender reassignment benefits set companies apart," *HR Magazine,* June 2001, p. 9). Kim Mills, education director of the Human Rights Campaign, sees gender reassignment benefits as "a logical extension of what we have been working for–which is equal treat ment and equal benefits in the workplace for all g/l/b/t Americans . . ." (*ibid.*, p. 11).

50. *Manual,* p. 11. "According to a 1997 study by the National Lesbian and Gay Journalists Association, extending health-care benefits to same-sex couples raised overall health insurance costs by less than 0.5 percent, while covering both same-sex and opposite-sex couples increasedcosts by 1 percent to 3 percent" (*How to,* pp. 9–10). However, these figures may not reflect the true cost of DP benefits (Michael Hamrick, *The Hidden Cost of Domestic Partner Benefits,* Forthcoming).

51. Gallagher, p. 9. GM offers the benefits only to same-sex partners.

52. *Manual,* p. 1 (emphasis added).

53. Nor is it clear that the subsequent steps are quite so well orchestrated as the procedure for obtaining DP benefits.

54. HRC WorkNet, "Gay, lesbian, bisexual, employee support groups and workplace diversity programs," p. 2, www.hrc.org/worknet/empgroup/emp_howto.asp.

55. Out & Equal, seminar on "Extending the Reach of ERG's," slide 16. GLBT advocates view events like Gay Pride marches as "important in helping move the [GLBT] community forward" (Tonia Holbrook, "March celebrates gains in gay rights: About 500 people mark Fairness group's 10 years," *The Courier-Journal,* Louisville, Ky., June 25, 2001, www.courierjournal.com/localnews/2001/06/ 25/ke062501s42429.htm).

56. Ford GLOBE Home Page, fordglobe.org; Ford Out & Equal advertisements.

57. *Lambda Update,* "Donor Profile: United Airlines," Summer 2000, p. 18.

58. The idea of silencing opposition to GLBT relationships is not new. In *After the Ball,* the authors define any opposition to GLBT relationships as bigotry or "homohatred" (*After the Ball,* p. xxv). Those who will not change their minds about opposing GLBT relationships are denominated "Intransigents" (*ibid.*, p. 176). The authors are explicit about their goal of silencing such opponents: "Our primary objective regarding diehard homohaters of this sort is to cow and *silence* them as far as possible, not to convert or even desensitize them" (*ibid.*, p. 176, emphasis original). The authors also stated their intent "to make the very expression of homohatred so discreditable that even Intransigents will eventually be silenced in public–much as rabid racists and anti-Semites are today" (*ibid.*, p. 189).

59. United Employment Policies, www.united.com/site/primary/0,10017,1404,00.html.

60. Out & Equal seminar on "Extending the Reach of ERG's," slides 16–17.

61. Eskridge states his belief that there can be no valid opposition to GLBT relationships—or same-sex marriage—as follows: "the nonsense frequently found in the objections examined in this book may suggest that arguments against same-sex marriage rest only on ignorance and antihomosexual hysteria. That is probably the case for many people. The only

strategy for persuading such persons is to urge them to work through their homophobia with a therapist" (*The Case for Same-Sex Marriage,* p. 183). Eskridge further states, without citation, that "medical professionals generally consider antihomosexual feelings mentally unhealthy" (*ibid.,* p. 185).

62. Katherine A. O'Hanlan, M.D., et al., *Homophobia As a Health Hazard,* Report of the Gay & Lesbian Medical Association, p. 3, www.ohanlan.com/phobiahzd.htm.

63. *Ibid.,* p. 3.

64. *After the Ball,* p. xxv.

65. Laura Dean, et al., "Lesbian, Gay, Bisexual, and Transgender Health: Findings & Concerns," *Journal of the Gay & Lesbian Medical Association,* Vol. 4, No. 3, p. 102 (2000) ("'Homophobic' and 'antigay' are terms commonly used in this document and elsewhere to describe *negative attitudes* toward lesbians and gay men") (emphasis added); National Lesbian and Gay Journalists Association *Stylebook Addenda* similarly defines homophobia as the "Fear, hatred or *dislike of homosexuality,* gay men and lesbians" (emphasis added).

66. On October 13, 1998, the San Francisco Board of Supervisors passed a resolution attacking an "advertisement campaign to encourage gays and lesbians to change their sexual orientation" as an "anti-gay campaign[]" that results "in violence and even death" (Resolution No. 873–98, City and County of San Francisco). Without citing any authority for any proposition in the resolution, the Board stated, "Advertising campaigns which insinuate sexual orientation can be changed by conversion therapy or other means are erroneous and full of lies; and . . . Advertising campaigns which insinuate a gay or lesbian orientation is immoral and undesirable create an atmosphere which val idates oppression of gays and lesbians and encourages maltreatment of gays and lesbians . . ." (*ibid.*). A similar perspective by an employer would prohibit any employee from expressing opposition to gay sex or GLBT relation ships.

67. The Safe Space® program is licensed to LEAGUE at AT&T by EQUAL at Lucent.

68. AT&T Safe Space® Program, www.league-att.org/safespace/index.html, p. 1.

69. *Ibid.,* p. 2 (emphasis added).

70. Xerox "Galaxe," www.galaxe.org/programs/safe_space/index.html.

71. Personal interview with former Xerox employee.

72. AT&T's Safe Space® Program, p. 1. The description goes on to say that diversity "is about recognizing, valuing and taking full advantage of the unique and individual contri butions that each person brings to the workplace" (*ibid.,* p. 1). However, the next paragraph, which states that "homo phobia and hostility will not be tolerated in the work place," makes clear that only diversity supportive of GLBT relationships is permissible.

73. Hewlett Packard January 12, 1999 letter, p.2.

74. *Ibid.,* p. 4.

75. *Ibid.,* p. 3 (emphasis added).

76. EEOC Affidavit, December 8, 2000. The employee did not inform Trilogy that his reference to "the lies of homo sexuality" expressed a religious belief.

77. The employee allegedly was not very proficient with the e-mail program and did not realize that he was sending the "cc."

78. *After the Ball*, pp. 176, 189, 381.

79. Many "straight" employees, who constitute the majority of the workforce, are offended when told that their corporation must adopt sexual orientation and DP benefit poli cies to attract or retain the "brightest and best" employees. In addition, some supervisors are reluctant to discipline the misconduct of GLBT employees because of fear that they will be accused of discrimination (personal interviews with employees from several Fortune 500 companies).

80. Personal interviews with former employees of American Airlines and Xerox.

81. Lawrence Morahan, "Domestic Partnerships Bill 'Would Hurt Families,'" *CNSNews.com*, April 17, 2001. GLBT advocates often criticize opponents for objecting to GLBT relationships on moral grounds. They claim that no one has the right to impose their morals on GLBT persons. Yet, GLBT advocates repeatedly refer to "fairness" or "the fair thing to do" as a reason for giving domestic partner bene fits. Arguments relying upon "fairness" are inherently based upon the moral beliefs of the proponent.

82. "Scottsdale plan a good one: Health care for domestic partners serves society," *Arizona Republic*, April 12, 2001.

83. See page 5 and endnotes 44–46 above.

POSTSCRIPT

Should Corporations Ensure Equal Rights for Their Lesbian, Gay, Bisexual, and Transgender Employees?

As with other social issues affecting the LGBT community—such as same-sex marriage and the military's "Don't Ask, Don't Tell" policy—ensuring equal rights to LGBT employees remains a controversial one.

Is there really a need for workplace nondiscrimination policies? Lavy posits that workplace protections against discrimination based on sexual orientation or gender identity are not needed as LGBT employees can be protected under general corporate policies which promote respect and dignity for all employees. What do you think about this? If legislation is not needed, should the Civil Rights Act of 1964 and the Americans with Disabilities Act—which grant protections from discrimination based on race, color, religion, sex, nation of origin, and disability—have been signed into law? Should they be repealed?

Are workplace nondiscrimination policies for LGBT employees part of a larger social agenda, as Lavy suggests? He contends that by offering equal rights to LGBT employees, corporations are signing on to support broader social changes sought by LGBT individuals, noting that equal rights for LGBT employees will inevitably lead to same-sex marriage. Do you agree that there is a connection between workplace equality and same-sex marriage? If so, should corporations be involved in such social issues, or other social issues, such as sustainable energy and fair trade? If there is not a connection, how are the issues of workplace equality and same-sex marriage different or distinct?

Lavy references the 1989 book *After the Ball: How America Will Conquer its Fear & Hatred of Gays in the 90's* to outline the social goals of the LGBT community, often referred to as the "gay agenda." He indicates that the gay agenda includes removing the age of sexual consent, revolutionizing the concepts of masculinity and femininity, and legalizing same-sex marriage in an attempt to "radically alter the archaic institution [of marriage]." Is it a realistic assumption that marginalized groups have an "agenda"—one clear set of goals they *all* hope to achieve? Might these goals and beliefs be held by some members of a community, but not necessarily representative of the entire community? One political cartoon embraces the feelings of many lesbian and gay individuals. It shows a person with a list marked "Gay Agenda," with only one entry : "1. Leave me alone."

Where should we draw the line between expressing religious views and nondiscrimination policies? Lavy criticizes corporations for reprimanding and in some cases terminating employees who expressed their religious opinions about the LGBT issues. Recalling that nondiscrimination policies protect employees of different religious views, do you think these employees were wrongfully reprimanded for merely expressing their religious beliefs, or were they in violation of company *harassment* policies, rather than *nondiscrimination* policies?

Who benefits from equal rights extended to LGBT employees? Hall outlines both the human rights and business benefits of offering equal rights to LGBT employees, include hiring and retaining key talent, and increasing LGBT employee productivity. While reports of the percentage of the workforce that is LGBT can range from 2 to 10 percent, equal rights for LGBT employees may have a broader reach than the LGBT population alone, impacting *all* employees. Many employees want to work for companies that represent their personal beliefs, and statistics show that many people believe workplace discrimination is inappropriate. A 2007 study found that 79 percent believe lesbian, gay, or bisexual employees should be judged by their work performance, not their sexual orientation, and 67 percent felt similarly about transgender employees (Out & Equal, 2007). Should corporations appeal to the incoming talent pool, which often values workplace diversity? What do you see as the advantages and/or disadvantages of offering equal rights to LGBT employees? Do they reach beyond LGBT specific employees?

Finally, are equal rights in the workplace an important issue for you? Would it be important that your company represent your personal beliefs? What other issues do you think need to be addressed in the workplace to ensure equality?

References

Out & Equal, "Significant Majority of All Adult Americans Believe It Is Unfair that Federal Law Allows Employers to Fire Someone Because They are Gay or Lesbian," Sixth Annual Out & Equal/Harris Interactive/Witeck-Combs Communications Survey Explores Workplace Attitudes toward GLBT People. Press Release. http://www.witeckcombs.com/news/releases/20070910_outequal.pdf

Suggested Readings

M.M. Clark, Religion vs. Sexual Orientation, *HR Magazine* (vol. 4, no. 6, 2004)

B. DiSarro, "Private Interest, Public Good, or Both? An Analysis of Fortune 500 Anti-Discrimination and Benefits Policies," paper presented at the annual meeting of the American Political Science Association, Marriott, Loews Philadelphia, and the Pennsylvania Convention Center, Philadelphia, PA, August 31, 2006, accessed at http://www.allacademic.com/meta/p153608_index.html (February 2, 2009).

M. Gunther, "Queer Inc," *CNN Money* (November 30, 2006).

Human Rights Campaign, The State of the Workplace for Lesbian, Gay, Bisexual and Transgender Americans: 2007–2008. A Human Rights Campaign Foundation Report, February 2009 (revised February 20, 2009).

Out & Equal, "Significant Majority of All Americans Believe It Is Unfair That Federal Law Allows Employers to Fire Someone Because They Are Gay or Lesbian" (2007).

Supporting a Diverse Workforce: What Type of Support Is Most Meaningful for Lesbian and Gay Employees? Human Resource Management (vol. 47, no. 2). Special Issue: Part One: Breaking Barriers for Purposes of Inclusiveness, published online, May 15, 2008.

L. Winfield, *Straight Talk about Gays in the Workplace* (Binghamton, NY: Haworth Press, 2005).

ISSUE 20

Should Same-Sex Marriage Be Legal?

YES: Human Rights Campaign, from *Answers to Questions about Marriage Equality* (Human Rights Campaign, 2009)

NO: John Cornyn, from "In Defense of Marriage," *National Review* (July 2009)

ISSUE SUMMARY

YES: The Human Rights Campaign (HRC), America's largest gay and lesbian organization, explains why same-sex couples should be afforded the same legal right to marry as heterosexual couples.

NO: John Cornyn, United States senator from Texas, says a constitutional amendment is needed to define marriage as permissible only between a man and a woman. Senator Cornyn contends that the traditional institution of marriage needs to be protected from activist courts that would seek to redefine it.

On May 17, 2004, Massachusetts became the first state in the United States to grant marriage licenses to same-sex couples. The state acted under the direction of its supreme court, which had found that withholding marriage licenses from lesbian and gay couples violated the state constitution. More than 600 same-sex couples applied for marriage licenses that first day alone. The first same-sex couple to be issued marriage licenses was Marcia Kadish and Tanya McClosky. That couple had waited over 18 years for the day to arrive. Since then, over 3,000 same-sex marriages have been performed in Massachusetts.

After the Massachusetts ruling, gay and lesbian couples across the country sought marriage licenses from their municipalities. Many were denied, while others found loopholes in laws that allowed them to file for licenses. In Oregon, for example, the law stated that marriage is a "civil contract entered into in person by males at least 17 years of age and females at least 17 years of age." Since the law did not state that males had to marry females, gay and lesbian marriages were never technically against the law. Marriage licenses were also issued in counties in California, New Jersey, New York, and Washington. In San Francisco, Mayor Gavin Newsom challenged state law and allowed city officials to wed same-sex couples. For the time being, the gay and lesbian marriages and marriage licenses in all states other than Massachusetts were ruled illegal and invalid.

The court ruling that paved the way for same-sex marriage in Massachusetts opened a firestorm of controversy. Supporters heralded the decision as a step toward equality for all Americans. Opponents of gay and lesbian nuptials spoke out against the redefinition and destruction of traditional marriage. President Bush endorsed a constitutional amendment that would define marriage as being between a man and a woman saying that "the sacred institution of marriage should not be redefined by a few activist judges."

Several years earlier, President Bill Clinton had signed the Defense of Marriage Act (DOMA), which said that states were not required to recognize same-sex marriages performed in other states. Nevertheless, supporters of the constitutional amendment believe DOMA is not enough to keep courts from redefining traditional marriage. Gay rights supporters oppose the amendment, which they feel unjustly writes discrimination into the Constitution. Even many conservatives oppose the amendment because they believe it to be too strong of a federal intrusion into the rights of states.

Since Massachusetts's landmark decision in 2004, six additional states have legalized same-sex marriage, including Connecticut, California, and Iowa. Vermont and Maine will begin issuing marriage licenses in the summer and fall of 2009, respectively. New Hampshire's law will take effect on January 1, 2010. At the time of this printing, the legislatures of two more states—New Jersey and New York—are considering legalizing same-sex marriage. California's legalization of same-sex marriage, however, was short-lived. After voters narrowly approved Proposition 8, the state's constitution was amended and gay marriage was once again banned, leaving those couples who had been married in limbo. Opponents of Proposition 8 appealed to California's Supreme Court, but the voters' decision was upheld. Interestingly, the justices also ruled that the same-sex marriages already performed were to remain valid, leaving 18,000 couples legally wed, despite the ban.

In the following essays, the Human Rights Campaign (HRC) answers common questions about same-sex marriage and the law, religion, and family. HRC also reviews the benefits that same-sex marriages could potentially have for gay and lesbian couples and society. Senator John Cornyn argues that the traditional definition of marriage is threatened by activist judges who seek to redefine the most fundamental union the world has ever known. Cornyn states that protecting marriage is about ensuring that relationships consisting of husband and wife will remain the "gold standard" for raising children.

Answers to Questions about Marriage Equality

10 Facts

1. Same-sex couples live in 99.3 percent of all counties nationwide.
2. There are an estimated 3.1 million people living together in same-sex relationships in the United States.
3. Fifteen percent of these same-sex couples live in rural settings.
4. One out of three lesbian couples is raising children. One out of five gay male couples is raising children.
5. Between 1 million and 9 million children are being raised by gay, lesbian and bisexual parents in the United States today.
6. At least one same-sex couple is raising children in 96 percent of all counties nationwide.
7. The highest percentages of same-sex couples raising children live in the South.
8. Nearly one in four same-sex couples includes a partner 55 years old or older, and nearly one in five same-sex couples is composed of two people 55 or older.
9. More than one in 10 same-sex couples include a partner 65 years old or older, and nearly one in 10 same-sex couples is composed of two people 65 or older.
10. The states with the highest numbers of same-sex senior couples are also the most popular for heterosexual senior couples: California, New York and Florida.

Why Same-Sex Couples Want to Marry

Many same-sex couples want the right to legally marry because they are in love—either they just met the love of their lives, or more likely, they have spent the last 10, 20 or 50 years with that person—and they want to honor their relationship in the greatest way our society has to offer, by making a

---

These facts are based on analyses of the 2000 Census conducted by the Urban Institute and the Human Rights Campaign. The estimated number of people in same-sex relationships has been adjusted by 62 percent to compensate for the widely-reported undercount in the Census. . . .

From *Human Rights Campaign Report*, 2009, pp. i, 1–17. Copyright © 2009 by Human Rights Campaign Foundation. Reprinted by permission.

public commitment to stand together in good times and bad, through all the joys and challenges family life brings.

Many parents want the right to marry because they know it offers children a vital safety net and guarantees protections that unmarried parents cannot provide.

And still other people—both gay and straight—are fighting for the right of same-sex couples to marry because they recognize that it is simply not fair to deny some families the protections all other families are eligible to enjoy.

Currently in the United States, same-sex couples in long-term, committed relationships pay higher taxes and are denied basic protections and rights granted to married heterosexual couples. Among them:

- **Hospital visitation.** Married couples have the automatic right to visit each other in the hospital and make medical decisions. Same-sex couples can be denied the right to visit a sick or injured loved one in the hospital.
- **Social Security benefits.** Married people receive Social Security payments upon the death of a spouse. Despite paying payroll taxes, gay and lesbian partners receive no Social Security survivor benefits—resulting in an average annual income loss of $5,528 upon the death of a partner.
- **Immigration.** Americans in binational relationships are not permitted to petition for their same-sex partners to immigrate. As a result, they are often forced to separate or move to another country.
- **Health insurance.** Many public and private employers provide medical coverage to the spouses of their employees, but most employers do not provide coverage to the life partners of gay and lesbian employees. Gay employees who do receive health coverage for their partners must pay federal income taxes on the value of the insurance.
- **Estate taxes.** A married person automatically inherits all the property of his or her deceased spouse without paying estate taxes. A gay or lesbian taxpayer is forced to pay estate taxes on property inherited from a deceased partner.
- **Retirement savings.** While a married person can roll a deceased spouse's 401(k) funds into an IRA without paying taxes, a gay or lesbian American who inherits a 401(k) can end up paying up to 70 percent of it in taxes and penalties.
- **Family leave.** Married workers are legally entitled to unpaid leave from their jobs to care for an ill spouse. Gay and lesbian workers are not entitled to family leave to care for their partners.
- **Nursing homes.** Married couples have a legal right to live together in nursing homes. Because they are not legal spouses, elderly gay or lesbian couples do not have the right to spend their last days living together in nursing homes.
- **Home protection.** Laws protect married seniors from being forced to sell their homes to pay high nursing home bills; gay and lesbian seniors have no such protection.
- **Pensions.** After the death of a worker, most pension plans pay survivor benefits only to a legal spouse of the participant. Gay and lesbian partners are excluded from such pension benefits.

Why Civil Unions Aren't Enough

Comparing marriage to civil unions is a bit like comparing diamonds to rhinestones. One is, quite simply, the real deal; the other is not. Consider:

- Couples eligible to marry may have their marriage performed in any state and have it recognized in every other state in the nation and every country in the world.
- Couples who are joined in a civil union in Vermont (the only state that offers civil unions) have no guarantee that its protections will even travel with them to neighboring New York or New Hampshire—let alone California or any other state.

Moreover, even couples who have a civil union and remain in Vermont receive only second-class protections in comparison to their married friends and neighbors. While they receive state-level protections, they do not receive any of the *more than 1,100 federal benefits and protections of marriage.*

In short, civil unions are not separate but equal—they are separate and unequal. And our society has tried separate before. It just doesn't work.

Marriage:	Civil unions:
• State grants marriage licenses to couples.	• State would grant civil union licenses to couples.
• Couples receive legal protections and rights under state and federal law.	• Couples receive legal protections and rights under state law only.
• Couples are recognized as being married by the federal government and all state governments.	• Civil unions are not recognized by other states or the federal government.
• Religious institutions are not required to perform marriage ceremonies.	• Religious institutions are not required to perform civil union ceremonies.

"I Believe God Meant Marriage for Men and Women. How Can I Support Marriage for Same-Sex Couples?"

Many people who believe in God—and fairness and justice for all—ask this question. They feel a tension between religious beliefs and democratic values that has been experienced in many different ways throughout our nation's history. That is why the framers of our Constitution established the principle of separation of church and state. That principle applies no less to the marriage issue than it does to any other.

Indeed, the answer to the apparent dilemma between religious beliefs and support for equal protections for all families lies in recognizing that marriage has a significant religious meaning for many people, but that it is also a legal contract. And it is strictly the legal—not the religious—dimension of marriage that is being debated now.

Granting marriage rights to same-sex couples would *not* require Christianity, Judaism, Islam or any other religion to perform these marriages. It would not require religious institutions to permit these ceremonies to be held on their grounds. It would not even require that religious communities discuss the issue. People of faith would remain free to make their own judgments about what makes a marriage in the eyes of God—just as they are today.

Consider, for example, the difference in how the Catholic Church and the U.S. government view couples who have divorced and remarried. Because church tenets do not sanction divorce, the second marriage is not valid in the church's view. The government, however, recognizes the marriage by extending to the remarried couple the same rights and protections as those granted to every other married couple in America. In this situation—as would be the case in marriage for same-sex couples—the church remains free to establish its own teachings on the religious dimension of marriage while the government upholds equality under law.

It should also be noted that there are a growing number of religious communities that have decided to bless same-sex unions. Among them are Reform Judaism, the Unitarian Universalist Association and the Metropolitan Community Church. The Presbyterian Church (USA) also allows ceremonies to be performed, although they are not considered the same as marriage. The Episcopal Church and United Church of Christ allow individual churches to set their own policies on same-sex unions.

"This Is Different from Interracial Marriage. Sexual Orientation Is a Choice."

"We cannot keep turning our backs on gay and lesbian Americans. I have fought too hard and too long against discrimination based on race and color not to stand up against discrimination based on sexual orientation. I've heard the reasons for opposing civil marriage for same-sex couples. Cut through the distractions, and they stink of the same fear, hatred, and intolerance I have known in racism and in bigotry."

— Rep. John Lewis, D-Ga., a leader of the black civil rights movement, writing in *The Boston Globe,* Nov. 25, 2003

Decades of research all point to the fact that sexual orientation is not a choice, and that a person's sexual orientation cannot be changed. Who one is drawn to is a fundamental aspect of who we are.

In this way, the struggle for marriage equality for same-sex couples is just as basic as the fight for interracial marriage was. It recognizes that Americans should not be coerced into false and unhappy marriages but should be free to marry the person they love—thereby building marriage on a true and stable foundation.

"Won't This Create a Free-for-All and Make the Whole Idea of Marriage Meaningless?"

Many people share this concern because opponents of gay and lesbian people have used this argument as a scare tactic. But it is not true. Granting same-sex couples the right to marry would in no way change the number of people who could enter into a marriage (or eliminate restrictions on the age or familial relationships of those who may marry). Marriage would continue to recognize the highest possible commitment that can be made between two adults, plain and simple.

Organizations That Support Same-Sex Parenting

American Academy of Pediatrics
American Academy of Family Physicians
Child Welfare League of America
National Association of Social Workers
North American Council on Adoptable Children
American Bar Association
American Psychological Association
American Psychiatric Association
American Psychoanalytic Association

"I Strongly Believe Children Need a Mother and a Father."

Many of us grew up believing that everyone needs a mother and father, regardless of whether we ourselves happened to have two parents, or two *good* parents.

But as families have grown more diverse in recent decades, and researchers have studied how these different family relationships affect children, it has become clear that the *quality* of a family's relationship is more important than the particular *structure* of families that exist today. In other words, the qualities that help children grow into good and responsible adults—learning how to learn, to have compassion for others, to contribute to society and be respectful of others and their differences—do not depend on the sexual orientation of their parents but on their parents' ability to provide a loving, stable and happy home, something no class of Americans has an exclusive hold on.

That is why research studies have consistently shown that children raised by gay and lesbian parents do just as well on all conventional measures of child development, such as academic achievement, psychological well-being and social abilities, as children raised by heterosexual parents.

That is also why the nation's leading child welfare organizations, including the American Academy of Pediatrics, the American Academy of Family Physicians and others, have issued statements that dismiss assertions that only heterosexual couples can be good parents—and declare that the focus should now be on providing greater protections for the 1 million to 9 million children being raised by gay and lesbian parents in the United States today.

"What Would Be Wrong with a Constitutional Amendment to Define Marriage as a Union of a Man and Woman?"

In more than 200 years of American history, the U.S. Constitution has been amended only 17 times since the Bill of Rights—and in each instance (except for Prohibition, which was repealed), it was to extend rights and liberties to the American people, not restrict them. For example, our Constitution was amended to end our nation's tragic history of slavery. It was also amended to guarantee people of color, young people and women the right to vote.

The amendment currently under consideration (called the Federal Marriage Amendment) would be the only one that would single out one class of Americans for discrimination by ensuring that same-sex couples would not be granted the equal protections that marriage brings to American families.

Moreover, the amendment could go even further by stripping same-sex couples of some of the more limited protections they now have, such as access to health insurance for domestic partners and their children.

Neither enshrining discrimination in our Constitution nor stripping millions of families of basic protections would serve our nation's best interest. The Constitution is supposed to protect and ensure equal treatment for *all* people. It should not be used to single out a group of people for different treatment.

TEXT OF PROPOSED FEDERAL MARRIAGE AMENDMENT

"Marriage in the United States shall consist only of the union of a man and a woman.

Neither this [C]onstitution [n]or the constitution of any state, nor state or federal law, shall be construed to require that marital status or the legal incidents thereof be conferred upon unmarried couples or groups."

— H.J. Resolution 56, introduced by Rep. Marilyn Musgrave, R-Colo., in May 2003. It has more than 100 co-sponsors. A similar bill was introduced in the U.S. Senate in November 2003. In February 2004, President Bush said that he would support a constitutional amendment to define marriage as between only a man and a woman.

"How Could Marriage for Same-Sex Couples Possibly Be Good for the American Family—or Our Country?"

"We shouldn't just allow gay marriage. We should insist on gay marriage. We should regard it as scandalous that two people could claim to love each other and not want to sanctify their love with marriage and fidelity."

— Conservative Columnist David Brooks, writing in
The New York Times, Nov. 22, 2003.

The prospect of a significant change in our laws and customs has often caused people to worry more about dire consequences that could result than about the potential positive outcomes. In fact, precisely the same anxiety arose when some people fought to overturn the laws prohibiting marriage between people of different races in the 1950s and 1960s. (One Virginia judge even declared that "God intended to separate the races.")

But in reality, opening marriage to couples who are so willing to fight for it could only strengthen the institution for all. It would open the doors to more supporters, not opponents. And it would help keep the age-old institution alive.

As history has repeatedly proven, institutions that fail to take account of the changing needs of the population are those that grow weak; those that recognize and accommodate changing needs grow strong. For example, the U.S. military, like American colleges and universities, grew stronger after permitting African Americans and women to join its ranks.

Similarly, granting same-sex couples the right to marry would strengthen the institution of marriage by allowing it to better meet the needs of the true diversity of family structures in America today.

"Can't Same-Sex Couples Go to a Lawyer to Secure All the Rights They Need?"

Not by a long shot. When a gay or lesbian person gets seriously ill, there is no legal document that can make their partner eligible to take leave from work under the federal Family and Medical Leave Act to provide care—because that law applies only to married couples.

When gay or lesbian people grow old and in need of nursing home care, there is no legal document that can give them the right to Medicaid coverage without potentially causing their partner to be forced from their home—because the federal Medicaid law only permits married spouses to keep their home without becoming ineligible for benefits.

And when a gay or lesbian person dies, there is no legal document that can extend Social Security survivor benefits or the right to inherit a retirement plan without severe tax burdens that stem from being "unmarried" in the eyes of the law.

These are only a few examples of the critical protections that are granted through more than 1,100 federal laws that protect only married couples. In the absence of the right to marry, same-sex couples can only put in place a handful of the most basic arrangements, such as naming each other in a will or a power of attorney. And even these documents remain vulnerable to challenges in court by disgruntled family members.

"Won't This Cost Taxpayers Too Much Money?"

No, it wouldn't necessarily cost much at all. In fact, treating same-sex couples as families under law could even save taxpayers money because marriage would require them to assume legal responsibility for their joint living expenses and reduce their dependence on public assistance programs, such as Medicaid, Temporary Assistance to Needy Families, Supplemental Security Income disability payments and food stamps.

Put another way, the money it would cost to extend benefits to same-sex couples could be outweighed by the money that would be saved as these families rely more fully on each other instead of state or federal government assistance.

For example, two studies conducted in 2003 by professors at the University of Massachusetts, Amherst, and the University of California, Los Angeles, found that extending domestic partner benefits to same-sex couples in California and New Jersey would save taxpayers millions of dollars a year.

Specifically, the studies projected that the California state budget would save an estimated $8.1 million to $10.6 million each year by enacting the most comprehensive domestic partner law in the nation. In New Jersey, which passed a new domestic partner law in 2004, the savings were projected to be even higher—more than $61 million each year.

(Sources: "Equal Rights, Fiscal Responsibility: The Impact of A.B. 205 on California's Budget," by M. V. Lee Badgett, Ph.D., IGLSS, Department of Economics, University of Massachusetts, and R. Bradley Sears, J.D., Williams Project, UCLA School of Law, University of California, Los Angeles, May 2003, and "Supporting Families, Saving Funds: A Fiscal Analysis of New Jersey's Domestic Partnership Act," by Badgett and Sears with Suzanne Goldberg, J.D., Rutgers School of Law-Newark, December 2003.)

"Where Can Same-Sex Couples Marry Today?"

In 2001, the Netherlands became the first country to extend marriage rights to same-sex couples. Belgium passed a similar law two years later. The laws in both of these countries, however, have strict citizenship or residency requirements that do not permit American couples to take advantage of the protections provided.

In June 2003, Ontario became the first Canadian province to grant marriage to same-sex couples, and in July 2003, British Columbia followed suit—becoming the first places that American same-sex couples could go to get married.

In November 2003, the Massachusetts Supreme Judicial Court recognized the right of same-sex couples to marry—giving the state six months to begin issuing marriage licenses to same-sex couples. It began issuing licenses May 17, 2004.

In February 2004, the city of San Francisco began issuing marriage licenses to same-sex couples after the mayor declared that the state constitution forbade him to discriminate. The issue is being addressed by California courts, and a number of other cities have either taken or are considering taking steps in the same direction.

Follow the latest developments in California, Oregon, New Jersey, New Mexico, New York and in other communities across the country on the HRC Marriage Center. . . .

Other nations have also taken steps toward extending equal protections to all couples, though the protections they provide are more limited than marriage. Canada, Denmark, Finland, France, Germany, Iceland, Norway, Portugal and Sweden all have nationwide laws that grant same-sex partners a range of important rights, protections and obligations.

For example, in France, registered same-sex (and opposite-sex) couples can be joined in a civil "solidarity pact" that grants them the right to file joint tax returns, extend social security coverage to each other and receive the same health, employment and welfare benefits as legal spouses. It also commits the couple to assume responsibility for household debts.

Other countries, including Switzerland, Scotland and the Czech Republic, also have considered legislation that would legally recognize same-sex unions.

"What Protections Other Than Marriage Are Available to Same-Sex Couples?"

At the federal level, there are no protections at all available to same-sex couples. In fact, a federal law called the "Defense of Marriage Act" says that the federal government will discriminate against same-sex couples who marry by refusing to recognize their marriages or providing them with the federal protections of marriage. Some members of Congress are trying to go even further by attempting to pass a Federal Marriage Amendment that would write discrimination against same-sex couples into the U.S. Constitution.

At the state level, only Vermont offers civil unions, which provide important state benefits but no federal protections, such as Social Security survivor benefits. There is also no guarantee that civil unions will be recognized outside Vermont. Thirty-nine states also have "defense of marriage" laws explicitly prohibiting the recognition of marriages between same-sex partners.

Domestic partner laws have been enacted in California, Connecticut, New Jersey, Hawaii and the District of Columbia. The benefits conferred by these laws vary; some offer access to family health insurance, others confer co-parenting rights. These benefits are limited to residents of the state. A family that moves out of these states immediately loses the protections.

10 Things You Can Do

Every Family Deserves Equal Protections.
How Can I Help?

1. Urge your members of Congress to oppose the Federal Marriage Amendment, or any constitutional amendment to ban marriage for same-sex couples. Make a personal visit if you can. HRC's field team can help you. Or fax a message through HRC's Action Network. . . .
2. Sign the Million for Marriage petition . . . and ask 10 friends and family to do the same.

3. Talk to your friends and family members about the importance of marriage for same-sex couples and their children. Recent polls of the GLBT community show that many people have not yet talked to parents, siblings or other family members about the discrimination they face. Nothing moves the hearts and minds of potential straight allies more than hearing the stories of someone they know who is gay, lesbian, bisexual or transgender. For more information, download "Talking about Marriage Equality" from HRC's Online Action Center.
4. Write a letter to the editor of your local newspaper saying why you support marriage for same-sex couples and why a constitutional amendment against it is a bad idea.
5. Next time you hear someone say marriage is only meant for heterosexual couples, speak up. If you hear this on a radio program, call in. If you hear it on television, call or send an e-mail. If it comes up in conversation, set the record straight.
6. Host a house party to educate your friends and family about marriage equality. Invite a diverse group and inspire them to write letters to Congress and your state government at your house party. . . .
7. Meet with clergy and other opinion leaders in your community and ask them to join you in speaking out in support of marriage equality and against the Federal Marriage Amendment. Let HRC know the results. . . .
8. Share your story about why marriage equality matters to you and send it to HRC's family project. . . . Personal stories are what move hearts and minds.
9. Become a member of HRC and support our work on behalf of marriage equality. . . .
10. Register to vote and support fair-minded candidates. . . .

Additional National Resources

Human Rights Campaign . . .

HRC is the nation's largest national organization working to advance equality based on sexual orientation and gender expression and identity to ensure that gay, lesbian, bisexual and transgender Americans can be open, honest and safe at home, at work and in their communities. Of particular interest to people following the marriage issue:

The Human Rights Campaign Foundation's FamilyNet

Project . . . offers the most comprehensive resources about GLBT families, covering marriage, parenting, aging and more. HRC's Action Center . . ., offers important updates about what's happening in legislatures nationwide and the latest online grassroots advocacy tools.

Other important resources include:

American Civil Liberties Union . . .

ACLU works in courts, legislatures and communities throughout the country to defend and preserve the individual rights and liberties guaranteed by the Constitution and laws of the United States.

Freedom to Marry Collaborative . . .

A gay and non-gay partnership working to win marriage equality.

Children of Lesbians and Gays Everywhere (COLAGE) . . .

Fosters the growth of daughters and sons of GLBT parents by providing education, support and community, advocating for their rights and rights of their families.

Dignity USA . . .

Works for respect and justice for all GLBT persons in the Catholic Church and the world through education, advocacy and support.

Family Pride Coalition . . .

A national education and civil rights organization that advances the well-being of GLBT parents and their families through mutual support, community collaboration and public understanding.

Federation of Statewide LGBT Advocacy Organizations . . .

The GLBT advocacy network of state/territory organizations committed to working with each other and with national and local groups to strengthen statewide advocacy organizing and secure full civil rights in every U.S. state and territory.

Gay & Lesbian Advocates & Defenders . . .

The GLBT legal organization that successfully brought the case that led to the civil union law in Vermont and the recognition of marriage equality in Massachusetts.

Gay & Lesbian Victory Fund . . .

Committed to increasing the number of openly gay and lesbian public officials at federal, state and local levels of government.

Lambda Legal . . .

A national legal group committed to achieving full recognition of the civil rights of, and combating the discrimination against, the GLBT community and people with HIV/AIDS, through impact litigation, education and public policy work.

Log Cabin Republicans . . .

Operates within the Republican Party for the equal rights of all Americans, including gay men and women, according to the principles of limited government, individual liberty, individual responsibility, free markets and a strong national defense.

Marriage Equality USA . . .

Works to secure the freedom and the right of same-sex couples to engage in civil marriage through a program of education, media campaigns and community partnerships.

National Center for Lesbian Rights . . .

A national legal resource center devoted to advancing the rights and safety of lesbians and their families through a program of litigation, public policy advocacy, free legal advice and counseling and public education.

National Black Justice Coalition . . .

An ad hoc coalition of black GLBT leaders who have come together to fight against discrimination in our communities, to build black support for marriage equality and to educate the community on the dangers of the proposal to amend the U.S. Constitution to discriminate against GLBT people.

National Gay & Lesbian Task Force . . .

Dedicated to building a national civil rights movement of GLBT people through the empowerment and training of state and local leaders, and research and development of national policy.

National Latina/o Lesbian, Gay, Bisexual & Transgender Organization (LLEGÓ) . . .

Develops solutions to social, health and political disparities that exist due to discrimination based on ethnicity, sexual orientation and gender identity affecting the lives and well-being of Latina/o GLBT people and their families.

Parents, Families & Friends of Lesbians & Gays (PFLAG) . . .

Promotes the health and well-being of GLBT people, their families and friends, through support, education and advocacy with the intention of ending discrimination and securing equal civil rights.

Soulforce . . .

An interfaith movement committed to ending spiritual violence perpetuated by religious policies and teachings against GLBT people through the application of the principles of non-violence.

Universal Fellowship of Metropolitan Community Churches . . .

A worldwide fellowship of Christian churches with a special outreach to the world's GLBT communities.

John Cornyn  **NO**

In Defense of Marriage: The Amendment That Will Protect a Fundamental Institution

In 1996, three fourths of the House and Senate joined President Bill Clinton in a strong bipartisan effort to defend the traditional institution of marriage, by enacting the federal Defense of Marriage Act (DOMA). That act defined, as a matter of federal law, the institution of marriage as the union of one man and one woman—reflecting the views of the vast majority of Americans across the country. Today, as it debates a constitutional amendment to defend marriage, the Senate will revisit precisely the same question: Should the institution of marriage continue to be defined as the union of one man and one woman—as it has been defined for thousands of years?

Since the 1996 vote, two things have changed. First, activist courts have so dramatically altered the meaning of the Constitution, that traditional marriage laws are now under serious threat of being invalidated by judicial fiat nationwide—indeed, the process has already begun in numerous states across the country. Second, the broad bipartisan consensus behind marriage that was exhibited in 1996 has begun to fracture. Some who supported DOMA just a few years ago are, for partisan reasons, unwilling to defend marriage today. Although the defense of marriage should continue to be a bipartisan endeavor—and kept out of the hands of activist lawyers and judges—there is no question that both the legal and the political landscapes have changed dramatically in recent years.

Commitment to Marriage

One thing has never changed, however: Throughout our nation's history, across diverse cultures, communities, and political affiliations, Americans of all stripes have remained committed to the traditional institution of marriage. Most Americans strongly and instinctively support the following two fundamental propositions: Every human being is worthy of respect, and the traditional institution of marriage is worthy of protection. In communities across America, adults form caring relationships of all kinds, while children are raised through the heroic efforts of parents of all kinds—including single parents,

From *The National Review*, July 2004. Copyright © 2004 by Senator John Cornyn. Reprinted by permission of the author.

foster parents, and adoptive parents. We admire, honor, and respect those relationships and those efforts.

At the same time, most Americans believe that children are best raised by their mother and father. Mankind has known no stronger human bond than that between a child and the two adults who have brought that child into the world together. For that reason, family and marriage experts have referred to the traditional institution of marriage as the "gold standard" for raising children. Social science simply confirms common sense. Social science also confirms that, when society stops privileging the traditional institution of marriage (as we have witnessed in a few European nations in recent years), the gold standard is diluted, and the ideal for raising children is threatened.

There are a number of important issues facing our nation—and the raising and nurturing of our next generation is one of them. Nearly 120 years ago, in the case of *Murphy v. Ramsey*, the U.S. Supreme Court unanimously concluded that "no legislation can be supposed more wholesome and necessary in the founding of a free, self-governing commonwealth" than "the idea of the family, as consisting in and springing from *the union for life of one man and one woman in the holy estate of matrimony*" (emphasis added). That union is "the sure foundation of all that is stable and noble in our civilization; the best guaranty of that reverent morality which is the source of all beneficent progress in social and political improvement." Moreover, that same Court unanimously praised efforts to shield the traditional institution of marriage from the winds of political change, by upholding a law "which endeavors to withdraw all political influence from those who are practically hostile to its attainment."

False Arguments

Today, however, the consensus behind marriage appears to be unraveling. Of course, those who no longer support traditional marriage laws do not say so outright. Instead, they resort to legalistic and procedural arguments for opposing a marriage amendment. They hope to confuse the issue in the minds of well-meaning Americans and to distract them from the importance of defending marriage, by unleashing a barrage of false arguments.

For example:

- *Why do we need a federal constitutional amendment, when we already have DOMA?*

The need for a federal constitutional amendment is simple: The traditional institution of marriage is under constitutional attack. It is now a national problem that requires a national solution. Legal experts and constitutional scholars across the political spectrum recognize and predict that the *only way* to preserve the status quo—the *only way* to preserve the traditional institution of marriage—is a constitutional amendment.

Immediately after the U.S. Supreme Court announced its decision in *Lawrence* v. *Texas* in June 2003, legal experts and commentators predicted that, under *Lawrence,* courts would begin to strike down traditional marriage laws around the country.

In *Lawrence,* the Court explicitly and unequivocally listed "marriage" as one of the "constitutional" rights that, absent a constitutional amendment, must be granted to same-sex couples and opposite-sex couples alike. Specifically, the Court stated that "our laws and tradition afford constitutional protection to personal decisions relating to *marriage,* procreation, contraception, family relationships, child rearing, and education. . . . Persons in a homosexual relationship may seek autonomy for these purposes, just as heterosexual persons do" (emphasis added). The *Lawrence* majority thus adopted the view endorsed decades ago by one of its members—Justice Ruth Bader Ginsburg. While serving as general counsel of the American Civil Liberties Union, she wrote that traditional marriage laws, such as anti-bigamy laws, are unconstitutional and must be struck down by courts.

It does not take a Supreme Court expert to understand the meaning of these words. And Supreme Court experts agree in any event. Legal scholars are a notoriously argumentative bunch. So it is particularly remarkable that the nation's most recognized constitutional experts—including several liberal legal scholars, like Laurence Tribe, Cass Sunstein, Erwin Chemerinsky, and William Eskridge—are in remarkable harmony on this issue. They predict that, like it or not, DOMA or other traditional marriage laws across the country will be struck down as unconstitutional by courts across the country.

Indeed, the process of invalidating and eradicating traditional marriage laws nationwide has already begun. Most notably, four justices of the Massachusetts Supreme Judicial Court invalidated that state's marriage law in its *Goodridge* decision issued last November, which it reaffirmed in February.

Those decisions were breathtaking, not just in their ultimate conclusion, but in their rhetoric as well. The court concluded that the "deep-seated religious, moral, and ethical convictions" that underlie traditional marriage are "no rational reason" for the institution's continued existence. It argued that traditional marriage is a "stain" on our laws that must be "eradicated." It contended that traditional marriage is "rooted in persistent prejudices" and "invidious discrimination," rather than in the best interest of children. Amazingly, it even suggested abolishing the institution of marriage outright, stating that "if the Legislature were to jettison the term 'marriage' altogether, it might well be rational and permissible." And for good measure, the court went out of its way to characterize DOMA itself as unconstitutionally discriminatory.

Without a federal constitutional amendment, activist courts, and judges will only continue striking down traditional marriage laws across the country—including DOMA itself. Lawsuits challenging traditional marriage laws are now pending in courtrooms across America—including four lawsuits in federal court.

In 2000, Nebraska voters ratified a state constitutional amendment protecting marriage in that state. Yet that state constitutional amendment has been challenged in federal district court as violating federal constitutional law. As Nebraska's attorney general, Jon Bruning, testified last March, the state expects the federal district judge to strike down its constitutional amendment. A federal lawsuit has also been filed in Florida to strike down DOMA as unconstitutional under *Lawrence*. Lawyers are similarly claiming that DOMA is unconstitutional in a pending federal bankruptcy case in Washington state. And in Utah, lawyers have filed suit arguing that traditional marriage laws, such as that state's anti-polygamy law, must be struck down under *Lawrence*. And that just covers lawsuits in federal court—in addition, dozens of suits have been filed in state courts around the country.

A representative of the Lambda Legal organization—a champion of the ongoing nationwide litigation campaign to abolish traditional marriage laws across the country—recently stated: "We won't stop until we have [same-sex] marriage nationwide." This nationwide litigation campaign also enjoys the tacit, if not explicit, support of leading Democrats—including Sens. John Kerry and Ted Kennedy, Rep. Jerrold Nadler, and former presidential candidates Howard Dean and Carol Moseley Braun. All of them have attacked DOMA as unconstitutional, and thus presumably *want* DOMA to be invalidated by the courts—and without a constitutional amendment, their wishes may very well come true. The only way to stop the lawsuits, and to ensure the protection of marriage, is a constitutional amendment.

- *Why do we need an amendment now?*

Last September, the Senate subcommittee on the Constitution, Civil Rights and Property Rights examined the threat posed to the traditional institution of marriage by the *Lawrence* decision.

Detractors of the hearing scoffed that the threat was a pure fabrication, motivated by partisan politics. But then, just two months later, the Massachusetts *Goodridge* decision, relying specifically on *Lawrence,* struck down that state's traditional marriage law—precisely as predicted at the hearing.

Detractors then scoffed that the *Goodridge* decision would not stick. They argued that the state's own constitutional amendment process would be sufficient to control their courts. But then, the Massachusetts court reaffirmed its decision in February. The court even refused to bend after the Massachusetts legislature formally approved a state constitutional amendment—an amendment that can only take effect, if ever, no earlier than 2006.

Detractors then scoffed that DOMA had not been challenged, so there was no reason to take constitutional action at the federal level. But then, lawyers began to challenge DOMA. Cases are now pending in federal courts in Florida and Washington. Additional challenges are, of course, inevitable.

The truth is that, for these detractors, there will never be a good time to protect the traditional institution of marriage—because they don't want to protect the traditional institution of marriage. The constitutional amendment to protect marriage is not a "preemptive strike" on the Constitution, as detractors allege—it's a precautionary solution. Parents take responsible precautions to protect their children. Spouses take responsible precautions to protect their marriage. Likewise, government has the responsibility to take precautions to protect the institution of marriage.

- *Why can't the states handle this? After all, isn't marriage traditionally a state issue?*

This argument borders on the fraudulent. There is nothing that a state can do to fully protect itself against federal courts hostile to its laws except a federal constitutional amendment. Nebraska has already done everything it can, on its own, to defend marriage—up to and including a state constitutional amendment. Yet its amendment has already been challenged in federal court, where it is expected to be struck down. As state and local officials across the country have repeatedly urged, when it comes to defending marriage, the real threat to states' rights is judicial activism—not Congress, and certainly not the democratic process.

Moreover, the Constitution cannot be amended without the consent of three-fourths of the state legislatures. States can protect marriage against judicial activism—but only if Congress provides them the opportunity to consider a federal constitutional amendment protecting marriage.

- *Isn't our Constitution too sacred for such a political issue as defending marriage?*

No one is suggesting that the Constitution should be amended lightly. But the defense of marriage should not be ridiculed as a political issue. Nor should we disparage the most democratic process established under our Constitution by our Founding Fathers.

Our Founding Fathers specifically insisted on including an amendment process in the Constitution, because they humbly believed that no man-made document could ever be perfect. The constitutional amendment process was deliberatively considered and wisely crafted, and we have no reason to fear it.

We have amended the Constitution no fewer than 27 times—most recently in 1992 to regulate Congressional pay increases. The sky will not fall if Americans exercise their democratic rights to amend it again. Surely, the protection of marriage is at least as important to our nation as the regulation of Congressional pay, the specific manner in which we coin our money, or the countless other matters that can be found in our nation's charter.

Moreover, there is a robust tradition of constitutional amendments to reverse constitutional decisions by the courts with which the American people disagree—including the 11th, 14th, 16th, 19th, 24th, and 26th Amendments.

Opponents of the marriage amendment apparently have no objection to the courts amending the Constitution. Yet the power to amend the Constitution belongs to the American people, through the democratic process—not the courts. The courts alter the Constitution—under the guise of interpretation—far more often than the people have. Because of *Lawrence,* it is inevitable that the Constitution will be amended on the issue of marriage—the only question is how, and by whom. Legal scholars across the political spectrum agree that a constitutional amendment by the people is the only way to fully protect marriage against the courts.

- *Why would we ever want to write discrimination into the Constitution? Why would we ever want to roll back the Bill of Rights?*

This argument is offensive, pernicious—and revealing.

Marriage is not about discrimination—it is about children. It is offensive to characterize the vast majorities of Americans who support traditional marriage—individuals like Reverend Ray Hammond of the Bethel African Methodist Episcopal Church in Boston, Reverend Richard Richardson of the St. Paul African Methodist Episcopal Church in Boston, and Pastor Daniel de Leon, Sr., of Alianza de Ministerios Evangélicos Nacionales (AMEN) and Templo Calvario in Santa Ana, California—as bigots. It is offensive to characterize the laws, precedents, and customs of all fifty states as discriminatory. And it is offensive to slander the 85 senators who voted for DOMA as hateful.

Moreover, it is *precisely because* some activists believe that traditional marriage is about discrimination, and not about children, that they believe that all traditional marriage laws are unconstitutional and therefore must be abolished by the courts. These activists leave the American people with no middle ground. They accuse others of writing discrimination into the Constitution—yet they are the ones writing the American people out of our constitutional democracy.

Just last week, representatives of Sens. John Kerry and John Edwards said that the marriage amendment would "roll back rights." If you believe that traditional marriage is only about discrimination and about violating the rights of adults—as Sens. Kerry and Edwards apparently believe—then you have no choice but to oppose all traditional marriage laws. Any other position is incoherent at best—and deceptive at worst.

Marriage Protection

So the issue has been joined—precisely as it was in 1996. Despite typical Washington Beltway tricks to overcomplicate and confuse matters, the question remains a simple one: Should marriage, defined as the union of one man and one woman, be protected against judicial activism and the will of legal and political elites? If you believe that the answer is yes—as vast majorities of Americans do—then you have no legal option but to support a federal constitutional amendment protecting marriage.

The American people believe that every human being deserves respect, and the traditional institution of marriage deserves protection. As members of Congress continue to debate this issue, we should also remember what else the American people deserve: honesty.

The Honorable John Cornyn is a United States senator from Texas and chairman of the Senate Judiciary subcommittee on the Constitution, Civil Rights and Property Rights. He is a former state-supreme-court justice and state attorney general. Since September 2003, he has chaired three hearings to examine the legal threat to the traditional institution of marriage.

POSTSCRIPT

Should Same-Sex Marriage Be Legal?

Several European countries have given legal status to same-sex couples, including Denmark, France, Germany, the Netherlands, Sweden, Iceland, Belgium, and Norway. In 2003, Canada removed from its laws language that restricted marriage to a man and a woman.

In the U.S., attitudes remain divided. According to a Gallup poll conducted in July 2004, 62 percent of Americans believed that same-sex marriages should not be recognized. By May of 2008, the number had fallen to 56 percent. According to the 2004 poll, only 48 percent supported a constitutional amendment that would define marriage as being only between a man and a woman. In May of 2009, that number had increased to 49 percent.

Support appears slightly stronger for civil unions—a concept intended as a legal equivalent to marriage, in all but name. While some regard civil unions as an acceptable compromise to this divisive debate, to others such arrangements stir up memories of the "separate but equal" days of racial segregation.

Opponents of same-sex marriage frequently rely on biblical references to condemn the practice. They cite passages that describe marriage as between man and woman (1 Cor 7:2), and others that denounce homosexuality in general (Lev 18:22; Cor 6:9; 1 Tim 1:9–11). Yet, if the Bible is to be relied upon for enacting marital legislation, other biblical passages may give legislators pause, such as those that endorse polygamy (Gen 29:17–28; 2 Sam 3:2–5) and a man's right to have concubines (2 Sam 5:13; 1 Kings 11:3; 2 Chron 11:21), or those that prohibit divorce (Deut 22:19; Mark 10:9) or mandate female virginity in order for a marriage to be valid (if a wife is not a virgin, she can be executed, the Bible says) (Deut 22:13–21).

Biblical references and implications notwithstanding, the Human Rights Campaign says that fully recognized same-sex marriages are essential to ensuring the same legal protections and benefits that are available to heterosexual married couples. Do you agree? Do you believe civil unions are a just substitution? Why or why not?

Cornyn argues that while the efforts of single, foster, and adoptive parents are heroic, the relationship between a child and its biological mother and father are the "gold standard." Do you believe that single-parent families, adoptive families, and gay and lesbian families cause that gold standard to be "diluted," as Cornyn states?

How do you view the argument to amend the U.S. Constitution? What potential benefits or difficulties do you foresee resulting from this action? Finally, what do you believe is the *purpose* of marriage? Is marriage primarily about love? Rights? Children and family? Monogamy? Other considerations? Do you regard it as primarily a religious institution or a legal institution? Is there any *single, predominant* purpose of marriage, or are there many purposes worthy of consideration?

Suggested Readings

D. Bush, "Same-Sex Marriage and Racial Justice Find Common Ground," *New York Times* (May 17, 2008).

S. Feldhan and D. Glass, "Why is Reality TV Marriage OK When Gay Marriage is Not?" *Atlanta Journal-Constitution* (December 2003).

A. Kramer, "The Gay Marriage Apocalypse Is Coming!" *Salon* (April 14, 2009).

H. Kurtz, "An Exclusive Club," *Washington Post,* (January 8, 2009).

J. Jacoby, "The Timeless Meaning of Marriage," *Boston Globe* (November 2003).

J. McKinley, "California Ruling on Same-Sex Marriage Fuels a Battle, Rather Than Ending It," *New York Times* (May 18, 2008).

V. Rossmeier, "Same-Sex Marriage Coming to New York?" *Salon* (April 14, 2009).

Contributors to This Volume

EDITOR

WILLIAM J. TAVERNER, M.A., is the editor of the *American Journal of Sexuality Education* and Director of The Center for Family Life Education at Planned Parenthood of Greater Northern New Jersey. Taverner is the author or co author of numerous sex education manuals, including *Making Sense of Abstinence; Older, Wiser, Sexually Smarter; Sex Ed 101;* and *Streetwise to Sex-Wise.* Taverner is also the editor of several editions of *Taking Sides: Clashing Views in Human Sexuality.* He has received the American Association of Sexuality Educators, Counselors and Therapists Founder's Award and the Golden Apple Award from the Association for Planned Parenthood Leaders in Education (APPLE). He was also named "one of the country's preeminent sex educators, trainers, and sex education theorists."

An adjunct professor of human sexuality at Fairleigh Dickinson University, currently on sabbatical, Taverner has trained sexual health professionals throughout the nation. He received his Master of Arts degree in human sexuality from New York University and can be reached at sexedjournal@hotmail.com.

EDITOR

RYAN W. MCKEE, M.S, is an adjunct professor of human sexuality at Montclair State University. He has taught courses at Kean University, Fairleigh Dickinson University, Touro College, and Richard Bland College.

While earning his Master of Science degree in sociology from Virginia Commonwealth University, McKee worked as a Research Assistant on numerous projects including the Virginia Transgender Health Initiative, the Virginia Teen Pregnancy Prevention Initiative, the Youth Risk Behavior Survey, and the Virginia Community Youth Survey. He has written for Columbia University Health Services' award-winning GoAskAlice! web page (www.goaskalice.columbia.edu) and was recently published in the four volume *Sexuality Education: Past, Present, and Future* anthology.

In addition to teaching, McKee works as a sexuality education consultant and program evaluator. He is currently enrolled in Widener University's Doctoral program in Human Sexuality Education and is a member of the American Association of Sex Educators, Counselors, and Therapists (AASECT), and the Society for the Scientific Study of Sexuality (SSSS). He can be reached at mckeer@mail.montclair.edu.

AUTHORS

THE ADMINISTRATION FOR CHILDREN AND FAMILIES works within the United States Department of Health and Human Services and is responsible for federal programs that promote the economic and social well-being of families, children, individuals, and communities.

MERCEDES ALLEN is the founder of AlbertaTrans.org, a network designed to help foster and support the transgender community in Edmonton, Calgary, and rural Alberta, Canada.

THE AMERICAN FAMILY ASSOCIATION advocates for traditional family values, focusing primarily on the influence of television and other media— including pornography—on American society.

ELOKIN CAPECE is a Health Educator with Planned Parenthood Greater Memphis Region. She holds an MA in Women's Studies from the University of Memphis and has an undergraduate degree in History, Greek and Roman Studies, and Education.

PATRICK J. CARNES is a nationally known speaker on the topic of sex addiction. He is the author of numerous books, including *Facing the Shadow: Starting Sexual and Relationship Recovery and In the Shadows of the Net: Breaking Free of Compulsive Online Sexual Behavior.*

RHONDA CHITTENDEN is a regional educator for Planned Parenthood of Greater Iowa and is a regular columnist for *Sexing the Political,* an online journal of Gen X feminists on sexuality.

JOHN CORNYN is a United States Senator from Texas, who chairs the Senate Judiciary subcommittee on the Constitution, Civil Rights and Property Rights. He is a former state supreme court justice and state attorney general.

CYNTHIA DAILARD is a senior public policy associate at the Guttmacher Institute's Washington, DC, office and is responsible for issues related to domestic family planning programs, sex education, and teenager's sexual behavior.

JENS ALAN DANA is a former student at Brigham Young University, where he was also an editor for the student newspaper, *The Daily Universe.*

MARCY DARNOVSKY is the associate executive director of the Center for Genetics and Society in Oakland, California.

DONALD A. DYSON is an Assistant Professor in the Widener University Program in Human Sexuality, and serves as the Director of Doctoral Studies in the Center for Education. He also serves as an adjunct faculty member at Widener's Center for Social Work Education.

J. PAUL FEDEROFF is Director of the Forensic Research Unit at the Institute of Mental Health Research, University of Ottawa, and Director of the Sexual Behaviours Clinic at the Royal Ottawa Hospital.

NORA GELPERIN is the director of training and education for Answer at Rutgers University and has presented workshops at local, state, and national conferences.

DOUGLAS GROOTHUIS is Professor of Philosophy at Denver Seminary and the author of 10 books, including *Truth Decay* (InterVarsity Press, 2000).

REBECCA HAGELIN is a public speaker on family and culture and is the author of *30 Ways in 30 Days to Save Your Family.*

DAVID M. HALL a recipient of teaching and humanitarian awards, is the author of *Allies at Work: Creating a Lesbian, Gay, Bisexual and Transgender Inclusive Work Environment.*

MARK HAMILTON is the chair of the British Fertility Society and a consulting gynecologist with Aberdeen Maternity Hospital, Scotland.

DONNA M. HUGHES is the Eleanor M. and Oscar M. Carlson Endowed Chair at the University of Rhode Island and one of the world's leading researchers on sex trafficking.

HUMAN RIGHTS CAMPAIGN is the largest national lesbian, gay, bisexual and transgender civil rights organization, representing a grassroots force of over 750,000 members and supporters nationwide.

MAUREEN A. KELLY is the vice president for education and training for Planned Parenthood of the Southern Finger Lakes in Ithaca, New York.

EILEEN P. KELLY is a professor at Ithaca College who teaches courses in Applied Ethical Issues in Management, Labor Relations, Strategic Management, and Employment Law.

GLEN LAVY

JUDITH LEVINE is the author of *Harmful to Minors: The Perils of Protecting Children from Sex,* which won the 2002 Los Angeles Times Book Prize.

MARSHALL MILLER is the co-founder of the Alternatives to Marriage Project (www.unmarried.org) and co-author of *Unmarried to Each Other: The Essential Guide to Living Together as an Unmarried Couple.*

SUSAN A. MILSTEIN is an associate professor in the Health Department at Montgomery College and is the lead consultant for Milstein Health Consulting and an advisory board member for the Men's Health Network.

NATIONAL WOMEN'S LAW CENTER is a nonprofit organization that works to expand the possibilities for women and focuses on family economic security, education, employment opportunities, and health, with special attention given to the concerns of low-income women.

WAYNE V. PAWLOWSKI is an independent consultant, trainer, and clinical social worker based in the Washington, DC, area, with over 20 years in sexuality education, reproductive heath, and family planning.

DAVID POPENOE is co-director of the National Marriage Project and a professor of sociology at Rutgers University. He is the author of several books, including *Life Without Father: Compelling New Evidence That Fatherhood and Marriage are Indispensable for the Good of Children and Society.*

RONI RABIN is a journalist whose work has appeared in *Newsday* and the *New York Times.*

LARA RISCOL is a freelance writer who explores societal conflicts and controversies surrounding sexuality. She has been published in AlterNet, *The Nation,* and *Salon* and other media outlets worldwide, and is working on a book called *Ten Sex Myths That Screw America.*

JOHN A. ROBERTSON holds the Vinson & Elkins Chair at The University of Texas School of Law at Austin. A graduate of Dartmouth College and Harvard Law School, he has written and lectured widely on law and bioethical issues.

DAVID L. ROWLAND is a Professor of Psychology and Dean of the Graduate School at Valparaiso University, Valparaiso.

WILLIAM SALETAN is a national correspondent for *Slate* magazine and is the author of *Bearing Right: How Conservatives Won the Abortion War.*

BRENT A. SATTERLY is an Associate Professor and Program Director at Widener University's Center for Social Work Education. He also serves as adjunct faculty in Widener University's Human Sexuality Program.

LAWRENCE A. SIEGEL is the president and CEO of the Sage Institute for Family Development in Boynton Beach, Florida.

RICHARD M. SIEGEL is the vice president of education, training, and counseling services for Planned Parenthood of South Palm Beach & Broward Counties, Inc. in Boca Raton, Florida.

CHARALAMBOS SIRISTATIDIS is affiliated with the Assisted Reproduction Unit, part of the Department of Obstetrics and Gynaecology at Aberdeen Maternity Hospital in Scotland.

DORIAN SOLOT is the executive director of the Alternatives to Marriage Project (www.unmarried.org) and co-author of *Unmarried to Each Other: The Essential Guide to Living Together as an Unmarried Couple.*

LEONORE TIEFER is a Clinical Associate Professor of Psychiatry at New York University School of Medicine and the author of *Sex is Not a Natural Act.*

JENNIFER WEBSTER is the Projects Coordinator for the Network for Reproductive Options, a grassroots feminist organization seeking to ensure reproductive justice for the women of Oregon.

BARBARA DEFOE WHITEHEAD is co-director of the National Marriage Project. She is the author of numerous essays, articles and of two books, including *Why There are No Good Men Left: The Romantic Plight of the New Single Woman.*

KELLEY WINTERS, formerly under pen-name Katherine Wilson, is a writer on issues of transgender medical policy, founder of GID Reform Advocates, and an Advisory Board Member for the Matthew Shepard Foundation and TransYouth Family Advocates.